THE CLAIMS *of* POVERTY

The figures of Waster (left) and Hunger from *Piers Plowman,* MS Douce 104, fols. 37v and 38r. Reproduced with the permission of the Bodleian Library, University of Oxford.

THE CLAIMS *of* POVERTY

Literature, Culture, and Ideology in Late Medieval England

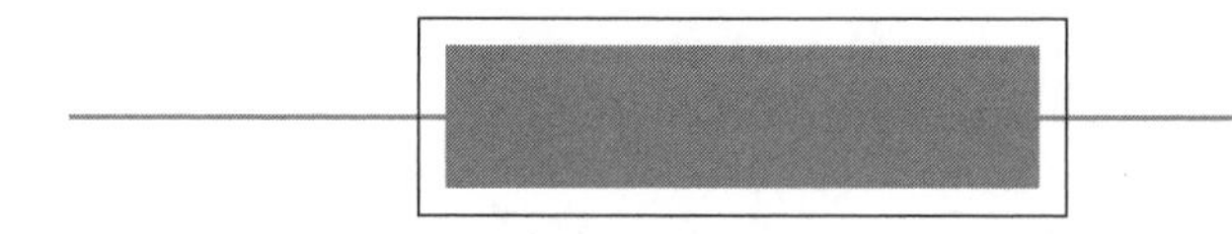

KATE CRASSONS

University of Notre Dame Press
Notre Dame, Indiana

Notre Dame, Indiana 46556
www.undpress.nd.edu

Manufactured in the United States of America

Library of Congress Cataloging-in-Publication Data

Crassons, Kate.
The claims of poverty : literature, culture, and ideology in late medieval England / Kate Crassons.
p. cm.
Includes bibliographical references and index.
ISBN-13: 978-0-268-02302-7 (pbk. : alk. paper)
ISBN-10: 0-268-02302-6 (pbk. : alk. paper)
1. English literature--Middle English, 1100–1500—History and criticism.
2. Poverty in literature. 3. Social problems in literature. 4. Ideology in literature.
5. Civilization, Medieval, in literature. 6. Literature and society—England—History—To 1500. 7. England—Social conditions—1066–1485. 8. Poverty—England—History—To 1500. 9. Poverty—Religious aspects—Christianity—History of doctrines—Middle Ages, 600–1500. I. Title.
PR275.S63C73 2010
820.9'3556--dc22

2010007655

∞ *The paper in this book meets the guidelines for permanence and durability of the Committee on Production Guidelines for Book Longevity of the Council on Library Resources.*

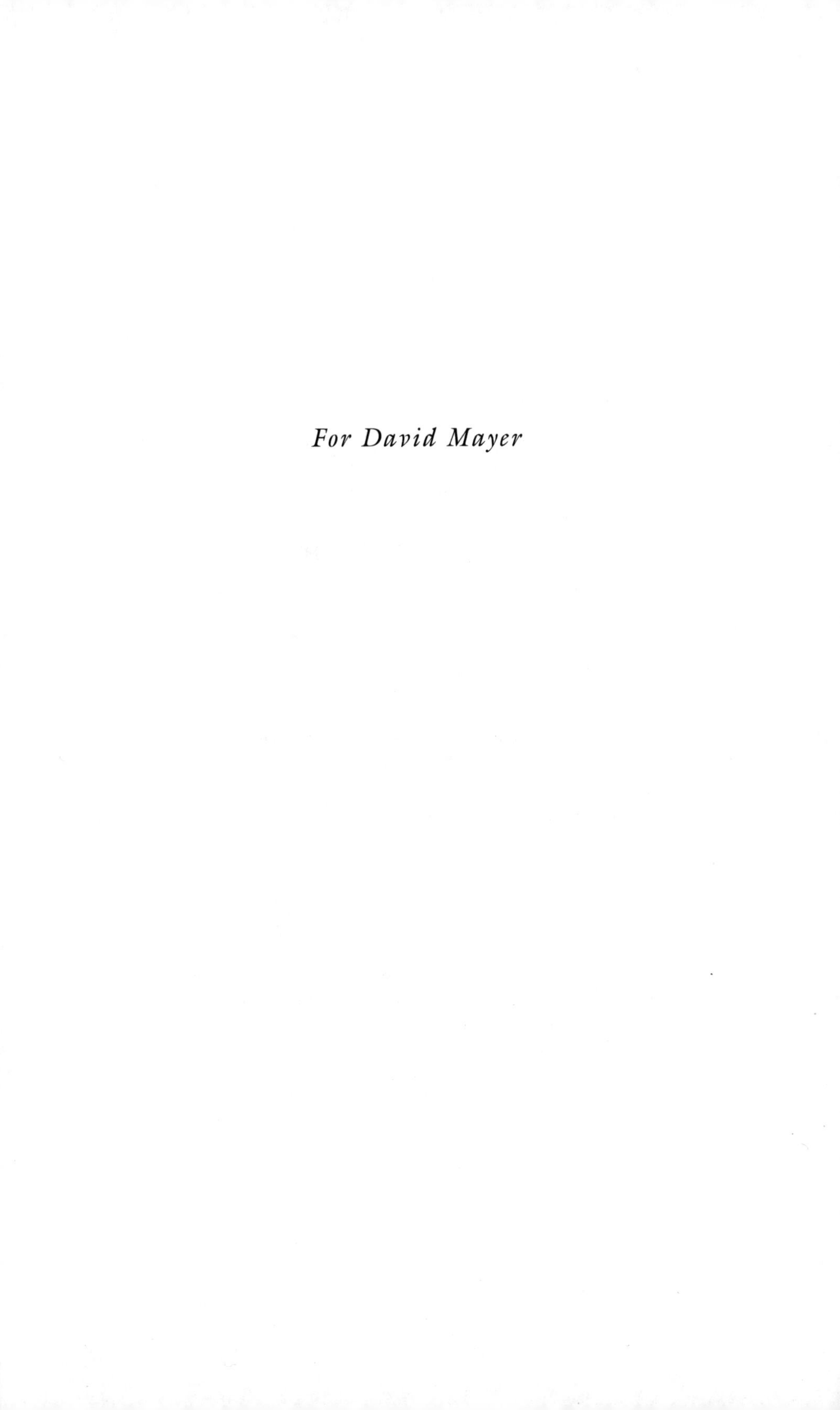

For David Mayer

CONTENTS

ACKNOWLEDGMENTS

In writing a book on poverty, I have accrued many debts, yet these are a sign of my great fortune in having so many people who have offered help along the way. I owe tremendous thanks to my teachers, whose wisdom and guidance have been nothing short of inspiring. Bruce Holsinger and Beth Robertson first introduced me to the fascinating world of medieval literature. It was Beth in particular who inspired me to become a medievalist, and her thoughtfulness and curiosity as a scholar are qualities that I hope to emulate in my own work. Judith Bennett offered supremely knowledgeable advice about this particular project and academic life more generally. Sarah Beckwith often seemed to recognize dimensions of my work that I had yet fully to grasp, and I am incredibly grateful for her perceptive readings. Sarah's patience, generosity, and willingness to push me have made this book far richer than it otherwise would have been.

My greatest thanks goes to David Aers who supervised this project from its beginning as a dissertation at Duke University and who continued to offer indispensible guidance with amazing efficiency and thoroughness. I am deeply thankful for his friendship along with that of his wife, Christine Derham. Without David's great knowledge and kindness, this book would not have been possible. And if I can pass on to my students a fraction of what I've learned from him, I will consider myself a successful teacher.

I've also benefitted from the generosity of other scholars and friends. The anonymous readers for the University of Notre Dame press provided invaluable criticism of the manuscript. Barbara Hanrahan shepherded this project through the publication process with great care and attention. I also appreciate Matt Dowd's meticulous editorial work. Fiona Somerset and Maureen Quilligan offered helpful comments in the early stages of this project. Richard Newhauser's NEH seminar held at Cambridge University in 2006 usefully influenced my thinking about the relationship between poverty and sin. Dorrie Armstrong, Dan Breen, Alex Feerst, Cara Hersh, Katie Little, Jana Mathews, Vin Nardizzi, Julie Paulson, and Amy Vines have all read parts of this book and, more generally, enriched my academic life with their scholarly insights and good humor. I am also grateful to Ashley Mills for her friendship and much-needed diversions in New Orleans.

At Lehigh University my work has been supported by the Faculty Research Grant program and the Franz/Class of 1968 Fellowship. In the English department, I have benefited greatly from friendship and intellectual exchange with Beth Dolan, Suzanne Edwards, Dawn Keetley, and Seth Moglen. The participants in the department's Premodern Studies Colloquium offered lively and thoughtful criticism of my work. I also want to thank Addison and Mary Louise Bross, Alex Doty, Jan Fergus, Monica Najar, Rosemary and Bob Mundhenk, and Kathy Olson for all of their advice and camaraderie.

Early versions of material in chapters 3 and 5 appeared as, respectively, "'The Workman is Worth His Mede': Poverty, Labor, and Charity in the Sermon of William Taylor," in *The Middle Ages at Work*, edited by Kellie Robertson and Michael Uebel, and published by Palgrave Macmillan; and "The Challenges of Social Unity: *The Last Judgment* Paegant and Guild Relations in York," in *The Journal of Medieval and Early Modern Studies* 37. I am also grateful to the British Library and the Bodleian Library at Oxford University for permission to use their manuscripts.

Finally, I would like to thank my family for all that they've done for me over the years. My grandparents, Pete and Glory Wilbert, my sister, Ann Crassons, and most especially my parents, Norman and Gloria Crassons, have always offered me their support—emotional, financial, and otherwise. Nothing would be possible without the solid foundation of love they've provided.

My greatest debt is to my husband, David Mayer, to whom this book is dedicated. Over the past several years, we've had many conversations about this book, and I can't imagine that there are too many other Jewish men from Queens, New York, who would be as happy to talk about Jesus and medieval poverty. I am incredibly grateful for his generosity of spirit, his encouragement, and his ability always to make me laugh. It's difficult to articulate the wealth of blessings that he's brought me, but his love and the joy we share in our son, Henry, stand out as the most "nidefole" things in my life.

Introduction

In 1206 the man who would become St. Francis of Assisi was brought before the bishop to face punishment for his increasingly disruptive behavior. The stories of the saint's life famously record how Francis's father, a prosperous cloth merchant, sought legal recourse in response to his son's actions. After giving away his own belongings, Francis took cloth from his father's shop, sold it, and eventually threw the proceeds out of a church window. Though he eventually recovered the money, Francis's father sought retribution for his son's careless and rebellious conduct, and he insisted that Francis be stripped of his inheritance. While Francis replied willingly to his father's demands, his acquiescence entailed a further challenge to earthly authority and the possessions on which it depended. In the presence of his father, the bishop, and those gathered at the court, Francis "took off and threw down all his clothes and returned them to his father. He did not even keep his trousers on, and he was completely stripped bare before everyone."[1] In this dramatic act Francis inaugurated a conception of poverty that would become a hallmark of religious life in the Middle Ages. Evoking the image of Jesus as a naked and persecuted figure, Francis transformed poverty into a sacred ideal performed in imitation of Christ. This theological premise embodied the saint's own commitment to simplicity, for it defined poverty in the plainest of terms: to be poor was to share in the perfection of Christ himself.

Yet, once institutionalized, this straightforward philosophy would provoke a massive controversy, and antifraternal writers came to dispute the legitimacy of voluntary poverty and its effects on both the church and the lay community.[2] As I shall discuss later, these debates are obviously central to the poverty controversies of the Middle Ages, but they also remain significant in modern scholarship on poverty, revealing an essential lesson about the fundamental ambiguity of poverty, especially as a force in the medieval period. Whether exploring the economic situation of medieval Assisi or the consequences of globalization in the present day, writers have continued to invoke Francis, but they have done so in utterly divergent ways. Such opinions are worth consideration because they illustrate how a claim of poverty, even if articulated with apparent straightforwardness, bears no direct relationship to material reality. As a result, its precise meaning and its ethical implications become a source of interpretive conflict.

The enduring nature of such conflicts is evident in the work of modern writers who have continued to debate the significance of Francis's legacy, revealing its particular ethical stakes for the twenty-first century. Some have condemned the Franciscan ideal as a form of economic exploitation, while others have praised it as a sacred practice that undermines such oppression. Kenneth Wolf, for example, has recently criticized Francis's conception of poverty, arguing that it constituted another form of power and prestige for the rich. He concentrates on the specifically voluntary nature of Franciscan poverty to consider how its claims of sanctity very likely had negative effects on those who did not choose to be poor:

> Francis's extreme love of poverty, pursued for the sake of his own spiritual progress . . . potentially made the lives of those suffering from involuntary poverty even more difficult. For one thing, Francis could not help but attract the attention of almsgivers, many of whom appreciated the vicarious spiritual advantages of supporting him in his quest for perfect poverty, as opposed to trying to alleviate the poverty of someone who did not want to be poor. Second, if the kind of "spiritual economy" that Francis epitomized, based as it was on deliberate divestment from this world and investment in

> the next, required that Christians have something invested in this world in the first place, how were the poor expected to compete with the rich for entrance into the next life?

Wolf answers his own question by exposing what he sees as Franciscanism's utter disregard for the spiritual welfare of the involuntary poor: "in a religious tradition where sacrifice meant little or nothing unless it was undertaken voluntarily, it was not at all obvious how the plight of the *poor* poor (as opposed to the formerly rich poor) was to be alleviated in the next world."[3]

In this account, we can begin to see the ambiguities that trouble medieval conceptions of poverty as Wolf strains to find a more precise vocabulary to distinguish what he calls the "poor poor" from those who falsely appropriate the "true" condition of poverty. He thus argues that the form of poverty established by Francis was not poverty at all but rather a strategic choice that made indigence spiritually valuable only when it was undertaken willingly by the elite. Having no option about living in poverty, the "true" poor could make no claims to spiritual perfection, and the "formerly rich poor" co-opted the alms that such people desperately needed. Given what he sees as the economic and ethical reality of Francis's poverty, Wolf finds the saint's continued popularity in the present day to be deeply troubling. To venerate Francis, he implies, is to be complicit in an exploitative tradition that has long denied the needs and worthiness of the "true" poor.

Discussing Francis in the very different context of postmodern globalization, Michael Hardt and Antonio Negri work against this perspective by heralding the saint as an ideal for the present age. At the end of *Empire,* they invoke Francis as a figure representing the promise of the final triumph over capitalism. Hardt and Negri see the saint's voluntary poverty as a legitimate and, indeed, deeply ethical form of life; it becomes a sign of solidarity with the poor, functioning as a decisive movement against the forms of domination and social division structuring relations in a capitalist society:

> There is an ancient legend that might serve to illuminate the future life of communist militancy: that of St. Francis of Assisi. Consider

> his work. To denounce the poverty of the multitude he adopted that common condition and discovered there the ontological power of a new society. The communist militant does the same, identifying in the common condition of the multitude its enormous wealth. Francis in opposition to nascent capitalism refused every instrumental discipline, and in opposition to the mortification of the flesh (in poverty and in the constituted order) he posed a joyous life, including all of being and nature, the animals, sister moon, brother sun, the birds of the field, the poor and exploited humans, together against the will of power and corruption. Once again in postmodernity we find ourselves in Francis's situation, posing against the misery of power the joy of being. This is a revolution that no power will control—because biopower and communism, cooperation and evolution remain together, in love, simplicity and also innocence. This is the irrepressible lightness and joy of being communists.[4]

In this powerful tribute to the saint, Franciscanism becomes, so to speak, a modern call to arms because it functions to bring down a society defined by economic exploitation.

For Hardt and Negri, Francis's poverty does not therefore promote elitism or reaffirm the privilege of the rich, as Wolf suggests; rather, it is a sign of unity with the involuntary poor, "a common condition" that he adopts so as to unleash a political revolution. To follow Francis's call in the present day is thus to perform the work of justice. Considering Wolf's perspective against that of Hardt and Negri, we see that the contradictions characterizing Franciscan poverty prove to be as salient in the twenty-first century as they were in the fourteenth: Francis emerges as both an elite man who exploited the poor to enhance his own social credit and as a saint who undertook a groundbreaking quest to ensure the protection of society's most vulnerable members.

I begin my discussion of medieval culture with these brief modern vignettes about St. Francis because they crystallize a truth about poverty more generally in the Middle Ages: it is a highly flexible concept that tests our capacity to define material reality and to assess its ethical implications. Franciscanism forms only one strand in a complex—and equally contradictory—web of ideas about the nature and status of poverty in the Middle Ages. In this book, I specifically investigate how writers in late medieval England negotiate competing ideologies of poverty, an issue that proves to be central to the social and moral visions developed within a range of poetic, polemical, and dramatic texts. Discussing poverty in post-plague England, medieval writers drew on theological and political discourse to participate in a wider cultural debate that questioned the virtues of poverty with increasing rigor and hostility. As antifraternal arguments fused with objections to the rising power and mobility of lay workers, poverty and mendicancy came to be described more readily as signs of sinfulness than as hallmarks of Christian sanctity. With the enactment of labor laws that criminalized able-bodied begging and indiscriminate charity, one can see the development of a powerful social imaginary in fourteenth-century England.[5] Constituting what critics have termed a "shift in values" or a "newer ethos," labor became a sign of virtue while poverty emerged as a symptom of idleness and other sins.[6]

I also explore the nature of the cultural shift concerning poverty in late medieval England and uncover new intricacies central to this ideological transformation by showing how literature is a crucial resource for understanding poverty and the particular anxieties it provoked. This book argues that literature reveals—and indeed embodies—the most urgent concerns defining the late medieval debates on poverty. While readers may tend to think of poverty primarily as an economic or historical issue, I contend that it is a subject intimately bound up with concerns about representation. In this sense, the book does not offer a comprehensive overview of historical shifts in attitudes toward poverty. Rather, I aim to complicate the traditional text-context relationship by suggesting that we need texts themselves to understand why poverty emerged as a site of historical and cultural crisis in late medieval England.

Literary texts are essential to the study of poverty because poverty is as much an economic force as it is an epistemological issue that challenges our ability to know and fix the precise nature of material reality. We only discern what we conceptualize as the economic through symbolic representation. As Louise Fradenburg explains, "representation—the signifier—is intrinsic to the practices of exchange that produce culturally variable definitions of wealth and poverty."[7] It is within discourse that these "culturally variable definitions of wealth and poverty" come to life in especially fascinating ways, as texts make use of sophisticated rhetorical strategies and literary techniques in order to present arguments about the nature of need—an extremely slippery category. As the title of this book suggests, I invoke the notion of a claim as the most appropriate way of conveying both the complexity of poverty and its ideological urgency in the Middle Ages. Functioning both as a noun and a verb, the word "claim" encompasses an extraordinary range of meanings that illuminate how poverty makes material reality and ethical action inextricable from questions of representation and hermeneutics—questions central to literary practice itself.

If we consider the meaning of the word "claim" in relationship to poverty, we see that poverty can be understood in one way as a force that makes claims in and of itself. In this sense, poverty is something that "demands recognition" of an "alleged right, title, possession, [or] attribute."[8] In fourteenth- and fifteenth-century England, the claims that poverty could make were especially capacious, as evidenced by the major medieval discourses concerning poverty. For example, within the mendicant orders poverty asserted itself as a form of spiritual perfection. It was perceived as an authorizing force entitling at least the voluntary poor to material, symbolic, and spiritual rewards. The Franciscan Rule of 1223 offers a succinct account of this perspective, explaining how poverty enables the friars to claim holiness as well as the need for charitable assistance: "As pilgrims and strangers in this world, serving the Lord in poverty and humility, let [the friars] go seeking alms with confidence, and they should not be ashamed because, for our sakes, our Lord made Himself poor in this world." The Rule goes on to praise the "sublime height of most exalted poverty" as a condition that makes the friars "poor in temporal things but exalted in virtue."[9] By undertaking poverty in sacred imitation of Jesus, the friars made claims to charitable aid, Christ-like sanctity, and perhaps even heavenly reward.

However, in the massive body of antifraternal thought that developed in the wake of the Franciscans' popularity and the establishment of other fraternal orders, critics of the friars rejected such claims, denying that poverty and begging were evangelical virtues to be emulated in the medieval church. Asserting that the friars' claims of spiritual perfection were at odds with the gospel message and that their claims of need were at odds with material reality, the secular masters at the University of Paris were the first antifraternalists to attack the legitimacy of voluntary poverty. They began to undermine the notion that poverty was a virtue, viewing it not as a claim of sanctity but as a sign of idleness, covetousness, and other sins. The most outspoken critic in the early conflicts with the friars was William of St. Amour, and within the wide range of his antifraternal thought he developed a distinctive portrait of Christ and the apostles. Insisting that they worked for their food instead of begging from others, William argued that it was labor, and not poverty, that should be revered as a work of humility.[10] In 1323 Pope John XXII affirmed such ideas when he declared heretical the Franciscan understanding of Christ's poverty.[11] Later, in fourteenth-century England, the archbishop Richard FitzRalph continued to criticize the friars' way of life by describing poverty as "þe effect of sin." He argued that God called human beings not to live in indigence but to labor and accumulate wealth since "riches is good having & worþi to be loued of God."[12] In the long history of writing against the friars, poverty, especially in its voluntary form, was understood as an essentially sinful condition that made empty claims of sanctity. Poverty thus became, most centrally, a violation of Christian practice, not its perfect fulfillment.

While antifraternalists rejected the claims that poverty could make as a religious practice, secular lawmakers applied similar criticisms to their vision of poverty as a problem affecting lay society in the changed economic circumstances of post-plague England.[13] The labor statutes did not react to poverty's claims as a form of spiritual perfection, but rather objected to the rights and assertions that lay beggars were supposedly making with increasing intensity and frequency. In this sense, then, poverty can also be understood as a force that makes claims on behalf of the laity—even potentially on behalf of the involuntary poor. Indeed, those who experienced poverty not as a matter of choice could still make claims to alms and also possibly to sanctity based on their professed need and perhaps on their own association with the poor Christ (Matthew 25). The now obsolete sense that to claim is "to call for, cry for, [or] beg loudly" reveals how the act of begging might be understood not only as a form of supplication but as an explicit claim by which the poor asserted their presumed rights to charitable assistance.[14]

Shaped by the anxieties of elite employers, the labor laws construct a particular image of poverty that condemns beggars precisely because they were perceived as claiming such rights illicitly. As part of its overall project to control workers and set their wages at pre-plague levels, the legislation consistently depicts an alleged class of lay people who rejected labor altogether so as to live in greater ease by begging.[15] For example, the 1349 labor ordinance identifies a problem with people who are "willing to beg in Idleness rather than earn their Living by Labour."[16] In describing this problem, the legislation clearly draws on antifraternal writing to develop a representation of poverty almost certainly at odds with socioeconomic reality.[17] The ideological work of the labor laws is important because it sought to restrict the claims that poverty could make by describing the poor, with very few exceptions, as fraudulent and sinful idlers. The 1349 ordinance goes on to condemn those people who "as long as they may live of begging, do refuse to labor, giving themselves to Idleness and Vice, and sometime to Theft and other Abominations."[18] In this framework, poverty is a choice that facilitates moral depravity. As it is feigned by reluctant workers, poverty becomes a claim of sinfulness, a declaration of idleness, and a challenge to the law itself.[19]

Clearly, the discourses of antifraternalism and labor legislation contributed to the anti-poverty ethos by constructing poverty as a form of vice willfully chosen by those attempting to avoid labor. However, these discourses made an important exception in their denigration of poverty by acknowledging that it could be a legitimate and unavoidable hardship for some people, namely those incapable of working. In making this acknowledgment, lawmakers and antifraternalists implicitly called attention to a second meaning of the word "claim"—a meaning that reveals how poverty could make claims on the poor themselves. In this sense, the word "claim" loses its association with human agency and entitlement, becoming instead an undesirable consequence imposed on someone.[20] Here poverty is not itself a claim but rather it makes claims on those who are subject to its force. For the involuntary poor especially, poverty grants few rights but takes from its victims, exacting various forms of hardship and suffering. This suffering might entail physical deprivation, as poverty left people hungry, thirsty, and exposed to the elements. In extreme cases such suffering could cause people to die, and in this sense the claims of poverty were catastrophic, literally stripping the poor of their own lives. In other circumstances, the poor could experience physical suffering along with psychological and emotional pain resulting from the ill-effects of social division. Neglected by the rich, the poor might feel a sense of alienation and invisibility; or they might experience despair and shame if they provoked the ire of people disdainful of their presence.

Both antifraternal discourse and labor legislation imaginatively attempted to limit the ways in which poverty could make such claims on the poor by restricting the legitimate experience of need to those unable to work. This restrictive definition of poverty can be observed in theories advocating the practice of discriminate charity.[21] For example, William of St. Amour argued that charity should not be given to just anyone. Making a person's right to charitable aid contingent on his inability to labor, William declared that "the right of the prospective recipient to alms should be carefully scrutinized, and he should be advised to find work to support himself."[22] The labor laws codified this policy on charity, mandating that alms be given "only to such as cannot assist themselves or work."[23] These brief statements reveal how antifraternal discourse and labor legislation redefined the ethical response to need by reshaping the very conception of poverty and limiting its legitimate claims.

This necessary connection between issues of poverty and charity introduces yet another claim of poverty. Because poverty makes claims on behalf of the poor, and because it makes claims on the poor themselves, poverty is also a force that is significant for making claims on the wider community. Poverty privileges the category of human response; it is an issue fraught with deep epistemological and ethical complexity because it demands acts of interpretation that bear moral and material consequences for poor and rich alike. As a force that makes potentially dire material claims on the poor, poverty pricks the conscience of the Christian community. It reminds people of their charitable obligation to alleviate Christ's own suffering by easing the suffering of the poor and showing mercy to those in need. As a condition that also makes claims to material and symbolic rewards, poverty puts those charitable obligations to the test. It demands that people make interpretive acts, forcing them to acknowledge the reality of suffering, to deny its presence, or to suspend judgment willfully.

The labor statutes in particular register great anxiety about the epistemological challenges triggered by the presence of poverty.[24] The laws not only highlight the alleged dangers posed by wandering and anonymous beggars, they also attempt to supply such people with a distinct identity so as to clarify the appropriate response to claims of need. The 1376 Commons' Petition against Vagrants seeks to make the exercise of discriminate charity possible by exposing the poor as people whose sinister acts and illicit demands harm the entire community:

> And let it be known to the king and his parliament that many of the said wandering laborers have become mendicant beggars in order to lead an idle life; and they usually go away from their own districts into cities, boroughs, and other good towns to beg, although they are able-bodied and might well ease the commons by living on their labor and services, if they were willing to serve. Many of them become "staff strikers" and lead an idle life, commonly robbing poor people in simple villages, by two, by three or four together, so that their malice is very hard to bear. The majority of the said servants generally become strong thieves, increasing their robberies and felonies everyday on all sides, to the destruction of the kingdom.[25]

In this passage we find a portrait of ominously shifting identities that are gradually channeled into a clear trajectory that we will revisit in the half-acre scene of *Piers Plowman*. Notice that the passage repeatedly refers to a process of becoming inaugurated by the movement from labor to begging: "wandering laborers have become mendicant beggars"; "many of [the mendicant beggars] become 'staff strikers'"; "the majority of the said servants generally become strong thieves." Able-bodied begging is but one step on a path of moral degeneration. The passage conveys the severity of this moral decline by following its depiction of an evolutionary process with an account that describes the multiplication of false beggars and their intrusion into various communities. With a kind of teeming pervasiveness they move in ever greater numbers into all places at all times: they rob people "by two, by three or four together . . . increasing their robberies and felonies everyday on all sides."

While the petition attempts to construct a rhetorical identity for vagrant beggars, later legislation established other technologies of discernment with practical applications for people responding to actual claims of poverty or need. The much discussed 1388 Cambridge Statute enacted all of the proposals listed in the 1376 petition; and this law was innovative, among other reasons, for establishing an ambitious system of documentary identification that required mobile workers and approved religious mendicants to carry letters of authorization.[26] While the law's attempt to regulate social identity has many implications, it is most significant for this discussion because it sought to simplify the response to poverty. Its new system of identification attempted to make discriminate charity practicable by creating the fantasy that social identity can be easily fixed and authorized. The single act of asking for some identification was meant to replace other more challenging forms of human response that required people to exercise moral judgment by acknowledging need, dismissing its real presence, or refusing to scrutinize what they thought ultimately unknowable.

In addition to occluding the difficulty of discernment, the emphasis on discriminate charity found in both labor legislation and antifraternal writing also promoted a restricted definition of poverty that obscured other categories of need. Most obvious is the refusal to acknowledge the possibility that poverty can make claims on people who work. In the century after the plague, it is true that this category of people would have been comparatively small, given that workers could take advantage of higher wages, lower food prices, and increased demand for labor.[27] Yet this improved economic picture was hardly consistent or universal, and poverty would have nonetheless been a reality for many working people.[28] The major late medieval discourses discussing poverty, however, disregard its pervasiveness and variability as a condition that could stem from many different factors including changes in the life cycle, unforeseen calamities, and gender inequality.[29] In failing to acknowledge such realities, and in shaping cultural perceptions and social policies, such discourses may have functioned to increase the hardship of those not explicitly included in their restricted category of need.[30] As we have seen, in both antifraternal thought and labor legislation, "true" poverty makes claims only on those who cannot work to prevent its presence. And it is only this group of "deserving" people who can make claims on the charitable intentions and material resources of the wider community.

Writers in antifraternal and legislative discourse thus make claims about poverty that attempt to limit the concept's potentially fluid meaning. Turning to the literature of late medieval England, we will see that specific writers sometimes affirm these discourses and sometimes challenge them. In the chapters that follow, I examine a range of generically diverse texts united by their explicit attention to poverty as an issue of cultural contestation. In my exploration of works ranging from *Piers Plowman* and Wycliffite writings to *The Book of Margery Kempe* and the York plays, we find a range of complex arguments about poverty that give us a lens into a moment of cultural change.[31] Discussing these texts in chronological order serves as a means of engaging with—and complicating—the narrative of cultural transition supplied by critics recounting the history of poverty in late medieval England. If one were to look for a sense of historical development across the texts I discuss, he or she would be likely to find a hardening of attitudes toward poverty by comparing, for example, *Piers Plowman* and the York cycle, the starting and end points of this book's investigation into medieval literature. Indeed, Langland offers some sympathetic portraits of poverty and takes the ideals of Franciscanism seriously (even if he finally rejects those ideals), while the York plays, which continued to be performed roughly two hundred years after *Piers Plowman*, depended on a highly regulated guild system predicated on the primacy of labor, competition for commercial success, and the outright exclusion of the poor. Yet, in my view, recapitulating a tale about the ultimate triumph of the market is less interesting and less relevant to the complexities of poverty itself than exploring the intricacies that actually constitute a moment of cultural change. In short, then, this book does not argue *that* poverty falls from a virtue to a vice so much as it shows *how* that decline occurs in a variety of discursive arenas.

There are, admittedly, costs to such a methodology, and this book may not satisfy readers looking for a clear trajectory or a single argument that neatly sums up the literature of poverty in late medieval England. But it should also be acknowledged that such streamlined approaches have their own costs in that they can overlook continuities, ambiguities, and nuances that might defy easy assimilation into a grand narrative of change. This book attempts to resist the lure of such grand narratives and instead primarily focuses on the subtle rhetorical maneuvers of texts. This methodological decision is motivated by both ethical and intellectual concerns. We have seen, for example, how religious and secular discourse promotes the claim that poverty is a singular condition legitimate only for the disabled. Yet this idea, which derives power from its straightforwardness, is deeply problematic for assuming that poverty stems solely from the refusal or inability to work. Its clear and efficient argument thus comes with dangerous liabilities that occlude other categories of need experienced, for example, by the working poor. In pursuing multiple lines of inquiry and in exploring the contours of cultural transformation, *The Claims of Poverty* aims to show the importance of attending to specificities and varied possibilities for meaning.

Sensitivity to complexity is also essential to this book because it seeks to follow the mandates of its own subject; in this sense it approaches poverty as a force that necessitates careful attention to the processes of representation and interpretation. Shaped by aesthetic forms, rhetorical strategies, and linguistic slippages, literary texts place the signs of poverty before readers; and they demand that readers both interpret these signs and assess their ethical implications, in the same way that an almsgiver would evaluate the signs of need in the body and speech of the poor themselves. When viewed in this light, literature becomes far more than the repository of shifting historical attitudes toward poverty. Rather, a text's complex use of signs embodies the very anxieties around representation that are at the heart of poverty itself. In the chapters that follow, I primarily attend to these signs through the practice of close reading. This practice is essential because it marks the first step in determining the very object of historical inquiry; the work of discerning a text's formal operations helps readers understand that text's ideological investments and ethical commitments.[32]

This is certainly the case with the C-text of *Piers Plowman* and the later Wycliffite poem *Pierce the Ploughman's Crede*. The first two chapters of *The Claims of Poverty* explore the relationship between these works, offering the book's most concentrated focus on interpretive issues. My reading of these texts serves as an extended exposition of the idea that questions of poverty are simultaneously questions of poetic practice. While I attend to the subtle maneuvers of texts throughout the book, these opening chapters are distinctive for honing in on the poems themselves to consider how their formal dynamics are inextricable from their ideological assumptions. In the first chapter I argue that Langland's use of allegory works as an ethical intervention in the dominant late medieval discourses on poverty that erode the subject's epistemological and moral complexity. While Langland ultimately rejects the viability of the Franciscan ideal, his work is notable not so much for denigrating the virtues of poverty as for exposing the ideological limitations that structure the debates about poverty in the first place. The poem features a range of interlocutors who invoke Franciscanism, antifraternalism, anticlericalism, and labor legislation in order to claim poverty as either the highest virtue or the most wretched vice. Though they offer opposing arguments, Langland reveals how these ideological perspectives are ultimately united because they insist on rigid conceptions of need.

Langland's poem contrasts with these discourses by employing complex and dynamic signs of allegory that personify aspects of poverty including hunger and need itself. In the course of the poem, the semantic wanderings of such figures ultimately stress the fundamental opacity of need. Approaching poverty in its fullest sense as a material and spiritual condition as well as a voluntary and involuntary practice, Langland exposes the extreme difficulty of defining poverty and recognizing its presence. He also illuminates how these interpretive acts have important theological, ethical, and material consequences. In both conceptual and formal terms, his poem reveals that the dominant discourses on poverty create the potential for ethical catastrophe: if an almsgiver were to accept their basic assumptions, he might fail to recognize his fellow human beings most in need of charitable aid.

The second chapter shows how the later poem *Pierce the Ploughman's Crede* strategically attends to selective elements of Langland's work in order to discuss poverty within the limited context of antifraternal satire. Unlike its poetic predecessor, the *Crede* insists that the signs of poverty are readily discernible as it contrasts fraternal corruption with the virtue of the true poor, embodied by Pierce the ploughman. Furthermore, the *Crede* is able to affirm the sanctity of true poverty by equating material reality with interior identity so that, in the world of the poem, need always signals humility and wealth always indicates covetousness, pride, and other sins. The *Crede*'s antifraternal polemic is in some sense unusual because it comes in the form of a poem shaped by a deliberate aesthetic. This chapter reveals how the poem's faith in the immanent discernability of material signs corresponds to its faith in textual signs as "clear" and "open" purveyors of meaning. The *Crede* thus abandons Langland's allegorical and dialectical forms in favor of what we might see as a willfully "impoverished poetics." The *Crede* privileges a linear time scheme and discrete narrative episodes, while eschewing the massive shifts in time, place, and perspective made possible by the fluid modes of allegory and dream vision. This literary methodology is essential because it ultimately allows the writer to present the climactic recitation of the Creed and the poem itself as works that transparently expose the "Truth" about the friars' abuse of poverty.

The third chapter continues to show how poverty is a crucial topic in the Wycliffite program of ecclesiastical reform. Moving away from a primary focus on poetics to consider broader cultural contexts, I investigate two Wycliffite sermons and related texts so as to explore in greater detail how the demands of polemic shape writers' conceptions of poverty and foster a particular vision of social relations. Developing an attack on the church's wealth, Wycliffite writers seem to approach poverty as a Christian virtue: they want the church to abandon its wealth, and they passionately plead for the protection of the involuntary poor. However, by exploring the rhetorical strategies of their fervent call for reform, it becomes clear that their praise of poverty is far from straightforward; and this chapter ultimately challenges the dominant critical assumption that Wycliffism was a movement that highly valued poverty and the poor themselves.

While the Wycliffite writers express concern for the involuntary poor, they do so primarily in conjunction with their critique of the church's covetousness (and almost never as a criticism of the rich laity). This framework has troubling ethical consequences. First, it makes care for the poor as much a polemical strategy as a charitable duty. And, second, in blaming the church alone for all moral failures, it obscures certain forms of social relation, rendering invisible the obligations that the lay elite bear to the poor people in their community. Exploring how the writers strategically employ antifraternal theories of dominion along with a relativistic vocabulary of need, I show how the Wycliffites' social and moral vision is committed most fundamentally to protecting the power and interests of the lay elite. The sermons finally promote a form of non-mendicant poverty for the church that ideally functions to maximize the resources of the lay community, who should work to support themselves, pay their rents, and restore the status of impoverished lords.

Whereas the Wycliffites explicitly rejected the notion of voluntary poverty as an ideal for the laity, chapter four shows how *The Book of Margery Kempe* presents a different perspective, one that seems committed to Franciscan values. Aligning Kempe with St. Francis, the *Book* describes her conversion as a rejection of worldly ambition, trade, and pride in her family's elite status within the town of Lynn. Kempe's commitment to poverty grows stronger when she embarks on a highly unusual path for a woman by following Christ's command in Rome to give away all of her belongings and become a mendicant. Though Kempe's life seems greatly at odds with the Wycliffite rejection of poverty, reading the *Book* in light of Franciscan theology and theories of dominion reveals that it ultimately shares ideological territory with the texts explored in the previous chapter. Drawing on the resources of hagiography, the *Book* seeks to present Kempe as a saint, and it therefore highlights her miraculous immunity to material hardship. Yet this form of sanctity becomes problematic in the context of the *Book*'s attachment to Franciscan ideals. This is the case because the *Book* transforms a radical conception of need, vulnerability, and weakness into a form of poverty that ultimately affirms the values associated with the urban elite. As such, Kempe's poverty allows her to maintain financial security, to wield civil dominion, and to attain social acceptance.

Characterizing Kempe's material poverty as strangely benign, the text ultimately redefines need as a form of powerlessness. Though she remains financially secure, Kempe's status at the end of her life as an elderly and illiterate laywoman confirms her vulnerability and her dependence on other people. Perhaps Kempe's greatest need can be found toward the end of her life when she searches for a scribe who is both morally and intellectually capable of recording her life story. Indeed, this search exposes the complex nature of Kempe's need as a form of poverty shaped by divergent interests. In this sense, the text uneasily combines a rigorous form of Franciscanism with the conventions of female hagiography, amalgamates traditional idealizations of poverty with urban mercantile values, and brings material deprivation together with the seemingly greater hardships of age, gender, and illiteracy.

Continuing to explore poverty within an urban context, the final chapter examines York's Corpus Christi theater and approaches the civic drama as both a theatrical and economic production. Drama brings distinctive resources to bear on the exploration of poverty, because to stage poverty is to give presence to absence; by placing the signs of need in the bodies and speech of actors, the theater makes poverty visible. It moves throughout the streets of York; it permeates the spaces of the city. Drama also offers complex and multiple opportunities for meaning, as actors engage with other actors, as they interact with audience members, and as audience members respond to one another. Constituted by these varied points of contact, the performance of a play anatomizes social relations, making it difficult to obscure any facet of the community. This encompassing social dynamic, however, does not necessarily signal an idealized concept of social unity. Rather, the plays are at once a theological ideal and a material reality subject to the socioeconomic tensions that defined late medieval York.

Examining how the plays animate the relationship between rich and poor, this chapter finds that the pageant texts offer a sharp critique of the anti-poverty ethos as they acknowledge the reality of the able-bodied poor and articulate a powerful theory of indiscriminate almsgiving. The plays' conception of poverty and charity, however, proves to be at odds with the political and social formations that structure the city. Investigating guild documents relevant to the plays, I show how the civic records produce a competing discourse of poverty and charity that renders the ideals of the pageants impracticable as widespread civic values.

By discussing a wide array of texts, this book reveals the far-reaching claims of poverty in late medieval literature and culture. It shows how the particular urgency associated with poverty derives primarily from the epistemological anxieties that this issue generates. Indeed, as a whole, the texts explored in this book exploit the very capaciousness of poverty, pulling the concept in different directions so as to advocate a variety of political, ethical, and theological positions. Specifically, their claims of poverty can be said to expose the fundamental instability of need, to uncover the fraudulence of the friars, to lament the decline of the lay elite, to redefine the miraculous nature of female sanctity, and to reveal the limits of community. Despite the diversity of these conceptual positions, the texts explored in this book are united in mounting a serious inquiry into the moral value of poverty, an inquiry that ultimately excludes poverty as a virtue to be cultivated by the Christian community. Though their arguments participate in a wider movement denigrating poverty, the texts I consider nonetheless attest to the enduring power of this issue, which remained a force of tremendous gravity in medieval culture. Shaped by the vagaries of representation, poverty is a highly fluid sign, but it is a sign that demands acknowledgement and response, for it incites charitable obligations potentially owed to Christ himself. Addressing a subject that makes claims extending into the material, spiritual, and moral realms, the literature of poverty in late medieval England deserves our careful attention, for it has a profound role to play in shaping the culture's economic practices, theological traditions, and ethical imagination.

The medieval literature of poverty also arguably has an important role to play in shaping our modern conceptions of poverty and social aid. Though *The Claims of Poverty* focuses primarily on medieval literature, there is an important aspect of this book that looks beyond the Middle Ages to insist that medieval texts offer valuable insights into many modern perspectives on poverty. It is not a coincidence, for example, that people still frequently think of poverty as a singular condition that stems from the inability or refusal to work. Barbara Ehrenreich's *Nickel and Dimed: On (Not) Getting by in America* attests to the long afterlife of this idea by arguing that there is an entire class of low-wage laborers consistently overlooked in modern discussions of poverty. In the epilogue of this book, I focus on *Nickel and Dimed* and the controversy it provoked in order to pursue some of the continuities between medieval and modern writing about poverty. It is fascinating, for example, that critics of *Nickel and Dimed* take a page from antifraternal polemic. While Ehrenreich claims to prove the insufficiency of the minimum wage by living temporarily as a low-wage worker, the book's critics view her experiment as nothing more than a fraudulent form of voluntary poverty. Similar to the debate about Francis with which I began this introduction, the criticism surrounding *Nickel and Dimed* raises questions relevant to those also being asked seven hundred years ago: How exactly should poverty be defined? Is work the primary antidote to poverty? How can writers and advocates of the poor bridge the cultural and economic divide that separates them?

This last question, I think, is of particular importance given the massive and ever-widening socioeconomic divisions that structure modern society, rendering the poor largely invisible. Ehrenreich describes how poverty has received decidedly little attention as a modern issue. She remarks that "some odd optical property of our highly polarized and unequal society makes the poor almost invisible to their economic superiors."[33] The force of Ehrenreich's comment was certainly affirmed in the recent past by Hurricane Katrina, an event that exposed this phenomenon of invisibility by making the pervasiveness of poverty suddenly clear. When it hit New Orleans in 2005, the storm ripped away the occlusions and ideological artifices that ordinarily push poverty to the margins. Television screens and newspapers revealed thousands of poor, elderly, and other vulnerable people—most of whom were African American—left abandoned in flood-ravaged areas where the federal and state governments dared not to go.

While localized to a particular time and place, this event exposed a larger, systemic problem sustained, in part, by ideological beliefs that gained currency during the medieval conflicts concerning poverty. In revealing the presence of poverty as a structural force, Hurricane Katrina also revealed the regular occlusion of poverty as a reality frequently denied by myths of equal opportunity—myths that promote hard work as the primary solution to economic deficiency. On a much less dramatic scale, my own students learned about such myths while taking an undergraduate course on poverty and medieval literature that featured a service learning component. As they worked at a variety of agencies serving the poor, they grew increasingly aware of poverty's presence within the local community, and my students were especially shocked to encounter workers from their very own university eating lunch at a soup kitchen near campus. Poverty would seem to be a nearly ubiquitous reality, but its claims go largely unheard in modern day America, where it takes an overwhelming natural disaster or, at least in the case of my course, a mandate of community service to reveal its actual presence.

Concentrating as it does on the medieval literature of poverty, this book, I believe, can help remedy the sense of invisibility that so often shrouds the reality of poverty. It can do so by making readers conscious of the ways in which ideology can function to obscure the varied and intricate claims of poverty so as to advance a particular social imaginary often at odds with material reality. The debates about poverty in medieval literature are still resurfacing today, and as they do, it is important to recognize how they continue to make claims on our present community. By attending to the representation of poverty in medieval literature, we can see how rigid definitions of need and universalizing assumptions about the poor have lasting ethical consequences that structure social relations and forge deep-seated divisions in our very own lives.

CHAPTER ONE

Forms of Need

The Allegorical Representation of Poverty in *Piers Plowman*

The parable of Dives and Lazarus in Luke 16 offers a haunting story about the failures of charity, the invisibility of the poor, and the divisions that fracture community. Describing how the rich man ignores the needy beggar at his gate, the gospel passage goes on to recount how Dives is damned while Lazarus finds respite enfolded in Abraham's bosom. This outcome serves as a highly appropriate punishment for Dives who now must beg Lazarus to relieve his great thirst. He asks Lazarus to dip one of his fingers into some cool water so as to drop a bit of it onto his tongue. Dives's request offers a strikingly intimate portrait of almsgiving: the rich man imagines the poor man approaching him and administering aid directly as a gift that passes from the poor man's body into his own. The physical closeness of this act stands in stark contrast to the isolation previously experienced by Lazarus, who was locked out of the rich man's gates and left alone to die. Intensifying Dives's punishment, Abraham denies the man alms and pronounces his continued separation from Lazarus (and all others who are "saved"). As Dives now becomes the figure trapped outside the gates, Abraham defines damnation as a permanent form of social isolation. He tells the rich man, "they who would pass from hence to you cannot, nor from thence come hither."[1]

This well-known story functions as a focal text in late medieval discussions about poverty. While writers invoke the parable for different exegetical ends, it is most often used to emphasize the catastrophic effects of the failure of mercy—a failure made all the more glaring by the rich man's ready ability to have saved Lazarus from starvation.[2] As a poem deeply interested in the relationship among wealth, poverty, mercy, and justice, *Piers Plowman* turns to this story repeatedly: various personifications mention the fate of Dives and Lazarus on four different occasions in the poem.[3] Langland, I think, is drawn to this story because it illustrates that charity is a form of love demanding recognition among different sectors of people. In the case of Lazarus, who is covered with sores and on the verge of starvation, his urgent need is clear. Yet Dives cannot discern his need, that is, he cannot recognize Lazarus as a fellow human being, as a person to whom his own life and salvation are bound.

Piers Plowman is a poem that is extremely sensitive to the challenges of defining and discerning need. It is also a poem that wants to correct the failures of Dives, as its frequent appeals to the rich make evident. At various points in the poem, an array of different figures offer statements of caution to the wealthy, proclaiming, "y rede yow riche;" or "Taketh hede, ȝe ryche;" or "beth ywar, ȝe wyse men . . . that rich ben."[4] In following these statements with calls for charitable work, Langland reinforces the importance of offering mercy and aid to the poor.[5] Yet the poem's insistence on moral action brings with it a troubling epistemological problem central to the story of Dives and Lazarus: how can someone know and come to recognize the presence of need? This question is complicated further by the possibility of fraud: how can a person detect need among ambiguous and potentially false signs of poverty? And in cases where suffering is indisputably present, as it is with Lazarus, there are still obstacles to detecting the reality of need: how, for example, can need become meaningfully visible, especially to those who are isolated from the poor and untouched by poverty themselves? *Piers Plowman* raises all of these questions, and in so doing poses an especially tricky epistemological challenge, one with serious ethical consequences. To give to the needy is a work of justice and love; to give to a false beggar perpetuates fraud and idleness; to fail to give to one in need destroys the bonds of community and the hope of salvation.

Piers Plowman is unique for treating such questions about poverty with a great deal of subtlety, as the poem's critical history attests. Indeed, much scholarship on the poem has explored Langland's representations of poverty in contexts ranging from contemporary labor conflicts and ecclesiological disputes to the hierarchy of allegorical signification.[6] Recent work within this extensive body of criticism has tended to focus particularly on assessing the overall status of poverty in the poem. Thus, critics have sought to determine whether *Piers Plowman* ultimately endorses poverty as the highest form of virtue or seeks to discredit it as such. In *Piers Plowman and the Poor*, for example, Anne Scott sees Langland as promoting the virtue of poverty: the poem affirms that "poverty, whether patiently borne, voluntarily chosen, or endured as inevitable, has, in itself, the power to save."[7] Lawrence Clopper makes a similar argument, though he approaches *Piers Plowman* specifically in relationship to Franciscanism. In his account, the poem offers a reformist praise of Franciscan ideals, and Clopper surmises that Langland himself belonged to a coterie of radical Franciscans.[8] David Aers, however, takes a different view of the poem. While he acknowledges that *Piers Plowman* is sympathetic to Franciscan values, he argues that it ultimately subordinates poverty to charity in the pursuit of Christian perfection. The poem's anxieties about Franciscanism, according to Aers, derive in large part from its suspicion that poverty encourages versions of Pelagianism that the poem rejects.[9]

This chapter contributes to these debates about the status of Franciscanism and poverty more generally in *Piers Plowman* by suggesting, in a similar vein to Aers, that the poem is largely suspicious of poverty's claims to perfection. My argument, however, importantly extends beyond reading *Piers Plowman* as a critique of poverty; instead, I emphasize the poem's distinctiveness among late medieval texts for portraying poverty as a subject irreducible to a single sign, meaning, or discourse. Rather than solely attempting to ascertain Langland's final attitude toward poverty, this chapter explores why Langland treats the issue with such urgency and complexity, especially in his final version of the poem. The answer to this question lies, I think, in the poem's engagement with contemporary discourses of poverty—discourses affiliated not only with Franciscanism but also with fourteenth-century labor legislation, antifraternalism, and anticlericalism.[10] Though they advance different moral visions, these discursive modes are aligned in presenting need as a transparent and straightforward subject. In his poem, however, Langland exposes the ethical liabilities of viewing need as a readily discernible condition. By closely attending to *Piers Plowman*'s poetic processes, this chapter explores how ethics and hermeneutics necessarily converge in the issue of need. I argue that *Piers Plowman* makes an important ethical intervention in late medieval discourse on poverty by approaching the subject through particularly fluid and complex modes of representation, including allegory, dialectic, and dream vision. The distinctiveness of Langland's approach to poverty and to poetry will become clear not only in this chapter through close readings of the poem but also in the next chapter, which features a comparative analysis of the Wycliffite poem *Pierce the Ploughman's Crede.*

As discussed in this book's introduction, the dominant late medieval discourses of poverty offer their own conceptions of need, understanding the term as a form of Christ-like sanctity that can be voluntarily undertaken (Franciscanism) or as a condition that can result only from the inability to work (labor legislation and antifraternalism/anticlericalism). Langland thoughtfully pursues each of these discursive definitions, and, in his attentive consideration of them, the poem generates a striking juxtaposition: along with its urgent awareness of the catastrophe resulting from failed charity, *Piers Plowman* features a scrupulosity that seeks to prevent the donation of alms to false beggars. These dual perspectives would seem to place a great deal of confidence in one's ability to distinguish between the deserving and the undeserving poor, lest an almsgiver mistakenly deny alms to a person truly in need. However, what becomes especially compelling about Langland's text is its attraction to a theory of discriminate giving that is rendered virtually impracticable by its own poetic modes and sacramental vision. At the same time that Langland is drawn to the idea that only the truly needy deserve alms, he develops a massive meditation on poverty that stresses the epistemological and ethical difficulties involved in discerning need.[11]

These difficulties come to life in the poem's construction of poverty as an array of shifting, elusive, and interrelated signs. In *Piers Plowman* allegorical figures such as Hunger, Rechelesnesse, Patience, and Nede personify different aspects of poverty; the dynamic shifts that develop among these figures cast poverty as a capacious concept shaped by evolving systems of meaning. In this sense, allegorical signification, as Maureen Quilligan describes, takes place on a horizontal surface of interaction, not simply on a vertical system of interpretation; in allegory "complicated patterns of interconnected meaning . . . spread like a web across their horizontal verbal surfaces."[12] With its allegorical figurations and its resistance to stable taxonomies, *Piers Plowman* revels in creating such "complicated patterns of interconnected meaning"—patterns that often reveal the semantic slippages endemic to claims of poverty. The poem's personifications of poverty, along with its depiction of the poor themselves, almost never figure forth the transparent meaning of neediness so often assumed in late medieval discourse on poverty. *Piers Plowman* thus makes an important ethical contribution to the contemporary debates on poverty: it acknowledges the epistemological limits of powerful moral visions current in legislative, Franciscan, and anticlerical discourse—visions to which the poem itself is drawn. Though deeply suspicious of poverty's claims, *Piers Plowman* ultimately warns against the ethical consequences of acceding to ideological pressures that impose on those very claims preconceived interpretations of need.

In the pages that follow, I shall examine the C-text, the version of the poem that features Langland's most expanded discussion of poverty. I will focus specifically on episodes of the poem that highlight its attention to the intricate signs of poverty, its awareness of need's invisibility, and its ultimate development of a sacramental theology that eschews the quick judgment of self and others. Rather than move sequentially through the poem, this chapter follows the presumed chronology of the C-text's composition to approach as a unit the new material that Langland added to Passus IX and V. This methodology helps to reveal the growing importance of poverty in Langland's poetic imagination. It also aims to show how the new material in the C-text shares important conceptual terrain foregrounding poverty in relation to the limits of discernment.[13]

Human Needs and Worldly Demands

In its opening scene, *Piers Plowman* famously recounts Wille's vision of the "fair feld ful of folk," and from the outset the poem explores the diverse social networks that comprise the Christian community. Wille directs his attention to "alle manere of men," including "þe mene and þe riche," and he enumerates all the types of people "Worchyng and wondryng as þe world ascuth" (Prologue.19–21). In the poem's opening Passus, Wille meets the authoritative figure of Holy Churche, who offers a skeptical interpretation of this initial vision. She cautions that the demands of the world can become an all-consuming force obscuring concern for salvation. She asks, "Wille, slepestou? Seestow þis peple, / Hou bisy þei ben aboute þe mase? / The moste party of this peple þat passeth on þis erthe, / Haue thei worschip in this world thei wilneth no bettere; / Of othere heuene then here halde thei no tale" (I.5–9). As Holy Churche explains, working within the world can all too readily make Christians blind to the wider obligations conferred on them in baptism and membership in the Christian faith. She aims to remind Wille of these obligations by integrating mankind's worldly occupations into an ethical vision, an institutional body, and an incarnational theology that stresses the interrelation of all people.

After explaining that the demands of the world can become a distraction unto themselves, Holy Churche introduces the crucially important issue of need, a subject that will haunt the poem until its final Passus. While this term is frequently co-opted into contemporary debates about labor and valid forms of poverty, it is significant that Holy Churche discusses need in a very different context. She shows how it is an issue relevant to all Christians, not just those claiming "need" for alms. In her view, if a community is to be based on justice and love, all people must be conscious of need, as it applies to themselves as well as others. Developing such consciousness and defining need, however, will prove to be difficult tasks; and, as William Rogers remarks, the ensuing dialogue between Wille and Holy Churche raises sharp questions about "meaning and money," "interpretation . . . and social justice."[14]

Holy Churche's unique approach to need becomes clear when she first mentions the issue in relation to the great wealth supplied to all people by God. Holy Churche presents the earth's resources as an abundant gift of God's grace, and she tells Wille that "þe elmentis" are there "to helpe ȝow alle tymes" and "to make ȝow attese" (I.17–19). She goes on to explain, however, that if humans want to enjoy the earth's plentitude, they must practice moderation; they must, in other words, take only what they need. Initially, Holy Churche defines this term with admirable clarity and directness, as she teaches Wille about the three "nidefole" things to which all men are entitled. She tells him that "The firste is fode and vesture þe seconde, / And [the third is] drynke þat doth the good" (I.23–24). She goes on to sum up the spirit of her discourse on need by offering the memorable epithet that "Mesure is medecyne" (I.33).

While Holy Churche offers sound teaching on moderation and the meaning of need, she ultimately exposes the difficulties of truly understanding these concepts so as to live them out as part of the church's ethical vision. For example, as soon as the figure names drink as the third item "nidefole" to all people, she follows her definition of need by acknowledging the powerful temptation to consume beyond the bounds of need. Thus, in the very same line in which she lists "drynke þat doth the good," she goes on to qualify her statement with the warning to "drynke nat out of tyme" (I.24). Similarly, after telling Wille that "Mesure is medecyne," she follows this half line with the direct admission, "thogh þow muche ȝerne" (I.33). In the very same moment that she defines need and measure—indeed, in the very same poetic line—Holy Churche repeatedly acknowledges humans' disinclination to recognize and abide by these concepts.[15] Holy Churche continues her lesson by naming Lot as an example of someone whose fall into gluttony led to incest and thereby "wrathed god almyhty" (I.26). She goes on to explain how bodily cravings, which often oppose the good of the soul, nevertheless triumph in a sign that the world, the flesh, and the devil have succeeded in their attempts to "bigyle" and "desseyue" people in prioritizing desire over need (I.37, 40).[16] And, finally, in describing the "castel of care," she also explains how Wrong, a historically powerful "lettere of loue," works to "combre men with coueytise" (I.67). Given these references to gluttony, covetousness, and the actual victims of these sins, Holy Churche's teaching on measure emerges as an extremely complicated lesson for the human will, a will that seems predisposed to misrecognize its own need.[17]

The obscurity of this concept becomes more troubling as Holy Churche instructs people to use the earth's abundant gifts for the fulfillment of need, not the pursuit of excess. At one point in their dialogue, Wille asks Holy Churche, "'to wham [does the world's] tresour bylongeth?' " (I.43), and she replies by explaining that wealth should be used in the appropriate arena by anyone "at nede" (I.52). This seemingly clear instruction, however, is once again complicated by the figure's acknowledgement that one's need may not be obvious. She explains that the will must rely on the intellect to authorize the distribution of treasure so as to satisfy personal need: " 'For riȝtfulliche resoun shoulde reule ȝow alle / And kynde witte be wardeyn, ȝoure welthe to kepe, / And tutor of ȝoure tresor, and take it ȝow at nede' " (I.50–52). The process of fulfilling one's needs can only be accomplished when individuals rely on reason and kind wit to determine how to use wealth legitimately. Yet once again we see the will's difficulty in living out such teachings, as Wille himself later mistakenly announces to Holy Churche that he lacks an essential faculty linked to reason and kind wit. Having already irritated Holy Churche by failing to recognize her as the institution he has entered through baptism, Wille makes his interlocutor even more angry by stating, "I haue no kynde knowyng," a faculty that unites understanding with an innate capacity to love God (I.137).[18] She sharply informs Wille that he does in fact possess this faculty, but Wille's ignorance looms as a factor that complicates Holy Churche's call for humans to employ their intellect in the diagnosis and satisfaction of need.

Holy Churche thus emerges as one of the poem's most authoritative figures, yet Wille does not recognize this personification; furthermore, her teaching betrays other difficulties of recognition highlighting the opacity of need. The question remains, how can individuals enact Holy Churche's teachings when the will itself seems ignorant of both Holy Churche and the range of its own faculties? Or, put another way, how do we reconcile Holy Churche's authority as an adept agent of interpretation with the figure's sharp lessons about the ambiguity that haunts the interpretive acts elicited by her discourse? In the midst of offering important moral lessons about moderation and measure, this moment of the allegory simultaneously exposes the real difficulty involved in defining need and reasonably fulfilling it, in knowing one's self and knowing one's church.

After revealing how frequently people confuse their own needs and live in various forms of excess, Holy Churche considers how Christians as a whole can live in measure. Implicit in her ethical vision is the awareness that misrecognizing one's own need affects others. As Louise Fradenburg remarks, "Only by establishing what is needful can one's obligations to one's own body and life and to the bodies and lives of others be calculated and acted upon."[19] Holy Churche thus turns to the reality of need among the poor, a reality that has emerged, in part, from the people's failure to distinguish their own need from the excesses so readily desired in the world of the prologue. Holy Churche finds in Christ a model of relieving the suffering of the poor, and she presents him as an exemplar of mercy and might combined.[20] It is significant that her reflection on Christ's love and virtue leads to one of the many moments in the poem where the rich are directly named as interlocutors. Holy Churche goes on to say, "y rede ȝow riche, haueth reuthe on þe pore; / Thow ȝe be myhty to mote, beth meke in ȝoure werkes, / For þe same mesure þat ȝe meteth, amis other elles, / ȝe shal be weye þerwith whenne ȝe wende hennes" (I.171–74). Here, Holy Churche explicitly enjoins the rich to imitate Christ in exercising their might mercifully and using their abundant resources to relieve the poor.

In her exhortations to practice charity, it also important to note that Holy Churche reintroduces the term "mesure," but this time she uses it in a different context: warning the rich, as Jesus did in Luke 6, that what measure they give to others will be given to them at the time of judgment. As a figure who has been deeply concerned with defining the concept of need, Holy Churche interestingly does not here designate any worthy recipients of the rich's charity beyond the "þe pore" themselves.[21] Once again, it seems that she is concerned with need in a much larger context, a context that links the measure given by the rich as alms to the measure that is medicine for all society. Indeed, Holy Churche returns to this latter meaning of the term by calling on the rich to distribute their excess belongings to the poor. She tells them to "louye leeliche and lene þe pore, / Of such good as god sent goodliche parte" (I.177–78). The work of charity is needed to remedy the inequalities that result from the blurring of need among all people, not simply among the poor, who are so often imagined in other discursive arenas as claiming poverty falsely. In this regard, Holy Churche's teaching is distinctive in *Piers Plowman* and in late medieval writing more generally because it does not confine need to a particular site of polemic; instead, the figure reminds us of the earth's plentitude, and she encourages charity because all people can readily lose sight of their need in a world so energetically directed toward getting and spending.

Hunger and the Need for Labor

The plowing of the half-acre episode confirms Holy Churche's teaching about the opacity of need, yet this section of the poem is markedly different from the first Passus in that it restricts its discussion of need to the realm of legislative discourse. The half-acre episode nonetheless ultimately exposes the costs of its more limited and politicized focus as it enacts through its dynamic allegory the troublingly seamless slippage from need to excess. These two conditions are famously represented in Passus VIII by the figures of Hunger and Wastour. In the Douce 104 manuscript of *Piers Plowman,* which is distinctive for its cycle of more than seventy illustrations, Wastour and Hunger are prominently depicted as figures leering ominously at one another.[22] Their oppositional position on folios 37v and 38r presents the two personifications as arch-enemies representing rival ideas and economic configurations (see the frontispiece to this volume). Wastour is an aggressive figure dressed in elegant and bright clothing. Glaring wide-eyed at his enemy, he carries some kind of weapon around his waist. In one hand he brandishes a stick that holds meat presumably taken from Piers without permission; Wastour's other hand reaches out for more goods, and seemingly attempts to "scoop up the lines of the poem as well."[23] Against the forceful image of Wastour, we encounter Hunger, who emerges on the following folio to combat his enemy's wasteful excess with the reality of deprivation. He defiantly meets Wastour's gaze and offers an image of contrast as he sits barefoot, dressed in simple garb.

Though these figures seem to be locked in an angry contest, upon closer inspection the illustrations function not as competing concepts but as unique representations of a similar phenomenon. If one looks beyond the superficial differences in their clothing and bodily position, it becomes clear that both Wastour and Hunger are allied in their possession and active consumption of food. Wastour, predictably, possesses an abundance of food carried on his stick. Perhaps surprisingly, however, Hunger also possesses things to eat even though he is a force of deprivation. While his sustenance looks to be much simpler fare in the form of radishes or turnips, it is striking that these oppositional figures are united by their visible ownership of food. The similarities between Hunger and Wastour multiply if we notice that they share an actively acquisitive spirit: each figure consumes or reaches out for food while also reserving additional supplies for future use. Once again, this behavior makes sense for Wastour who characteristically takes and consumes goods with no regard for moderation. In the case of Hunger, however, we find the figure eating in an attempt to relieve his Hunger or to remedy the very sense of deprivation meant to define him. While the artist perhaps thought it more effective to convey the painful effects of hunger by showing a figure desperate to eat, the sense of need encompassed by this personification begins to look very much like the acquisitive spirit associated with Wastour. For just as Wastour uses both his hands to gather and store more food than he actually needs, Hunger similarly uses both his hands in consuming and holding on to the fruits of Piers's labor. Allied in their visible accumulation of food, Hunger and Wastour ultimately seem to be defined by the very same characteristics. Their presumed opposition as enemies glaring at one another in challenge may instead be seen as a mirrored gaze, reflecting the acquisitive desire that can define excess and poverty alike.

The Douce artist's subtle rendering of the striking continuities between these putatively inimical figures touches on a powerful lesson enacted in the allegory of the half-acre itself. Encapsulated by the strange convergence of these illustrations, the half-acre episode explores how these oppositional figures can become more alike than different, how need can all too readily tip over into excess. This section of the poem explores this idea from the ideological perspective of fourteenth-century labor legislation and its preoccupation with need as a prerequisite for licit almsgiving.[24] As we shall see, the poem initially seems to endorse the ideology of the labor laws as Piers relies on the material effects of Hunger to force able-bodied beggars into work, thereby allowing him to distinguish confidently between those worthy and unworthy of his aid. After initially rejoicing in Hunger's effects, however, Piers begins to have doubts about the interpretive efficacy of Hunger and the ethics of his repressive actions. Ironically, as the figure attempts to defend his policies, he ultimately unravels both their ethical pretense and practical application by undermining any stable definition of need.[25] As the episode ends with the triumphant return of Wastour, the poem can be said to disrupt the confident claims of legislative discourse and its proposed solution to the problem of false beggars.

The half-acre episode begins as an ideal scene of production and social order, when Piers emphasizes the interdependence of community and the charitable impetus for labor. The plowman integrates all people into the work at hand; and he specifically tells the women, for example, that their labor not only serves the poor but also creates a sense of pleasure: "Consience conseyleth ȝow cloth for to make / For profit of the pore and plesaunce of ȝowsuluen" (VIII.13–14). Following Holy Churche's teaching on love, Piers then describes how he labors in order to sustain the poor and the larger community, who in turn should do their part to support him:

> For y shal lene hem lyflode but yf þe lond faylle
> As longe as y leue, for þe lordes loue of heuene.
> And alle manere men þat by þe molde is susteyned
> Helpeth hym worche wiȝtliche þat wynneth ȝoure fode.
> (VIII.15–18)

Invoking an image of a deeply interconnected society, Piers's remarks show that his vision of labor is inseparable from his vision of charity: according to the plowman, any form of work should be a labor of love that helps sustain one's fellow Christians.

The vision of productive labor becomes even further idealized and unlikely when Piers refuses to accept the knight's generous offer to help perform the work of plowing. In his exchange with the knight, Piers reveals that he is interested not just in producing food but in cultivating charity and mercy within the estates model. To this end, Piers cautions the knight not to abuse his high status by treating any common man badly. For, as Piers explains to the knight: "Thogh he be here thyn vnderlynge in heuene parauntur / He worth rather reseyued and reuerentloker sette. . . . / At churche in the Charnel cherles Aren euele to knowe / Or a knyhte fram a knaue or a quene from a queene" (VIII.43–46). Piers urges the knight to act mercifully by emphasizing the equality of all people after death. However, social differentiation is readily apparent on earth, and Piers ultimately reinforces traditional schemes of hierarchy—a message that ironically works against the social subversion implicit in the plowman's instruction of a knight.

Piers's regard for social differentiation becomes increasingly apparent when he goes on to articulate a confident policy of discriminate almsgiving. Though Piers agrees to provide food for the community, he restricts that vision of community to include only those individuals who sufficiently fulfill their obligations within Christian society. Piers distinguishes among different types of people to enumerate who is specifically entitled to the fruits of his labor and who is not:

> . . . alle kyne crafty men þat conne lyue in treuthe,
> Y shal fynde hem fode þat fayfulleche libbeth,
> Saue Iacke þe iogelour and ionet of þe stuyues
> And danyel þe dees playere and denote þe baude
> And frere faytour and folk of þat ordre,
> That lollares and losels lele men holdeth. . . .
> (VIII.69–74)

Arguing that all people can be divided into the categories of either "lollares" (a term I discuss later) or "lele men," Piers excludes from his charitable labor those who, in his view, make no valuable contribution to society. The existence of such people initially seems unimaginable as the plowing of the half-acre begins quite successfully, and "Vch man in his manere made hymsulue to done" (VIII.117). Such success is, however, short-lived, and the project quickly collapses with the emergence of wasters, who, like the aforementioned "lollares and losels," fail to work as productive members in Piers's agrarian community. After they put down their tools of labor in favor of singing and drinking ale, Piers confronts the wasters, and in so doing he tests out his theory of selective almsgiving, a policy that conspicuously echoes the ideology found in the labor laws of the fourteenth century.

Exploring the relations between this section of the poem and secular labor legislation reveals that, on the one hand, Langland deplores the self-interested, acquisitive behavior of the wasters because they do not value labor as a charitable activity benefiting the greater community; rather, they view work solely as a means to gain material goods and enjoy leisure for themselves. On the other hand, Langland's own portrayal of the idlers can also be said to reflect an anticommunitarian spirit that stems from a similarly acquisitive desire to protect the power of employers against workers who may justly resist the upper classes' tight control over the means of production. David Aers advances this latter argument in his reading of the half-acre scene. He explains that Langland uses "waster" as an "ideological and partisanly class term" in order to describe a negative version of the mobile, able-bodied workers who, according to fourteenth-century labor law, posed a great threat to the interests of the employing classes.[26] Indeed, Langland's commitment to the ideology of the labor legislation becomes increasingly apparent as the laborers in Piers's field grow more ominous. They fraudulently assume the signs of need by feigning physical disability and choosing to beg in avoidance of work (VIII.128–30). In this sense the poem imagines the poor much as the 1376 Vagrancy Petition and the 1388 Cambridge Statute do.[27] These documents, as we have seen, similarly call attention to the shifting identity of mobile workers who feign neediness and transform themselves into vagrant mendicants. Langland, as Aers suggests, thus describes the wasters with the same "terms in which horrified gentry and clerics perceived working people's increased expectations and assertiveness."[28] No longer just passive idlers, the wasters are transformed into aggressive and deceptive consumers who ask for "alms" by commanding the finest of foods.

Langland puts to the test Piers's model of discrimination when the plowman must decide whether to give alms to the wasters or let them starve. Without hesitation Piers refuses to offer charity to the former workers because he views them strictly as "wastours . . . [who] waste and deuouren / That lele land tilynge men leely byswynken" (VIII.139–40). Piers will give alms only to the poor who are "blynde or brokelegged or bolted with yren" (VIII.143). In maintaining these distinctions between wasters and the nonvoluntary, ailing poor, Piers reduces the definition of need to physical disability and fails to consider fully the categories of poor people and the specific conditions or causes of their poverty. Such writing thus "confirms convenient stereotypes" encouraged by the employing classes, who imagine the poor as idle rebels threatening the well-being of all society.[29]

The dynamic shifts of Langland's allegory indeed substantiate the landowners' fantasy by abstracting the reluctant workers into the single personification known as Wastour. This formal move brilliantly encompasses the ideological force of the labor legislation. Like these laws, the term Wastour seeks to label *all* workers who do not readily accede to the demands of employers as fundamentally uncontrollable and unproductive. As a single categorization, the term does away with any conception of workers as unique individuals claiming particular rights or needs in particular circumstances. With Wastour we have a highly efficient and concentrated representation of a homogenous workforce united in its efforts to waste the profits and charitable acts of loyal, hardworking Christians.

What is the solution to this subversive labor force? Both Piers and the labor laws offer the same answer: deprivation. As Wastour brazenly threatens Piers, the knight, and thus the entire social order, the plowman calls in Hunger who emerges allegorically as a result of both the lapse in labor and Piers's refusal to give alms. Drawing attention to the violence of Hunger's assault, Langland describes poverty in its most vicious effects on the human body: "Hunger in haste tho hente Wastour by þe mawe / And wronge him so by þe wombe þat al watrede his yes" (VIII.171–72). Hunger's painful attack miraculously "heals" the disabled beggars, who almost instantly resume their work in fear of starvation: "for a potte ful of potage þat Peres wyf made / An heep of Eremytes henten hem spades, / Spitteden and spradden donge in dispit of hunger" (VIII.182–84). Pleased with the benefits of the workers' panic about starvation, Piers is "proud" to "potte hem alle a werke . . . in alle kyne trewe craft þat man couthe deuyse" (VIII.197–200).[30] As a tool of social control, Hunger, for the moment, seems to have restored the fantasy of productive labor that we saw at the beginning of the Passus. His "success" comes from what Margaret Kim has aptly termed Hunger's "overall agenda of containment," which effectively suppresses the laborers' dissent.[31]

Hunger's powerful attack places all people in such a dire state of need that they immediately seek to combat it through work, if they are able. This extreme deprivation is also a welcome epistemological force, for it allows Piers to identify true need in the disabled people who are legitimately dependent on his alms for survival. Describing the aftermath of Hunger's assault, Langland indeed affirms that

> There was no ladde þat lyuede þat ne lowede hym to Peres
> To be his holde hewe thow he hadde no more
> But lyflode for his la[b]our and his loue at nones. . . .
> Was no beggare so bold, but yf a blynd were,
> Þat durse withsitte þat Peres sayde for fere of syre hunger.
> (VIII.194–202)

The figure of Hunger, who now notably is referred to as "syre," functions as a tyrannical lord enforcing obedience to Piers and making the true presence of need known within the community.

While Piers initially applauds Hunger's measures of control and interpretive efficacy, the plowman quickly recalls his Christian duty to cultivate charity, and he therefore begins to question the validity of Hunger's repressive policies. Concerned with the just distribution of resources as well as with the proper orientation of the will, Piers concedes that Hunger's plan has extreme practical and ethical limitations. For instance, after asking Hunger what to do about beggars and bidders, Piers expresses reservations that Hunger is not only a temporary fix, but also a force that makes people labor for "fere of famyen" rather than "for loue" (VIII.213–14).[32] At this point, Piers's confident classification of people as wasters begins to unravel when he acknowledges the rebellious workers as his "blody bretherne" (VIII.217). The plowman, furthermore, refuses to grant absolute primacy to material production and instead asks how he "myhte amaystre [his bloody bretherne] *to louye* and to labory" (VIII.220, my emphasis).

In response to Piers, Hunger defends his policies of discriminate charity, hard work, and deprivation. Attempting to sustain Piers's distinction between the deserving and fraudulent poor, Hunger encourages Piers to give alms first to those who are truly in need, that is, to the sick, lame, and blind poor who have not chosen a life of indigence. According to Hunger, Piers should offer "houndes bred" and "hors breed" to the "bolde beggares and bygge þat mowe here breed byswynke" (VIII.223–24). Piers nonetheless has misgivings about the ethics of Hunger's advice and asks the figure, "Myhte y synneles do as thow sayst?" (VIII.236). The plowman's resistance here bristles against the contemporary move toward discrimination in almsgiving because it demonstrates what Derek Pearsall sees as Langland's "continued scrupulous concern . . . for the 'undeserving poor.'" Noting Langland's anomalous position on the matter, Pearsall emphasizes that unlike the poem, legal documents criminalizing indiscriminate almsgiving have "no interest" in disputes about the claims of the undeserving poor to charity.[33]

It is also interesting to note that while Hunger advocates discrimination in almsgiving, the reality of hunger in many circumstances "does not discriminate between the moral and immoral among its victims."[34] As Hunger goes on to offer the poem's first mention of Dives and Lazarus, he exposes one of the most disturbing consequences of his existence: extreme deprivation causes people to die. Referring to Lazarus, the figure explicitly tells Piers, "y, hungur, culde hym" (VIII.279). Here, Hunger's teachings noticeably contradict the emphasis on work and need found within fourteenth-century labor legislation and up to this point Passus VIII itself. Hunger refers to a parable in which a man who is legitimately needy, that is, one of the blind, lame, or sick, dies of starvation. In this case Hunger "wronge" Lazarus "so by þe wombe" that he died. Significantly, Lazarus experienced Hunger's wrath not because he refused to work but because his fellow Christian refused to give him food.

It should be acknowledged that Hunger himself is not particularly concerned with Dives's failures in charity, as he explains that the rich man "for his delicat lyf"—and not for his failure to show mercy—"to þe deuel wente" (VIII.277). Yet the figure's reference to the parable exposes an important and entirely different side of Hunger. In the gospel passage hunger emerges not as a solution to the problem of wasting but as a problem in and of itself that wastes the life of an honest man. While Hunger initially aids Piers in discerning his truly needy brothers and sisters, in this parable Hunger stems from Dives's *inability* to discern need.[35] Amid the Passus's outrage at idlers and false beggars, amid Piers's confident schemes of social classification distinguishing the worthy from the unworthy poor, we now have a story of failed charity within the very presence of "real need." The consequences of this failure, Hunger reminds us, are severe as one man dies and another experiences damnation.

It is at this point that the poem's critique of the labor laws fully reveals its ethical force. The episode's conservative social imaginary, described so clearly by Aers, now gives way to express serious reservations about the law's ideological commitments. Mentioned by Hunger himself, Dives's moral lapse serves as an implicit warning about the potential for other failures when almsgivers might use the tool of hunger to distinguish for themselves the deserving from the undeserving poor. If a potential almsgiver calls in hunger by withholding alms, he may indeed impel a fraudulent beggar to work, as the imaginary of the labor laws suggests. However, his use of hunger might also be mistaken, too severe, or ineffective so that his scrupulosity actually leads one of his "bloody brethren" to starve. Perhaps Hunger's most important lesson concerns these larger consequences of imagining hunger primarily as a force with welcome hermeneutic power that enables almsgivers to detect the real presence of need. Hunger's very own discourse reveals that casually relying on deprivation as a tool of discrimination and social control makes people blind to the realities of hunger even when experienced by the truly needy. In other words, the dominant meaning of hunger found within the labor laws obfuscates the other meanings of the word, meanings reminding us that hunger is not simply a benign force that promotes labor and clarifies social identity. In the parable of Dives and Lazarus, Hunger's lack of discrimination and the suffering it produces do not aid justice and charity but emerge directly as the failure of these virtues.[36]

The striking acknowledgement of Hunger's indiscriminately fatal consequences turns out to be rather short-lived as Hunger goes on to take up the familiar refrain that hunger or poverty is strictly the result of a voluntary decision not to work. In articulating this enduringly powerful idea, Hunger ultimately reveals what his pictorial representation in Douce makes clear: the figure does not just create material deficiency but actually fosters a frantic desire within the community to accumulate possessions so as to escape Hunger's most severe effects. Hunger discusses the parable of talents (Matthew 25) in an attempt to justify his estimation of work as a means to acquire goods. When he recounts how the lord strips the slothful man of his possessions, Hunger cites with approval the lord's declaration that "He þat hath shal haue and helpe þer hym liketh" (VIII.255). The figure goes on to threaten those who fail to work—those who "shal nauht haue"—with the reality of physical deprivation. Implicitly proffering material goods as the reward for labor, Hunger says, for instance, that both the parable in Matthew and Psalm 127:2 "aren euidences . . . for hem þat wolle not swynke / That here lyflode be lene and lyte worth here clothes" (VIII.261–62). As Kim has cogently argued, such statements reveal that "insecurity and the acquisitive attitude are the defining aspects of 'hunger'" at this point in the poem. Clearly, as a form of material deprivation, the figure of Hunger lacks any positive spiritual dimensions. In contrast to penitential forms of hunger as experienced by Jesus when fasting in the desert (Luke 4), this type of deprivation does not affirm or elicit any larger pursuit of virtue. Rather, as Hunger's exegetical practices reveal, "what started as an apparently innocuous affirmation of honest labor in lieu of begging has become a celebration of the acquisitive spirit."[37] This dimension of Hunger recalls Holy Churche's earlier teaching describing the human inclination to live beyond one's needs.[38]

Indeed, Langland's allegory goes on to enact how Hunger contributes to an excessive urge for accumulation. Langland explains that "Pore folk for fere tho fedde honger ȝerne / With craym and with croddes, with cresses and oþere erbes" (VIII.319–20). At the time of harvest, the workers celebrate their plentiful acquisition of food and finally conquer Hunger only by slipping into the sin of gluttony: "By that hit nyhed neyh heruost and newe corn cam to chepyng. / Thenne was folke fayn and fedde hunger dentiefliche, / And thenne gloton with gode ale garte hunger slepe" (VIII.321–23). The opacity of need is once again evident as the attempt to relieve Hunger with necessary sustenance turns into an exercise in gluttony. Indeed, the above lines figure gluttony as the seemingly inevitable consequence of satisfying need. The folk eat, we are told, "and thenne" gloton emerges. The allegory dynamically enacts this phenomena when the crisis of the Passus begins anew with the sudden return of Wastour who again demands delicate food and refuses to work in favor of "wander[ing] aboute" (VIII.324).

As the scene concludes with an apocalyptic warning about crop failure and famine (another dimension of hunger not caused merely by idleness), Langland does not put an end to the conflicts surrounding the plowing of the half-acre.[39] Rather, he exposes the insufficiency of the legal discourse that advocates the imposition of hunger as an unproblematically ethical act. The episode thus raises questions and complications that are crucial to understanding the causes of poverty and determining the Christian community's ethical response to need. Among its most central questions, the Passus asks, how does a community live out Holy Churche's lesson that measure is medicine? What are the resources for cultivating a society whose members are oriented toward charity, moderation, and the simple fulfillment of need? And in a Passus where the church is entirely absent, how can Christians understand hunger, labor, and almsgiving as nuanced issues with ethical importance beyond the powerful yet partisan version of justice articulated within secular labor legislation?

Franciscan Orations and the Sanctity of Need

In Passus XII–XVI Langland moves away from the ideological preoccupations of secular labor legislation to discuss poverty in a mode that explicitly considers the discourse of Franciscanism.[40] While concerns about material hunger and agricultural labor remain relevant, this section of the poem does not approach poverty as a consequence of idle or rebellious workers, but instead views it as a sanctifying condition. Moving into new conceptual territory, the poem explores the experience of material poverty in relationship to the dispositions of rechelesnesse and patience, qualities that emerge as personified interlocutors in this section of the text. As these figures elaborate on poverty as a dimension of subjectivity, they make strong interpretative claims about need, heralding it as an unequivocally sacred sign. Yet just as Langland exposes the troubling occlusions of the legal discourse on poverty, which largely demonizes the poor, he similarly reveals how the idealization of poverty also rests on rather suspicious ethical claims. In juxtaposing the discourse of Rechelesnesse and Patience, the poem calls attention to the striking similarities of their arguments. The allegory thus blends the signs to expose what might be viewed as the recklessness of patient poverty. Despite the speakers' arguments to the contrary, we shall see how the Franciscan idealization of poverty ultimately inhibits the work of charity and the growth of virtue among rich and poor alike. The difficulties and ethical consequences of discernment remain a powerful theme in this part of the poem. While we encountered earlier in the poem the slippages between need and excess and hunger and gluttony, we now experience the challenge of distinguishing between recklessness and patience, poverty and apathy, virtue and vice.

When we meet the personification of Rechelesnesse, Langland offers additional hermeneutic complications by presenting us with a figure of poverty that encompasses varied meanings and ethical commitments.[41] On the one hand, Rechelesnesse could be a way of heeding Holy Churche's warnings against the all-consuming temptations of the world. In this sense the figure would represent a healthy disregard for temporal concerns that block the pursuit of salvation. However, Rechelesnesse also bears a decidedly negative valence, allowing for the possibility that an admirable sense of carelessness can become a dangerous form of spiritual negligence. Indeed, the allegorical figure allows for both of these semantic possibilities when he emerges in the poem to support the discourse of Trajan, who insists that salvation is possible without clerical learning. Affirming the pagan's arguments, Rechelesnesse emphasizes the fundamental importance of love, mercy, and poverty as criteria for salvation. Yet he advocates these virtues as part of a larger argument rejecting religious education, knowledge, and sacramental works. How does one reconcile the figure's praise of some virtues at the direct expense of others?

The difficulties involved in defining Rechelesnesse remain apparent in the figure's extensive discourse on poverty. Initially, Rechelesnesse begins his discussion of poverty by addressing the importance of almsgiving and emphasizing the neediness and worthiness of the poor as alms recipients. Evoking Luke 14 as a guide for almsgiving, he calls on his fellow Christians to invite not just the "carefole" and the "crokede" to their feasts, but also the undifferentiated group of the "pore" (XII.104). His rationale for almsgiving stems from a social vision that emphasizes the unity of all people through Christ. Using the same term invoked by Piers in Passus VIII, he advances a reckless disregard for social hierarchy on earth and declares that "we [are Christ's] blody bretherne, as wel beggares as lordes. / Forthy loue we as leue childerne, lende hem þat nedeth, / And euery man helpe other for hennes shal we alle / To haue as as we haen serued" (XII.116–19). Rechelesnesse certainly displays no scrupulosity toward potential alms recipients, and he goes on to emphasize the fundamental worthiness of the poor by presenting them as figures of Christ.

The figure's Franciscan affiliations become explicit when he cites Matthew 19, one of the gospel texts central to the Franciscan movement. He argues that Christian perfection can only be attained through the renunciation of material possessions:

> "Yf thow likest to lyue," quod god, "þe lyf þat is parfit,
> Al þat thow hast here, hastly go and sulle hit;
> ȝef pore peple þe panes, þerof pors þou none,
> Ac ȝef hem forth to pore folk þat for my loue hit aske;
> Forsaek al and sue me and so is the best."
> (XII.163–67)

In calling his followers to "forsake al" and in adopting a life of need himself, Rechelesnesse's Christ makes poverty an integral part of Christian virtue.

As he elaborates on the nature of poverty as a holy state, Rechelesnesse considers how the virtue of patience is essential to Christian perfection. He makes it clear that the reckless disregard for material things must also entail the patient acceptance of deprivation. In the figure's well known comparison of poverty to a walnut, Rechelesnesse describes how the willing experience of need ultimately offers spiritual sustenance to the soul, so that poverty functions as a "spiritually restorative" condition:[42]

> Althouh hit (patient poverty) be sour to soffre, þer cometh a swete aftur.
> As on a walnote withoute is a bittere barke

> And aftur þat bittere barke, be þe scale aweye,
> Is a cornel of confort, kynde to restore,
> So aftur, pouerte or penaunce pacientliche ytake
> Maketh man to haue mynde in god and his mercy to craue,
> The which is þe cornel of confort for alle cristene soules.
> (XII.145–51)

In subsequent descriptions of poverty, Rechelesnesse continues to emphasize its spiritual benefits, and he develops a theory of salvation guaranteed almost entirely by the patient suffering of poverty. He offers specific analogies to explicate this theological notion. For example, he compares the patient poor to a seed that grows into a hardy plant only after surviving winter winds and frost (XII.187–200). His teaching on salvation repeatedly insists that those who suffer in poverty and those who delight in wealth will be repaid with the opposite situation after death: "Riht so, sothly, þat soffry may penaunce / Worth allowed of oure lord at here laste ende" (XII.194–95). And again, "Mescheues and myshappes and many tribulacions / Bitokeneth treuly in tyme comying aftur / Murthe for his morning, and þat much plentee" (XII.202–4). Lending further support to this idea, Rechelesnesse offers Abraham and Job as exemplars of patient poverty whose suffering eventually earns them great rewards. Though Abraham was "in greet pouerte . . . put," he was eventually delivered from his hardship "with moche welthe aftur" (XIII.8–14). Job similarly loses his wealth to face unimaginable suffering, but his sorrowful song eventually turns to "solace," and Job "bykam as a iolyf man and al his ioye newe" (XIII.19–20).

While Rechelesnesse mentions Abraham and Job to lend biblical authority to his ideas, the cracks in his teaching begin to show when he remarks on the outcome of their suffering. This outcome poses problems for his theory about the relationship between poverty and salvation because Abraham and Job do not simply receive heavenly rewards for their earthly hardship; rather, compensation comes when their wealth is restored and, in the case of Job, multiplied while they are still alive. Abraham himself remarks in Passus XVIII that God promised him material possessions and dominion as a reward for his faith: "Myen affiaunce and my faith is ferme in this bileue, / For hymsulue saide y sholde haue, y and myn issue bothe, / Lond and lordschip ynow and lyf withouten ende" (XVIII.254–56).[43] Most poor people could probably not expect such gracious material gifts from God while still on earth. In telling a story that promises such explicitly tangible rewards, Rechelesnesse's teaching on virtuous poverty becomes compromised, for it recalls Hunger's lessons on the acquisitiveness of need. Furthermore, because their riches were restored while they were alive, Abraham and Job died as wealthy patriarchs. This fact certainly complicates Rechelesnesse's extensive commentary on wealth as an obstacle to salvation. Indeed, the condemnation of wealth functions as a central aspect of the figure's discourse. While he sometimes claims that he does not oppose wealth in and of itself (XIII.26–27), he nonetheless tends to do just that. For instance, in a characteristic statement, Rechelesnesse unabashedly declares that "Riht as wedes waxeth in wose and in donge, / So of rychesse ope rychesse ariste alle vices" (XII.229–30).

In making such assertions, Rechelesnesse begins to reveal the more ethically suspect dimensions of his identity, and his carelessness ultimately proves to entail disregard for moral action.[44] While Holy Churche also warned against maintaining superfluous possessions, Rechelesnesse's critique of riches works differently because it imagines wealth primarily as a moral danger leading automatically to guile, covetousness, and even murder. For example, as he goes on to describe the particular dangers of wealth that is misspent or undistributed, Rechelesnesse strikingly fails to account for the activity of the human will:

> For, how euere hit be ywonne, but hit be wel dispened,
> Worldy wele ys wykked thing to hem þat hit kepeth.
> For if he be fer þerfro, fol ofte hath he drede
> That fals folk fecche aweye felonliche his godes;
> And ȝut more hit maketh men mony tymes and ofte
> To synege, and to souche sotiltees of Gyle,
> For coueytyse of þat catel to culle hym þat hit kepeth.
> And so is many man ymorthred for his moneye and his godes
> And tho that dede þe dede ydampned þerfore aftur,
> And he for his hard holdying in helle, parauntur.
> So coueytise of catel was combraunce to hem alle.
> (XII.235–45)

As Rechelesnesse describes the hypothetical murder of a rich man, he affirms the danger that wealth poses to the soul by noting that the punishment for murder (damnation of the killers) is the same as the punishment for storing up goods (damnation of the rich man). Making a kind of equation between murder and wealth, Rechelesnesse locates sinfulness not in the choice to steal and kill, but in the wealth itself which "maketh men mony tymes and ofte / To synege" (XII.239–40). Suggesting that the possession of material goods not only impels the owner into avarice but also inspires his fellow men to act on a murderous form of covetousness, Rechelesnesse offers no account of the interior processes by which a person resists or consents to sin. Therefore his praise of poverty, which relies on this repudiation of wealth, strangely nullifies moral action and accountability at the same time that it claims perfection in these arenas. The figure's concluding statements in Passus XII confirm this tendency to displace agency and culpability onto inanimate, material things. Rechelesnesse remarks, "Lo, how pans purchaseth fayre places and drede, / That rote is of robbares the rychesse withynne!" (XII.246–47). In this formulation, it is the "rychesse withynne" the beautiful houses that functions as the root or source of the robbers' nature.

As these examples suggest, Rechelesnesse's praise of patient poverty leads into some rather treacherous ethical territory that ultimately dismisses the work of virtue for both rich and poor alike. The figure's meaning as an admirable form of carelessness or lack of solicitude begins to look more and more like reckless passivity or, as I shall argue below, moral negligence. For Rechelesnesse, the poor person attains sanctity not finally because of his own goodness or penitence, but because of what Pearsall has aptly termed "want of opportunity for sin."[45] Rechelesnesse's teaching in this regard conveys a sense of apathy, and indeed Langland highlights such meaning by linking Rechelesnesse with wanhope, the consequence of sloth (XI.199). The lethargy that characterizes Rechelesnesse's teaching becomes most clear in his exemplum of the merchant and messenger. In Rechelesnesse's interpretation, the messenger, a figure for the poor, reaches his destination with significantly less anxiety and delay since he is unencumbered with material goods. He can more easily "rikene byfore resoun a resonable acounte" of what he possesses, while the rich merchant "mote nede be ylet lenger" than the messenger (XIII.35, 37). Furthermore, under the stipulation,

"*Necessitas non habet legem*" (an argument that Nede himself will later address), the messenger can freely take wheat from others' fields, while the merchant "mote forgo" "his hatt or his hoed or elles his gloues . . . or moneye of his porse" in exchange for the food (XIII.44–49). Finally, the messenger is "merye" and proceeds with "his mouth ful of songes" (XIII.59), while the merchant's many possessions cause him to "dredeth to be ded þerfore . . . and in derke mette / With robbares and reuares þat ryche men despoilen" (XIII.57–58). Burdened by his possessions and the anxiety they induce, the merchant can work to ensure his safety only by taking on the additional expense and effort of hiring "hors and hardy men" to protect him (XIII.62).

In his explication of the exemplum, Rechelesnesse significantly interprets the merchant's extra efforts to ensure his own safety as the rich person's necessary obedience to *all* Christian law in order to reach heaven. Emphasizing that the merchant/rich have to work especially hard to attain what seems to come so easily for the messenger/poor, he explains that

> The marchaunt is no more to mene but men þat ben ryche
> Aren alle accountable to crist and to þe kyng of heune,
> That hold mote þe hey way, euene the ten hestes,
> Both louye and lene lele and vnlele
> And haue reuthe and releue with his rychesse by his power
> All maner men yn meschief yfalle. . . .
>
> (XIII.66–71)

Here, Rechelesnesse seeks to argue, not unreasonably, that rich and poor have different obligations, and that the poor, in particular, should not be held accountable to laws that their need prevents them from fulfilling. Indeed, Lawrence Clopper finds Rechelesnesse's teachings persuasive for suggesting that the rich must fulfill the "letter of the law," while the poor can perform charitable acts in the "will alone."[46] However, in Rechelesnesse's account of these groups' distinctive obligations, the poor are exempted from some seemingly universal Christian duties that they could certainly perform in both will and deed. For example, Rechelesnesse argues that it is the rich who "aren alle accountable to

Criste," and he adds that it is they who are expected to uphold the "ten hestes" along with the command to "louye" (XIII.68–69). In specifying that such obligations pertain to the rich alone, Rechelesnesse gives us the sense that the poor can live in a kind of undemanding and carefree existence. The result is that the figure ends up making poverty into what Aers calls a "spiritual abstraction," devoid of all hardship and suffering.[47] The rich, however, enjoy no such freedom as they must "Fynde beggares bred, bakkes for þe colde, / Tythen here goed treuliche . . . And ȝut more . . . maken pees and quyten menne dettes / And spele and spare to spene vppon þe nedfole" (XIII.72–77). Many of these activities would be difficult for the poor to perform, but this account remains problematic because it makes the active work of charity—loving one's neighbor, giving alms, promoting peace—look like a series of tedious tasks on a demanding to-do list. Here, it seems as though the poor have the better life not necessarily because they suffer in Christlike poverty, but because they can bypass the most strenuous Christian duties as people who "beth nat ybounde as beth þe riche, to bothe two (bowe to) lawes" (XIII.80).

In this formulation poverty is truly reckless, for it gives no concern to what seem to be basic Christian duties. While Rechelesnesse obviously admires the freedom found through poverty, one wonders if this path to salvation is not more appropriately a path of indifference. Revealed in his parable and in the semantic range of his very name, Rechelesnesse hardly makes lack of solicitude seem like Christian perfection. The poem's suspicion of Franciscan ideology emerges with its recognition that detachment from worldly things might also entail detachment from one's fellow Christians and the moral obligations conferred on all people—rich and poor alike.

After Ymagenatyf makes a brief appearance in the poem, we next encounter Patience, who recapitulates many of Rechelesnesse's views on poverty. In returning to these subjects, Langland's allegory reveals the power and flexibility of Franciscan ideals, which are presented here not explicitly as a reckless disregard for things of the world but as a lesson in the interior virtue of patience, appropriately articulated by Patience himself. Seeing the relationship between Rechelesnesse and Patience as a progression of virtue, Clopper views Patience as a morally sound version of his predecessor—as the perfect fulfillment of Franciscan poverty.[48] However, when examined closely, the discourse of these figures betrays a strking similarity, leading us to question if the patience praised within Franciscanism is really anything other than a reckless form of spirituality. Exploring the meaning and implications of Patience, we can see that Langland's allegory will put pressure on the figure's account of sanctity, subtly exposing how his arguments may actually inhibit the work of virtue. Once again, we are being asked to see the slippages between signs that are central to late medieval writing about poverty.

Patience's associations with Franciscan poverty become clear when we first encounter the figure as a mendicant begging for food and, rather troublingly, for money as well (XV.35).[49] In his subsequent conversation with Activa Vita, an individual defined by material labor, Patience criticizes his solicitude for temporal things. Though Actyf tries to defend his production of food as a form of charitable work, Patience is unimpressed by his arguments. Actyf angers Patience further and reveals his thorough immersion in the material world when he goes on to advocate the use of hunger as a tool of moral reform. Making a now familiar argument, he maintains that pride can be "puyreliche fordo and þat thorw payn defaute" (XV.229). Reiterating a lesson learned from the half-acre episode, Patience objects to Actyf's comment by exposing the ineffectiveness of Hunger as a moral tool. Rather impatiently, Patience tells Actyf, "Pees! . . . Y preye, ȝow, sire Actyf! / For þoȝ nere payn of plouh ne potage were, / Pruyde wold potte hymsulf forth though no plough erye" (XV.232–34).

Rather than continuing to elaborate on both the practical and ethical limitations of hunger, Patience takes us further into Franciscan discourse as he offers himself as the solution to the problem of need. He tells Actyf, "Hit am y þat fynde alle folke and fram hunger saue" (XV.235). On hearing this statement, one wonders how Patience can save people from hunger, especially when we think of the patient figure of Lazarus, who finally died from hunger's effects. Patience is unconcerned with such material exigencies, however, and he offers Actyf a line from the Pater Noster, "*fiat voluntas tua*," telling him, "eet þis when þe hungreth / Or when thow clomsest for colde or clingest for drouthe" (XV.250–51).

In offering the words of prayer as sustenance to the hungry, naked, and thirsty, Patience makes it clear that neither almsgiving nor labor is the solution to poverty. Rather, patient Christians will receive sustenance from God's miraculous gifts. Patience names the Israelites as an example of this ideal existence and explains how they were fed by a miracle, not by working for their food: "Hit is founde þat fourty winter folke lyuede and tylde nat, / And oute of þe flynt spronge þe floed þat folk and bestes dronke" (XV.263–64). With his dismissal of Actyf's labor and his disregard for the mortal consequences of those who might not experience such miracles,[50] Patience exemplifies par excellence the Franciscan lack of solicitude for earthly things.

Yet, interestingly, the figure's discourse begins to shift, and Patience returns us, at least briefly, to the material world where some people wield wealth and others suffer from the physical and emotional consequences of poverty. The figure thus becomes increasingly complex as he seems to retreat from his rigorous idealization of poverty as a welcome experience that should simply be suffered with patience. Taking us back to the lessons of Holy Churche, Patience first explains that poverty is the result of immoderate desire and consumption: "yf men lyuede as mesure wolde sholde neuere be defaute / Amonges cristene creatures" (XV.270–71). At this moment, Patience does not exactly advocate the patient acceptance of poverty, but demands an organization of resources based on principles of moderation presumably enacted through charitable giving.[51] Patience goes on to paint a realistic portrait of poverty by describing those people who stand to benefit most from a measured distribution of wealth: "beggares about myssomur bredles they soupe / And ȝut is wynter for hem worse, for weetshoed þey gange, / Afurste and afyngered and foule rebuked / And arated of ryche men, þat reuthe is to here" (XVI.13–16). Here, Patience is attentive to both the physical and emotional hardship of the poor.

Following such a description, one might expect to find a "reckless" repudiation of the rich, but once again Patience surprises us. Rather than strictly promoting ideals of material poverty, Patience offers a more inclusive vision of sanctity that primarily requires spiritual humility. Opposing Rechelesnesse's attitudes toward the rich, Patience follows his description of beggars by stating: "Ac for þe beste, as y hope, aren som pore and ryche. / Riht so haue reuthe on thy renkes alle / And amende vs of thy mercy and make vs alle meke, / Lowe and lele and louynge and of herte pore" (XVI.21–24). Patience's prayer that "alle" can become poor in heart strikingly demonstrates the figure's concern with the interior self and prepares us for yet another discursive shift into the poem's sacramental vision.

Establishing spiritual poverty as a goal for rich and poor alike, Patience goes on to speak like a confessor, and he emphasizes how the sacrament of penance functions to make one "pore of herte." In a detailed treatment of the sacrament, Patience names its component parts and comments on the unique spiritual benefits of each. He asks God to "sende vs contricion clereliche to clanse with oure soules / And confessioun to kulle alle kyne synnes / And satisfaccioun þe whiche folfilleth þe fader will of heuene" (XVI.25–27). Patience then goes on to determine that confession, contrition, and satisfaction "ben dowel and dobet and dobest of alle" (XVI.28). He does not stop there, however, and Patience ultimately links penance with poverty itself, declaring that "*Cordis contricio, Oris confessio, Operis satisfaccio* . . . withoute doute tholieth alle pouerte / And lereth lewed and lered, hey and lowe to knowe / Ho doth wel or bet or beste aboue alle" (XVI.31a–34).

Emphasizing the sacrament's applicability to "lewed and lerned, hey and lowe," Patience explicitly turns the discussion of poverty into a consideration of the will and its reformation through penance. At this point of the poem, Patience suggests that the amount of one's material possessions is not the final arbiter of salvation, though it is certainly a factor. Rather, for Patience a contrite heart and participation in penance make up the essential conditions for attaining heaven. In reference to contrition, confession, and satisfaction, he says, for instance, "[A]nd bote these thre þat y spak of at domesday vs defende / Elles is al an ydel al oure lyuynge here" (XVI.36–37).

In highlighting how the sacrament of penance functions as an important tool of moral reform, Patience challenges the ethical visions articulated by both Hunger and Rechelesnesse. However, Langland once again reveals the ideological power of the Franciscan imaginary as Patience's sacramental teachings only emerge as a temporary anomaly in a speech that is otherwise insistent on prioritizing need as the highest form of sanctity. After his powerful oration on the centrality of penance,

Patience reintroduces the troubling moral theology we encountered in Rechelesnesse's discourse on poverty. Specifically, he undermines his own teaching by offering material poverty as the all-encompassing antidote to sin.[52] After declaring that "none of þe seuene synnes sitte" "in pouerte þer pacience is" (XVI.60–61), he explains precisely how poverty combats each vice. He tells us that "pruyde in rychesse regneth," for poverty is "buxom" and "buxumnesse and boest ben eueremore at were" (XVI.57, 63–64). Wrath does not dwell in the poor man because "lowlyche he loketh and louelych is his speche" (XVI.66–69). Gluttony is similarly unwelcome with the poor because "his rents wol nat reche ryche metes to bugge" (XVI.71–72). While Covetous "is of a kene will / And hath hondes and Armes of a longe lenthe," poverty "is but bote a pety thynge, appereth nat to his nauele" (XVI.81–83). And while Avarice "hath almaries and yrebounden coffres," poverty "hat bote pokes to potten in his godes" (XVI.86, 87). Because the needy lack the fine food and drink that stir up lust, "Lechereye loueth no pore" (XVI.90). And, finally, though sloth "sewe pouerte," misfortune intervenes to prevent the poor man from acting on his thought, reminding him instead of his ultimate dependence on God (XVI.94).

It is not surprising that the poem generates this detailed reflection on the deadly sins after Patience has focused on the importance of penance. For, in the widespread tradition of penitential literature, and indeed in Passus V of *Piers Plowman* itself, the sins emerge as a useful framework enabling the penitent to examine his conscience and make a complete confession. But in Patience's discourse, the sins do not at all function as part of an interior hermeneutic exercise that leads the penitent to assess both the motives and effects of his behavior. Rather, the sins are enumerated within a paradigm that ultimately nullifies the sacrament of penance. Following Patience's arguments, it seems reasonable to ask what poor person would ever need to confess, since poverty offers him or her direct immunity to sin?

The nature of poverty's moral benefits also becomes troubling if we look closely at Patience's vision of sinlessness. Given the similarities between his and Rechelesnesse's arguments, we must ask once again what version of virtue does the poem's Franciscan discourse produce? Patience's treatment of pride offers an answer to this question for it shows that material poverty does not necessarily encourage the poverty of spirit associated with penitence. Instead, poverty demands outwardly humble behavior because the poor literally cannot afford to act otherwise. As Patience explains, "þe pore is ay prest to plese the þe ryche / And buxom at his biddyng for his breed and his drynke" (XVI.62–63). Here poverty encourages only the signs of humility that the poor offer the rich in exchange for food and drink. Patience's discussion of wrath rests on a similar logic: "For lowlyche he loketh and louelyche is his speche / That mete or moneye of straugne men moet begge" (XVI.69–70). Once again, the point is not that the poor never experience anger but that the expression of anger must be suppressed if one expects to acquire "mete or moneye" from "straunge" men. In these examples of what amounts to a deeply suspect form of patience, it is significant that Patience's interpretation of poverty as a holy condition only leads to additional hermeneutic complexity. This is because Patience's poverty merely *displays* the absence of sin. His specious logic also becomes more pronounced if we notice his failure to mention envy, a sin to which the poor might understandably be tempted.

In addition to questioning the nature of poverty's supposed perfection, we should also consider the paradigm in which Patience presents his most strenuous arguments for the value of need. We have seen how Patience's discussion of the seven deadly sins unusually works against penitential theology at this point in the poem. But it is also interesting to note that Patience presents the poem's highest praise of poverty as the absence of sin. This framework is telling within a poem deeply interested in the nature of virtue as an affirmative concept. In other sections of the poem, Langland allegorizes the theological virtues, writing with breathtaking sophistication about the relations among faith, hope, and charity within the realm of biblical history and the liturgy. Given our previous encounter with Rechelesnesse as a form of apathetic negligence, we should be extremely cautious of viewing poverty as a counter to sin, not an affirmative path of virtue.

What are the implications of this specific ethical framework? Could this notion of poverty as perfection actually obscure the importance of the remedial or contrary virtues more commonly invoked as the antidote to sin? In this longstanding tradition, temperance emerges as the remedy to covetousness, peace counteracts the effects of wrath, faith disrupts the power of pride, and so on.[53] Does Patience's praise of poverty somehow make these virtues irrelevant? Because the poor are sanctified by their poverty alone, are they excluded from participating in charity, faith, or prudence, for example? While Patience may be well intentioned in suggesting that the poor suffer enough without the added pressure of cultivating particular forms of virtue, does he ultimately dehumanize the poor by discounting them as moral beings beyond the confines of their poverty? Such questions clearly challenge Clopper's claim that Patience's perfect "rechelesnesse" is not "a passive acceptance of whatever comes one's way."[54] On the contrary, it would seem that Patience's all-encompassing praise of poverty carries with it some troubling omissions that obfuscate how the poor can pursue specific forms of virtue as acts of the will.

If Patience's teachings about the poor surprisingly dismiss their potential for sanctity, then his comments about the rich also surprisingly de-emphasize their hope for salvation through almsgiving. The rich who may remain unpersuaded by Patience's exhortations to poverty find themselves in a difficult position. In many instances, Patience echoes Rechelesnesse's repudiation of wealth and the wealthy themselves. He makes the familiar statements that the rich cannot have two heavens but must pay the price for their joy and ease while on earth (XVI.1–12). One of the most disturbing facets of this argument comes with Patience's insistence that the rich's suffering after death will not be mitigated by their (patient?) performance of the works of mercy that seek to alleviate the suffering of the poor. Patience makes the poem's second reference to the parable of Dives and Lazarus to warn the rich of the spiritual danger they face. While most commentaries on the parable, as we have seen, attribute Dives's damnation to his failures in charity and not to his wealth itself, Patience seems uninterested in the story's charitable lessons—lessons that might, incidentally, encourage almsgiving and relieve the suffering of the poor with something more than patience, that is, with material food and drink (the very items for which Patience has begged). Positing a cycle of strict substitution in the afterlife, Patience explains,

> Angeles þat in helle now ben hadden somtyme ioye,
> And dyues in deyntees lyuede and in *douce vie*
> And now he buyth hit bittere; he is a beggare of helle.

Many man hath his ioye here *for al here wel dedes*
And lordes and ladyes ben cald for ledes þat they haue
And slepeth, as hit semeth, and somur euere hem followeth.
Ac when deth awaketh hem of here wele þat were er so ryche
Then aren hit puyre pore thynges in purgatorie or in hell.
(XV.298–305, my emphasis)

If the rich, as Patience declares, suffer purgatory or damnation in spite of their good deeds, then it remains to be seen why they should practice charity at all.

The danger of Patience's views becomes further apparent when he applies similar logic to the poor, arguing that they can claim salvation based solely on their material state. After he notes how the poor are called by poverty to recognize that God will always help them, functioning even as their own servant, Patience goes on to say that the poor's relationship to God does not especially matter, for their poverty guarantees them salvation above all else:

Mescheif is ay a mene and maketh hym to thenk
That god is his gretteste helpe and no gome elles,
And he his seruant, as he saith, and of his seute bothe.
And where he be or be nat, a bereth þe signe of pouerte
And in þat secte our saueour saued al mankynde.
(XVI.95–99, my emphasis)

While he begins by stating that poverty induces dependence on God, Patience then abandons this very idea by advocating poverty above and beyond any awareness of one's own connection to God. Scott summarizes the point of the above passage when she explains that the poor "may be saved, in spite of themselves, because they wear Christ's livery." She adds that "This is the case whether they consider themselves God's servants or not, because they are wearing the badge of poverty."[55] This idea is shocking, though it is unacknowledged as such by Scott. Poverty here seems to surpass any sense that even one's identity as a Christian matters in the scheme of salvation. It is for this reason that Aers has called attention to this passage's troubling Pelagianism.[56] Indeed, Patience's theological commitments compromise his status as a form of virtue; if material poverty alone offers such great rewards, then it matters not if one's patience is reckless, passive, or ultimately negligent. Once again, the poem has exposed how discourse on poverty—in this case within the mode of Franciscanism—offers need as a quintessential moral solution that poses deep interpretive, theological, and ethical problems.

Charity, Church, and the Limits of Anticlericalism

The absence of affirmative forms of virtue in Patience's teaching becomes more noticeable with the emergence of figures who shift the poem's focus to charity and the other theological virtues. While Patience and Rechelesnesse presented poverty itself as charity, as the highest form of virtue, Liberum Arbitrium, Abraham (Faith), and the Samaritan further undermine Franciscan ideology with authoritative teaching about love as a lived practice in the material world. This section of the chapter focuses primarily on Liberum Arbitrium and the Samaritan to show that these figures are united in their rejection of poverty and mendicancy as sacred practices; each of these figures, moreover, gains credibility by offering more sophisticated theological models that present virtue as something other than the absence of goods that in turn leads to the absence of sin. In their teachings on love, they propose models of sanctity based not on the renunciation of all possessions but on their charitable distribution.

Their corrective role in the poem, however, is not without its own complications. Difficulty arises when Liberum Arbitrium in particular approaches poverty largely within the framework of anticlerical discourse. Making arguments that we will encounter again in chapters two and three, Liberum Arbitrium describes the church as a corrupt institution poisoned by its obsession with material goods. Yet in spite of the figure's conventional anticlericalism, the poem nonetheless reveals the limitations of this ideological perspective in the same way that it has revealed the limitations of labor legislation and Franciscan thought. While critics such as Wendy Scase find in the C-text a "broader and more fully developed anticlericalism," my reading shows that the poem's anticlerical arguments are in tension with its capacious approach to poverty and its powerful spiritual vision foregrounding the importance of the church and sacraments.[57] Though Liberum Arbitrium does criticize the church, he ultimately moves past the institution's flaws to acknowledge the role of the laity who exploit the poor and to make the sacraments central to his conception of charitable practice. The Samaritan completes this movement away from anticlerical discourse, as he allegorically enacts the poem's sacramental vision—a vision that imagines baptism, penance, and the Eucharist as acts of social aid.

These figures, I argue, make an important contribution to *Piers Plowman*'s investigation of poverty because they promote the primacy of charity over poverty itself, and they provide a unique theological rationale for almsgiving as a form of social relation inextricable from the sacraments themselves. In so doing, they reveal the costs of anticlericalism's epistemological and ethical confidence when it comes to the subject of poverty. With its focus on exposing the fraudulence of the clergy's need, anticlerical critique proves to be problematic because it tends to overlook other agents exploiting the poor, and it tends to locate all possibility for moral reform in the single act of restricting the church's possessions.

When we meet the personification of Liberum Arbitrium, the distinctiveness of his thought becomes readily apparent as he contradicts his poverty-focused predecessors by declaring that it is a "vyce and a foule shame / To begge or to borwe, but of god one" (XVI.373–74). Liberum Arbitrium's denunciation of mendicancy signals a wider suspicion about Franciscanism and fraternal life.[58] This suspicion is embodied in the figure's own semantic and ontological complexity as the personification of shifting intellectual, affective, and moral powers.[59] The very nature of a figure who "Of fele tyme [chooses] to fihte . . . falsnesse to destruye, / And *som tyme* to soffre bothe sorwe and tene" challenges the ideal of patient and perpetual suffering insisted on by Rechelesnesse and Patience himself (XVI.174–75, my emphasis). Indeed, the distinctiveness of Liberum Arbitrium's perspective becomes more apparent when he instructs Wille about the virtues of charity. Referencing 1 Corinthians 13, Liberum Arbitirum attributes to charity what

Patience ascribes to poverty: "Charite . . . chargeth not, ne chyt, thow me greue hym . . . *Non inflatur, non est ambiciosa*" (XVI.290–291a).

This definition leads Wille to express reservations about mankind's ability to cultivate charity, and it is the will that returns the poem to explicitly material concerns by telling Liberum Arbitrium, "I knewe neuere, by Crist, clerk noþer lewed / That he ne askede aftur his and oþerewhiles coueytede / Thyng that nedede hym nauhte, and nyme hit yf a myhte!" (XVI.292–94). Here, Wille recalls Holy Churche's earlier teaching to define love as the recognition and fulfillment of need, acts that are extremely difficult, as Wille himself attests. Liberum Arbitrium continues to educate Wille about the nature of charity, but he hardly eases Wille's doubts when he explains that charity is an interior state connected to earthly possessions but not determined by desire for such goods: "Charite is a childische thyng . . . As proud of a peny as of a pounde of golde, / And as glad of a goune of a gray russet / As of a cote of cammaca or of clene scarlet" (XVI.298–301).[60] While characteristic of the highest theological virtue, this form of detachment remains elusive; and Liberum Arbitrium seems to confirm Wille's initial reservations about the practicability of charity, as he goes on to condemn the church's failure to live according to its needs.

In the next Passus, Liberum Arbitrium presents the miraculous feeding of holy men and women as a call for discriminate almsgiving. He notes that birds fed people such as Paul "In tokenynge þat trewe man alle tymes sholde / Fynde honest men, holy men and oþer rihtfole peple" (XVII.33–34). After specifying the recipients of charity as honest, holy, and righteous people, Liberum Arbitrium focuses primarily on the church to clarify its role within schemes of almsgiving. He quotes a section of Tobias 3, and then glosses the scripture by saying, "This is no more to mene bote men of holy churche/ Sholde reseue right nauht but þat riht wolde / And refuse reuerences and raueners offrynges" (XVII.41–43).[61] While these guidelines seem straightforward, it becomes apparent that the contemporary church has had difficulty in following them. Liberum Arbitrium displays his anticlerical tendencies when he criticizes the church for its rampant covetousness. Using puns to emphasize how Christ's cross has been turned into a cash-like commodity, Liberum Arbitrium complains that it "is reuthe to rede how the rede noble / Is reuerenced byfore the rode and resceyued for the worthiore / To amende and to make, as with men of holy churche / Thenne Cristes crosse"(XVII.200–203). The clergy must learn to "louye mesure," and, to facilitate this objective, Liberum Arbitrium calls on the laity to withhold alms from the clergy who are not really in need. The poem once again addresses the rich directly as Liberum Arbitrium advocates a prioritized system of discriminate almsgiving with the church functioning as the least worthy recipient:

> "Allas! Lordes and ladyes, lewede consayle haue ȝe
> To feffe suche and fede þat founded ben to þe fulle
> With þat ȝoure bernes and ȝoure bloed by goed lawe may clayme!
> For god bad his blessed, as þe boek techeth . . .
> To helpe thy fader formost byfore freres or monkes
> Or ar prestes or pardoners or eny peple elles.
> Helpe thy kyn, Crist bid, for þer comseth charite,
> And afturward awayte ho hath moest nede
> And þer help yf thow hast; and þat halde y charite."
> (XVII.56–64)

Liberum Arbitrium presents the church as a body that usurps from lords and ladies the goods that are rightfully owed to their children. He insists that charity begins by helping one's kin and then by aiding those who "hath moest nede."[62] The church ranks near the bottom as an object of charity because the clergy are not poor; rather, as Liberum Arbitrium explains, they are "founded . . . to þe fulle."

According to Liberum Arbitrium, the church should be an agent that disperses its goods to the poor.[63] The figure names St. Lawrence as an example of the "largenesse" that characterizes charity, a virtue that in turn should characterize the church itself (XVII.65). As his legend makes clear, Lawrence achieved sanctity for his discriminate use of the church's treasure in refusing to give it to the Roman emperor and in distributing it to the truly needy. The legend describes Lawrence's charity as an active and intimate association with the poor: "Blessed Laurence . . . sought out Christians by day and by night, and ministered to all according to their needs. . . . He also washed the feet of the poor and gave alms to all."[64] The saint's commitment to the poor becomes even more clear when, after the emperor demands the church's treasure, Lawrence gathers up the needy people, presenting the poor themselves as the true treasure of the institution.

This story is a powerful allusion in Liberum Arbitrium's discourse for it suggests that the church should not claim poverty for itself but should view the poor as its most valuable possession to be protected and aided by the giving of alms. In this spirit, Liberum Arbitrium focuses explicitly on the rights of the poor, insisting not that they subsist merely on patience, but that they deserve a share of the church's wealth. While Patience said that the poor could claim salvation "by puyr rihte" (XVI.100),[65] Liberum Arbitrium corrects his Pelagian statements at the same time that he seeks to improve the lives of the poor. He calls for the church to perform the active work of charity when he says, "Y dar not carpe of clerkes now þat cristes tresor kepe / That pore peple *by puyre riht* here part myhte aske" (XVII.69–70; my emphasis). In acknowledging that the poor have a claim to part of the church's treasure (not to heaven itself), Liberum Arbitrium seeks to remedy the injustice caused by the institution's covetousness, and in so doing he also exposes the error of Patience's poverty-centered theology. For Liberum Arbitrium the church itself must be a form of charity that brings together a sense of social unity, a commitment to faith, and an array of economic practices guided primarily by love. When Wille asks Liberum Arbitrium for a definition of holy church, the figure responds by saying that it is "Charite . . . Lif in and leutee in o byleue and lawe, / A loueknotte of luetee and of lele byleue, / Alle kyne cristene cleuyinge on o will, Withoute gyle and gabbyng gyue and sulle and lene" (XVII.125–29). This last aspect of charity and church reaffirms that the institution must adopt a new economic program that foregrounds moderation and aid to the poor. Later in his speech, the figure wanders into near Wycliffite territory when he advocates the disendowment of the church, commanding "Taketh [the clergy's] londe, ȝe lordes, and lat hem lyue by dymes" (XVII.227).[66]

Despite the heights reached by his anticlerical fervor at this point in the poem, Liberum Arbitrium nonetheless constrains his criticism of the church to reveal that contemporary problems with poverty are not simply a matter of clerical covetousness to be resolved by the church's disendowment. His speech diverges from traditional anticlerical discourse as it expands to consider the faults of the lay elite and to detach the discussion of charity solely from the corruption of the church. While Liberum Arbitrium certainly complains about the church's covetousness and wealth, he interestingly connects the institution's failings with the failings that are rampant in lay society as well. He emphasizes the interrelations between the church and the laity when he explains how the institution's discriminate reception of alms will produce widespread moral rehabilitation:

> Thenne wolde lordes and ladyes be loth to agulte
> And to take of here tenauntes more then treuthe wolde,
> And marchauntʒ merciable woulde be and men of lawe bothe,
> Wolde religious refuse rauenours Almesses.
> Thenne grace sholde grow ʒut and grene loue wexe
> And charite þat chield is now shoulde chaufen of hymsulue
> And conforte alle cristene, woulde holy kirke amende.
> (XVII.44–50)

While the church is imagined as the necessary catalyst of moral reform, thus bearing some responsibility for the actions of the wider community, its ethical failures are not constructed in opposition to the presumed perfection of lay society. Even though Liberum Arbitrium, as we have seen, at one point encourages lords to disendow the church, he also notes that they, too, are implicated in exploiting the poor by, for example, "tak[ing] of here tenauntes more then treuthe wolde." The sins of the church are thus intertwined with the sins of the laity, and the reformation of the religious institution entails the necessary moral rehabilitation of the elite as well.

Liberum Arbitrium also restricts his anticlerical vehemence by making it clear that charity does not strictly entail discriminate almsgiving and the disendowment of the church. While it might include such acts, the virtue also importantly involves cultivating a generous disposition aimed at treating others with love. Liberum Arbitrium thus introduces the concept of charity by explaining that it is distinctive for its empathetic awareness of others: "He is glad with alle glade, as gurles þat lawhen alle, / And sory when he seth men sory—as thow seest childerne / Lawhe þer men lawheth and loure þer oþere louren" (XVI.302–4). As a condition that binds people together in the mutual experience of sorrow or joy, charity also entails a generosity of spirit that sees one's fellow Christians as fundamentally honest and trustworthy people:

> And when a man swereth "forsoth" for sooth he hit troweth;
> Weneth he þat no wyhte woulde lye and swerie,
> Ne þat eny gome woulde gyle ne greue oþere
> For drede of god þat so goed is. . . .
>
> (XVI.305–8)

Implicitly trusting the motives, speech, and actions of others, charity here is defined by the absence of scrupulosity or suspicion. This disposition is clearly in tension with the figure's own antagonism toward the clergy and his insistence on discriminate almsgiving.

Yet this sense of trustworthiness and empathy is also what drives acts of charity, which are not limited in the figure's discourse to reforming the church. Liberum Arbiturum describes how charity appropriately performs the works of mercy: "his wone is to wynde on pilgrimages / There pore men and prisones ben, and paye for here fode, / Clotheth hem and conforeth hem" (XVI.324–26). These activities are good and holy works that stress the interaction of rich and poor. Yet even such moments of generosity do not fully constitute charity. The figure instead emphasizes the importance of the sacraments in cultivating the highest of virtues:

> And when [charity] hath visited thus fetured folke and
> oþer folke pore,
> Thenne ȝerneth he into ȝouthe and ȝeepliche he secheth
> Pryude with alle þe purtinaunces, and pakketh hem togyderes
> And laueth hem in þe lauendrie, *laboraui in gemitu meo,*
> Bouketh hem at his breste and beteth hem ofte,
> And with warm water of his yes woketh hem til they white. . . .
>
> (XVI.330–35)

The sequence of events in this passage is important. Penitence surprisingly follows—rather than motivates—the performance of the works of mercy. This order implies that doing good works can lead to pride, and it shows that contrition emerges as an important dimension of charity, with penance washing away sin, a moral failure experienced by the almsgiver himself. This discussion thus carefully places limits on the sanctifying power of doing good works.

It also reveals that Liberum Arbitrium's programs for ecclesiastical reform are not strictly constituted by economic changes. Throughout his commentary on the church, Liberum Arbitrium makes it clear that the clergy must actively perform the sacraments to sustain the growth of charity. So, in addition to aiding the poor and sick, they must preach to the people and spread the faith. In particular, "Euery bisshope bi þe lawe sholde buxumliche walke / And pacientliche thorw his prouynce and to his people hym shewe, / Feden hem and follen hem and fere hem fro synne" (XVII.283–85). For Liberum Arbitrium, the church's role in giving alms and performing the works of mercy cannot be separated from its larger mission of offering the people spiritual sustenance by performing the sacraments and preaching. This sacramental focus not only undermines the anticlericalism in this section of the poem but also once again exposes problems with Rechelesnesse's and Patience's praise of poverty as the antidote to sin. Liberum Arbitrium shows that a person cannot simply suffer poverty and claim salvation, nor can a person practice charity and expect to be saved. In Liberum Arbitrium's discourse, it is the clergy's work and participation in the sacraments that "destruye dedly synne" (XVII.291). Overall, Liberum Arbitrium occupies a unique position in the poem as someone who is suspicious of Franciscan ideals yet also reluctant to transform that suspicion solely into anti-poverty polemic. While his discussion of poverty and charity includes principles of antifraternal and anticlerical thought, Liberum Arbitrium moves beyond the constraints of these discursive arenas to articulate an ethical vision that prioritizes both care for the needy and participation in the sacraments.

The poem goes on to explore the nature of faith, hope, and charity, and, as it does, it reveals more clearly how the theological virtues and the sacraments encompass forms of social relation often imagined as the rich's merciful treatment of the poor. While poverty thus persists as a key focus in the poem, the experience of need remains excluded as the primary site of sanctity; the poem instead continues to praise the alleviation of poverty performed as a dimension of faith. When Wille meets Faith himself on a "myddelenton sonenday" (XVIII.181), Langland takes us into liturgical time, and the structure of the poem itself becomes shaped by the rhythms of the church that lead us through Christ's passion, crucifixion, and resurrection. We must pause now, however, before the advent of Christ to explore how the virtue of faith works in relationship to charity and poverty.

The personification of faith in *Piers Plowman* is figured as Abraham, and, while this identification is traditional, it conveys a particular resonance in the poem because Abraham is the same man who comforts Lazarus in the wake of Dives's charitable failures. The poem explicitly foregrounds Abraham's relationship with the poor man, whom Wille sees sitting in the patriarch's lap. Wille notes that Abraham "baer a thynge þat a blessed euere," and he asks about the person to whom Abraham shows such affection (XVIII.270). Abraham replies to Wille that Lazarus is a "present of moche pris," and he describes how he comforts him along with "many a carfol þere þat aftur [Christ's] comyng loken" (XVIII.266).

The representation of Lazarus in this part of the poem is important because Abraham emphasizes not only that the poor man suffers, but that he too shares in the poor man's suffering as they both await Christ's fulfillment. It is interesting to note that earlier in the poem, however, Hunger viewed Lazarus's place in Abraham's lap as one of honor and peacefulness. He described the poor man as "sitt[ing] as he a syre were / In al manere ese" (VIII.280–81). Yet when understanding the parable through the evolving allegorical process, that is from the perspective of faith rather than hunger, this later Passus shows that the poor man, along with Abraham, actually remains wretched without Christ. The two figures find themselves in the same predicament of waiting for God's own mercy. As Abraham explains,

> ". . . the pouke [Lazarus] hath atached,
> And me þerwith . . . . may no wed vs quyte
> Ne noen bern ben oure borw ne bryngen vs fro his daunger—
> Fro þe poukes pondefuld no maynprise may vs feche—

> Til he come þat y carpe of, Crist is his name
> That shal delyuere vs som day out of þe deueles power. . . ."
> (XVIII.277–82)

In place of the "ese" imagined by Hunger, we find Abraham and Lazarus under siege, in a state of desperate longing. Lazarus in particular hardly seems like the jubilant figure sanctified by his earthly poverty and suffering. Rather, Abraham and Lazarus's situation demonstrates that poverty, kindness, and faith itself hold little force without the presence of Christ. Indeed, as the poor man stays "lollyng in [Abraham's] lappe," Wille begins to weep at the painfulness of waiting for "the myhte of goddes mercy that myhte vs alle amende" (XVIII.285, 287).

As it continues to move through the virtues and liturgical time, *Piers Plowman* does grant Wille a vision of Christ whose mercy alleviates suffering through the promise of salvation. Christ's mercy is presented as a manifestation of charity, and the Samaritan emerges in the poem to offer the text's most authoritative teaching on love—a form of love that combines the work of the sacraments with the work of nonscrupulous almsgiving. In a retelling of Luke 10, the Samaritan encounters the ailing figure of *semyuief* who represents the human will encumbered by sin. As such he remains totally incapable of healing himself or directing himself toward virtue. The Samaritan tends to *semyuief,* and the allegorical dimensions of the episode become clear as the man's regeneration occurs through the sacraments: "Withoute þe bloed of a barn he beth nat ysaued . . . And with þe bloed of þat barn enbaumed and ybaptised." (XIX.86–88). Emphasizing the progressive nature of the sacraments, the Samaritan moves beyond baptism to foreground the importance of the Eucharist in enabling the man to be healed from sin: "And thouh he stande and steppe riȝt stronge worth he neuere / Til he haue eten al þat barn and his bloed dronken" (XIX.89–90). In the Samaritan's account, the will is absolutely powerless in resisting sin without the guidance of the church. The figure's comments not only support Liberum Arbitrium's teaching on the importance of the church, but also undercut Rechelesnesse's and Patience's arguments about the salvific power of poverty. As Aers puts it, "[this] scene makes all talk about fallen human beings voluntarily embracing a state of perfection in poverty seem rather hollow."[67]

The poem thus clearly emphasizes the absolute centrality of baptism, penance, and the Eucharist for *semyuief's* health and rehabilitation. The mode in which the poem teaches this theological lesson is also important, however. In retelling the Samaritan parable as an allegory of sacramental theology, the poem simultaneously constrains the allegorical dimensions of the episode to present the sacraments literally as a form of social relation constituted by one person's charitable aid of another. Indeed, Langland's central teaching on love and sacramental efficacy is presented as the greatest act of almsgiving in the poem. Earlier in the text, Liberum Arbitrium describes the fruit of the tree of charity as "werkes / Of holynesse, of hendenesse, of helpe-hym-þat-nedeth" (XVIII.12–13). The Samaritan fulfills all of these works when, unlike Faith and Hope, he attends to *semyuief,* whose need is depicted in strikingly physical terms. He lies "naked as an nedle and noen helpe abouten" (XIX.58). The text places great emphasis on how the Samaritan embodies the nonscrupulous empathy that Liberum Arbitrium cited as the defining characteristic of charity. Against the reluctance of the other virtues, the Samaritan displays an immediate readiness to help the needy man: "*so sone so* the samaritaen hadde sihte of this carefole, / Alihte adoun of lyard and ladde hym in his hande / And to the wey a wente" (XIX.65–67, my emphasis).[68] His desire to help the man seems almost involuntary, and he offers aid with no hesitation, reservation, or inquiry into the cause of his suffering.

While this episode never casts doubt on *semyuief's* extreme need, Langland nonetheless emphasizes the distinctive hermeneutic work necessarily performed by the Samaritan. In this case, the hermeneutic process is not directed at determining if *semyuief's* need is legitimate; rather, it works as a form of deeply personal interaction when the Samaritan reads the signs of the man's body. In contrast to Dives's neglect of Lazarus, the Samaritan approaches *semyuief* "his woundes to byholde, / And parseued by his poues he was in perel to deye" (XIX.67–68). Throughout this episode, the Samaritan functions as a foil for Dives since he recognizes the man's dire need and helps him without scrutinizing the man's identity, status, or worthiness. He simply sees a person in need, diagnoses its severity, and immediately provides him with relief.

The poem continues to accommodate both the literal and allegorical levels as the Samaritan's offer of sacramental healing is accompanied by direct physical assistance as well. We learn that he "Enbaumed hym and boend his heued and on bayard hym sette," taking the man to a grange or inn representing the church and the sacrament of baptism (XIX.72). As he is left to heal, the episode refuses to let go of material reality and explains that the Samaritan pays for the man's lodging and promises the innkeeper further compensation for any additional expenses during his stay (XIX.74–76). The Samaritan's material resources, which enable his charitable act, certainly disprove Clopper's claim that he is one of the poem's "figures of charity manifested as the patient poor."[69] Rather, the text could not emphasize any more clearly that the Samaritan's kind treatment of *semyuief* is made possible precisely because he is not poor. The restorative effects of the sacraments are thus configured simultaneously as charitable relations among men, relations that entail one person offering material assistance to another.[70] The healing power of baptism and the Eucharist is not a theological topic to be separated from the social interaction of Christians and the work of almsgiving.[71]

Indeed, the poem goes on to focus a great deal of its energy encouraging people to treat one another with kindness. While the Samaritan serves as an exemplary figure of love, he offers a counterexample by returning to the parable of Dives and Lazarus for the fourth time in the text. Offering the poem's most authoritative commentary on the biblical story, the Samaritan makes it quite clear that Dives's grave sin is a failure of kindness, a failure to give where there was need.[72] Speaking directly to the wealthy, he asks, "Minne ȝe nat, riche men, to which a myschaunce / That diues deyede, and dampned for his vnkyndenesse / Of his mete and his mone to men þat hit nedede?" (XIX.233–35). The Samaritan is quick to point out that Dives was damned despite the fact that he earned his wealth rightfully. This acknowledgement prompts further warnings to the wealthy who may find themselves in even greater moral danger for attaining their goods by false means. While Dives is thus "godes tretor . . . for al his trewe catel," the Samaritan asks, "how wol riche nouthe / Excuse hem þat ben vnkynde and ȝut here catel ywonne / With wyles and with luyther whitus . . . ?" (XIX.242, 246–48). Unlike Patience and Hunger, who view the parable as evidence for the sanctifying power of poverty, the Samaritan understands it as an urgent warning that the rich must acquire their goods licitly and then use those resources to help the poor.

The Samaritan stresses the utter importance of almsgiving by showing how it is a matter of life and death for poor and rich alike. His attention to the parable of Dives and Lazarus not only recalls Lazarus's terrible death but also foregrounds the spiritual death of the rich who fail to be merciful. As he reminds the wealthy, "For þat ben vnkynde to [God's servants], hope ȝe noen oþer / Bote they dwelle there diues is dayes withouten ende" (XIX.253–54). By reexamining the parable of Dives and Lazarus and by stressing the dire consequences of failing to give aid, the Samaritan offers a powerful lesson about charity as an issue not confined to debates about fraudulent begging and the legitimacy of need. While the Samaritan does not explicitly advocate indiscriminate almsgiving, he emphasizes that the needy themselves all too often go unaided to the detriment of rich and poor alike. His warnings to the wealthy help make them conscious of need so that their concerns in the world do not make them blind to the Lazaruses and the *semyuiefs* who may lie beyond their own gates or beside the paths they travel down.

As he continues to explore the precise causes and forms of unkindness, the Samaritan also offers some important correctives to Rechelesnesse's earlier teaching when he discusses this gravest of sins as the will's deliberate rejection of charity. At this point in the poem, we are being taken through a subtle hermeneutic process as the Samaritan reinterprets some of Rechelesnesse's most specious arguments. In his definition of the sin against the Holy Spirit, the Samaritan comments specifically on those unkind individuals who choose out of covetousness to rob and murder the rich:

> Thus is vnkyndnesse the contrarie that quencheth, as hit were,
> The grace of the holy goest, godes owene kynde.
> For þat kynde doth vnkynde fordoth, as this corsede theues,
> Vnkynde cristene men, for coueytise and enuye
> Sleth a man for his mebles with mouthe or with handes.
> For that the holy goest hath to kepe tho harlotes distruyeth,
> The which is lyf and loue, the leye of mannes body. . . .
> (XIX.255–61)

The Samaritan goes on to discuss murder more specifically and adds: "this (murder) is the worste wyse þat eny wiht myhte / Synegen aȝen þe seynte spirit—assente to destruye / For coueytise of eny kyne thynge, þat Crist dere bouhte (XIX.267–69).

Focusing on the nature of the sin and its implications, the Samaritan does not view wealth itself or the "kyne thinge[s]" as the cause of homicide, as Rechelesnesse does. Rather, for the Samaritan, murder results from the will's deliberate choice to reject charity and become unkind. The Samaritan counsels rich men to be especially wary of covetousness, a sin that the poem has described as particularly powerful. While the incapacitating effects of sin have been made apparent through the figure of *semyuief,* the Samaritan nonetheless urges the wealthy to promote charity by donating their excess possessions as alms. Riches, then, are not simply the "root of sin," but function as a resource enabling the giver to "brenne[th] . . . and blase[th] clere" in love (XIX.226).

The Personification of Need

If the Samaritan's interaction with *semyuief* works in part to stress the importance of giving alms without scrutinizing the causes and legitimacy of need, then the closing Passus of the poem might be said to confirm this view, for it directly presents need as an elusive and shifting condition, not easily recognized by readers and almsgivers alike. The final Passus of *Piers Plowman* recapitulates its engagement with the dominant late medieval discourses of poverty, offering a concentrated representation of the legislative, Franciscan, and anticlerical discourse explored throughout the wider poem. Presenting need itself as an allegorical personification, the Passus reminds us how this powerful concept is central to each of these discursive modes. Nede is accordingly a dynamic and flexible figure who functions as an individual circumstance associated with Wille's own mendicancy, as a condition arguably immune from human law, and as an institutional state associated with the fraternal orders. In addition to stressing the concept's complexity as a personal experience, a legal precept, and an ecclesiological structure, the Passus also highlights the term's moral ambiguity in these arenas.[73] Nede makes circular and sometimes contradictory arguments that raise questions about the figure's status as a form of vice or virtue. In its final Passus the poem still grants no easy answers to these questions, but its unwillingness to resolve the ambiguity of need is important for revealing the stakes of the hermeneutic obstacles erased by the dominant discourses of poverty.

Evident in the substantial amount of criticism on the subject, Wille's encounter with Nede at the beginning of Passus XXII constitutes one of the most complex episodes of the poem.[74] In its first appearance the personification emerges as Wille's material need for food, but much like the figure of Hunger, he also seeks to justify his position, and, in this case, he works to rationalize and defend the legitimacy of Wille's poverty. With the appearance of this multidimensional personification, the allegory's ongoing inquiry into the nature of need becomes especially dynamic. By imagining need as an allegorical figure, the concept becomes both a problem for potential almsgivers and an interpretive difficulty for the reader as well. In other words, this section of the poem directly forces us to attempt to determine what need actually is. In considering what this personification represents we are also asking, what kind of condition is need? How do we identify need, and can we readily judge it as worthy or false?

Discerning the nature of Nede becomes one of the most challenging interpretive acts in the poem due to the figure's unusual construction as an allegorical personification. Kim has fruitfully outlined the distinctive qualities of this figure: "Langland calls attention to Nede's lack of 'self'; unique in *Piers Plowman,* Nede consistently refers to himself in the third person." Signaling Nede's representation of deficiency, Nede's "lack of self" also allows the figure to offer a "circular definition of himself with himself (need with need)." This self-contained identification jeopardizes Nede's authority and its precise meaning because it fails to specify the status of neediness in relation to any material "conditions outside poverty." The figure's identity, in Kim's reading, thus has particularly negative implications because it "dangerously renders null the notion of social accountability. . . . Since a needy person justifies himself with neediness, he is under no obligation to explain his neediness in terms other than his subjective expression, in terms that may bridge the gap between himself and the rest of his community."[75] Kim here acknowledges how need is a condition that necessarily connects personal experience to communal practices and obligations. In this sense, as Fradenburg explains, "the problem of 'need' names something central to the economy of the subject's relation to the other." And need has the "potential . . . to shatter that economy, to derange fatally the subject's relation to community and to providential order."[76]

Indeed, Nede's self-referentiality highlights the inherent ambiguity of the concept, and that ambiguity can always be exploited to foster anticommunal and self-justifying modes of existence. However, the figure initially attempts to avoid such pitfalls by making legal and ethical claims that stress the fundamental legitimacy and meaning of need. In his confrontation with Wille, Nede initially seeks to legitimize the experience of poverty by explaining that extreme deprivation entitles one to take the necessities of life freely. In accord with canon law, the figure declares that "nede hath no lawe" (XXII.10). He momentarily offers important clarifications for his theories about the essential legitimacy of poverty. He insists, for example, that only the most severe forms of lack permit a poor person to take "þre thinges . . . his lyf for to saue" (XXII.11). While he makes no explicit reference to the church or to God's generous gifts, he echoes Holy Churche's teaching in Passus I by listing the three things "nidefole" to all people. He also recalls her teaching on moderation and measure when he explains that those who are entitled to these goods must actively pursue temperance (XXII.20–22).[77] The figure's estimation of this virtue importantly emphasizes that the will should be disciplined and measured when acting out of material poverty, an undertaking that the poem has shown to be extremely difficult.

Following this discussion, however, Nede begins to oppose his own arguments and, as a result, compromises any sense of authority he may have tenuously possessed. Nede prioritizes temperance as the highest virtue and in so doing suspiciously disregards the fundamental importance of justice, fortitude, and prudence as well as the operations of Conscience, which are obviously essential to the sacrament of penance:

> So nede at greet nede may nyme as for his owne
> Withouten consail of Consience or cardinale vertues
> So þat he sewe and saue *Spiritus temperancie.*
> For is no vertue be ver to *Spiritus temperancie,*
> Noyther *Spiritus iusticie* ne *Spiritus fortinudinis.*
> (XXII. 20–24)

Nede praises temperance because, as he goes on to claim, it somehow singularly resists earthly corruption and abuse (XXII.29–35).[78] After making such a specious assertion, Nede notably abandons the subject of temperance altogether and shifts into Franciscan discourse to argue, as did Rechelesnesse and Patience, that need alone induces virtue. He states that "anoen [nede] meketh / And as louh as a lamb for lakkyng þat hym nedeth; / For nede maketh neede fele nedes louh-herted" (XXII.35–37). The figure attempts to bolster his arguments by offering a portrait of what looks very much like a Franciscan Christ who confirms the sanctity of need (XXII.40–49). In this light, poverty should be praised, and the needy should "be nat basched to byde and to be nedy / Sethe he þat wrouhte al þe worlde was willefolliche nedy" (XXII.48–49).

However, in describing Jesus, Nede once again exposes the limits of Franciscan discourse as he conspicuously fails to mention any of the charitable dispositions and sacramental relations so important in the authoritative teachings of the Samaritan. With this disregard for charity and praise of deprivation, Nede revisits problems of the half-acre episode, and the coming of antichrist sparks similarly desperate attempts to reform the community. When Conscience calls on disease, age, and death, he relies on agents of material coercion, not unlike Hunger, to transform the will of the people; the result is predictably ineffective. In fact, once Kynde's castigations abate, the sins reemerge among "imparfit prestes and prelates" who seek to destroy holy church (XXII.229).

Nede notably reappears at the height of this crisis and yet again offers a different account of how poverty intervenes in the production of charity. Dealing now with the question of mendicancy and institutionalized forms of need, the figure shifts into antifraternal discourse when he argues that the friars' sinfulness directly results from their lack of a "fyndynge": "And for thei aren pore, parauntur, for patrimonye hem faileth, / Thei wol flatere, to fare wel, folk þat ben riche" (XXII.234–35). Directly opposing his opening arguments, Nede here argues that need does not sanctify one's life and promote virtues of patience and humility. Rather, as in Holy Churche's teaching and in the dramatic events of the half-acre episode, need leads seamlessly to covetousness and excess. At the conclusion of the poem, Conscience recapitulates this notion and goes out to search for Piers Plowman who can not only destroy pride, but give the "freres . . . a fyndynge, þat for nede flateren / And contre-pledeth [Conscience]" (XXII.383–84). Nede suggests that the friars' commitment to total poverty has gone awry and serves as an excuse allowing them to beg relentlessly for goods that they claim not to have.[79] Their economic situation corrupts penance and perverts the entire sacramental order—an order that the previous section of the poem has imagined as the charitable relations among men. It is Friar Flatterer who disrupts such relations and abandons his sacramental duties by turning confession into an opportunity for personal profit. He thus gives Contrition a "plastre / Of a pryue payement" and tells him (XXII.364):

> ". . . y shal preye for ȝow,
> And for hem þat ȝe aren holde to, al my lyf tyme,
> And make of ȝow *memoria* in masse and in matynes
> As freres of oure fraternite, for a litel suluer."
> (XXII.364–67)

The friar's seemingly innocuous request "for a litel suluer"—confined to the final half-line of the passage—betrays his covetousness, a sin that has ruinous effects on the sacrament of penance. Friar Flatterer eventually "goeth and gedereth and gloseth þer he shyrueth / Til Contricioun hadde clene forȝete to crye and to wepe / And wake for his wikkede werkes, as he was woned to do" (XXII.368–70). Earlier, in exploring Patience's Franciscanism, the poem criticized how poverty can presume to nullify the poor's need for penance; at this later point, the poem exposes another means by which poverty perverts the same sacrament with distastrous consequences for lay penitents.

Facilitating outcomes ranging from tempered humility to outright covetousness, Nede is not a transparently consistent state in the poem, as the final Passus reminds us. The contradictory nature of this allegorical figure—its discordant theories, positions, and ideologies—reflect need's instability as a form of virtue. Crystallizing the poem's wider engagement with the discourses of poverty, the representation of Nede signals many different things: if the will is directed toward temperance, need can at best facilitate humility; in some cases, it can enforce obedient behavior on an undisciplined will; and at the other extreme, as an institutionalized state, it can actually inhibit the growth of charity.

Set against this portrayal of need's insufficiency and instability as a virtue, (the) will remains disoriented and unsure about where to direct him/itself. While the church is under siege by antichrist, Kynde nevertheless tells Wille to "wende into Vnite" and to "conne som craft ar thow come thennes" (XXII.204–6). When Wille inquires about what craft he should learn, Kynde affirms the teachings of Liberum Arbitrium and the Samaritan by urging the will to charity (XXII.207). He tells him: "lerne to love . . . and leef all othere. . . . And thow loue lelly, lacke shal the neuere / Wede ne worldly mete while thy lif lasteth" (XXII.208–12). The will's orientation to love is paramount as a penitential disposition and material practice that, as Liberum Arbitrium has shown us, entail supporting oneself and giving to others.[80] In developing an image of love that fulfills all lack, Kynde offers Wille a sense of solace at the poem's catastrophic ending. Yet such solace is perhaps fleeting for the poem's readers, who are themselves left in a state of ethical and interpretive conflict generated by Nede's competing claims.

Classifying Acts

This anxiety about the meaning and instability of need becomes increasingly palpable in the material that Langland added to Passus IX and Passus V of the C-text. Though separated in the poem's narrative sequence, the additions to these Passus are aligned in offering what is perhaps the poem's most urgent exploration of the difficulties involved in defining need. We find in this material a particularly strenuous desire to categorize the poor, to establish social boundaries, and to fix identity. In Passus IX, for example, Langland develops an elaborate taxonomy of the poor, and in Passus V, the theoretical classification of beggars becomes an active exercise in discernment as Reason and Conscience question Wille's mode of existence. Furthermore, in each of these cases Langland invokes the problematic term "lollar" in an attempt to separate the deserving from the undeserving poor.[81] The new material of Passus IX and Passus V reveals that Langland's final attempt to know the meaning of need ultimately fails; in these sections of the poem, the text's poetic modes and sacramental vision disrupt with particular acuteness the neat classifications central to contemporary poverty discourse.

The opening section of Passus IX engages most directly with the theory of discriminate charity that underwrites legislative, antifraternal, and anticlerical discourse in late medieval England. This section of the poem and the discourses promoting discriminate charity are motivated by anxiety about need's fundamental unknowability—an unknowability that threatens the charitable bonds among Christians. As Middleton explains, medieval culture found the "threat of fraud" much more dangerous than the threat of violence in the mobile beggar; fraudulent "wanderers, by preying upon the sympathies of the individual and the charitable motives and resources of a community, violated a far more fundamental trust than the physical security of body and property."[82] False claims of need undermine the theological, ethical, and material fabric of society, and it is for this reason that Langland attempts to separate the false from the needy once and for all. He thus develops an involved taxonomy of the poor as the poem meditates on the types of people who are covered by Piers's pardon. This section of the text is explicitly addressed to the rich, and, as it seeks to distinguish between the deserving and undeserving poor, it creates a guide for almsgivers that would ideally thwart the abuse of charity. While Kathleen Hewett-Smith reads this section of Passus IX as part of the poem's more general turn, in its central visions, to a figural, allegorical, and idealized account of poverty, the passage is directly connected to historical and material reality; it both explores with ethical sensitivity the growing cultural importance of discriminate charity and foregrounds the actual presence of need as a complex epistemological force.[83]

The passage's interest in discrimination is made clear from the outset as Langland omits the lines from the B-text emphasizing Gregory's commands to give to "alle / That askeþ for his loue þat vs al leneþ."[84] In the C-text Langland does not support the donation of alms to the undeserving because the false beggar "defraudeth the nedy / And also gileth hym þat gyueth and taketh agayne his wille" (IX.64–65). Indeed, according to Langland, a truly charitable giver "for goddes loue wolde nat gyue, his thankes, / Bote ther he wiste were wel grete nede / And most merytorie to men þat he ȝeueth fore" (IX.66–68). Citing Cato's command, *cui des videto,* Langland in fact does attempt to look into the nature of alms recipients and seeks, through his poem, to fix and authorize their social identity. This process, however, becomes riddled with practical and moral problems.[85]

Such difficulties emerge when the taxonomic project virtually admits its failure from the outset. It begins with an unnamed narrator making a statement that contradicts his own goals of categorization: "Woet no man, as y wene, who is worthy to haue" (IX.70). The next line, though, begins with the first of a long series of "acs," and the rest of the section nonetheless sets out to determine what we have just been told is indeterminate. The validity of the distinctions that follow is therefore immediately called into question by the speaker's opening statement about his and all people's inability to define worthiness. Nevertheless, the poet is driven by a powerful ethical vision that seeks to separate the legitimately poor from fraudulent beggars so as to facilitate the just operations of charity. He pursues the problem, as Pearsall states, "with characteristic tenacity, probing, questioning, objecting, qualifying so that one has the liveliest sense that Langland is working at the problem . . . rather than presenting in a rhetorically persuasive manner a conclusion he has already arrived at."[86]

Indeed, largely because of the passage's "ruminative" qualities,[87] the fundamental distinction that Langland wants to make between the worthy and unworthy poor is hardly secure. He does initially set up a *general* division between those who have true need and those whom he calls "lollares." He invokes the standard assumption in labor legislation and antifraternal discourse to define true need as a condition resulting from physical disability; and he characterizes all others who beg as "lollares":

> . . . beggares with bagges, þe whiche brewhouses ben
> here churches,
> But they be blynde or tobroke or elles be syke,
> Thouh he falle for defaute þat fayteth for his lyflode,
> Reche ȝe neuere, ȝe riche, thouh such [lollares] sterue.
> For alle þat haen here hele and here yesyhte
> And lymes to labory with, and lollares lyf vsen,
> Lyuen aȝen goddess lawe and þe lore of holi churche.
> (IX.98–104)[88]

This broad division among the truly needy and "lollares," or the fraudulent poor, sounds simple enough, yet as the passage continues, we have to work to uncover that distinction, for the poet considers numerous subdivisions of people and then stops to imagine their alternatives. For instance, Langland repeatedly makes statements of contradiction and reversal such as: our needy neighbors are in the pardon, "*ac* beggares with bagges" are not (IX.98); those who make their children into "beggars of kynde" are not covered by the pardon, "*ac* olde and hore, þat helples ben and nedy" are; holy hermits make it in, "*ac* ermytes þat inhabiten by the heye weye" do not (IX.169, 176, 189, my emphasis).[89] This meandering form, which structures the entire passage, implies a certain reluctance on Langland's part to make hard and fast distinctions among the poor. Unwilling to create a totalizing scheme that definitely separates one categorization of the worthy poor from another categorization of the false poor, Langland constantly crosses back and forth over the line that supposedly divides the two; the result is that he almost blends the groups of people whom he seeks to segregate.[90] Furthermore, Langland breaks down the fundamental dichotomy he tentatively establishes by broadening the meaning of the already ambiguous term, "lollar."

The division between fraudulent "lollares" and those who are truly needy begins to blur when Langland begins a section of the taxonomy with a typical reversal. After discussing the corrupt "beggares with bagges, þe whiche brewhouses ben here churches," Langland says: "*An ȝut* ar ther oþere beggares" (IX.98, 105, my emphasis). As he goes on to describe this new group, Langland notably complicates the categorical terms of his inquiry into charity by labeling these people "lunatyk lollars." Langland defines these beggars as insane individuals, whose madness seems to make them admirably unconcerned with things of the world.[91] Characterizing the "lunatyk lollares" as possessing a kind of apostolic holiness, Langland writes,

> Careth they for no colde ne counteth of non hete
> And aren meuynge aftur þe mone; moneyles þey walke,
> With a good will, witteles, mony wyde contreyes,
> Riht as Peter dede and poul. . . .
>
> (IX.109–12)

As he changes the meaning of "lollar," the crucial term that initially defined the primary difference between true neediness and false indigence, Langland here destabilizes the taxonomy as a whole.[92] Indicating the collapse of these essential distinctions, David Lawton remarks on the failure of the taxonomy by affirming that "this whole passage is hardly clear: lollards are bad; lollards are good."[93] If we recall the distinctions made by Hunger and indeed by the speaker of this Passus—distinctions that divide corrupt beggars from the sick, lame, and blind poor—we see that these easy definitions quickly erode away in this taxonomy. We can no longer ask simply who is a true beggar and who is a false one. Rather we must also consider, who is a true beggar and who is a "lollar"? Additionally, from here we now have to wonder who is a false "lollar" and who is a true one?[94] While Langland has attempted to distinguish between kinds of beggars by labeling them as "lollars," the distinction only leads to the need for further discrimination. Instead of clarifying how almsgivers can discern a truly needy beggar, Langland's taxonomy leaves us wondering most importantly about what a "lollar" actually is.

Langland himself seems especially concerned to clarify what proves to be a highly problematic term. He provides a detailed definition of the word and creates an etymology for the noun "lollar" based on its purported association with the verb "lollen":

> Kyndeliche, by Crist ben suche ycald lollares.
> As by þe englisch of oure eldres, of olde mennes techynge.
> He þat lolleth is lame or his leg out of ioynte
> Or ymaymed in some member, for to meschief hit souneth.
> Rihte so, sothly, such manere Ermytes
> Lollen aȝen þe byleue and þe lawe of holy churche.
>
> (IX.214–19)

While this description may ingeniously encompass many of the characteristics of false beggars, who defraud the true poor—those "ymaymed in some member"—by faking their own lameness or disability,[95] Langland's definition is far from comprehensive. Rather, as critics have shown, it functions as one of many attempts to win "the semantic contest over the referents of [a] term that seems to have been in its most volatile phase" during the composition of the C-text.[96]

Scholars have written a great deal about Langland's use of the word "lollar," and it is worth pursuing their arguments in some detail because they focus on the term's problematic homology with the word "lollard." Scase, for instance, finds two possible meanings of "lollar," arguing that the term designates the English equivalent of a gyrovage or a member of the Wycliffite heresy. In her reading, Langland uses the term to promote the gyrovague meaning, though she explains that the "*Piers Plowman* sense [of the word] soon lost ground in competition with the other usage" of "lollar" as a derogatory term for a Wycliffite.[97] Middleton adds to these possibilities and mentions yet another potential meaning of the "lollar" as an individual who disruptively "practices religion 'out of place.'" Noting that there is a fundamental similarity among these and other definitions of the term, she explains furthermore that there are multiple senses of the verb "lolling," which can signify "prayer-mumbling, lameness of gait, languishing, and tares or weeds." Such terms, according to Middleton, reflect a "linguistic displacement of a genuine and fundamental social contest." Like Langland's own invented definition, they are thus "consciously applied to assert intellectual control" over perceived causes of social disruption, which for Langland revolve around the persistent problem of fraudulent begging.[98]

Andrew Cole has also approached the word "lollar" as a potentially capacious term signifying either a Wycliffite or an idle friar, categories of people that were indeed identified as sources of social anxiety. Cole, however, argues against Scase in asserting that Langland "registers and responds explicitly" to the sense of "lollar" as it defines Wycliffites.[99] Cole takes issue with Scase's suggestion that Langland's sense of the word "lollar" seems to "predate the anti-Wycliffite sense of the 1380s." Offering a fresh account of the word's history, Cole argues that, when Langland writes the C-text, "lollar" has been given specific associations with Wycliffism. However, he contends that this meaning is a "backformation" invented in the mid-1380s, when legal records and chronicles use it retrospectively to describe the Wycliffites condemned at the Blackfriars council in 1382. However, Cole goes on to show that the term is not limited to this particular definition, and he demonstrates the word's common applicability to anti-Wycliffite and antifraternal discourse. He defines "lollar" as a "fusion of Wycliffite and fraternal identities and practices," summing up the meaning of the term as "an anti-Wycliffite expression of the first order that is nonetheless laden with antifraternal sentiment."[100] After tracing these shared discursive fields, however, Cole ultimately argues that Langland favors the antifraternal connotations of the term, as he applies the word "lollar" not to Wycliffites but to idle friars who choose mendicancy over labor. In making this interpretive decision, Langland, Cole concludes, "neutralizes the anti-Wycliffite term," for he "see[s] 'lollare' heresy as a fault of friars, not Wycliffites."[101]

While this critical debate has fascinating implications for Langland's own relationship to Wycliffite thought, what is missing from these accounts is a serious consideration of what this vexed term is doing within a section of the poem that aims to clarify meaning and identity.[102] If we recall that "lollar" functions as a crucial part of Langland's taxonomy, which seeks to identify and "assert control over" the threatening indeterminacy of false beggars, then the poet's choice of the term as a classification remains especially puzzling. The critical debates about the meaning of "lollar" in relation to Wycliffism demonstrate some of the major interpretative problems. For example, while Cole's argument about Langland's antifraternal use of the word is, in many ways, compelling and relevant to this discussion, the involved interpretive work he undertakes to prove this point affirms the term's very inefficacy as a mode of categorization.[103]

The question remains, why would Langland choose such an opaque and highly contestable term as a means of *specifying* particular kinds of beggars? Although he invents his own etymology for the word, he also, as we have seen, creates multiple meanings for his unique definition by introducing the category of the "lunatyk," who is deserving of charity. Furthermore, in the passage itself, the intricate and evolving association of "lollars" with bag-wielding beggars, hermits by the highway, wasters, and friars does not make for a particularly successful form of classification, especially given the narrative detours along the way describing groups of worthy people. Ultimately demonstrating that distinctions may not be as recognizable, as easy to make, or as hard and fast as he wishes, Langland's taxonomic system begins to unravel with its "specification" of this very term, "lollar."

This happens largely because the desire to find clarity in rigid systems of classification and to supply one's own meaning for a highly contentious term proves to be impracticable in light of the poem's commitment to epistemological and formal complexity. The ability to make ready distinctions among the poor is a tempting fantasy but a fantasy nonetheless, for it dismisses the intricacy and fluidity of signs, a semiotic reality that the poem finds necessary in so far as it renders possible the dynamic operations of Langland's allegory. The semantic range of the word "lollar" and the range of the signs of poverty ultimately pose deep hermeneutic challenges to readers and almsgivers alike. Although troubling, the message that is perhaps most clear from Passus IX is that the nature and motives of a beggar do not become any clearer by labeling him with a designation that potentially signifies anything from a heretic, a social irritant, and an idler to a fraudulent beggar, a friar, or a kind of holy and innocent madman.[104]

Just as Langland's category of the "lollar" seems plagued by indeterminacy, the poet's classification of the deserving poor in Passus IX also finally demonstrates the fundamental difficulty in discerning need. As Langland sets out to describe different types of legitimate poverty, he begins with a moving portrait of the righteous, working poor. This description is unusual in late medieval writing, and it is especially distinctive within Passus IX itself, for it contradicts the speaker's determination that legitimate need results from the inability to work. As he initially insists that we *can* recognize true need in the forms of our own neighbors, Langland gives us an image of women who use their small profits from spinning to feed their hungry children and, if enough is left over, themselves as well. The poet here seems ideologically worlds away from the abstraction and demonization of Wastour in Passus VIII as he now considers the reality of the working poor—individuals who labor honestly and continuously, but still cannot avoid the threat of hunger and possibly death. As Geoffrey Shepherd has noted, passages like this one are unique because the writing does not simply "exploit" the topic of poverty as part of a larger satire or "argument for affluence," but rather actually "presents the inner life of the unvocal unassertive people who live in powerlessness and poverty."[105] Focusing particularly on "the wo of this women þat wonneth in cotes," this depiction of need is also significant because it takes gender into account and exposes that poverty entails different difficulties for different people. In this case it affects mothers whose work extends beyond a specific trade and encompasses the raising of children as well.

Langland describes these people in detail to mark a clear contrast between their righteous poverty and the falseness of those who lead a lollarne life. Yet even this seemingly straightforward representation of need poses hermeneutic problems. Although Langland on one level does display what makes these individuals worthy, their true need, part of what the poet finds so admirable about them is their very tendency to hide their own neediness. Thus, at the same time that Langland attempts to expose their poverty and their legitimacy as poor people, he explains that the reality of their need is far from transparent. Describing how the working poor possess a kind of righteous pride, Langland explains that there are

> . . . monye oþer men þat much wo soffren,
> Bothe afyngered and afurste, to turne þe fayre outward,
> And ben abasched for to begge and wollen nat be aknowe
> What hem nedeth at here neyhebores at noon and at eue.
> (IX.84–87)

Citing the very concealment of true need as one of its characteristics, Langland implicitly highlights the obscurity of deserving poverty. As Kim notes, this "embarrassingly intimate" portrait of the needy is "published against their will."[106] The sense of disclosure in the passage thus works paradoxically to highlight the silent invisibility of the working poor in their daily lives.

Langland goes on to list other categories of poor people who are deserving of alms, yet he similarly works against his own goals of making clear and useful classifications by equating worthiness with patience and humility—internal dispositions that would be virtually impossible for an almsgiver to discern. In addition to validating the poor who are disabled in some sense—the helpless elderly; pregnant women unable to work; and the ever familiar blind, bedridden, and broken boned—Langland also praises another category of people, "the pacient pore," a group similarly esteemed by Rechelesnesse and Patience himself. With regard to the categorization of beggars and the practice of discriminate charity, patience becomes a key factor in determining who is deserving of alms. Langland, for instance, praises those who suffer "meschiefes mekeliche and myldeliche at herte" (IX.184). He also asserts that "For loue of here lowe hertes oure lord hath hem ygraunted / Here penaunce and here purgatorye vppon this puyre erthe / And pardon with the plouhman" (IX.185–87). Underscoring the proper orientation of the will toward humility and patience, Langland notably argues that an interior state determines one's worthiness as a poor person. However, the choice of an internal attribute here may not necessarily help an almsgiver clarify whether a potential recipient is deserving or not. And, as we have seen in the discourse of Patience himself, the virtue of patient poverty in this poem is especially problematic for its display of a sense of humility that may not be sincerely felt.

The difficulty in determining an individual's overall neediness or worthiness becomes even more apparent in what is likely to have been Langland's final addition to the C-text—Wille's apologia in Passus V.[107] In this episode of the poem, the theoretical classification of beggars in Passus IX becomes an active exercise in discernment when Reason and Conscience seek to determine Wille's precise role in society and question the validity of his existence as a seemingly idle man.[108] As it examines Wille's legitimacy as an itinerant beggar and as a maker of verse, the scene has implications for thinking about the nature of Langland's own status as a poet himself.[109] The episode, however, functions as much more than an autobiographical representation, and it has been discussed as part of the poem's engagement with post-plague labor legislation. Middleton has pursued the episode's legislative connections most fully, arguing that Reason and Conscience's interrogation of Wille functions as an "incipient prosecution" under the major stipulations of the 1388 Cambridge Statute.[110] Middleton's work not only explores the potentially fascinating relations between the statute and Langland's text, but goes on to posit that Langland's decision to prosecute Wille under the terms of secular vagrancy law marks a strategic avoidance of a potentially more serious ecclesiastical condemnation of his vernacular text as heresy.

As Middleton has shown, the apologia shares with the 1388 Cambridge Statute an interest in authorizing identity. Both texts "exemplif[y] a quixotic effort to give permanent and irrevocable textual stability and fixity—and thereby perpetual accountability before the law—to social identity."[111] The identity of a figure like Wille is especially problematic because he declares himself to be a mobile beggar who not only dresses like "lollares" and lives among them, but who also writes against them and therefore earns their scorn (V.2–5). Describing his existence as somehow both like and very different from the life of the ambiguous "lollares," Wille conspicuously resists placement within the classifying schemes pursued in Passus IX. When he meets Reason, we also find out that he "hadde [his] hele / And lymes to labory with and louede wel fare / And no dede to do but to drynke and to slepe" (V.7–9). Not surprisingly, Reason becomes suspicious of Wille, and he is especially concerned to ascertain both who he is and how he fits into the social hierarchy. He asks Wille if he can perform a series of primarily agricultural activities so that he "betere therby þat byleue [him] fynden" (V.21).[112] Reason seeks to remind Wille that social obligations are mutual; he wonders what Wille does to acknowledge and serve those who fulfill his own need for food.

When Wille proceeds to defend his existence as a cleric arguably unsuited for and exempt from agricultural labor, it becomes clear that his identity and legitimacy as a mendicant maker resist any straightforward authorizing regimes including those of the Cambridge vagrancy statute. Reason questions Wille's arguments, and he invokes some of the taxonomic categories explored in Passus IX, when he tells Wille,

> ". . . an ydel man þow semest,
> A spendour þat spene mot or a spilletyme—
> Or beggest thy bylyue aboute at men hacches
> Or faytest vppon frydayes or festedayes in churches,
> The whiche is lollarne lyf þat lytel is preysed
> There ryhtfulnesse rewardeth ryht as men deserueth. . . ."
> (V.27–32)

Reason imagines Wille as one of the "lollares" who fail to contribute productively to Christian society. Ruminating in much the same way that Passus IX meanders through different classifications, Reason then takes a different tack and questions if Wille is disabled and therefore entitled to beg. As an able-bodied mendicant, Wille responds defensively, giving an account of his clerical training and the activities appropriate to his vocation. These activities, he says, exclude manual labor, and he goes on to adopt a superficially authoritative voice that bemoans all mobility and fluid social identity—the very things that Wille himself represents (V.61–81). In a move that adds yet another layer of complexity and ambiguity to his identity, Wille speaks the ideology of the vagrancy law that, in Middleton's argument, seeks to prosecute him for violating its terms. For critics such as Scase, this seemingly hypocritical tirade against social instability locates Wille firmly within the tradition of gyrovague satire, which works in this instance to mock "the Cornhill loller's claim that his status is different from that of other idlers."[113]

Middleton and Scase usefully draw attention to the passage's satirical elements and legislative connections; yet if we understand Reason and Conscience as the allegory suggests, that is, as rational and moral faculties, then we can see that this episode is not simply a satirical attack on Wille's hypocrisy or a secular prosecution of Wille under the 1388 Cambridge Statute. Rather, Reason and Conscience emerge as figures that provoke a moral crisis *within* Wille, ultimately leading him to penitence. When read in this light, Wille's "prosecution" does not necessarily distract us from the vernacular poem's potentially dangerous theological components, as Middleton suggests it does. The episode instead can be seen as foregrounding the painful process of self-examination central to the experience of contrition. By the end of the episode, Wille's apparent hypocrisy and seemingly insufficient apologia somehow evolve into a serious confession that prompts Reason and Conscience to sanction Wille's ostensibly unproductive labor. In focusing on the internal and penitential dimensions of the allegory, we can see that Wille's apologia emerges as a final lesson about the complexities of discernment: Wille must struggle to determine even for himself whether his existence is indeed licit and ethical.

The success of Wille's apologia and the fundamental nature of Wille's character remain puzzling to many critics because, as in Passus IX, the poem does not work so much to resolve ambiguities as it does to reflect the larger challenges of discernment. The allegory's operations as an interior examination of the self strikingly emphasize the difficulty involved in any attempt—legislative, poetic, or otherwise—to fix an individual's identity.[114] Functioning here not just as a prosecution leveled by the king's deputies, Reason and Conscience, the allegory also operates as a self-generated form of moral inquiry. Wille thus meets Reason "inwit"; he is "romynge in rememberance."[115] In this sense, the will is in dialogue with reason and conscience, and Wille himself evaluates the actions that have both shaped his identity and determined his relations with others. As the episode makes clear, this is a difficult process vexed by self-delusion, when, for example, Wille's claims of moral perfection work to justify a potentially self-centered and solipsistic existence.[116] In the early stages of his dialogue with Reason, Wille confidently defends his way of life and angrily declares, "rebuke me ryhte nauhte, resoun, y ȝow praye, / For in my Conscience y knowe what Crist wolde y wrouhte. / Preyeres of a parfit man and penaunce discrete / Is the leuest labor þat oure lord pleseth" (V.82–85). Insisting that he follows the dictates of conscience, Wille declares that he knows and abides by Christ's will.

His adamant declarations of perfection, however, quickly lose their force when Conscience himself intervenes in the discussion. Wille is forced to consider whether he truly lives as the "parfit man" he claims to be, when Conscience knowingly exposes his moral shortcomings, telling Wille: "y can nat se this lyeth; /Ac it semeth no sad parfitnesse in Citees to begge, / But he be obediencer to prior or to mynistre" (V.89–91). Under the guidance of Conscience, Wille's justifications for his mendicant existence begin to unravel, and we learn that he begs without any attachment to a religious community or rule. While he cites scriptural lines central to Franciscan idealizations of poverty (V.86–88), Conscience makes it clear that such teachings function for Wille as rather thin ethical claims. His claims to virtue perpetuate his status as someone who potentially values receiving over giving and who first judges others without subjecting oneself to the moral scrutiny necessitated by penance.

Given the episode's exploration of the occlusions and ambiguities that define the self, Wille's apologia powerfully demonstrates that questions of identity, legitimacy, and value are often not at all clear even to the subject in question. In this regard, legislation like the Cambridge Statute feels like a futile attempt to define what in some cases is for an individual himself unknown and potentially unknowable. Scripture's warning to Wille in Passus XI perhaps puts the problem most clearly: "*Multi multa sciunt et seipsos nesciunt*" (XI.165). It is, however, Wille's moral crisis that offers him a sense of self-knowledge. He accepts Conscience's rebuke, undergoes a transformation, and does seem to attain some justification for his life when Reason and Conscience ultimately release him into the life of "labor" that according to Middleton eventually produces this poem.[117] Testifying to the futility of vagrancy legislation and the centrality of more "religious" concerns, Wille's reprieve does not finally come from his compliance with the statute but seems to result from his orientation toward penitence. In a solemn acknowledgment of sin, loss, and hope for God's grace, Wille responds to the revelations of his conscience by saying,

> "That is soth . . . and so y beknowe
> That y haue ytynt tyme and tyme myspened;
> Ac ȝut y hope, as he þat ofte hath ychaffared
> And ay loste and loste, and at þe laste hym happed
> A boute suche a bargayn he was þe bet euere,
> And sette al his los at a leef at the laste ende,
> Such a wynnyng him warth throw wyrdes of grace. . . .
> So hope y to haue of hym þat is almighty
> A gobet of his grace, and bigynne a tyme
> That alle tymes of my tyme to profit shal turne."
> (V.92–101)

Articulated in some of *Piers Plowman*'s most haunting lines, Wille's self-examination dramatically moves the poem away from the satirical and anticlerical registers of the episode. Wille looks much less like the gyrovague figure described by Scase as he becomes repentant both for his way of life and for the unreasonable justifications advanced in its defense.[118] The noticeably economic language of Wille's speech does not necessarily refer to wages to be gained in the field but to the spiritual rewards of God's treasure of grace.[119] The spiritual dimensions of this language also become apparent, if we consider the placement of the apologia within the wider poem. Wille's penitence aptly follows the reformation of the monarchy in Passus IV and anticipates the confession of the sins in Passus VI in order to highlight the sacramental teachings that will be unfolded more fully by Liberum Arbitrium and the Samaritan.

The importance of penance and its accordant interior hermeneutics becomes clear when Wille undertakes a "new" existence strangely indistinguishable from his prior way of life. After Reason encourages Wille to begin the "lyf þat is louble and leele to [his] soule," he does not suddenly take up a new agrarian vocation, but goes to church (V.102–3).[120] As Wille explains, "And to the kyrke y gan go god to honoure; / Byfore the cross on my knees knokked y my brest, / Syhing for my synnes, seggyng my paternoster, / Wepyng and waylyng til y was aslepe" (V.105–8). Only after he weeps, wails, and sighs for his sin does Wille continue living as a mendicant and writing down his visions. By validating Wille's suspect labor and itinerant existence only after he participates in the sacrament of penance, Langland once again exposes the practical and ethical limitations of other discursive modes that seek to legitimate identity by approaching need as a readily meaningful subject. Statutes, taxonomies, and claims to spiritual perfection do not go very far in authorizing Wille's ambiguous existence. Rather, *Piers Plowman* offers the penitential process as the most efficacious means of determining the true meaning of one's need and acknowledging one's communal responsibilities.

Approaching poverty as a topic central to a range of discursive modes, *Piers Plowman* highlights the semantic, theological, and cultural complexity of discerning need. The poem insists on treating poverty as a capacious subject, as it brings together legislative, Franciscan, antifraternal, and anticlerical thought; in addressing these discourses, the text also reveals their limits, for each confines its attention to need within a specific polemical objective or narrow vision of sanctity. In the case of post-plague legislation, "affordable" labor is the all-consuming priority, and need is understood primarily as the inability to work. In the case of Franciscanism, mendicancy is a form of perfection, and need is revered as the guarantor of salvation. In the case of anticlericalism and antifraternalism, clerical covetousness is the central preoccupation, and need becomes a state to be enforced on the clergy so as to aid the truly needy who have been injured by the church's excess.

Against such restrictive conceptions of poverty, Langland's poem repeatedly demonstrates that need is not a transparent or singular condition. Its meditations on discriminate giving in Passus IX are only one example of how the text acknowledges the limitations that humans face in distinguishing between true and false poverty and in recognizing true need despite the social invisibility of the poor. It is most significant, however, that Langland does not simply reflect on such difficulties but enacts them poetically through the fluid and dynamic operations of his allegorical personifications. The shifts among figures such as Hunger and Nede, the affinities between Patience and Rechelesnesse; and Wille's inability to know his own will all *perform* the very problems that Langland finds in the late fourteenth-century discourses of poverty. As a poem built on the volatilities of language, semantic slippages, and the clashing of allegorical modes, *Piers Plowman* makes the intricacy of need a firsthand experience for its readers, who seek meaning in the poem's allegorical representations of poverty. Furthermore, as an affirmation of the text's own structural modes, the sacramental vision that develops over the course of *Piers Plowman* also emphasizes the impossibility of rendering quick judgments of both self and other. The Samaritan's unhesitating ability to help *semyuief* and Wille's penitential examination in Passus V offer major qualifications of any notion that a person's need or moral status can be readily ascertained by almsgivers, polemicists, and lawmakers alike.

The epistemological difficulties associated with need remain palpable throughout *Piers Plowman* because the poem consistently reminds us that poverty is a hermeneutic issue inextricably linked to ethical practice and the question of salvation. With the specter of Lazarus haunting the poem, Langland never lets go of the consequences of failed charity. In this figure of the ailing poor, who ultimately dies and awaits Christ's coming in painful expectation, Langland reveals the devastating costs of failing to acknowledge need as a state of suffering not necessarily associated with reluctance to labor, clerical covetousness, or the promise of salvation. Langland writes as he does about poverty because he seeks to liberate the concept from such ideological constraints; he strives to make the challenging realities of need recognizable beyond the semantic limitations of labor law, Franciscanism, and anticlerical thought. The distinctiveness of this poetic project will become apparent in the chapters that follow and particularly in the next chapter, when we turn to a poem that subsumes lessons of *Piers Plowman* within the epistemological confidence of antifraternal polemic.

CHAPTER TWO

Poverty Exposed

The Evangelical and Epistemological Ideal of *Pierce the Ploughman's Crede*

The Wycliffite poem *Pierce the Plougman's Crede* offers an enthusiastic response to the calls for ecclesiastical reform articulated in *Piers Plowman*. Written by an anonymous author sometime after 1393, the *Crede* self-consciously follows in the footsteps of Langland's work, condemning the corruption of the institutional church and affirming the authority of a plowman whose virtue and spiritual knowledge surpass that of the clergy.[1] These shared preoccupations, along with other similarities, have earned the *Crede* a prominent place within what critics have termed the "Piers Plowman Tradition."[2]

As further evidence for their place in a shared socioliterary domain, both *Piers Plowman* and the *Crede* feature a deep concern with poverty, labor, and mendicancy—issues that readily transgress the boundary between Langland's orthodox text and Wycliffite writing more generally.[3] The *Crede* in particular addresses these subjects in its exploration of fraternal abuses, which it then sets against the righteousness of the working poor. The later poem thus extends the work of *Piers Plowman* in so far as it condemns the friars' accumulation of wealth, identifies the worthy poor as sympathetic figures, and promotes a vision of labor at once industrious and charitable. It is likely that Langland would have shared the *Crede* author's disgust at the friars' desire for profit, and that he would also have sympathized with the writer's praise of the poor plowman's honesty and humility.

Given these correspondences, one might argue that *Piers Plowman* and the *Crede* possess similar ideological goals. This view would certainly contribute to recent critical work arguing that Langland's poem should be read in a broader context that recognizes the direct literary influence of *Piers Plowman* on Wycliffite writing. Critics such as Fiona Somerset and Shannon Gayk have suggested that Wycliffite texts share not only a reformist sensibility with *Piers Plowman,* but a self-conscious literary and linguistic style that includes the use of Latin quotation, alliteration, and instances of personification allegory.[4] While such work identifies compelling points of similarity between *Piers Plowman* and Wycliffite writing, in this chapter I emphasize the substantive differences between Langlandian and Wycliffite thought.[5] In my view, the overt similarities between *Piers Plowman* and the *Crede* are largely superficial areas of overlapping concern that mask major discontinuities in how these works understand poverty and charity.

While *Piers Plowman* is unique for interrogating the major fourteenth-century discourses of poverty, the *Crede* distills Langland's expansive cast of wasters, beggars, lollares, and laborers into a single group of friars, a plowman, and a narrator, all of whom make claims of poverty. The claims of poverty articulated in the *Crede* prove to be strikingly straightforward and thus contrast sharply with the competing and often ambiguous assertions of poverty in *Piers Plowman*. The Wycliffite poem, as I shall argue, deliberately omits the epistemological and ethical difficulties that Langland vigorously pursues in his exploration of need. This is the case because the *Crede* constrains its representation of poverty within the narrow ideological arena of antifraternal satire.[6] This mode demands that the friars' assertions of need be exposed as fraudulent, and the *Crede* does this skillfully by making the friars' wealth utterly obvious in the landscape they occupy, the clothes they wear, and the words they say. To clarify the true meaning of need, the poem also contrasts the friars' false claims of poverty with the real poverty of the plowman, which is also made utterly obvious in his exposed and suffering body.

In presenting a set of unequivocally wealthy friars and an obviously poor plowman, the *Crede* creates a world where the signs of poverty and wealth are immediately discernible. Moreover, these visible signs accurately indicate corresponding internal dispositions. While *Piers Plowman* explores the varying relations between economic conditions and interior states such as pride, charity, and humility, the Wycliffite poet posits a static relation between material reality and the state of the soul. Thus, in the *Crede*, those who are materially poor are also poor in spirit, and those who are rich in possessions are subsumed with pride and covetousness. The ethically and epistemologically tricky terrain of *Piers Plowman* gives way in the *Crede* to clearly demarcated representations of poverty and wealth, goodness and corruption.

Driven by the demands of antifraternal satire, the *Crede*'s insistence on the transparency of need and moral behavior has important implications for thinking about Wycliffite models of theology, ecclesiology, and poetics. To take the first of these issues, we shall see that the *Crede*'s clear definitions of poverty and fraud make Langland's emphasis on the processes and potential occlusions of the will virtually irrelevant to its theological vision. In this poem's version of the relations between the self and world, ethical practice is clear without the mediating assistance of self-examination or penitence. The poem sidelines virtually all questions about the will in favor of outlining problems within the contemporary church.[7] Thus, Langland's exploration of epistemological complexity, applied both to the material world and to the innermost self, all but disappears in the *Crede* where the slippage between need and excess, virtue and vice becomes a consequence of fraternal corruption alone.

Second, the *Crede*'s moral outrage at the friars' abuse of poverty is so extreme that it can offer virtually no affirmative spiritual guidance beyond the climactic recitation of the Creed itself. This leaves the poem's ecclesiology entirely unelaborated.[8] Are we meant to see Pierce as an ideal representative of the priesthood of all believers? And if so, what are the implications of presenting such a radically de-institutionalized image of spiritual authority? What resources does the poem offer for pursuing theological knowledge and moral goodness? The *Crede* offers no explicit answers to these questions. We can only assume from the antifraternal teaching of the plowman and his exemplary life that virtue comes from living in poverty, working industriously in the fields, and knowing the words of the Apostolic Creed.

Finally, the poem's emphasis on the importance of the prayer as a sign of faith and charity affirms the *Crede*'s faith that all signs—even poetic signs—are fundamentally legible. The *Crede*'s own formal dynamics, as I shall argue in the final section of this chapter, attempt to replicate the transparency that the poem ascribes to the signs of poverty and wealth in the material world. Langland's and the *Crede* poet's distinctive treatments of poverty thus correspond to a more general divergence in the formal methods of each work. The *Crede* poet's dismissal of the difficult epistemological questions critical to Langland's treatment of poverty entails his rejection of the dynamic literary forms that constitute *Piers Plowman*. While critics have recently sought to uncover the aesthetic intricacies of polemical texts such as the *Crede,* my argument finds the poem less hermeneutically challenging than Langland's work.[9] Yet in making such a claim, my intention is not to dismiss the poetic achievements of the *Crede,* which in the words of Bruce Holsinger, has "suffered by poetic comparison to its Langlandian model."[10] As Holsinger shows, there are moments when the *Crede* develops a brilliantly artful aesthetic;[11] however, such moments are confined to a poem that, in its overall shape, deliberately cultivates a sense of transparency, directness, and simplicity. It does this not because the *Crede* poet is presumably less capable of Langland's poetic feats or because the *Crede* is simply a form of polemic that might as well be written in prose. Rather, the text's antifraternal approach to poverty, which depends on exposing the signs of true and false need, entails a broader approach to signs that necessarily emphasizes their transparency.

The *Crede* offers a stark literary methodology—what we might see as a willfully impoverished poetics—as it seeks to articulate the plain truth and to establish a single "graith." The *Crede* trades *Piers Plowman*'s allegory for narrative, its dream vision for waking life, and its dialectical argument for unyielding dualism. In choosing these more straightforward literary modes, the poem attempts, in its very structure, to embody the arguments it makes about the immanence of the visible signs that signal poverty, wealth, and interior identity. As the previous chapter has shown, Langland's text forces its readers to experience firsthand the difficulties in understanding the value of hunger or in discerning need for ourselves, as we struggle to interpret the shifting signs of his allegory. In contrast, the formal modes of the *Crede* seek to minimize the kind of readerly discernment demanded by Langland's work. While the *Crede*'s polysemous linguistic signs inevitably reach beyond the text's claims of a single truth, the poem works hard to make us forget about the instability of language. It wants us to forget about the interpretive, ecclesiological, and theological problems raised by a plowman's recitation of a single, unelaborated prayer. It wants us to forget that the poetic signs placed before us demand response and that they carry within them the potential for multiple and contradictory meanings. The *Crede*'s poetic processes create an illusion of transparency where the signs of need and the signs of virtue seem to require very little interpretive action.

Many of the issues in this chapter concerning Wycliffite poverty polemic will be developed and contextualized in the following chapter, which considers a broader range of Wycliffite works in relationship to late medieval debates about mendicancy. What I hope to offer here is further reflection on why poverty is a matter of epistemology and poetic practice. Accordingly, as in the previous chapter, my primary methodology is close reading. The *Crede* deserves our careful attention precisely because it seeks to deny all epistemological ambiguity. To borrow the words of James Simpson, "it is clear that the self-presentation of simplicity is anything but simple."[12] Though Simpson's remark describes sixteenth-century evangelical polemic, it resonates with this earlier Wycliffite poem and helps us see how some of Wycliffism's ideological commitments depend on complex and artificial pronouncements of clarity. Such pronouncements have wider social, religious, and ethical implications. Indeed, through the practice of reading the poem's purportedly limpid signs, the *Crede* ultimately prepares Christians to mistrust virtually all claims of poverty, for true need—in the world of this text—always renders itself obvious.

The Transparent World of *Pierce the Ploughman's Crede*

The author of the *Crede* bases his text on the scene in *Piers Plowman* when Wille asks two Franciscan friars where he can find Dowel.[13] In a significant transformation that has implications for the poem's hermeneutical principles, the Wycliffite author changes the object of his narrator's search from the ongoing action of Dowel to the stable text of the

Apostolic Creed.[14] In his quest to learn the Creed, an unnamed pilgrim encounters a member of each fraternal order, who consistently proves to be unwilling or unable to teach him the prayer. In critiquing all the fraternal orders, the poem often singles out a particular group of friars for possessing a particular flaw. For example, the Dominicans prove to be the most covetous, and the Franciscans turn out to be the most proud. The Austins emerge as the greatest backbiters, while the Carmelites are the most aggressive beggars.[15] Despite these specificities, however, the *Crede* makes it clear that all of the orders are united in their failure to fulfill their vow of poverty.

This failure becomes evident in the first section of the text, which essentially reenacts the same scene as different friars ask the narrator for alms. A Franciscan begs the narrator to "amenden" his order; an Austin friar bids him to "helpe vs hertliche"; and a Carmelite friar urges the pilgrim to "amenden oure hous."[16] We have seen in the previous chapter how a request for alms in late fourteenth-century England could be a tricky matter quite possibly forcing the donor to negotiate competing theories of almsgiving or to engage in difficult acts of discernment. Langland, in particular, considers whether all of his "bloody bretherne" deserve at least some kind of alms; he explores how indiscriminate giving may unfairly harm the giver and nullify the practice of charity; and he questions how a potential almsgiver can effectively determine a beggar's "worthiness." The *Crede*, however, does not have to pursue these difficult questions because it strategically replays the same scenario in which an obviously corrupt and wealthy friar asks the innocent and poor narrator for alms. The first section of the *Crede* presents almsgiving strictly as an exchange between these static stereotypes taken from the tradition of estates satire.[17] The poem therefore has no need for Langland's complex taxonomy of the poor elaborated in Passus IX; in this text there are no slippages between the identities of loyal workers, idle wasters, and bloody brethren. Rather, the *Crede* implicitly supports a model of discriminate almsgiving as it exposes the fraudulence that lies at the heart of each and every request for alms made in the poem. The *Crede* makes this fraudulence clear by portraying the opulence of the fraternal landscape, the disguise of the fraternal garb, and the hypocrisy of fraternal speech.

The Fraternal Landscape

In the search to learn his creed, the poem's unnamed pilgrim encounters a Dominican friar, but, long before he meets the friar personally, the pilgrim wanders through the order's costly lands, holdings, and buildings. As it surveys the Dominican compound, the poem offers an architectural description that appears to match that of the London house of Blackfriars.[18] In so doing, it presents the Dominicans' territory as a kind of text signifying the friars' decisive lack of need. It is not surprising that the *Crede* devotes so much hostile attention to the Dominican house because it served as the location of the so-called earthquake council (1382), which marked the first official condemnation of Wyclif and his followers.[19] Indeed, the Dominicans are treated with particular antipathy in the poem, and, as Helen Barr notes, they are the only order said to be founded by the devil.[20]

The *Crede* poet certainly spares no energy in showing how the shape, layout, and adornment of the Dominican "estate" function as a testament to the order's fundamental interest in worldly excess and prestige. Much of this episode is worth quoting here because the sixty lines devoted to describing the Dominican surroundings demonstrate how the poem allows the setting to speak for itself: the landscape has been literally shaped out of the Dominicans' excessive wealth and sinful behavior. When he first comes upon their residence, the narrator cannot hide his astonishment at its exceptional opulence. Alluding to what we will see is a fully elaborated theme in other Wycliffite writings—the church's wrongful assumption of temporal power and wealth—the narrator tells us that after coming to the Dominican "court:"

> . . . y gaped aboute.
> Swich a bild bold, y-buld opon erthe heighte
> Say I nought in certeine siththe a longe tyme.
> Y yemede vpon that house and yerne theron loked,
> Whough the pileres weren y-peynt and pulched ful clene,
> And queynteli i-coruen with curiouse knottes,
> With wyndowes well y-wrought wide vp o-lofte. . . .
> (156–62)

The narrator speaks in some of the poem's most sumptuous language to convey his amazement at the building's unusual extravagance.[21] His account of how its various parts are painted, polished, and embellished exposes the friars' sinful obsession with objects of wealth and splendor.

After the pilgrim enters the convent, we see that the spatial design of the order's compound takes on deeper moral significance. The walled seclusion of their residence fosters an atmosphere of secrecy and courtly intrigue:

> And thanne y entrid in and even-forth went,
> And all was walled that wone though it wid were,
> With posterns in pryuytie to pasen when hem liste;
> Orcheyardes and erberes euesed well clene,
> And a curious cros craftly entayled,
> With tabernacles y-tight to toten all abouten.
> (163–68)

The friars' walled isolation and their immaculate gardens provide them with a freedom to come and go "in pryuytie"—a freedom that is "incompatible with the fraternal vow of obedience and unworldliness."[22] Indeed, the narrator's observation conjures an image of friars sneaking in and out of secret doors so as to engage in elicit and covert activities. Instead of ministering in public to the needs of the Christian community, the friars have removed themselves to a discrete place where they are deliberately inaccessible and their activities deliberately inscrutable.

As the narrator proceeds into the depths of the Dominican residence, he exposes the opulence that literally constitutes the specifically religious space of the order. The Dominicans' commitment to temporal goods and authority perhaps becomes most clear in the narrator's detailed account of the church. When he approaches the sacred building, he explains that it functions as a place where worldly wealth and power are the primary objects of worship. Relying heavily on alliteration to replicate its sumptuous nature, the narrator paints a fetishized portrait of the church:

> Thanne y munte me forth the mynstre to knowen,
> And a-waytede a woon wonderlie well y-beld,

With arches on eueriche half and belliche y-corven,
With crochetes on corners with knottes of golde,
Wyde wyndowes y-wrought y-written full thikke,
Schynen with schapen scheldes to schewen aboute,
With merkes of marchauntes y-medled bytwene,
Mo than twenty and two twyes y-noumbred . . . .
Tombes opon tabernacles tyld opon lofte,
Housed in hirnes harde set abouten,
Of armede alabaustre alfor for the nones,
Made vpon marbel in many maner wyse,
Knyghtes in her conisantes clad for the nones,
All it semed seyntes y-sacred opon erthe. . . .
(171–86)[23]

From the narrator's account, the religious space is designed to sanctify nobility, wealth, and commerce. It is significant that at this point in the poem, the narrator does not launch into a conventional Wycliffite attack on images, candles, or other religious decoration. Rather, he criticizes the institution in more severe terms by showing that the Dominicans employ ornamentation to honor only their financial donors. In this church there are not even any relics, icons, or images of Jesus to complain about! Instead, the Dominican church features the emblazoned names of its contributors as engraving in the windows. Coats of arms and the emblems of merchants supersede any images of Christ, the apostles, or even Dominic himself. The only saintly figures, according to the narrator, are the entombed knights "y-sacred opon erthe" (186). This is a church primarily focused on preserving, promoting, and replicating the values associated with the lay nobility.

Making a criticism that the Wycliffite sermons in the next chapter will echo more explicitly, the narrator ultimately shows how the Dominican residence is a hybrid space that sinfully amalgamates temporal and spiritual concerns. For example, the narrator enters the chapter-house and notes that it has been "wrought as a greet chirche, / Coruen and couered and queyntliche entayled" (199–200). The chapter-house, furthermore, is not only like a church but is "[a]s a Parlement-hous y-peynted aboute" (202). The meeting space thus embodies the order's desire to wield temporal power under the guise of religious devotion.

The pilgrim repeatedly criticizes the friars' surroundings along these same lines; each of their buildings and rooms is inappropriately extravagant for its designated function, and each represents a disoriented fusion of spiritual concerns and worldly ambition. The refectory, for instance, evokes images of both a royal household and a church. The narrator "fond there . . . An halle for an heygh kinge an householde to holden, / With brode bordes aboute y-benched wel clene, / With windowes of glas wrought as a chirche" (203–6). The narrator sums up his impression of the Dominican territory by explaining that the friars' living quarters are indistinguishable from a royal palace: he "walkede . . . ferrer and went all abouten, / And seigh halles ful hyghe and houses full noble. . . . / And kychens for an highe kinge in castells to holden, ... / And othere houses y-nowe to herberwe the queene" (207–15). In the eyes of the pilgrim, the architectural splendor of the Dominicans' residence rivals the most elaborate centers of lay authority and dominion.

Within his detailed description of the Dominican order, the narrator pauses briefly on three occasions to compare the friars' vast wealth to the agricultural and financial resources of the lay community. Lest the sumptuous poetic portrayal of the Dominican surroundings become seductive to readers, the narrator makes these assessments to reveal how the Dominicans' holdings drastically eclipse the honest labor and productivity of the nonfraternal population.[24] He gives the Dominicans' wealth a sense of wasteful excess by measuring it against the comparatively moderate yet inherently more fruitful resources of the community at large. Speculating on the financial value of a single pillar, the pilgrim first compares its worth to an area of plow-land: "The pris of a plough-lond of penyes so rounde / To aparaile that pyler were pure lytel" (169–70). He then follows this statement with a similar comment about the comparative value of the Dominican cloister. He remarks, "I trowe the gaynage of the ground in a gret schire / Nolde aparaile that place oo point til other ende" (197–98). These brief asides are important in calling our attention to the realities of agricultural production and physical labor, activities that are conspicuously irrelevant to the friars. The comparisons, furthermore, highlight the pervasive sense of emptiness encapsulated in the Dominicans' ornate surroundings. The plow-land, like the "ground in the gret schire," has value not only for its price in "penyes" as property, but as a fertile and renewable source of food for the community. In contrast to the productive benefits of the land, the Dominicans use material goods strictly for decorative purposes. Furthermore, it should be noted that the order has come to possess these temporal goods not through its own labor but through outside donations from individuals who work at the plow or some other occupation to support themselves. The members of lay society voluntarily share the fruits of their labor, which the friars then transform into empty objects of visible beauty.[25] Paradoxically, the poem's ornate description works as a clear critique of aesthetic pleasure within the domain of the friars. The elaborate architectural design of their residence conveys a willful disregard for the reality of human need; the narrator's comparisons conjure implicit images of the poor who could be fed and clothed with the resources used to decorate a single portion of the Dominican house.[26]

In the third and final reference to the resources of the lay community, the narrator raises the issue of taxation, thereby calling attention to the order's excessive wealth and its disavowal of any larger financial obligation to the government or community. In another evaluative comment about the friars' property, he notes that "Though the tax of ten yer were trewly y-gadered, / Nolde it nought maken that hous half, as y trowe" (189–90). This remark is similar to his other two comparisons in that it emphasizes the sheer enormity of the Dominicans' wealth: he argues that all the revenue generated by ten years of taxes does not even account for half of the order's decorative value. The reference to taxes also contains a more forceful criticism aimed at exposing the friars' release from the same financial obligations imposed on the nonfraternal populations. While the lay community, as the narrator implies, must labor and then pay taxes on their income, the friars are exempt from any form of civil taxation since they are directly under the auspices of the pope.[27] The narrator's comparison betrays a sense that the orders shirk financial responsibilities for their own material benefit. The artful poetic description in this part of the text offers a subtle critique by suggesting that the friars sinfully emulate the lay community in seeking wealth and temporal power; however, they do so without accepting the responsibilities (such as labor and taxation) that come with that form of life.

Thus, the friars get the best of both worlds as they pursue and enjoy the privileges of lay power while disavowing their financial obligation to civil authority and the community at large.

The Fraternal Disguise

The *Crede*'s faith in visible appearance holds true when the poem shifts its gaze from fraternal territory and property to the friars as individuals. Once the narrator finally meets a Dominican who lives in the infamous residence described in such detail, he is initially drawn to the "cleanness" of the friar's attire. The poem plays on the different meanings of the word "clene" to suggest that the friar's fine and neatly folded garments reveal his lack of moral purity.[28] The pilgrim first notes that "[the friar's] cope that biclypped him wel *clene* was it folden, / Of double worstede y-dyght doun to the hele; / His kyrtel of *clene* whijt *clenlyche* y-sewed" (227–29, my emphasis). The narrator reveals how the delicacy and elegance of the friar's garments (sartorial cleanness) undercut his supposed commitment to poverty and purity (moral cleanness). He affirms the superficiality of the friar's cleanness when he makes yet another evaluative statement that calls attention to the vanity of the friar's dress. Alluding once again to the realm of agricultural production, the narrator explains that his kyrtel "was good y-now of ground greyn for to beren" (230). The pilgrim associates the fraternal garb with agricultural labor as he explains that the friar's garments are strong enough to carry grain. When he visualizes the garment as an object employed usefully in the transport of an essential food source, the poet implicitly highlights how such cloth functions as an empty symbol of holiness. This brief description of the Dominican's attire clearly has something in common with the poem's earlier description of the order's property and lands. Just as the exterior buildings demonstrate that the Dominican friars value worldly goods and prestige, the apparel worn by the members of the order similarly operates as a sign affirming their corruption and decisive lack of need.

As it recounts the pilgrim's meetings with members of the other fraternal orders, the poem more fully develops an interpretive guide that approaches the friars' clothing as a sign of their false poverty.[29] The text, for instance, makes repeated references to the opulent garb worn by some types of friars, and it gives particular attention to the Franciscans, for this group most grievously seems to violate its founder's call to humility. An Austin friar explains that "in cotynge of [a Franciscan's] cope is more cloth y-folden / Than was in Fraunces froc whan he hem first made." While "Fraunces bad his bretheren barfote to wenden," he explains that "Non han thei bucled schon for bleynynge of her heles, / And hosen in harde weder y-hamled by the ancle" (292–300). Noting that the Franciscan's body is covered, contained, and protected from the elements, the Austin describes one way in which the rival order visibly violates its professed commitment to poverty. Pierce himself later adds to these sartorial portraits by insisting that friars of all the orders "schapen her chapolories and streccheth hem brode, / And launceth heighe her hemmes with babelyng in stretes" (550–51). Just as the windows in their opulent churches sparkle and glitter, the friars' clothing has "ben y-sewed with whight silk and semes full queynte, / Y-stongen with stiches that stareth as siluer" (552–53). Wearing clothing that shines like silver, the friars literally project an aura of opulence and extravagance. While the poem's sumptuous descriptions of the friars' extravagant dress might once again appear to lead readers into a perverse sense of pleasure, the exhaustive enumeration of their shoes, coats, and other accessories is meant, I think, to produce a sense of righteous anger. As the poet continues to offer such detailed accounts of their clothing, the sheer volume of the orders' possessions becomes overwhelming and thereby signals their reprehensible covetousness and material excess.[30]

The sparkling white elegance of the friars' robes not only displays their obvious wealth, but also indicates the orders' attempts to appropriate the symbols of holiness without possessing the interior substance of sanctity. In addition to pointing out the clear external signs of their wealth, the *Crede* then exposes the fact that some friars disguise their affluence under a plain robe and attempt to usurp, through their dress, the signs of purity, poverty, and humility.[31] The Austin friar explains that some members of the Franciscan order attempt to look poor by covering their sumptuous apparel with an outer habit made of the simplest cloth: "vnder [his] cope hath he furred, / With foyns, or with fitchewes other fyn beuer, / And that is cutted to the kne and queyntly y-botend, /

Lest any spirituall man aspie that gile" (294–97). Describing this friar's attire as a form of "guile," the poem characterizes all friars as potential masters of disguise; under the façade of purity and holy poverty lie wealth, covetousness, and corruption.

In underscoring the friars' abuse of signs, the poem develops an epistemological model that resonates with what Sarah Beckwith sees as a theory of disguise emerging in the wake of the Reformation. As an event that entailed "profound changes in . . . signifying systems," the Reformation "create[d] a sense of gap between inner conviction and outer conformity." Though written a century earlier in a very different context, the *Crede* anticipates such epistemological changes by imagining the friars as performers who put on a "covering," "disguise," or "mask" that hides their true identity. In acting as holy men, the friars attempt to pass themselves off as such. Wearing shining white cloth or ragged garments, they turn signs into disguises and make them something that "we [must] look past, behind, or through and not at."[32]

On one level, the text's acknowledgement of the friars' deceit may be seen as disrupting the comfortable correspondences that the poem seeks to make between appearance and reality. Indeed, as Beckwith explains, the disguise is meant to raise epistemological uncertainty: "[it] poses identity as conundrum. It says that there is a gap between what you see and what you can know." Having acknowledged that the friars' plain white robes may be just a cover, the *Crede* admits the possibility that a potential almsgiver may not "aspie that gile" and may therefore be duped into aiding someone secretly dressed in the finest of furs. The poem, however, ultimately works to uncover the friars' disguise and eradicate the possibility for future uncertainty about their identities. Referring again to the gap between what can be seen and what can be known, Beckwith describes how this uncovering ultimately resolves any ambiguity about identity or knowledge: "[the disguise] unsettles and then satisfies our desires to close that gap by its logic of exposure. For most disguises, epistemological ambiguity disappears with their exposure."[33] In the *Crede,* one of Pierce's central duties is to enact the exposure that Beckwith describes. He functions to decode the friars' misuse of signs and symbols and to uncover their deceit.

Part of what makes the plowman's speech so authoritative, then, is its unmasking of the friars. He explains to the narrator that their attire does not finally designate poverty and humility but instead signals the deliberate concealment of covetousness and pride:

> . . . for falshed of freres y fele in my soule,
> Seynge the synfull lijf that sorweth myn herte,
> How thei ben clothed in cloth that clennest scheweth;
> For aungells and arcangells all thei whijt vseth,
> And alle aldermen that bene ante tronum.
> Thise tokens hauen freres taken but y trowe that a fewe
> Folwen fully that cloth but falsliche that vseth.
> (687–93)

Cloaking themselves in the signs of cleanness, the friars claim the sanctity of angels and those saved at the Apocalypse, yet they fail to live by the symbols with which they choose to cover their bodies.[34]

By exposing the nature of the friars' sartorial treachery, Pierce attempts to train the narrator and the poem's readers in deciphering the friars' devious use of signs.[35] The *Crede* is confident that the friars' disguises can be uncovered and their true nature discerned. Pierce acknowledges his faith in the efficacy of sensory perception when he confidently declares that if anyone can "fynd foure freres" that live in meekness, "than haue y tynt all my tast, touche and assaie" (537). Similarly confident in both its readers' perceptive abilities and the discernibility of fraternal signs, the poem offers a key to almsgivers faced with the prospect of giving charity to a friar: either his apparent wealth will clearly expose his lack of need, or his apparent poverty and humility will clearly expose his fraudulent assumption of the signs of indigence. In both extremes, the text teaches us that friars are never needy. It is not likely, then, that careful readers of the *Crede* would ever be lured into giving alms to the friars, for the poem has trained us to discern in their varied appearances "[t]he image of ypocricie ymped vpon fendes" (305).

Fraternal Speech and Petitions for Alms

When the narrator actually speaks with the friars themselves and asks if they can teach him the Creed, their responses and behavior confirm the covetousness and hypocrisy that he has already discerned in their landscape and appearance. In his encounters with the friars, the narrator witnesses how they repeatedly backbite and malign members of the other orders. This satiric methodology has the benefit of allowing the friars to expose their own corrosive judgmentalism and propensity for slander.[36] At the same time, the text nonetheless affirms the veracity of the friars' vituperative speech. The poem thus gets the best of both worlds as the friars unwittingly reveal their own moral ineptitude while enumerating additional flaws within the other orders.[37]

Among their many complaints, the friars repeatedly charge that their peers commit the sin of covetousness and thus abuse the poor. For example, when the Franciscan friar alerts the narrator to the problems within the Carmelite order, he echoes the language of *Piers Plowman* in asserting that the friars immerse themselves in a sinful cycle of getting and spending. He tells the narrator that the Carmelites "wynnen werldliche god and wasten it in synne" (61). The Franciscan exposes their deep-rooted avarice and their fundamental disregard for charity, when he adds that "what glut of tho gomes may any good kachen, / He will kepen it hym-self and cofren it faste, / And theigh his felawes fayle good for him he may steruen" (67–69). Based on this account, the Carmelites negate the lessons of love taught by Langland's Samaritan. Such sinfulness is not, however, endemic to the Carmelites, and other friars make similar accusations against each of the remaining orders.[38]

Rounding out the cycle of complaints, the Carmelite speaks out against the pride and worldly ambition of the Dominican friars. After accusing them of committing simony and currying favor with the king, he declares that the Dominicans consciously avoid the poor because they cannot offer the order any material benefits. He poses a rhetorical question to the narrator, asking, "Y pray the, where ben thei pryue with any pore wightes, / That maie not amenden her hous ne amenden hemseluen?" (368–69). In making such critiques of the individual orders, the friars betray their collective sin as people who "werldliche worchype wilneth in erthe" (371). They not only neglect the poor—the very people with whom they should most readily identify—but they usurp from them the alms that they desperately need.

As if the friars' houses, clothing, and slanderous speech do not fully convey their lack of material need and their great supply of covetousness and other sins, their outrageous requests for alms finally demonstrate their fundamental "unworthiness" as beggars. In the scenes in which the friars ask the narrator for charity, it is significant that the mendicants consistently do away with any pretense of goodness, sanctity, or need and instead offer what seem to be explicit admissions of their sinful behavior. In his exchange with the narrator, the Franciscan friar initially claims to lead a life of poverty and prayer by saying that he and his brothers "hauen forsaken the worlde and in wo lyvveth, / In penaunce and pouerte and precheth the puple / By ensample of our life soules to helpen" (110–12). This bold assertion quickly unravels, however, as the Franciscan reveals that his Order trades in prayer for gifts and other material goods: "in pouertie [we] praien for alle oure parteners / That gyueth vs any good . . . Other bell other booke or breed to our fode, / Other catell other cloth to coveren with our bones, / Money or money-worthe" (113–17). The donations that the friar lists clearly violate the Franciscan Rule, which prohibits the friars from receiving "money or pens; neiþer bi hem self ne mene persone putt bitwixe."[39] Books, bells, and money count as illicit gifts exceeding the friars' entitlement to the necessities of life.

The friar's violation of his vows becomes even more obvious when he proceeds to outline the order's extravagant architectural plans for a church that promises to rival the splendor of the Dominicans' place of worship. In a highly alliterative speech designed once again to replicate architectural splendor, the Franciscan tells the narrator:

> . . . we buldeth a burwgh—a brod and a large—
> A chirche and a chapaile with chambers a-lofte,
> With wide windowes y-wrought and walles well heye,
> That mote bene portreid and paynt and pulched ful clene,
> With gaie glittering glas glowing as the sonne.
>
> (118–22)

Following this magnificent description, the friar asks the narrator directly for money in exchange for the opportunity to worship in the beautiful church and earn the protection of St. Francis himself:

> And myghtestou amenden vs with money of thyn owne,
> Thou chuldest cnely before Crist in compass of gold

In the wide windowe westwarde wel nighe in the myddell,
And seynt Fraunces himself schall folden the in his cope,
And present the to the trynitie and praie for thy synnes.
(123–27)

Offering St. Francis himself as a divine intercessor for any donor, the friar makes an appeal for "charity" only after the poem exposes the order's outright rejection of poverty.[40] This friar is clearly not an indigent figure depending upon his fellow Christians for only the most basic provisions. As a potential almsgiver, the pilgrim therefore hardly has to agonize over whether the friar actually needs his help.

This is also the case with the other friars that he goes on to meet. In fact, the mendicants' requests for alms become even more troubling because the friars invoke their performance of the sacraments as commodities in an economic exchange. Directly prior to his request for charity, the Austin friar, for instance, explains how penance is a reward for those who make financial or material contributions to the order:[41]

We have power of the pope purliche assoilen
All that helpen our hous in helpe of her soules,
To dispensen hem with in dedes of synne;
All that amendeth oure hous in money other elles,
With corne other catell or clothes of beddes,
Other bedys or broche of breed for our fode.
(318–23)

Here, the sacrament of penance functions as a privilege for those who have the resources, in effect, to purchase absolution and spiritual guidance from the friars. The Austin's statement thus serves as an implicit threat to the narrator warning him that absolution will be denied to those who fail to give.

A Carmelite similarly presents his penitential services in exchange for the narrator's gifts. Offering to take the narrator's penance on himself, the friar establishes the financial requirements of this arrangement by making the following proposition to the narrator: "And thou wilt gyuen vs any good y would the here graunten / To taken all thy penance" (393–94). The friar goes on to dismiss the narrator's ignorance of the Creed as an unimportant detail; as long as the narrator gives the friar some kind of material reward, he is prepared to grant the pilgrim absolution. Once again the Carmelite foregrounds the narrator's financial obligations by explaining: "And though thou conne nought thy *Crede* clene the assoile, / So that thou mowe amenden our hous with mony other elles, / With som kattell other corne or cuppes of siluer" (395–97). In an exchange that Langland would find immensely troubling, the Carmelite, like the Austin, returns us to the world of mede in *Piers Plowman*: his propositions to the pilgrim suggest that money is a viable substitute for the sacraments and faith itself. The friar demonstrates not only that a donation translates into penance, but also that this specious form of absolution makes up for failing to know the most basic tenets of Christian faith. In the friar's view, as long as he receives his money, no spiritual elision or moral failure is too great. The Carmelite sums up his corrupt view of his religious vocation and responsibilities by stating, "Oure power lasteth nought so feer but we some peny fongen" (407).

The friars' individual requests for charity generate a larger pattern concerning fraternal mendicancy and the practice of almsgiving. The poem implicitly develops and promotes a model of discriminate charity by working to expose the friars' complete lack of need. The friars are not like the indeterminate figure of Langland's Wille, nor are they even close to the beggars with bags who raise Langland's suspicion. Rather, they are the embodiment of wealth, whether that wealth is in their obvious display of opulence or in their feeble attempts to conceal it. Unlike Langland's false mendicants, these beggars have traded in bags for extensive buildings, elaborate costumes, and outrageous speech—all of which work to betray the friars' unworthiness as recipients of charity. The poem goes so far as to present the friars as figures who have no conception of need. Their requests for alms conspicuously avoid protestations of poverty; instead they function as outright propositions offering penance in exchange for various forms of financial payment.

While the *Crede* works to emphasize that the friars do not deserve charity, it does not portray a dramatic moment in which the narrator refuses to aid them based on ethical grounds.[42] There is no climactic moment as in *Piers Plowman* when Hunger is called in to punish fraudulent beggars. Rather, the poem reserves this moral authority for Pierce himself, who, as we shall see, speaks freely about the sins of the friars and their unworthiness as recipients of charity. In contrast, the humble narrator does not give "aid" to the friars for completely different reasons. He tells the Carmelite,

> Trewely, frere . . . to tellen the the soothe,
> Ther is no peny in my palke to payen for my mete;
> I haue no good ne no gold but go thus abouten,
> And travaile full trewlye to wynnen withe my fode.
> (398–401)

As he repeatedly emphasizes that he speaks and lives "trewely," the pilgrim proclaims that he is an unequivocally poor individual. This characterization is crucial because it establishes the legitimate poverty of the narrator in contrast to the fraudulence of the friars. Furthermore, it marks a critical departure from *Piers Plowman* as the *Crede* transforms the ambiguous figure of Wille into a truly needy pilgrim who never begs or lives as a waster. It is significant that the only information that the narrator reveals about his personal life comes in this instance when he declares that he is a poor laborer who works for his food and accumulates nothing more. Supplying this single detail about the narrator, the *Crede* makes sure to emphasize that he is unlike Langland's wasters and lollares, who refuse to labor yet still boast bags full of goods. This pilgrim works, and he does not have a ready supply of food or money.

With this admission, the *Crede* begins to promote what looks like an ideal representation of the honest, laboring poor—a group similarly praised by Langland. Unlike *Piers Plowman,* however, the *Crede* does not criticize the unjust reality of working poverty or show sympathy for those trying to make ends meet. Rather, the hard-working narrator's lack of resources is admirable in this poem because it ensures his moral purity as someone who does not have to render judgment about the friars. It is the pilgrim's explicit need that precludes him from responding to fraternal claims of poverty by performing his own interpretive acts and confronting their ethical consequences. The narrator's neediness thus affirms the purity of his charitable intentions and also allows Pierce to step in as the final authority figure, who affirms that the friars are unworthy of charity.

The Body of Poverty and the Spirit of Generosity

When the narrator finally encounters Pierce the plowman and his family, the poem presents an even more striking contrast between the ideal of working poverty and the idle existence of the fraternal orders. Having made the wealth of the covetous friars clear and the indigence of the honest narrator apparent, the *Crede* goes on to present Pierce and his family's neediness as a kind of living and visible presence. From the narrator's very first glimpse of Pierce, we can immediately see that the plowman's way of life completely opposes the existence of the friars. Unlike the friars who seem to cultivate empty and wasteful possessions, Pierce spends his days engaged in the fruitful work of agricultural production.

The narrator first sees Pierce when, after leaving the friars, he is distraught at their ignorance and corruption. He tells us that he "wente be the waie wepynge for sorowe" (420). Before discussing his actual encounter with the plowman, it is worth pointing out that the pilgrim's emotion markedly differs from the moments in *Piers Plowman* in which Wille cries out of shame, penitence, or other frustration at the difficult and seemingly endless process of learning he undertakes.[43] In contrast, the *Crede* pilgrim's tears stem from anger directed outward at the sins of the friars and their failure to teach him the Creed. His reaction corresponds to Katherine Little's findings in her analysis of sin in the Wycliffite sermon cycle. Little argues that the sermons foreground the church's institutional failures, while de-emphasizing the introspective reflections central to orthodox penitential discourse.[44] Indeed, after mentioning the pilgrim's sadness at the *friars'* sinfulness, the *Crede* immediately forecloses the possibility of discussing his own morality and interior thoughts.

Instead, the narrator quickly shifts his focus to the scene that appears before him:

> I seigh a sely man me my opon the plow hongen.
> His cote was of a cloute that cary was y-called,
> His hod was full of holes and his heer oute,
> With his knopped schon clouted full thykke;
> His ton toteden out as he the londe treddede,
> His hosen ouerhongen his hokschynes on eueriche a side,

> Al beslombered in fen as he the plow folwede;
> Twey myteynes, as mete, maad all of cloutes;
> The fyngers weren for-werd and ful of fen honged.
> (421–29)

This detailed depiction of the plowman's deprivation paradoxically highlights the powerful presence of the absence of material goods. While the friars, as we have seen, fraudulently enshroud themselves in garments that hide their wealth and sinfulness, Pierce's body refuses any form of covering. We have left the realm of ecclesiastical disguise and entered a world where there is no gap between "inner conviction and outward gesture." This is a place where the body faithfully serves as the "field of expression of the human soul."[45] Protruding from tattered clothes that can conceal nothing, Pierce's physical body literally exposes itself as a sign of true need. The plowman's hair sticks out of his hood, his toes peep out of his shoes, the backs of his heels slip out of his hose, and his fingers come through his worn mittens. This picture of deserving poverty certainly offers a stark contrast to Langland's account of the working poor (Passus IX) whose need remains invisible and unknown to potential almsgivers.

While he labors "in the fen almost to the ancle" (430), Pierce's body remains on display as veritable proof of his poverty. This strikingly physical image of Pierce would seem to oppose Kellie Robertson's view that late medieval culture imagined the "good laborer's body . . . as a disembodied ideal." Moreover, it complicates her claim that in medieval poetry, "the bad laborer is a narrativizing or narrativized body, while good laboring bodies are either silent or invisible or both."[46] In the *Crede*, the myopic focus on Pierce's exposed, laboring body is central to the text's polemical goals because it suggests that the plowman is fundamentally immune to the kind of theatricalizing disguises worn by the idle friars.[47] This portrait of Pierce is also important in a larger critical context precisely because it makes poverty visible, thereby highlighting a subject that modern cultural theory, at least in Terry Eagleton's view, has tended to ignore. As Eagleton wryly remarks, "it is usually the erotic body, not the famished one" that dominates current critical interests.[48]

The *Crede* poem, however, puts the famished body prominently on display, and one would clearly be hard pressed to characterize the description of the plowman as erotic. To discount eroticism, however, is not to disregard the connection between economics and gender issues—a connection that both Eagleton and the *Crede* itself eventually make clear. This connection begins to emerge when the narrator next describes the plowman's livestock and family. Perhaps revealing his primary concern with the plowman's work and the particulars of agricultural labor, the narrator attends first to Pierce's emaciated heifers and notes that the animals have become so "feble" that "[m]en myghte reken ich a ryb so reufull they weren" (432). He then turns to Pierce's wife and points out that she too is also pitifully needy. He explains that she

> . . . walked him with with a longe gode,
> In a cutted cote cutted full heyghe,
> Wrapped in a wynwe schete to weren hire fro weders,
> Barfote on the bare ijs that the blod folwede.
> (433–36)

Pierce's wife is similarly exposed to the elements. She wears only a short coat and walks barefoot on the ice leaving bloody footprints behind as a tangible trace of her need. She serves as a more genuine emblem of Franciscan poverty than the friars who claim to live by Francis's own rule but wear "buckled schon for blynynge of her heles" (299).[49] Emphasizing both the agricultural and domestic dimensions of labor, the narrator also mentions that the plowman's three children are present singing a sorrowful song until Pierce asks for their silence at the pilgrim's arrival (442).

This family portrait interestingly conjures an image of the proletariat as Eagleton defines it within premodern society. Eagleton explains that this group was formed by "those who were too poor to serve the state by holding property, and who served instead by producing children as labor power." He goes on to explain how this economic status is at once a gendered and dehumanizing condition: members of the proletariat are "those who have nothing to give but their bodies. Proletarians and women are thus intimately allied. . . . The ultimate poverty or loss of being is . . . to work directly with your body, like the other animals."[50] While Pierce at least seems to own his own livestock and plow, the *Crede* nonetheless implicitly makes the connections described by Eagleton, especially as it juxtaposes the exposed bodies of the plowman and his wife with the painfully thin bodies of the animals they drive. It is difficult, however, to discern the poem's precise attitude toward the status of the plowman and his family. At this point in the text, one wonders if Pierce's poverty is to be lamented as the effect of the friars' misappropriations, or if it is to be praised as a state that motivates his labor or confers a sense of sanctity on him.

Just as the obvious poverty of Pierce and his family contrasts with the obvious wealth of the friars, the narrator's exchange with Pierce disrupts the pattern of corruption and hypocrisy sustained by the friars. While the narrator's encounter with Pierce indeed marks this shift in the poem, it also nonetheless preserves continuity by maintaining the fantasy that almsgiving is a straightforward and unambiguous practice. Reversing the terms of the friars' fraudulent requests for alms, Pierce—despite his own indigence—instantaneously offers charity to the despairing pilgrim.[51] The narrator explains that "This man loked opon me and leet the plow stonden, / And seyde, 'Sely man, why syghest thou so harde? / Yif the lakke lijflode lene the ich will / Swich good as God hath sent'" (443–46). This brief exchange affirms the correspondence between Pierce's material poverty and his inner sanctity because it is the poor plowman who fulfills the charitable obligation to love one's neighbor as one's self. He seems conspicuously unattached to any possessions that he may have, and he offers the narrator a share of his food understood not as his own personal belongings but as "[s]wich good as God hath sent" (446). The scene further idealizes the act of almsgiving because Pierce as the donor initiates charity himself—in this instance, the narrator does not ask for alms, and no one has to engage in the potentially reprehensible practice of mendicancy (600). The text thus chooses once again to foreclose an interpretive act, this time to be performed by the plowman. We do not know how Pierce would respond to a beggar's direct request for alms. Would he scrutinize the purported neediness of the pilgrim? Would it be obvious? If not, would he support someone like Langland's Wille who seems to live the life of an able-bodied mendicant? Would he heed, with the same charitable spirit, the request of just any beggar? Would he go so far as to offer aid to the friars who may indeed appear to be needy?

Refusing even to pose such questions, the *Crede* takes additional measures to ensure the purity of this charitable episode when the narrator declines the plowman's gift because he does not need it. Though we know he possesses nothing to give to the friars, the pilgrim explains that his sorrow at not knowing the Creed is much greater than any sense of material need he may experience (447). With this acknowledgement, the poem once again refuses to explore the hermeneutic and ethical ramifications of an imperfect instance of almsgiving. What would happen to the poem's tight contrast between friars and honest men if the narrator (someone who is not a friar) had accepted Pierce's offer under the mere pretense of poverty? How would the poem then address the problem of discernment? Furthermore, how would Pierce's authority be affected if the narrator—to use Langland's words—had "gil[ed] hym þat gyueth and take[n] agayne his wille?" (IX.65). Would such a donation somehow compromise Pierce's charity? These too, however, are questions that the *Crede* does not want to explore. Based strictly on the content and situations that the poem does choose to depict, it seems almost unimaginable that an abuse of charity could ever occur outside of the fraternal population.

The Plowman's "Sermon" and the Elision of the Will

Pierce seems to function as a figuration of the ideal Wycliffite priest, for he surpasses the friars in charity, fraternal responsibility, and knowledge of the Christian faith.[52] Prior to teaching the narrator the Creed at the end of the poem, Pierce preaches a kind of sermon, offering the pilgrim moral guidance about the fraternal orders. The poem grants Pierce a sense of authority by casting traditional antifraternal arguments as the plainspoken and earnest opinions of an ordinary plowman. His speech thus strengthens the binary that the text has created between unequivocally fraudulent friars and fundamentally charitable Christians. The plowman's instruction is informed by the poem's insistence on the transparency of goodness and the transparency of need; his moral lessons begin to reveal the theological implications of the *Crede*'s distinctive epistemology of poverty.

Pierce discusses at length how the mendicants' abuse of poverty contrasts with an idealized vision of Christian behavior. Yet as he specifies both the parameters of the friars' corruption and the moral virtues that their behavior violates, Pierce fails to consider the role of the will in resisting or yielding to sin. While his instruction functions as the most authoritative discourse in the poem, it omits critical problems and lessons that Langland examined in relation to the human will. Recalling the arguments of Rechelesnesse and Patience in *Piers Plowman,* Pierce's sermon suggests that virtue develops out of material conditions and bodily practices such as poverty, hunger, and labor. The poem develops this problematic theological view in an attempt to affirm Pierce's holy poverty while also decrying the unjust ramifications of fraternal covetousness.

Pierce espouses conventional tenets of antifraternal thought when he condemns the friars because they make their living through begging. He explains the basis of his critique by referring to an evangelical vision that the next chapter will discuss more fully. In short, Pierce claims that God made mendicancy an illicit practice: "[b]agges and beggyng he bad his folk leuen" (600). Pierce then goes on to make an argument familiar from Passus VIII and IX of *Piers Plowman.* He echoes the ideology of both labor legislation and antifraternalism when he declares that begging is legitimate for only a select group of individuals. Pierce outlines the qualifications that the poor must meet in order to receive God's blessing and the material consolation of alms:

> All tho blessed beth that bodyliche hungreth;—
> That ben the pore penyles that han ouer-passed
> The poynt of her pris lijf in penaunce of werkes,
> And mown nought swynken ne sweten but ben swythe feble,
> Other maymed at myschef or meseles syke,
> And here good is a-gon and greueth hem to beggen.
> (619–24)

In an assertion that will prove to be pervasive in Wycliffite writing on poverty, Pierce insists that begging can be legitimate only when illness, weakness, or other physical conditions prevent people from working and force them reluctantly into mendicancy.[53] Pierce concludes his enumeration of these authorizing qualities with the confident declaration that "[t]her is no frer in feith that fareth in this wise" (625). Though the friars are capable of supporting themselves through work, the plowman explains that they beg to amplify their own pleasures and riches. He asks, "Whereto beggen thise men and ben nought so feble; / Hem faileth no furrynge ne clothes at full, / But for a lustfull lijf in lustes to dwellen?" (603–5). The friars' obvious healthfulness and prosperity confirm that their mendicancy is a sham.

Indeed, the plowman goes on to criticize most harshly the friars' rejection of physical labor. To make this point, he evokes the plowing of the half-acre episode in *Piers Plowman*; but for Pierce it is strictly the friars who are wasters, consuming the resources and profits of others. Once again, Pierce decodes the friars' deceptive use of signs by explaining that the mendicants are essentially wasters, despite their attempts to signal otherwise:

> Thei vsen russet also somme of this freres,
> That bitokeneth trauaile and trewthe opon erthe.
> Bote loke whou this lorels labouren the erthe,
> But freten the frute that the folk full lellich biswynketh.
> With trauail of trewe men thei tymbren her houses,
> And of the curious clothe her copes thei biggen,
> And als his getynge is greet he schal ben good holden.
> (719–25)

By disguising themselves as laborers, the friars, according to Pierce, enjoy the benefits of others' productive efforts. Their "work" ironically entails appropriating the fruits of "trewe" men's labor so that their houses and appearances are formed literally out of goods stolen from the lay community.

As it elaborates on their idleness, the *Crede* continues to direct at the fraternal orders a familiar social imaginary articulated in labor legislation and the half-acre episode of *Piers Plowman*. Pierce goes on to discuss how the friars are essentially parasites draining the resources of a productive community. He references the traditional image of society as a beehive, when he explains,[54]

> And right as dranes doth nought but drynketh vp the huny,
> Whan been with her bysynesse han brought it to hepe,
> Right so fareth freres with folke opon erthe;
> They freten vp the furste-froyt and falsliche lybbeth.
> (726–29)

As they reap the fruits of busy bees without working themselves, the friars waste the community's productive labor. In likening the fraternal orders to a kind of bee that is inherently unable to produce honey, Pierce promotes a static vision of social identity. Specifically, his analogy suggests that the friars are, in kind or by their very nature, a drain on the resources of society; the friars cannot amend their bad habits and maintain their identity as friars. Because the friars are incapable of change, the implication is that the fraternal orders must be abolished.[55]

Mum and the Sothsegger, another poem assigned to the Piers Plowman Tradition, uses this same image of the drone and reveals, to an extreme degree, the ethical liabilities of this mode of thought. As the narrator of *Mum* sleeps, he has a vision of a beekeeper who discusses the virtues and challenges in maintaining a well-ordered and governed society.[56] Similar to Langland's half-acre episode, the vision begins with a utopian fantasy in which the beekeeper characterizes the bee as the most praiseworthy insect because it willingly performs its designated labors in the hive (1020). Echoing Langland's discussion of wasters and the *Crede*'s treatment of friars, the beekeeper goes on to acknowledge, however, that there are drones that undermine the work of the loyal bees. The beekeeper outrageously characterizes the drones as wasters who have their own bags in which to store the stolen honey: "in thaire wide wombs thay wol hide more / Thenne twenty bees and trauaillen not no tyme of the day, / but gaderyn al to the gutte and growen grete and fatte / And fillen thaire bagges brede-ful of that the bees wyrchen" (1045–49).

In response to the drones, the beekeeper, as the protector of the hive, initiates a program of violence that aims simply to eliminate the drones/wasters without much concern for the ethical status of his actions. The beekeeper thus protects the honey and maintains the hive by killing the drones. When the narrator first sees him, he describes how the beekeeper "houed ouer a hyue, the hony forto kepe / Fro dranes that destrued hit and dide not elles; / He thrast thaym with his thumbe as thicke as they come, / He lafte noon a-live for thaire lither taicches" (966–69). In response to the beekeeper's violent action, we get no hint, as in *Piers Plowman*, that even these wasters are "bloody brethren" who possibly deserve mercy. In reference to the drones, the beekeeper simply declares: "deye mote they alle" (982). The allegory here makes it hard to remember that the text is talking about people and, in particular, the narrator's fellow Christians. The tendency toward demonizing "idle workers" or covetous friars is full-blown in *Mum*, as the text casts these individuals as insects that are most usefully exterminated.

In the *Crede*, Pierce stops short of advocating such violence against the drones/friars, but he proposes other reformist measures that similarly seek to dismantle the friars' form of life. Pierce recalls Hunger's ineffective and ethically suspect programs in the half-acre scene of *Piers Plowman* when he argues that the friars should be subjected to material deprivation and physical labor. The plowman affirms the text's valuation of agricultural work by making a connection between labor and virtuous forms of living. In reference to the friars, he proclaims, "Y might tymen tho troiflardes to toilen with the erthe, / Tylyen and trewliche liven and her flesh tempren" (742–43). The friars should live simply and work hard, because, as Pierce goes on to state, such pursuits are more appropriate for the members of their kind.

It is significant that at this point in the poem, the plowman launches into a conservative social imaginary, one that signals perhaps surprising affinities between Wycliffite thought and the ideology of late medieval labor legislation. The *Crede* briefly pauses from its focus on the fraudulent friars and deserving members of the peasantry to complain about the degeneration of the estates model. In so doing the poem reveals its commitment to the interests of the lay elite—a commitment that will become more pronounced in the following chapter. In a passage that echoes Wille's social critique in Passus V, we encounter the poor plowman lamenting the social aspirations of the working class and the reduced status of knights:

> "Now mot ich soutere his sone setten to schole,
> And ich a beggers brol on the booke lerne. . . .

> So of that beggers brol a bychop schal worthen . . .
> And lordes sones lowly to tho losels aloute,
> Knightes crouketh hem to and crucheth full lowe,
> And his syre a soutere y-suled in grees,
> His teeth with toylinge of lether tattered as a sawe."
> (744–53)

This remarkable passage—spoken by an impoverished plowman—expresses sympathy for knights and lords' sons who now find themselves forced to kneel before the sons of cobblers and beggars. This compassion for the elite reveals the poem's implicit acceptance of wealth as long as it is not held by the clergy. As we shall see in the next chapter, this perspective is more fully elaborated in other Wycliffite works, yet beyond this passage the *Crede* does not explicitly elaborate on its commitment to lay elite.[57] To do so would compromise the direct connection the poem wants to make between material conditions and interior dispositions: what would a class of morally secure and prosperous lords look like in the world of this text? Might their presence detract from the poem's antifraternalism by potentially presenting poverty as a consequence of the excesses of the first estate, and not simply the covetousness of the friars?

In the final lines of the above passage, the plowman's attitude toward workers is also striking, especially given that the poem has idealized labor up to this point. While the *Crede* approvingly examines the effects of labor on Pierce's obviously needy body, here it presents the labor of a cobbler as grotesque, as it pollutes the workman's body with "grees" and deforms his teeth.[58] This disparity does not indicate a sense of confusion in the poem but significantly reveals that its praise of labor is contingent on the precise role that labor plays in preserving traditional forms of social order. Thus, work is sanctified when undertaken by a poor plowman; when performed by an ambitious cobbler, seeking his son's advancement, it is a perversion revealing how both the human and social body has been distorted.

The plowman's critique of lay labor and the dissolution of social hierarchy is ultimately brief. The problematic implications of this passage are left behind just as quickly as they are raised when Pierce returns to the subject of the friars whom he identifies as the root of all social defects. He elaborates on his plan to amend the friars, and he claims that the fraternal drones are naturally suited to perform manual labor and to eat basic foods not much better than animal scraps. The plowman recapitulates Hunger's advice that Piers feed the wasters "houndes bred and hors breed" (IX.225):

> . . . her kynde were more to y-clense diches
> Than ben to sopers y-set first and serued with siluer.
> A great bolle-full of benen were betere in his wombe,
> And with the bandes of bakun his baly for to fillen,
> Than pertriches or plouers or pekokes y-rosted. . . .
> (760–64)

Pierce follows Hunger's logic in assuming that harsh material conditions will force the friars into proper Christian behavior. He wants to eliminate the practice of mendicancy and make the friars into hard-working, humble individuals who should not be distinguished from other Christians like the narrator and himself. The plowman concludes his "sermon" with a brief summary explaining how to restore the friars to the "pouerte of spirit" that Francis, Dominic, Elijah, and Austen once possessed:

> [The friars] schulden deluen and diggen and dongen the erthe,
> And mene-mong corn bred to her mete fongen,
> And wortes flechles wroughte and water to drinken,
> And werchen and wolward gon as we wrecches vsen;
> An aunter yif ther wolde on amonge an hol hundred
> Lyuen so for Godes loue in tyme of a wynter.
> (785–90)

Satirically emphasizing the deep-seated corruption of the mendicants (and not a lack of confidence in his own scheme), Pierce expresses hope that his plan will successfully reform at least one friar in a hundred. In the poem's view, hard work, plain food, and simple clothing can engender charity in the friars.

At this point, Pierce does not elaborate further on his plan for reform and chooses not to consider the practical and ethical problems that arise from Hunger's similar scheme in *Piers Plowman*. For instance, Pierce stops short of discussing how the friars would fare if deficiency were not the dominant material condition. Pierce and the narrator also display no concern that the repressive regimes of starvation and compulsory labor may oppose the laws of charity and Christian fraternity. Furthermore, and perhaps most importantly, the poem offers no critical reflection on this plan's dismissal of the will. Patience's lesson in *Piers Plowman,* which is well worth repeating, has no place in the Wycliffite poem: "For þoȝ nere payn ne plouh ne potage were, / Pryde woulde potte hymsulf forth" (XV.234–35). Pierce seeks the containment and repression of the friars' sinful behavior, which for him seems to derive from their material state. The plowman gives no account of how the friars might experience an interior moral reformation; he wants them simply to stop acting like wasters by contributing productively and visibly to the community.

When Pierce does turn to the subject of interior virtues, he enumerates a list of the beatitudes and explains how the friars are excluded from Christ's blessing by rejecting penitence, patience, and contentment with mere necessities. Pierce declares, for instance, that "Crist bad blissen bodies on erthe / That wepen for wykkednes that he byforne wroughte" (611–12). He then notes that the friars, however, refuse sorrow and penitence, "And therefore of that blissinge . . . may trussen her part in a terre powghe!" (617–18). Pierce also mentions the friars' wrathfulness, and he discusses in particular their ire at being criticized or reproached. He then adds that these fraternal "waspe[s]" are excluded from the "pesible blessed [by Christ] / That bene sufrant and sobre and susteyne anger" (645–46). Pierce furthermore declares that in contrast to the avaricious friars,

> Crist the clene hertes curteysliche blessed,
> That coueten no katel but Cristes full blisse,
> That leeueth fulliche on God and lellyche thenketh
> On his lore and his lawe and lyueth opon trewthe.
> (637–40)

Not surprisingly, the plowman is then quick to point out that the mendicants are not among this group for "[f]reres han foryeten this and folweth an other; / That thei may henten, they holden, and by-hirneth it sone" (641–42).

While the images of virtue and blessedness invoked by Pierce certainly accord with Langland's notions of Christian perfection, the *Crede* is uninterested in elaborating on these forms of what we could call "doing well." Because the plowman's vision of moral reformation consists in the friars' assumption of true poverty and labor, Pierce does not address how these forms of righteousness apply to Christians more generally. Given the poem's support for the estates model, presumably not all people should labor in the fields and restrict themselves to the bare necessities. Furthermore, with regard to the friars specifically, it is not clear how they can cultivate habits of penitence, restraint, and humility—virtues that do not necessarily proceed from hard labor and indigence. The plowman's commentary on the friars' avarice and abuse of mendicancy does not seek to clarify how a person, whether rich or poor, can limit the *desire* for material goods and "coveten no katel but Cristes fulle blisse" (638). The *Crede* erects religious and social ideals primarily to expose their absence within the fraternal orders. As a result, the poem reveals its disinterest in establishing how a person can cultivate dispositions blessed by Christ so as to become a peacemaker, a penitent, and member of the poor in spirit.

Wycliffite Spiritual Guidance and the Hermeneutic Ideal

In addition to promoting a theological ideal that dismisses the operations of the will, the *Crede*'s insistence on the clarity of poverty and its moral efficacy has further implications for understanding the poem's approach to signs more generally. In foregrounding the Creed itself as the culminating moment of the text, the poem displays its wholehearted faith in the transparency of linguistic signs. As we shall see in the final sections of this chapter, this faith produces not only a deeply ambiguous ecclesiology but a distinctive form of poetics that purports to minimize both the need for interpretation and the difficulty of discernment.

Among the many criticisms that the *Crede* levels against the friars, their abuse of language stands out as a particularly troubling manifestation of the orders' sinfulness.[59] The poem shows again and again how the friars' covetousness is apparent not only in their luxurious clothing and buildings, but in their distortion of writing, speech, and "truth."

In the world of the friars, language serves primarily as a vehicle for accruing worldly profit and prestige. The Dominicans, as we have seen, misuse linguistic signs by engraving the church windows with the names of wealthy donors and merchants. Furthermore, this list of financial contributors emerges as the most prominent text in their church. The narrator, as Barr explains, "is invited to read his name in the glazing of the visible church as a substitute for being taught the text he needs to know."[60] The word of God is conspicuously absent in the church of an order known particularly for its scholastic learning and preaching. To signal the spiritual corruption of all the fraternal orders, the poem amasses other examples of the friars' textual abuse.[61] Overall, the *Crede* makes it clear that the friars withdraw the "moral and theological significance" from all verbal signs.[62] In the poem, theological texts and God's word itself become commodities signaling the spiritual bankruptcy of the orders. The narrator realizes the extent to which the friars misuse language when he concludes that "Heere pride is the pater-noster in preyinge of synne; / Here Crede is coueytise" (336–37).[63] The friars have distorted the sacred language of prayer, and their desire for worldly profit has transformed the Christian faith into pride and covetousness.

In keeping with the poem's binary presentation of corrupt and virtuous forms of life, Pierce's "sermon" emerges as a corrective to the fraternal abuse of language. His plainspoken moral instruction about the greed and hypocrisy of the friars also functions as a hermeneutic lesson outlining how righteous Christians should read and interpret texts. In this sense, the *Crede*'s theories about verbal signs are relevant to its instruction about interpreting the signs of need. Just as Pierce uncovers the fraternal disguise by decoding the friars' perversion of sartorial symbols, he also exposes their distortion of linguistic signs. His speech is therefore central to the poem's larger goal of "distinguish[ing] between those texts which mislead and those which can be trusted."[64]

Pierce's commentary on language and interpretation reflects a major Wycliffite concern with accessing the "grounded" truth of scripture.[65] Promoting a central idea within Wycliffism, Pierce articulates a hermeneutic logic insisting that the "graith" of scripture can be readily apprehended. Academic debate, intellectual discussion, and glossing only serve to obscure the text's "open" meaning. According to Pierce, these activities are the specialty of the friars. He repeatedly blames them for "turning" God's word and wrenching it away from its essential truth. He warns that "now the glose is so greit in gladding tales / That turneth vp two-folde vnteyned opon trwethe, / That thei (the friars) bene cursed of Crist" (515–17).[66] Pierce follows this explicit condemnation with numerous attacks on the friars' hermeneutical practices. Among other critiques, he complains that the friars "godes wordes grysliche gloseth" (585); that they "Gods worde turneth" with "glosinge of godspells" (709); and that they consistently "studeyen and stumblen in tales" (591).

After making such condemnations, the plowman contrasts the friars' hermeneutical practices with what he sees as a model of right reading and "interpretation," if such a term is applicable to what is a largely unelaborated understanding of textual apprehension. He explains that

> God forbad to his folke and fullyche defended
> They schulden nought stodyen biforn ne sturen her wittes,
> But sodenlie the same word with her mowth schewe
> That weren yeuen hem of God thorugh gost of him-selue.
> (587–90)

Invoking Mark 13:11, Pierce asserts that the righteous Christian should not meddle with biblical study or commentary but rely solely on divine inspiration to apprehend God's word. This view affirms Wycliffism's commitment to *sola scriptura,* and it also interestingly anticipates evangelical polemic in the wake of the Reformation: both movements prioritize the text as a clear and open purveyor of meaning to those inspired by the Holy Spirit.[67]

The Prayer as Text

Pierce's perception that texts are immediately accessible, at least with the aid of the Holy Spirit, becomes even more apparent in his final recitation of the Creed. The poem as a whole foregrounds this hermeneutic ideal by diverging from *Piers Plowman* in making the object of the pilgrim's quest the Apostolic Creed, a twenty-three line text. As we have seen, Langland's Wille seeks to know what it means to "dowel." Exploring the operations of the will in relationship to material formations, communal obligations, and the sacraments, *Piers Plowman* investigates a process of becoming. In contrast, the Wycliffite text makes its end the Creed itself—a textual object that is efficiently recited to fulfill the pilgrim's fraught quest for spiritual knowledge. The poem, however, does not approach the Creed strictly as a changeless text, for Pierce recites it to the narrator. On one level, the poem thus refuses to treat the Creed as a textual object or as the kind of book that could be commodified and traded by the friars. The prayer consists of the words alone without any potentially distracting material dimensions. The poem, however, cannot eradicate the textual properties of the prayer, and it weaves the text of the Creed into the fabric of its own narrative. Clearly demarcating its presence in the poem with the title, "*Credo*," the poem fixes the prayer in language at the same time that it grants the Creed a kind of extratextual power that seeks to actualize the plowman's and the pilgrim's Christian perfection. While I do not wish to deny that texts, speech acts, and the language of prayer have genuine transformative power, the recitation of the Creed, as we shall see, is like the poem's approach to poverty in that it elides a number of interpretive and theological questions.

Pierce's attempt to restore and recuperate the friars' abuse of language culminates in his own recitation of the Creed. His iteration of the prayer is significant not only because it confirms his spiritual authority and knowledge (in contrast to the friars) but because it serves as the single occasion of affirmative moral "instruction" in the poem. Up to this point, the *Crede* has had very little to say about Christian virtue beyond contrasting examples of goodness with the sinful behavior of the friars. Having taught primarily through negative example, the plowman now recites the Creed thereby giving the pilgrim a more positive lesson beyond the bad example of the friars. In accordance with his preferred hermeneutic model, Pierce simply states the prayer without further explanation or elaboration, and the poem quickly comes to a close. The twenty-three lines of spoken text apparently satisfy the pilgrim's request for knowledge and suffice for teaching him the basis of the Christian faith. Indeed, much of the critical literature on the *Crede* attests to the seeming success and efficacy of the plowman's instruction.[68]

Many critics have agreed that the plowman's recitation of the prayer definitively stands in contrast to the friars' speech and inspires a true and active sense of faith in the narrator. Barr, for instance, comments on the unique significance of the plowman's prayer and its difference from the friars' use of language. She notes that "the illocutionary force of this recitation is not the ritualized rote learning exemplified by the narrator's knowledge of the Paternoster and the Ave Maria, nor the friars' parroted renditions of their rule and antiphonal responses. Instead, its significance is profound. . . . Opposed to the empty formalism of the friars, and their embellishments—sartorial, architectural, and verbal—is the 'graith' of a 'lewed' man."[69] In a comment similar to Barr's, George Kane gives an assessment of the Creed's "profound significance" by explaining that "it has nothing to do with disputes about dogma or the articles of faith, but relates to the fulfillment of belief in action, as in the Pauline definition of true religion."[70] Lampe concurs with this view and argues that the Creed is "designed to lead to the 'wisdom of God.'" Taking the final words of the poem to be those of the pilgrim, he describes how knowledge of the Creed enables the narrator to exemplify a form of Christian perfection: "Here is true humility, which has the ability to admit personal fallibility and at the same time balance this recognition with an absolute commitment to faith. Here is the new voice of a simple Christian, the words and actions of real rather than feigned belief."[71]

These kinds of readings are useful, I think, because they elucidate exactly what the poem wants to portray. In accordance with its hermeneutical idealizations, the *Crede* makes the simple recitation of a text into a spiritually transformative act that impels—to use the words of the above critics—"profound" significance, "belief in action," and "real rather than feigned faith." In order to contrast the great excess that defines both the friars' material belongings and their use of language, the *Crede* insists on the plowman's recitation of the prayer as a willfully unembellished act. However, in emphasizing simplicity and transparency as the consummate sign of virtue, the poem develops a moral strategy with some potentially troubling theological, hermeneutic, and ecclesiological implications that the above critics and the poem itself occlude.

Most explicitly, neither the critical work nor the poem itself gives any account of how the prayer translates into righteous Christian belief and practice. In other words, we have no insight into the process by which textual knowledge leads to faith and virtuous modes of being. Rather, the poem simply presents us with figures who simultaneously know and live by the Creed. What precisely is it about Pierce's recitation of the prayer that makes it more than an exercise in rote memorization? Or what, at least, prevents the pilgrim, or us as readers, from perceiving it as such? What activates the recitation and reception of these words so that they become "belief in action" or the complete fulfillment of the narrator's search? What has enabled a plowman to understand the prayer so fully that he can both embody it and teach it to others with such a firm sense of authority? How can the narrator, on hearing this prayer for the first time, apprehend the difficult theological concepts and doctrines it contains without further explanation, elaboration, or instruction? And perhaps, most importantly, why does he not state the prayer for himself in order to profess the words of faith that he has been so desperate to learn?

The word *credo,* which the poem prominently displays to announce the beginning of the Creed, is a verb form in the present tense spoken by the first person singular. These grammatical details importantly call attention to the creed as a speech act, as the pronouncement of individual faith. Applying J. L. Austin's theory of language, we can see that *credo* is not simply a descriptive or factual term marking off the final section of the poem, but a performative utterance with power to transform the pilgrim's identity and mode of being.[72] It is in this sense that Wilfred Cantwell Smith states that *credo* "fundamentally means to put one's heart on . . . bearing in mind quite firmly the notions of commitment . . . of self-involvement, the pledging of allegiance." Smith's particular discussion of both baptismal rites in the early church and the writing of Thomas Aquinas demonstrates that *credo* was perceived in Christian theology as a "decisive transformation" or "transforming drama"; *credo* was to "turn from all else in indifference if not disdain, becoming dead to that old life of darkness, and to plunge into the venture of beginning a quite new life, rising to live it in purity and joy and the freedom of a new allegiance."[73] As Smith explores this dynamic meaning of belief—

a meaning that he says loses force after the Middle Ages—he turns to the *Crede* itself. He specifically argues that the poem exemplifies how the Creed is much more than a declaration of belief as in the modern understanding of the word. Tracing the repetition of the word "leue," he reads the poem's conclusion as a "crescendo on love." The "holy beleue" articulated in the poem is the place "where one's heart is to be put." It is the "sacred reality to which one's allegiance is to be actively given."[74]

While Smith writes powerfully about the dynamic meaning of *credo* in general and in the poem itself, he does not recognize that the active giving of one's allegiance never directly happens in this poem: the narrator does not explicitly say the Creed. The poem's representation of *credo* thus transforms what should be a powerful act of self-commitment into a passive lesson. It thereby discounts the act of faith that the narrator must proclaim for himself. The poem's primary interest in relating the words of the prayer arguably disrupts its efficaciousness as a creed because it precludes the pilgrim's own utterance of the words. The poem thus prevents its readers from seeing how the pilgrim might truly come to know his creed, from seeing how this newly acquired "knowledge" transforms his life.

The poem also offers no hints about a larger ecclesiological structure giving form or meaning to the plowman and pilgrim's interaction. The *Crede* features the prayer as the only substantive form of spiritual guidance, and it implicitly posits a kind of circular reasoning to explain the connections between an unspoken text and the actualization of faithfulness and virtue. In its treatment of the prayer, the poem seems to accord with Wycliffite thought or at least support a particular hermeneutic model by substituting a "hermeneutics of life" for the "hermeneutics of the text." These terms, taken from Kantik Ghosh's study of Wycliffite interpretative methodology, describe how the Bible, in Wyclif's writing and in other Wycliffite works, tends to lose its status as a text requiring interpretation.[75] Instead, it becomes "the discourse of true belief originating in God and existing in the hearts of the faithful."[76] In this process the "principles of interpretation . . . become correspondingly elusive. Hermeneutics is . . . displaced by 'right living,' which provides, indeed embodies, the most dependable access to scriptural significance."[77]

The *Crede* arguably enacts this same principle in its approach to the prayer that concludes the poem.[78] The Apostolic Creed, as we have seen, does not need to be discussed, evaluated, or interpreted for the plowman and the narrator. Rather, these characters are able to apprehend the prayer as the true Christian faith because they are faithful. The absence of any kind of hermeneutical theory or practice concerning the prayer is predicated on the logic equating righteous Christian behavior with textual accessibility. In reference to scripture, Ghosh explains the circularity of the argument: "from scripture one elicits the principles of ideal humility, which principles in their turn underlie and dictate a correct hermeneutics."[79] The *Crede* generates a similar quandary. In the poem, the sinful friars are ignorant or willingly dismissive of the Creed, while the virtuous plowman and narrator readily accept it. This juxtaposition, especially in the case of the pilgrim, suggests that one must already live in charity to desire the Creed and to be able to comprehend it. Yet it is the Creed, the very foundation of Christian belief, that first establishes charity as a meaningful, practicable, and desirable virtue.

Beyond this central hermeneutic dilemma, the prayer raises other specific questions as an unelaborated and isolated instance of moral instruction in the poem. Perhaps most obviously, the plowman and the pilgrim seem to accept the difficult doctrinal matters in the prayer as self-evident truths or as precepts defying speculation and debate. The narrator hears the Creed for the first time and remarkably has no questions or concerns about some of the most complex tenets of the Christian faith. Theological concepts such as the incarnation, the resurrection, and the trinity are met with the pilgrim's silent acceptance and presumed understanding. This pilgrim is evidently very different from Langland's Wille who consistently struggles to grasp and live by the diverse teachings of figures such as Holy Churche, Patience, and Liberum Arbitrium. Wille's persistent questioning, his arguments with his interlocutors, and his moments of despair often demonstrate just how difficult it is to comprehend critical spiritual lessons and beliefs.[80]

The *Crede*'s attempt to dissolve or de-emphasize theological and linguistic complications becomes perhaps most clear when the plowman addresses the subject of the Eucharist. As he continues to recite the prayer, Pierce states rather matter-of-factly that Christians believe "in the sacrament also that sothfast God on is, / Fullich his fleche and his blod, that for vs dethe tholede" (817–18). Although debates about the Eucharist were central to Wycliffite thought and its opposition to orthodoxy, the plowman insists, without further elaboration and discussion, that all should believe in the sacrament, for, as he concludes, "it is [Christ's] blessed body." The plowman chooses to gloss over the uncertainty and ambiguity of his own statement about the nature of the Eucharist. He then returns to the sins of the friars and makes the Eucharist another vehicle for his antifraternalism. Speculation about the sacrament becomes yet another example of the friars' abuse of language:[81]

> And though this flaterynge freres wyln for her pride,
> Disputen of this deyte as dotardes schulden,
> The more the matere is moved the masedere hy worthen.
> Lat the losels alone and leue you the trewthe,
> For Crist seyde it is so, so mot it nede worthe;
> Therefore studye thou nought theron, ne stere thi wittes,
> It is his blessed body, so bad he vs beleuen.
> Thise maystres of dyvinitie many, als y trowe,
> Folwen nought fully the feith as fele of the lewede.
> (819–27)

In the plowman's view, the Eucharist is not a topic for debate; any speculation about the exact meaning of Christ's statement at the last supper incites only confusion and further misunderstanding.[82]

While Pierce's refusal to elaborate on his precise view of the Eucharist could be construed as a strategic or deliberate elision, it is difficult to know what purpose this might serve. David Aers has recently shown that Walter Brut de-emphasized the Eucharist as a consubstantiated or transubstantiated material because the importance of the sacrament for him involved "its reception in faith" and "the 'use' of the sacrament by the faithful."[83] Unlike Brut (whom the plowman notably praises), Pierce does not turn to discuss other aspects of the sacrament.[84] The poem remains deliberately elusive in its teachings on the Eucharist and on the church itself, an entity that the poem describes as something the pilgrim should "hold" in his mind (816).[85] In the *Crede,* the plowman and his recitation of the prayer emerge as the only resources available to the wandering pilgrim in need of spiritual aid. If Pierce is meant to serve as an ideal member of the priesthood of all believers, then the poem clearly advocates a radically de-institutionalized version of church.[86] While his instruction is apparently successful in the poem's terms, it retains deep ecclesiological ambiguities that lurk beneath the superficial clarity, confidence, and moral instruction that the *Crede* promotes.

In making the plowman's recitation of the Creed the final moment of the text, the poem stops short of exploring both practical and moral questions concerning the ongoing lives of the pilgrim, Pierce, and Christians in general. Because we see Pierce abstracted from any institution or community outside of his own family, we are not supplied with any central details explaining, for example, how Pierce himself first learned the Creed in a world where all clerics are woefully ignorant or remiss in their pastoral duties. Similarly, we are not told how the pilgrim first learned the Pater Noster and Ave Maria. He clearly has had access to enough religious training to know that what he does not know presents a major spiritual gap. How has he reached the seemingly paradoxical position of knowing what he has yet to learn?

While the poem certainly criticizes the friars for their ornate buildings, elaborate disguises, and wasteful ceremonies, the plowman's simple, spontaneous, and familiar teaching of the pilgrim seems perhaps excessively lacking in ritual or form. On the one hand, the absence of a formal religious structure is advantageous because it removes Pierce and the narrator from the possibility of being entangled in institutional corruption. On the other hand, this absence might also point toward a marginalization of religious practice and training within Wycliffite ideology. The poem clearly valorizes Pierce's sermon as an indispensable form of instruction shared between men who may belong to the priesthood of all believers. Is it worrisome, then, that Pierce's authoritative "preaching"—the most sacred activity in Wycliffite ideology—takes place as a chance encounter?[87] Is the seeming randomness of the poem's most morally significant exchange to be explained as a necessary consequence of the clergy's moral failings and the church's role as a persecutory agent?[88] In the world of the *Crede,* which claims to value simplicity and a sense of artless spontaneity, would Christians ideally learn the tenets of faith during unplanned meetings with laymen who have some access to knowledge that they do not? The exchange between the plowman and the pilgrim also raises questions about the priority of spiritual education and its parameters. Does the work of spiritual instruction routinely take precedence over Pierce's agricultural labor? Does it matter that the transmission of Christian faith in the poem occurs while the instructor takes a break from his pressing work in the fields? If we can read the exchange between these two characters as a lens into Wycliffite religious practice, then that practice entails potential problems emerging from the poem's ambiguous ecclesiology.

Poem as Text

The poem, as we have seen, offers the Apostolic Creed as its single source of spiritual edification. Presenting the words of the prayer without any significant interpretation or elaboration, the poem espouses an optimistic hermeneutic model that renders texts transparent and conveniently efficacious for those living in charity and spiritual poverty. While the *Crede* is clearly interested in articulating proper interpretive methods and distinguishing between good and bad texts, it remains to be seen how the Wycliffite poet understands his own literary endeavor. Scattergood concludes his study of the *Crede* by remarking that the author surprisingly "never appears to question his use of a poetic medium for his polemical diatribe."[89] While Scattergood is correct in that the *Crede* author never explicitly reflects on his own writing project, I think that the author does question his use of a poetic medium and that the very structure of the *Crede* reveals something about its approach to poetry.

Considering the text's formal dimensions as a poem consciously modeled, to a certain degree, after *Piers Plowman,* I want to conclude with some reflections on how the *Crede*'s hermeneutic of poverty informs its poetic methodology. Here, I will suggest that the *Crede*'s arguments about the transparency of poverty and wealth underwrite a poetic language and practice that, with few exceptions, prioritizes clarity, simplicity, and directness. As we have seen, the signs within the world of the poem—whether in the fraternal landscape, the clothing and speech of its characters, or the Creed itself—are presented as if they are immanently discernible, giving forth meaning without much complication or contradiction. As its own system of linguistic signs, the *Crede* similarly adopts a poetic methodology that seeks to pose minimal interpretive difficulty. Employing what I see as an "impoverished poetics," the *Crede* sparingly indulges in Langland's favored literary devices and replaces the hermeneutically demanding modes of dream vision, allegory, and dialectic with a stark, static, and more readily discernible system of dualism and contrast.

Before exploring the formal dynamics of the *Crede,* however, it is important to acknowledge that its goal of transparency is, of course, ultimately impossible to attain. In contrast to its professed aims of truth-telling and clarity, the poem, as Barr has explained, offers a wealth of linguistic complexity. In reference to the *Crede* and other poems in the Piers Plowman Tradition, she comments, "It is a mark of the textual force *Piers* exerted on these later poems that their language perpetuates plurality and serious play."[90] Holsinger has also read the *Crede*'s account of the Dominican order to show how a poem presumably opposed to artful intricacy provides just that in its passages of eckphrastic writing.[91] While Barr's and Holsinger's accounts describe the complexities of the *Crede*'s language with attention to how particular passages exhibit artfulness, puns, and other forms of linguistic play, I am not primarily concerned here to outline the technical ways in which we can deconstruct the text's claims to universal truth. Rather, I want to focus on the poet's overarching attempts to claim that his work can simply, clearly, and effectively translate the plain truth to its readers. In pursuing such objectives, the *Crede,* in my view, makes overt and substantive formal departures from *Piers Plowman* that signify a profound divergence between these texts. This divergence reveals that the *Crede* is not wholly amenable to the notions of linguistic complexity and aesthetic intricacy that Barr and Holsinger find within particular passages of the poem.

The *Crede*'s poetic objectives become most clear by considering its formal departures from *Piers Plowman.* Christina Von Nolcken has described how the *Crede* author chooses to adapt a particular episode from *Piers Plowman* that is unusual because it "contains relatively little Langlandian uncertainty." Indeed, the scene happens to be one of the longer waking moments in *Piers Plowman,* and it contains no allegorical personifications except for Wille himself.[92] Considering these formal details more closely, we can see that the *Crede* poet strategically attends to the atypical dimensions of *Piers Plowman* in order to de-emphasize the potentially opaque elements of his literary language.

As the *Crede* rejects the popular medieval genre of the dream vision, it limits the action of the poem to a single level of consciousness and does not therefore have to negotiate the complex relations between the world of dreams and waking reality.[93] The *Crede* confines itself to the conscious life of the pilgrim and thereby sidesteps some of the more fluid dimensions of Langland's text. Wille's sleep includes visions of the fair field of folk and scenes from the life of Jesus, all of which entail temporal and geographical shifts. In the *Crede,* the pilgrim's journey extends only as far as he can walk in his search to learn the prayer from another individual. Reporting the events in his waking life, the *Crede,* furthermore, refuses to follow Langland in exploring the intricacies of the human will as it functions in varying states of consciousness. We are not given a glimpse into the interior world of the pilgrim's dreams or into the psychological and spiritual preoccupations that shape them.

The lack of introspection within the *Crede* is due not only to its rejection of the dream vision genre, but also to the poem's abandonment of personification allegory. It should be noted that the *Crede* does very briefly indulge in personification when the narrator makes the following observations about the Franciscans: "y sey coueitise catel to fongen" and "charite and chastete ben chased out clene" (146, 150). However, such moments of allegory are highly unusual in this text, and they do not entail the fluid interaction of personifications that often makes Langland's allegorical representation so rich. The *Crede*'s overall departure from allegory gives it a different conceptual and temporal focus from *Piers Plowman,* making it concerned primarily with outward actions and events. The *Crede* noticeably eschews the interior terrain of the human will explored in many of *Piers Plowman*'s various personifications, including, most obviously, Wille himself. It thus disregards Langland's dense portraits of the relations between faculties such as reason and conscience. As a result, the Wycliffite poem denies us access to the thoughts, motivations, and conflicts within the pilgrim. The closest we get to any sense of his feelings or dispositions comes with the narrator's departure from the friars and his admission that: "Thanne turned y me forthe and talked to my-selue / Of the falshede of this folk—whou feithles they weren" (418–19). Unfortunately, we are not given the opportunity to hear the content of this internal dialogue. In general, the *Crede* excludes us from the pilgrim's introspective meditations, and when we are given access to his thoughts, we hear only more judgments against the friars (138, 335).

Because the *Crede* is committed to portraying the real life quest of a nonallegorical narrator, the poem is also fixed in time, working at a single level of action. Unlike Langland's allegory, the Wycliffite poem forestalls any fluid movements between past, present, and future. There are no passages that work like the tree of charity episode in *Piers Plowman,* when an apple falling in the present moment folds all at once into the time of human mortality, biblical history, and the liturgy.[94] The *Crede* confines itself to the literal actions and events of the pilgrim's journey, which is marked by an identifiable beginning and end. In contrast, *Piers Plowman* does not end with a definitive solution marking the completion of Wille's search. While the poem concludes in the mode of apocalypticism, Conscience initiates a new quest, and in this sense the poem ends "with no ending."[95] Although Langland is interested in exploring "a transcendent reality, with the divine as well as the human," A. C. Spearing explains that *Piers Plowman* does not conclude with any kind of omniscient vision: Langland "refuses to pretend to be able to stand firmly outside the confusing spectacle of human history, even in dreams, and to see the divinely ordained pattern complete, as God might see it."[96] The *Crede,* however, does not shy away from such a challenge and aims to effect a clear and seemingly permanent separation between false friars and loyal Christians.

While the *Crede* depicts a quest in real time and space, one cannot help but notice that the poem reaches beyond the present moment to signal that the conflict between the friars and virtuous Christians is essentially static. In the course of the poem it becomes hard to imagine any of its characters acting outside of a schematized agenda where the friars are thoroughly corrupt and the narrator, the plowman, and his family are thoroughly virtuous. Some critics have sensed this dimension of the poem and have accordingly perceived the characters as timeless abstractions. For example, in his discussion of Pierce's family, Lampe remarks that the plowman's wife can be understood as "Dame Poverty" herself.[97] While the poem does at times seem to operate at this level of abstraction, the characters do not work precisely as the fluid personifications often found in Langland's allegory, but function more readily as archetypes.[98] In its portrayal of the friars along with Pierce, his family, and the narrator, the poem, as Von Nolcken remarks, "sees through the temporal to a level of being in which [these characters] could never change."[99]

The *Crede*'s emphasis on a distinction between sinful friars and righteous laymen demands a readerly engagement that is very different from that required by the different allegorical modes found in *Piers Plowman*. While Barr thinks that the *Crede* has "absorbed very thoroughly the reading lessons offered by *Piers Plowman*," the larger formal differences in the poems demonstrate that the *Crede* resists many of Langland's lessons about reading, language, and signs.[100] For example, whereas Langland's exploration of poverty and ethical living is marked by fluid figures such as Nede and by evolving arguments about the spiritual advantages of being poor, the *Crede* relies solely on static characterization.[101] The nature of the *Crede*'s characters and, more specifically, their corruption by wealth or their sanctification by poverty seems to resist any development based on an individual's relations with others. Beyond the pilgrim's passive reception of the prayer, in the *Crede* there are virtually no transformations in meaning as the characters interact with one another. Furthermore, there is also the problem of social isolation, as we find a complete lack of interaction between the friars and the plowman. This lack, on the one hand may affirm the friars' neglect of the poor, but, on the other hand, it may also expose the incapacity of Pierce's moral teachings actually to influence and reform the friars in the here and now.

Indeed, the entire poem is structured as a binary narrative: presenting in the first 417 lines the corruption of the friars, it goes on in the final 433 lines to counter that corruption with the example and instruction of honest Pierce. In favor of this oppositional logic and organization, the *Crede* rejects the dialogism and dialectical methods of *Piers Plowman*. The complex multitude of voices in Langland's work gives way in the *Crede* to the simple dualism of the friars versus the plowman. As we have seen, this dualism is never and can never be synthesized. Langland's text, however, takes its readers through the oppositional arguments and debates articulated by personifications who speak with varying levels of authority. These conflicts do not end up as irresolvable binaries but constitute thoughtful ruminations on the contradictory elements of particular issues and ideas. For example, as I have argued in the previous chapter, the logical reversals and arguments of Passus IX attest to Langland's fraught deliberation on the ethics and workability of discriminate charity. Additionally, the debates among figures like Rechelesnesse, Patience, and Liberum Arbitrium do not stand as strictly oppositional arguments, but exist as part of an evolving mode of thought regarding the efficacy and value of Franciscan ideals of poverty. The *Crede,* however, seeks to impose the voice of "truth" on the corrupt friars, and Pierce's charitable wisdom simply displaces their "glosinge and gladdinge tales."[102] At the end of the poem, after Pierce recites the prayer, the text concludes in a culmination of monologism as the voices of plowman, pilgrim, and poet become one in the final lines: "But all that euer I haue sayd soth it me semeth, / And all that euer I haue written is soothe, as I trowe" (836–37).[103] These voices of truth, charity, and poverty easily cohere in opposition to the eternally false, covetous, and wealthy friars of antichrist's church.

Despite its prominent position in the Piers Plowman Tradition, the *Crede* diverges from its predecessor by approaching the practice of poverty and the practice of poetry from a very different perspective. In contrast to Langland's poem, the *Crede* restricts its scope to antifraternal satire. Within this world of fraudulent friars and poor plowmen, material states are readily discernible; furthermore, external reality accords with the state of the soul so that the needy plowman is poor in spirit and the wealthy friars are rich in sin. In this arena there is no need for Langland's exploration of the complex relations between shifting material realities and the interior processes of the will. There is also no need for self-examination and the sacraments, for one seems to achieve charity and humility in this poem by living in poverty, laboring in the fields, and avoiding the friars.

The *Crede*'s transparent signs of material and spiritual poverty are deeply significant, for they allow the poem to avoid some of the most difficult epistemological and ethical questions that Langland pursues in his exploration of charity and need. In the *Crede* social and interior identity are fixed, so that the poem can preclude the hermeneutic complexities that constitute Langland's text. Here only obviously wealthy friars beg alms from a poor pilgrim who has nothing to give them anyway. The obviously poor plowman offers charity to the obviously poor pilgrim, who despite his need refuses the plowman's generous gift. Within these carefully controlled systems of exchange there is no room for the ambiguities and ethical difficulties posed by Langland's wasters, lollares, faitours, and even Wille himself. The poem's hostility toward the friars trumps virtually all other concerns in the *Crede*. The result is that the poem denies the material, moral, and epistemological challenges of almsgiving. This insistence on clarity entails a potential danger, for the *Crede*'s claims about need's transparency actually occlude just how difficult and significant acts of discernment can be. As Langland's work has so anxiously revealed, judgments about need are not to be taken lightly because their consequences extend into this world and the next.

However, the *Crede*'s faith in the signs of need is powerful, and it generates a poetic that seeks to affirm faith in textual signs as well. In making the object of the narrator's search a prayer that is recited to him by the plowman, the poem conforms to a hermeneutic and poetic model suggesting that language is transparent, that words are immediately meaningful and transformative. The pilgrim needs no elaboration on the potentially tricky doctrines of the Creed, nor does he proclaim the act of faith for himself. It somehow suffices as a mode of learning for the narrator simply to hear the words of the prayer. The poem itself seeks to embody this faith in transparent linguistic signs by practicing a deliberately "impoverished poetics." The *Crede*'s formal modes eschew the jarring ambiguities and fluidity of Langland's text so as to produce a poem shaped by the commitment to narrative, waking life, and unyielding dualism. As we shall see, the dualistic structure of the friar versus the plowman continues to undergird even the more expansive forms of social relation outlined in the Wycliffite sermons I explore in the following chapter. Whereas the *Crede* primarily explores the friars' abuse of the laboring poor, the sermons ultimately explore the entire church's abuse of the lay community. While these works similarly condemn the church for its maltreatment of the needy, the category of "the poor" becomes increasingly elusive as does the relationship between the poor and the rich within the lay community.

CHAPTER THREE

"Clamerous" Beggars and "Nedi" Knights

Poverty and Wycliffite Reform

> We pore men, tresoreris of Cryst and his apostlis, denuncyn to þe lordis and þe comunys of þe parlement certain conclusionis and treuthis for þe reformaciun of holi chirche of Yngelond, þe qwiche haþ ben blynde and leprouse many ȝere be meyntenaunce of þe proude prelacye, born up with flatringe of priuate religion, þe qwich is multiplied to a gret charge and onerous to puple her in Yngelonde.

Posted on the doors of Parliament in 1395, the above statement proposing reforms for the institutional church begins with a striking declaration of authorial identity: "We pore men."[1] The proponents of what has come to be known as the *Twelve Conclusions of the Lollards* claim a position of authority for themselves by announcing their poverty. Revealing the complex associations of the term, their self-description as "pore" men does not merely refer to their degree of material need but allows them to assert a powerful ideological position that was especially prevalent in Wycliffite thought.[2] These "pore" men have the capacity to expose the pride and covetousness of the contemporary church. These "pore" men can see through the hypocrisy of the "blynde and leprouse" institution. These "pore" men can speak for the people of England who have suffered from the church's abuses. These "pore" men are, paradoxically, "tresoreris," who carry on the legacy of Christ and his apostles.

As we saw in the last chapter, *Pierce the Ploughman's Crede* similarly deploys poverty as an authorizing force. The needy plowman, like the "pore" men of the *Twelve Conclusions,* condemns the "private" sects of the friars and emerges as a "tresorer" of Christ by reciting the Creed. Yet, as we turn in this chapter to the larger body of Wycliffite prose, we shall see how the representation of the plowman in the *Crede* is actually distinctive because it focuses so explicitly on the reality of extreme material deprivation.

To suggest that the *Crede* is unusual in its focus on material need may seem surprising, given the pervasive concern with poverty in Wycliffite texts. Indeed, critics have long characterized Wycliffism as a movement that extols the virtues of poverty and advances the cause of the poor. Michel Mollat perhaps expresses this view most clearly when he argues that the Wycliffites retained "the goal of . . . leading their listeners to renounce the wealth and vanities of this world and donate all their belongings to the poor."[3] Other critics have similarly noted how Wycliffite writers frequently plead the case of the needy—a group that proves to be central to the movement's moral and ecclesiological reforms. For example, Margaret Aston contends that the Wycliffites possessed "a truly evangelical commitment to the poor,"[4] and Helen Barr's recent work would seem to affirm this view. In a study of Wycliffite representations of the commons, Barr argues that Wycliffite writers develop portraits of the third estate that are unusual within the wider scope of medieval literature. In contrast to the dominant tradition of anti-peasant discourse, Wycliffite texts offer "sustained idealization of the rural poor," and they consistently "uphold the sanctity of the third estate."[5]

These critics are correct in finding praise for poverty and concern for the poor within Wycliffite texts; however, their assessments of Wycliffism, I think, have tended to overlook the rhetorical subtlety of such polemical writing, which consciously employs poverty as a relativistic term. In its treatment of poverty the *Crede* poem, as we have seen, skillfully creates an aura of transparency, and it is tempting to seek a similar transparency in Wycliffite sermons as well. After all, on the surface these texts may indeed seem to be clear as they advance a relatively coherent set of goals and eschew the stylized medium of poetry.[6] Yet when examined closely, the sermons prove to be challenging and fluid texts shaped by a remarkable degree of rhetorical flexibility, particularly when it comes to the issue of poverty. As this chapter will show, the Wycliffites' own claims of poverty and the claims they make on behalf of the poor are neither simplistic nor straightforward declarations. Rather, one must look beyond the polemical confidence and the apparent directness of such claims so as to consider their status within the Wycliffites' overall plan for reform. This plan is concerned above all with restoring the poverty of the church. In pursuing this singular goal, the sermon writers, I shall argue, undertake skillful rhetorical maneuvers that ultimately occlude other forms of poverty, including, most importantly, the hardships of the needy themselves.[7]

In making such an argument, this chapter examines an array of Wycliffite prose in the context of orthodox antifraternalism and debates about mendicancy. Though the chapter considers a number of relevant texts, it focuses primarily on three sermons. The first is Archbishop Richard FitzRalph's *Defensio Curatorum,* which was preached in 1357 before the papal curia at Avignon as part of FitzRalph's and the secular clergy's longstanding feud with the friars.[8] The second is a Wycliffite sermon preached by William Taylor at St. Paul's cross in 1406.[9] Taylor's work stands out among other Wycliffite writings for revealing the the high stakes of preaching about poverty and mendicancy in late medieval England. After eventually being sentenced as a relapsed heretic, Taylor was burnt at Smithfield in 1423, and the list of articles condemning him includes his views on clerical ownership and mendicancy—topics central to his 1406 sermon.[10] In conjunction with Taylor's work, I also finally consider a third Wycliffite sermon known as *Omnis plantacio.* It is not clear if this anonymous text was actually preached, but it is roughly contemporary with Taylor's sermon, and both works are remarkably united in their approach to poverty, mendicancy, and other issues central to antifraternal thought.[11]

By focusing on these heretical works (and other relevant Wycliffite texts) within the larger context of antifraternalism, this chapter shows how Wycliffite writing ultimately generates a distinctive response to the historical conflicts associated with Franciscanism and fraternal begging.[12] FitzRalph's *Defensio Curatorum* is a particularly useful source of comparison since it was one of the most widely disseminated works of antifraternalism in the period.[13] The fact that it was translated by John Trevisa also makes it an appropriate text to consider alongside Wycliffite writings.[14] Since Trevisa was perhaps sympathetic to some of Wyclif's reforms, his translation helps reveal the affinity between FitzRalph's orthodox Latin sermon and the vernacular Wycliffite texts under consideration.[15] Indeed, one can see how these works occupy similar ideological territory, since the Wycliffite writers explored in this chapter follow FitzRalph quite closely by making traditional arguments against the legitimacy of the friars and Christ's own mendicancy.

However, traditional antifraternalism takes on new life when considered within the Wycliffites' larger plan for reforming the church. Perhaps most obviously, the Wycliffites extend antifraternal criticism into a wider form of anticlericalism that condemns the covetousness of all clergy. This shift also importantly broadens the range of those injured by the church's abuses. The victims are no longer members of the secular clergy, who condemned the friars for usurping clerical duties and revenues that belonged to parish churches. Instead, the Wycliffites speak from a wider viewpoint and denounce the entire clergy's exploitation of all poor people.[16] This wider anticlerical perspective and the vehemence with which it is articulated also make it possible, though, to look beyond the poor themselves in order to present the whole lay community as needy victims of clerical corruption. The Wycliffites' concern for the poor, then, becomes strangely flexible, confined not just to members of the third estate. Rather, it extends into a concern for the lay elite, whose power and resources, they contend, have been usurped by avaricious clerics. In this context, standard arguments against Christ's mendicancy have wider implications for understanding the cultural value of poverty. Such arguments, when expounded by Wycliffite writers, threaten to occlude Christ's poverty altogether and underwrite a social vision that ultimately challenges the humility, simplicity, and poverty that Wycliffites so often claim as authorizing forces.

The *Defensio Curatorum* and Orthodox Antifraternalism

Before turning to the intricacies of these Wycliffite texts, let us begin with Richard FitzRalph, the secular cleric beloved by later Wycliffite writers who referred to him variously as "sanctus Ricardus," "sanctus Armachamus, or "Seint Richart."[17] In his extensive debates with the friars, FitzRalph emerges an important figure who gives currency in late medieval England to earlier antifraternal arguments that developed when the secular masters objected to the friars at the University of Paris. These original conflicts focused largely on the Franciscans who embraced a doctrine of absolute poverty abdicating all forms of civil dominion. The friars based their order on the notion that Christ and the apostles were absolutely poor, owning nothing and begging for the necessities of life. They thus rejected ownership both individually and in common and maintained that they merely made use of goods without claiming dominion over them.[18] While Pope John XXII ultimately rejected the Franciscans' doctrine of absolute poverty and their distinction between dominion and use,[19] the version of poverty particular to Franciscanism would remain a live issue for years to come because even those Franciscans who were faithful to the pope were not entirely accepting of his determinations.[20] Furthermore, FitzRalph himself approached the Franciscan theory of poverty "as an intellectual basis for attacking all the orders of friars."[21]

In his condemnation of the friars, FitzRalph was influential for taking Franciscanism on its own terms in so far as he accepted the idea that a vow of poverty entailed the renunciation of dominion.[22] While James Dawson and Wendy Scase have offered detailed accounts of FitzRalph's arguments, revealing their distinctive relationship to the Franciscan theory of poverty, it will suffice here to give an overview of his approach to dominion—an issue important in both this chapter and the next.[23] In short, FitzRalph invokes the issue of dominion or lordship to discredit the claim that Christ was a mendicant. FitzRalph held that Christ could not have begged because he possessed dominion over the created world. In other words, Jesus was entitled to any temporal goods he needed.

The precise nature of Christ's dominion is more complicated, though, and in his *De pauperie salvatoris,* FitzRalph distinguishes between different kinds of dominion: there is civil dominion, by which one holds property, wields authority, and claims rights through the institution of human law; and there is original or natural dominion, which functions like the original lordship held by Adam, allowing humans to claim the right to the basic necessities of life.[24] According to FitzRalph, Christ relinquished civil dominion but retained original or natural dominion. When understood as a model for the fraternal orders, this conception of Jesus's dominion is important, for it theoretically allows Christ to remain poor (because he exercises no civil lordship) without having to practice mendicancy (because his original lordship entitles him to basic goods). FitzRalph's theories of lordship grow more involved as he considers the notion of dominion by grace, an idea that would later become central to Wyclif's reformist vision.[25] However, FitzRalph's view of dominion in all its forms would become extremely important to the Wycliffites, especially in regard to their vision of a disendowed church.

The *Defensio Curatorum* gives voice to some of FitzRalph's arguments about dominion, and it exposes many of the secular clergy's principle objections to the friars. One of the sermon's greatest complaints is that the friars usurp the roles of the secular clergy, particularly in the offices of confession, preaching, and burial. FitzRalph objects to the friars' unwelcome intrusion on his pastoral territory, declaring: "Hit is soþe þat þese riȝtes, þat freres haueþ y-procured, were þe riȝtes of curatours; þanne it was aȝenus Goddes heeste so to coueite þese riȝtes."[26] He goes on to complain that in appropriating the rights of the secular clergy, the friars violate their founding ideals of poverty by exercising civil dominion (62–63). He insists that "hauyng riȝt to preche and to cristen men may nouȝt stonde wiþ sich a foundment of beggerie" (62). If the friars undertake such duties, then they must acknowledge that they are entitled to goods by "the laws of God and the church."[27] For, as FitzRalph explains, "it is comyn lawe of holy cherche þat no man schulde fonge holy ordre, but he haue suffisaunt tytel to haue mete & drynke and cloþe"(66).[28] The priestly office entails dominion as it confers rights to the necessities of life.[29] FitzRalph therefore insists that the friars cannot be needy and perform pastoral work. The clerical office is a form of labor, and as such it merits material compensation, for Christ himself preached that "þe werkman is worþi his mede" (62). FitzRalph attempts to correct the friars' misappropriations of clerical duties by reminding them that they "makeþ [themselves] vnable to þe office of prest & to ech holy ordre" because they claim to renounce all ownership and civil dominion (92).

FitzRalph then goes on to attack the friars more directly, rejecting the basis of their mendicancy and the legitimacy of voluntary poverty itself. After explaining that mendicancy is incompatible with the clerical office, FitzRalph makes the argument, now familiar to us, that begging is not a viable pursuit for anyone who is capable of justly procuring the necessities of life for him or herself. Refuting the claim that Jesus was a mendicant, FitzRalph explains that "if Crist beggide wilfullich he was a verrey ypocryte, semyng a begger, & was no verrey begger, for Crist was neuer a verrey begger, for no man þat may haue y-nowȝ at his wille, is a verrey begger, þouȝ he begge. But he is a verrey faytour, & he þat beggeþ wilfullich may haue y-nowȝ at hys wille" (84). As Scase has remarked, FitzRalph here makes an extraordinary claim in attempting "to establish that voluntary need [is] *by definition* impossible; anyone who [is] voluntarily needy by definition [has] the wherewithal to avoid need, and [is] thus not a true beggar, but a false one."[30]

For FitzRalph, then, voluntary begging cannot be a licit Christian practice but is rather a sinful activity that explicitly violates some of God's most central commandments. FitzRalph argues that mendicancy opposes the fundamental Christian precept to love one's neighbor as oneself since "he þat axeþ of his neiȝbore vnskilfullich his neiȝbores goode wiþ-out nede, greueþ his neiȝbore" (82). Mendicancy actually disrupts charitable social relations because, in FitzRalph's view, it makes covetousness the central force that binds the Christian community together. The voluntary beggar "axeþ & . . . desireþ his neiȝbores þynge" and therefore "wilfullich doþ aȝenus Goddes heeste þat seiþ: 'þou schalt nouȝt coueite þi neiȝbores hous, noþer desire his wif, noþer his seruaunt man, noþer womman, noþer his oxe, noþer his asse, noþer any þyng þat is his'" (80–81). As a member of the secular clergy, FitzRalph claims to suffer the effects of such covetousness directly. As they beg alms, the friars "steal" money and other goods that Christians would ordinarily donate to their parish churches. Thus, for FitzRalph, "each gift to a friar is a theft from the institutional church."[31] Referring to the Decretal, he explicitly blames the friars for depriving parish churches of tithes:

> Þere it is seide þat "alle men of religioun þat haueþ no benefice, beþ a-cursed, ȝif þei wiþholdeþ, oþer wiþdraweþ, oþer fondeþ to

> appropre to hem wiþout a laweful cause, by any maner, colour, oþer sleiȝþe, riȝtes oþer teþinges, þat beþ dewe to holy chirche." & it semeþ no dowte, by Goddes owne lawe, þat teþinges of byqueestes & of fre ȝiftes is detty, & dewe to parische chirches, & to curatours þerof. . . . Þanne alle freres þat bynmeþ parische chirches þe teþinge of þat is y-ȝeue hem oþer biqueþe, beþ acursed. (44)

In FitzRalph's view, the friars are "acursed" for taking the revenue due to parish churches. While the increasingly wealthy friars "haveþ y-bilde fayre mynstres & rial palyces þouȝ hit were for kynges," they never "eni-oyneþ hem . . . to ȝeue . . . almes to amendment of parische chirches." Instead they keep such goods "al to hem-silf oþer to her owne ordre" (47–48).

While it offers such strident critiques of the fraternal life and its reliance on mendicancy, the *Defensio Curatorum* also rejects poverty more generally as a Christian value, for as FitzRalph states, "it is wrecchednesse to be pore . . . & and no man loueþ pouert for hit self" (80). He adds that "Crist neuer loued pouert for hit-self aloon," and he offers several different arguments to prove his point (80). FitzRalph explains that Jesus followed Joseph in the trade of carpentry and therefore "gat his liflode sometyme wiþ trauail and wiþ his hond werk" (87). FitzRalph also discusses Christ's divine power in order to reject theories of his mendicancy. Referencing the story of the fish and loaves, FitzRalph asks, "how schuld [Jesus] feede foure þousand men by myracle & may nouȝt fynde hym silf mete?" (83). In addition to arguing that Christ could not have been a truly indigent figure, FitzRalph also suggests that God himself rejects poverty in commanding to his people that "a nedy man & begger schal nouȝt be among ȝow" (81). FitzRalph affirms what he sees as the scripture's outright denunciation of poverty by remarkably defining it as "þe effect of sin" (80). FitzRalph argues that material need is a result of the fall and declares that "ȝif oure forme fader & moder hadde neuer y-synned, schuld neuer haue be pore man of oure kynde" (80). As Scase explains in a relevant discussion of FitzRalph's second London sermon, Adam's original lordship existed while he was in a state of grace, giving him access to all the goods of the world. After he sinned, however, his natural lordship was restricted, confining him to a state of poverty.[32]

Insisting that “pouert is euel,” FitzRalph finds value in wealth and in the labor that can bring about material gain. In his account of the pre-lapsarian world, he claims that mankind’s primary purpose was to labor and cultivate material goods. Promoting what David Aers has called a “new work ethic,”[33] FitzRalph declares that

> in þe first ordynaunce of man God ordeyned hym so þat anoon as man was made, God put hym in Paradys for he schuld worche & kepe Paradys; so hit is writen in þe bygynnyng of Hooly Writ. Hit semeþ me þat þere God tauȝt þat bodilich werk, possessioun and plente of riches & vnmebles, & warde & keping þerof for mannes vse, schuld be sett to-fore beggerie; for god sett man in Paradys for he schuld worche. (71)

FitzRalph reverses the commonplace that labor was actually the punishment for Adam’s and Eve’s sins. As a result, work becomes a divine reward: “man is y-bore to travail” so as to cultivate “possession and plente of riches.” He is not to cultivate poverty or practice mendicancy. Rather, he “schuld kepe Paradys as his owne & haue þere plente of good, & catel, meble & vnmeble” (71). Accordingly, wealth does not pose immediate danger to the soul, but, for FitzRalph, “riches is good having & worþi to be loued of God, for he is richest of alle” (80).

In presenting labor and material accumulation as sanctifying activities, the *Defensio Curatorum* establishes the groundwork for advocating a strict form of discriminate charity popular in antifraternal discourse and beyond. For FitzRalph, mendicancy in particular remains a problem because he views it as a deliberate rejection of labor—as a deceitful and slothful means of acquiring others’ justly earned possessions. Seeking to disqualify friars as legitimate recipients of alms, FitzRalph cites Luke 14 (a passage central to the Wycliffite sermons) and offers the gloss that only the poor who are “feble, blynde, and halt” should be given alms (88).[34] He is emphatic that “pore men þat beþ stalworþe and stronge schulde nouȝt be cleped to þe feste of beggers, for þei mowe quyte hit wiþ her trauail” (88). Marking only the disabled as deserving, FitzRalph offers a foundational articulation of an idea that, as we have seen, proves to be central to labor legislation, some parts of *Piers Plowman,* and the *Crede* alike.

Wycliffite Anticlericalism and Concern for the Poor

In its discussions of poverty, almsgiving, and labor, FitzRalph's *Defensio Curatorum* came to appeal to Wycliffite writers who viewed these topics as central to their own plans for ecclesiastical reform. Wycliffite texts such as Taylor's sermon, *Omnis plantacio,* and *De blasphemia contra fratres* engage many of the same issues and scriptural passages essential to FitzRalph's earlier conflicts with the friars. Yet antifraternalism plays a distinctive role in Wycliffite ideology. Indeed, as Scase has argued, FitzRalph's writing against the friars contains the potential for a wider anticlericalism, and we shall see precisely how Wycliffites exploit this potential to criticize all clerics for failing to uphold their varied claims of poverty.[35]

It is perhaps surprising to note that, at first glance, Taylor's sermon and *Omnis plantacio* seem quite removed from FitzRalph's anti-poverty ideology. Unlike the *Defensio Curatorum,* the Wycliffite texts give explicit warnings about wealth, particularly if it goes undistributed to the needy. As they explore the ethical status of material accumulation, the Wycliffite writers call attention to the dangerous moral consequences of retaining wealth—something that FitzRalph seemed only to praise. They turn specifically to Luke 12 to discuss the rich man with "plenteous fruytis," who decides to build bigger barns to store his goods. In his summary of the gospel account, Taylor describes the man's perspective as he says to himself, "Soule, þou hast manye goodis putt up into ful manye ȝeeris; reste, ete, drinke and make feeste."[36] The sermon then makes the moral consequences of such accumulation clear: "Forsoþe, God seide to him 'Fool! In þis nyȝt þei shulen take þi soule fro þee,' þat is to seie þe deuel" (13/ 368–69). Taylor presents the rich man as an avaricious figure who succumbs to the temptation to keep his wealth for himself alone. The *Omnis plantacio* affirms this characterization in its diagnosis of the man's sin: "for þe greet auarice þat he is encumbrid wiþ he mai not fynde in his herte to spende his goodis to Goddis worship, in releuyng of þo þat ben nedi."[37]

While FitzRalph would certainly not advocate the sin of avarice, he discusses the vice only in relation to fraternal mendicancy, and as a result the *Defensio Curatorum* does little to qualify its seemingly straightforward view that "riches [are] good having" (80). In contrast, the Wycliffite sermons offer a much more cautious attitude to wealth by showing how the rich man's possessions facilitate his solipsism and neglect of charitable duty. Taylor, for example, offers his commentary on Luke 12 as a cautionary tale to people in his own community. While he does not condemn wealth in and of itself (as Langland's Rechelesnesse and Patience do), he uses the damnation of the rich man to issue a particularly forceful warning against those who obtain wealth by sinful means:

> Certeyn, I doute me not, manye ben in þe caas of þis riche man or ellis in worse, þat laboren to encreece her poscesciouns and richessis, and to fulfille bernes and shoppis and gedren bisily, and holden hem noȝt apayed wiþ her owne goodis but bi extorcioun, wilis of þe lawe and ouerledyng of poore men, bi false and gileful weiȝtis, wily wordis, vnriȝtwise mesuris, vsurie, symonye and ypocrisie and oþere vnleeful meenys wiþoute noumbre geten hem goodis. (13/370–77)

Taylor exposes how people's "hertily bisynesse aboute þe world" may entail spiritual dangers, especially if their "bisynesse" allows them to acquire wealth unlawfully (13/378).

The sermons make additional qualifications to FitzRalph's enthusiastic support of wealth when they call attention to the real plight of the poor. They discuss the story of Dives and Lazarus in Luke 16, returning us to an area of concern that was central to *Piers Plowman*. In Langland's text, we saw how different personifications used the story for different ends, either to claim poverty as a guarantor of salvation or to emphasize the importance of charitable giving. The Wycliffite sermons seem to echo this latter perspective. For instance, the *Omnis plantacio* author treats Dives as another example of someone who has misused his goods, this time deploying them in the service of vanity and gluttony. Significantly, these activities cause the writer to denounce the rich man as a "*waastour* of Goddis goodis" (28/728, my emphasis). While I will discuss this term later in more detail, we can see that the writer gives a new connotation to the word Langland invoked in his exploration of the labor crisis in post-plague England. The sermon criticizes Dives because he "spendiþ [his goods] þere is no nede and upon hem þat haþ no nede, and to an yuel eende as for pompe and pride of þis world and for his owne veyn glorie, as dide þe riche, boostful, worldli, and glorious glotoun þat is biried in helle, of whom þe gospel spekiþ. (*Luc.* 16)" (28/728–32). While he criticized miserliness in discussing Luke 12, here the *Omnis plantacio* author condemns giving that is aimed at increasing the status of the donor. The misuse of wealth in the face of need once again results in damnation.

In his reading of Luke 16, Taylor similarly underscores the significance of almsgiving within the larger scheme of salvation as he explains "for þat duly fulfillid or þurȝ necgligence left, Crist bihotiþ us blisse or peyne euerlastinge"(12/342–43). Like Langland's Samaritan, Taylor argues that God dooms those who fail to show mercy to the poor:

> And bicause þat we shulden be war þat we be not vnmerciful, Crist techiþ us what bitidde of an vnmerciful man, riche and glotoun, þat delicatly and shynyngly fede himsilf wiþ his owne goodis, not reckynge of þe wrecchid Lazar ligginge at his ȝatis; and so þe riche man diede and was biried in helle. (12/344–49)

Dives's lack of mercy is encompassed by his gluttony. In contrast to Lazarus who experiences desperate hunger, Dives stuffs himself "delicatly and shynyngly" with food. The preacher clearly locates the rich man's sinfulness in his neglect of the poor, as he describes Dives as an otherwise virtuous man:

> Upon þis axiþ seint Austin þe cause of þe dampnyng of þis riche man, namely siþen þer is no mencioun maad in þe gospel þat he was a raueynour, wrongful chalenger and extorcioner, ne oppresser of fadirles and modirles children or of widowis, but he was riche. Wherof was he riche?—of his owne. What þanne was þe cause of þe dampnyng of him? Certeyn bicause þat he was vnmerciful, seynge þe mysese of his broþir and hauynge no mercy on him. (12/349–56)

The sermon once again warns about the dangers of misspent wealth as it explains that Dives is damned for failing to show mercy through almsgiving. By exposing the moral failures of Dives, both Taylor and the *Omnis plantacio* sermon grant visibility to the poor and demand their just treatment.[38] Their readings of Luke 12 and Luke 16 emerge as powerful lessons because they acknowledge a consequence that the *Defensio Curatorum* never spells out: the failure to distribute personal wealth results in final separation from God.

The sermons thus offer some potentially harsh warnings to the rich, and like *Piers Plowman* they emphasize the reality of need as a condition that demands almsgiving, not the denial of alms so as to force people to work. Their sharp moral lessons could certainly be applicable to lay elites, who must learn from Dives and relieve the suffering of the poor. The texts, though, do not explicitly pursue this line. The writers betray their ideological investments by presenting the clergy alone as sinful gluttons who waste the goods and even the lives of the poor. While the texts evince a passionate concern for the needy, it becomes clear that this concern almost always works in tandem with the writers' critique of the church.[39] When Taylor discusses the state of the church, he uses the very same terms with which he characterizes Dives, lamenting that there are clerics who, "*shynyngly* arrayed and *delicately* fed with pore mennys goodis, . . . areren up her vois in gladnesse" (8/201–3, my emphasis). Just like the rich men of Luke's gospel, these clerics "seien in effect þat . . . 'Blessid be God we ben maad riche,' and lyuen as *delicatly* and *rechelesly* as þouȝ þat þei weren in dispeir of liif to comynge" (8/211–13, my emphasis). Though Dives was not a cleric in the gospel, he implicitly becomes a figure for the late medieval clergy, not a model for rich laymen.[40]

The writers make additional complaints that both echo and expand the antifraternalism familiar to us from the *Crede*. The *Omnis plantacio* author characterizes the friars much as the *Crede* does: they approach their spiritual duties as an opportunity for economic gain. Speaking to the Christian community, the author declares that the friars "in couetise sillen and bien of ȝou in fayned wordis, for þei sillen her suffragiis or meritis, and bien þerwiþ ȝoure worldli good; and þus doen marchaundise wiþ ȝou or of ȝou in fayned wordis" (20/473–76). The sermons also often extend such arguments to all members of the clergy who are similarly obsessed with temporal wealth and power. Unlike Liberum Arbitrium's vision of the charitable church, which sells, lends, and gives with love, the "weylynge chirche" of Taylor's sermon laments its corruption by the clergy's commercial interests. The church complains, "Sones haue I norischid and enhaunsid, þei forsoþe han forsake me.

Þei han forsake me and defoulid me bi foul liif, foul wynnyng and foul marchaundise" (7–8/177–79).

In these accounts, the clergy have focused their energies so fervently on the pursuit of earthy goods and activities that they have lost their very identity as priests, friars, and men of God. Taylor protests that the devil "haþ wiþdrawun þe clergie from preestly office and brouȝt it into so greet worldlynesse . . . þat vnneþe reckiþ now ony man of þe office of preesthood to þe puple" (5/85–87). The *Omnis plantacio* author agrees, declaring that the clergy "encumbren and entriken hemsilf in worldli bisynesse and office, as in þe chaunserie, in tresorie and in oþir ful manye worldli office, aȝens þe pure staat of presthod and into greet wrong aȝens God and þe peple" (50/1184–87). Such comments suggest that the clergy have abandoned their spiritual obligations in favor of seeking power and wealth. Consequently, the church has been infected with what Taylor calls the "rootid scabbe" of hypocrisy (7/165); its leaders, according to *Omnis plantacio,* are "rulid in . . . apostasie, be anticristis lawe" (141/3015–16).

As the writers go on to complain, the church's worldliness is especially reprehensible because it injures the poor. The *Omnis plantacio* author censures the clergy for misusing donations to the church. Instead of giving such goods to their rightful recipients, that is, to the needy, the clergy once again act like Dives in keeping everything for themselves:

> al þat euere þei mai of worldli goodis þei scrapan into her corbanan, and þerwiþ lyuen as worldli, lordli, as ony kyngis or duykis; and to þe pore blynde, feble and lame þei ȝyuen wel nyȝ riȝt nouȝt, notwiþstondinge þat þei seien þat her goodis ben suche pore mennes goodis; and vndir colour of releuyng of suche pore men, þese goodis ben ȝoue into her conuenticlis. (53/1250–56)

Charity to the poor becomes a mere guise for enhancing the clergy's financial status. Taylor similarly objects to this situation and condemns the church as an insatiable force of consumption "swolowinge up þe substance of almes due bi Cristis wille to poore men" (19/596).[41]

The sermons criticize clerical covetousness more stridently by exposing its material consequences for the poor. They call attention to the plight of the poor by explaining that the church's covetous behavior actually endangers the lives of those most greatly in need. While the writers never give a precise definition of need in their sermons, at this point they seem to perceive the poor as those who suffer from extreme material deprivation. Like Lazarus, these are people whose survival is at stake without the assistance of alms. It is in this sense, then, that Taylor speaks in defense of the needy and objects, in explicitly political language, to what he sees as the church's outright abuse of the poor:

> as we seen aftir þe quantite of almes of poore men, þei multiplyen hem meynee as worldly as a temporal lord, and alle þe myȝtye of þe cuntree þei confederen to hem for to putte doun vndir foote þe poore, alwey bringing yn, in as moche as in hem is, newe bondage as Farao dide on þe children of Israel. And . . . þei han waastid þe bodyes of her sogetis, vsynge hem as beestis, and bi extorcioun haue take of her goodis and trauelis as moche as þei may. . . . Oo! how fer ben þese vnmerciful from þe condiciouns of merciful Iesu and his apostilis. (15–16/473–82)

Taylor underscores the physical suffering of the needy to remind his listeners that the treatment of the poor is not an abstract issue. He views the church's misappropriations as a matter of life and death: the bodies of the poor are "waastid" and "use[d] as beestis." He goes on to state explicitly that "summe of þese [clergy] . . . suffren pore men þat owen þese goodis to perisshe in body as we seen" (16/484–87).

The *Omnis plantacio* sermon is perhaps even more extreme in denouncing the church's mistreatment of the same contingent of the needy. Referring to those who have presumably died from starvation, the author views those church leaders who live in "greet plente and worldliness" as "mansleers." He declares that "þe blood of [Christ's] nedi chirche hangiþ on þis wickid peple, and upon her ouer worldli and waast arai in housyng, cloþing, in preciouse vessels and greet hors, and oþir þingis, þe whiche þei han in as greet plente and worldlynesse as ony seculer lordis" (114/2313–16). The writer's outrage causes him to lash out at the clergy, warning them of their potential damnation: "þese mansleers þat, bi defrauding of Cristis chirche, sleeþ Cristis sones, and hise briþeren, and han her handis baþid þus in þe pore and nedi peplis blood, ben riȝt vnable to be herd at God þe Fadir, for þei stiren not God to merci but raþer to venianunce" (114/2321–25). According to both writers, the role of the church has been subverted: rather than functioning as the steward of the poor, the church now steals directly from them and bathes its hands in their blood.

The Apostolic Ideal and Resistance to Poverty

In emphasizing the importance of almsgiving and in criticizing the church's wealth, the sermons certainly display a commitment to the ideal of the poor, apostolic church, and they passionately advocate the protection and just treatment of those in dire need. However, "their truly evangelical commitment to the poor" becomes less and less apparent when we investigate the authors' particular version of the apostolic church and their representation of Christ.[42] In the Wycliffites' vision of the evangelical church, it quickly becomes evident that poverty is not a value in and of itself; both sermons, like the *Defensio Curatorum,* emphasize that the members of the primitive church sought to eradicate all forms of need within the wider community. Taylor explains that "þe apostils . . . in whom was þer plente of perfeccioun of þe gospel . . . wiþ a comyn asent ordeyneden þat þer shulde be no needy man or womman amonge hem, for it was departid to euery as it was neede" (17/529–32). The *Omnis plantacio* writer also states that in the time of Christ and the apostles "þe comoun goodis were so wiisli delid among þe peple þat þer was no nedi among hem" (131/2730–31).[43] While these statements may seem like little more than an affirmation of the early church's commitment to charity, the Wycliffites go on to make it clear that they are ultimately focusing on the institution's denial that voluntary poverty is a legitimate Christian state.

Taylor asserts that Christ and the apostles rejected begging as an acceptable means of livelihood. The founders of the early church come to affirm antifraternal rhetoric as Taylor explains that "Þe cause whi þat Crist and his apostlis woulde no beggeris be may resonably be þe greuouse synnes þat comunly suen customable beggeris, as ypocrisie, flateringe, lyinge, enuye, drunkenesse and leccherie" (18/581–84).[44] The

Omnis plantacio author similarly remarks on the "mischif" and "greet synne" that "comeþ of beggerie" (131/2734, 2742). Based on these assertions, Christ and his apostles share goods and provide for the poor not just to relieve their need, but in order to prevent them from lapsing into the "sinful" practice of mendicancy.

The Wycliffite sermons also follow the *Defensio Curatorum* when they argue against the basis of the Franciscan movement by insisting that Jesus and his apostles never begged because Christ, in Taylor's words, "ordeynede sufficiently for his chirche" (16/502). The *Omnis plantacio* author also denies the validity of the friars' voluntary poverty and insists that their status as clerics grants them access to temporal goods: "þe clerkis weren sufficientli purueid for liiflood bi Cristis ordynaunce in þe gospel, for he is so perfit in al his worching þat he mai ordeyne noon astaat in his chirche, but if he ordeyne sufficient liiflood to þe same astaat" (100/2087–90). While both authors make it clear that figures like Jesus, Peter, and Paul eschewed temporal wealth, the writers explain that these early church leaders nonetheless retained a legitimate claim to possess basic material goods. By viewing the priestly office as a form of labor, Taylor, for instance, argues that Christ and his apostles were not destitute, but were entitled to receive "wagis ordeynede of Crist" (18/556), or more specifically "necessarie liiflode and hilyng" (9/238). He reiterates one of FitzRalph's central points when he makes the argument that "for þe clerkis Crist . . . ordeynede, enasumplynge hem and techynge hem to receyue þat þat was nedeful to liiflode bi title of þe gospel and not of beggyng, seiynge on þis wise 'Þe werkman is worþi his meede'" (16/505–8). The *Omnis plantacio* author also declares that Christ and the apostles rightfully earned food and clothing in exchange for their priestly work:

> And þis [liiflood and hilyng] þei took of þe peple, not bi titil of lordship or of beggerie, as oure maistir liers and her sectis doen, but bi titil of the gospel or of prestis office duli perfourmed to þe peple—þe which titil is þis, as Crist himsilf seiþ, 'þe werkman is worþi his meede or his mete.' (30/773–77)

While the writer ironically characterizes the fraternal position as somehow claiming dominion through mendicancy, he posits a form of dominion based on the priestly office and the spiritual labor it entails. This occupation entitles the clergy to possess basic goods so that they do not have to resort to mendicancy.

The authors make it clear that the priests of the early church had enough possessions to keep them from begging, but they are careful to point out that the clergy was not by any means wealthy. They take advantage of the broader anticlericalism that was only implicit in FitzRalph's antifraternal critique. Marking a central difference between the *Defensio Curatorum* and the Wycliffite texts, the sermon authors display no sympathy for the beneficed clerics who, in their opinion, retain excessive temporal wealth. The Wycliffites' discourse of poverty shifts once again as the writers explain that, in its evangelical form, poverty does not entail severe material need or abundant material possessions.[45] The *Omnis plantacio* author construes it as a type of fiscal moderation. He idealistically presents the early church as a self-sufficient and financially stable institution that rejects the extremes plaguing the contemporary medieval church: monastic superfluity and professed fraternal indigence. While the author exposes the fundamental differences between the possessioners' and the friars' opposed models of living, he nonetheless points out that the two groups have colluded to destroy Christ's law:

> notwiþstonding þat þei [þese new sectis] ben contrariousli foundid, þat oon upon possessiouns and þat oþer upon beggerie, as hemsilf seien, and notwiþstonding þat þei han wrouȝt ech aȝens oþir in scool and in preching, and þat long and ofte tymes to dispreue ech oþeris fundacioun and lyuyng, ȝit, bicause þat vnyte is so needful þat þe deuelis rewme mai not stonde if his retenu be dyuydid, þese sectis ben acordid, as Herodis and Pilat and þe pharisees and saduceis, and boþe bi oon assent maintenen oþeris fundacioun and lyuyng, and acorden in dampnyng of truþe of Goddis lawe and resoun. (27–28/706–14)

The possessioners and the mendicants exist in a symbiosis of sin, perverting the foundational ideals of the apostolic church.

The *Omnis plantacio* writer goes on to explain this ecclesiological problem in greater detail. He first notes that Christ and the apostles "lefte þe possessiouns and þe lordships, and so al maner of seculer lordlynesse or lordshiping, þe which mounkis and chanouns and oþir religiouse ypocritis þat ben possessioners ful lecherousli clippen to hem" (29/760–64). He is quick to add, however, that the apostolic church was not destitute since "Crist and such perfit folk leften þat oþir vicious extremyte þat is to seie beggerie" (30/769–70). Avoiding both civil dominion and mendicancy, the evangelical institution, he goes on to explain, is an exemplum of virtuous moderation: "And so þei leften þe two viciouse extremytees as grete and hidouse synnes, and chosen to hem þe virtuous mene, þat is to seie liiflood and hilyng, and helden hem apaied þerwiþ" (3/771–73).[46] Following this model, the contemporary clergy should remain content with the minimal payment owed to them by virtue of their office. Their office, moreover, as the *Omnis plantacio* sermon points out, "askþ greet labour and teenful busynesse" (128/2630–31). It requires that the clergy earn the necessities of life by "labour[ing] in word and doctryn" for the spiritual needs of the Christian community (Taylor, 3/21–22).

The Wycliffite writers thus present the apostolic church as a temperate, hardworking, and fiscally responsible institution. They are also especially concerned to portray the head of that church, Jesus himself, as a figure of lordship who competently provides for his own needs and those of the clergy. The writers seek to recuperate Christ from fraternal ideology and therefore reject the claim that he chose a life of absolute poverty. Distinguishing between the humanity and the divinity of Jesus, Taylor discusses the multifaceted nature of his rightful dominion.[47] He contends that Christ could not have begged "for þre causis:"

> First for Crist is God, wherfore he hadde ful lordship uppon alle creaturis bi title of creacioun. Bi title also of innocense he hadde as Adam ful lordship of alle þingis þat nediden to mannys vse. And þe þridde skile is for he was a trewe preest and bisshop to the Iewis, doynge duly his office to þe puple, þerfore he myȝte, as he dide bi title of þe gospel, receyue þat þat was needeful to hym in excucioun of his office. (21–22/700–707)

Taylor once again mentions the rights involved in Jesus's priestly office but adds to this type of dominion, recalling the natural lordship and the dominion of grace invoked earlier by FitzRalph. Taylor concludes that as God, the second Adam, and a priest, Christ by his very nature possesses varying degrees of dominion that prevent him from ever experiencing true need and living as a beggar. In nearly identical language, the *Omnis plantacio* author makes the same point when he asserts that as the creator Christ had lordship "bi titil of creacioun"; like Adam, he held lordship "bi titil of innocence"; as a "riȝtful man" he had lordship "bi riȝtwisnesse o[r] grace"; and finally as a "trewe prest and bishop" he held lordship "bi titil of þe gospel" (11/221–29).[48] Wielding authority in all of these modes, Christ, according to the writer, could not have been a beggar, even if he had tried.[49]

The writers then turn to the gospels for proof of Jesus's self-sufficiency, and in so doing they present a version of Christ very different from the poor and meek persona often associated with the fraternal ideal. In their interpretation of biblical passages central to the mendicant debates, Wycliffite writers, like their antifraternal predecessors, transform Christ into a commanding figure who is *never* in need of alms. Even when Christ is ostensibly asking for sustenance or lodging, the writers cast Jesus as the ultimate almsgiver who is always offering some form of charity to others. While such arguments certainly work to oppose the friars, it is important to note that they serve a new purpose as well. Within the Wycliffites' broader anticlericalism, Christ emerges as the model for the entire clergy's commitment to evangelical poverty. And because Wycliffite anticlericalism brings into focus the clergy's relationship with the laity, the traditionally antimendicant Christ now offers some important lessons for the Christian community as a whole. In the Wycliffite sermons, then, the commanding Christ looms especially large, for he now serves not only as a model for the clergy but as a figure who defines the proper relationship between clerics and the laity. His actions serve as lessons for both groups who seek to play their part in restoring the ideal of the apostolic community.

By looking at a few examples of their antimendicant arguments, we can first see how Taylor and other Wycliffite authors gloss scripture in order to create a fundamentally powerful and charitable Christ. Central to the mendicant debates are gospel passages that the friars take as evidence of Christ's begging. These include John 4 when Jesus asks the Samaritan woman for water, and Luke 19 when he requests lodging from

Zaccheus.[50] In his discussion of John 4, Taylor explains that: "for to coloure her vngroundid beggyng [mendicants] putten upon Crist þat he shulde haue beggid of þe womman of Samarie, whanne he seide to hir 'Womman ȝyue me drinke'" (19/607–10). Taylor rejects the friars' claim when he emphasizes Christ's power by explaining that Jesus "seide not in begginge maner but on comaundinge maner, 'Womman, ȝyue me drynke'" (19/615–17). The *Omnis plantacio* author makes the identical complaint that "þese maistir liers . . . maken a lesyng upon Crist, seiynge þat he shulde haue beggid watir of þe womman of Samarie, whanne he comaundide þe womman to ȝyue him drynk" (130/2698–2702).[51] What the friars see as requests, the antifraternalists see as demands.

In addition to focusing on Christ's commanding tone, the writers also rely on allegorical interpretation of the scripture to deny his mendicancy. Taylor, for instance, goes on to argue that "it was not bodily watir þat Crist princiaply axide of þe womman, but watir of sorewe for synne and of feiþ" (19/617–18).[52] While the *Omnis plantacio* sermon does not make this particular point,[53] Taylor's reasoning here does correspond to the arguments of another Wycliffite writer. In his treatment of John 4, the author of *De blasphemia* similarly claims that Christ "spake here of spiritual eetynge and drinkynge" and gave the woman "water of lif."[54] In these accounts, Christ does not merely beg or even command a glass or water; instead, he actually *gives* the Samaritan woman the opportunity to ask for his forgiveness and mercy.

If we compare these readings of the passage to orthodox interpretations not directly embroiled in the mendicant debates, we can see the distinctiveness of the antifraternal perspective. Augustine's earlier exegesis of John 4 provides an interesting contrast to the Wycliffite accounts. As Augustine explicates Christ's exchange with the woman, he begins by focusing on the dual nature of Jesus as a divine and human figure: "We find Jesus to be strength, and we find Jesus to be weak."[55] Unlike the Wycliffite writers, Augustine gives as much attention to the weak dimensions of Jesus as a human being as he does to his power and divinity. In a reference to Matthew 23:37, Augustine goes so far as to liken the incarnate Christ to a hen "with her wings drooping, her feathers ruffled, her note hoarse . . . her limbs so sunken and abject."[56] He adds that "in such manner was Jesus weak, wearied with his journey." For Augustine,

Jesus is an emblem of human weakness in this segment of the gospel. He notes that Christ came to the well "wearied because He carried weak flesh"; and he explains that Jesus sat down by the well "because He was humbled."[57]

When Augustine goes on to address Christ's actual request to the woman, he too determines that Jesus allegorically offers her faith, but he still acknowledges that Christ asks as a figure of weakness at the same time that he gives. Augustine explains that "he who was asking drink was thirsting for the faith of the woman herself." He goes on to outline the dual nature of Christ's offertory/request: Jesus "asks to drink and promises to give drink. He longs as one about to receive; He abounds as one about to satisfy."[58] Augustine's commentary on John 4 emphasizes Jesus's paradoxical position as both giver and receiver. His attention to both facets of Christ's identity reveals what the Wycliffite readings in the antifraternal tradition consistently foreclose: Jesus may have begged for water even as he offered the gift of faith.

As evidenced by Denis the Carthusian, late medieval readings of John 4 also contrast with the Wycliffite perspective in sharing Augustine's more even-handed view of Jesus's request/gift. Denis also begins his commentary on the episode by focusing on Jesus's weariness as a consequence of the incarnation. He makes the significant qualification, however, that Jesus's suffering cannot be attributed to ordinary need as experienced by any person; rather, it is a need born out of divine dispensation: "Omnis ergo corporalis defectus et passio corporis Christi, fuit dispensationis divinæ, non necessitatis humanæ. Esuriit igitur, sitivit, æstuavit et fatigatus est Jesus, non ex necessitate, sed propter multiplices causas" [Therefore every bodily defect and suffering of Christ's was of divine dispensation, not of human necessity. Therefore he hungered, thirsted, became hot, and grew tired not out of necessity but on account of multiple causes]. [59] Denis then goes on to enumerate the causes of Christ's poverty: he wanted, for instance, to demonstrate the true reality of human existence. He also wanted to be an example to laborers, encouraging them to face their troubles with strength and tolerance.[60]

Even though Denis presents Christ's suffering as if it were distinct from human need, he nonetheless draws attention to the physical deprivation that partly motivates Jesus's request for water. He does not therefore entirely dismiss the literal act of begging but, similarly to Augustine, emphasizes the dual nature of Christ's thirst: "Christus enim ad litteram corporaliter sitiebat; spiritualiter vero conversionem feminæ hujus omniumque animarum sitiebat errantium" [For according to the letter Christ was thirsting bodily, but (he was thirsting) spiritually for the conversion of this woman and all lost souls]. While Christ could have drunk water of his own accord before the arrival of the Samaritan woman, Denis explains his reasons for asking the woman to give him a drink: "noluit semper supernaturaliter agere, voluitque ad tempus se ipsum siti affligere propter commodum nostrum" [He did not always want to live supernaturally and he wanted to afflict himself for awhile with thirst for our blessing]. In this account, Jesus is actually thirsty and asks for actual water, but he suffers thirst and begs from the woman ultimately for her own spiritual edification: "Petiit . . . potum a femina, ut daret ei occasionem meriti copiosi" [He asked the woman for a drink so that he might give her an opportunity of copious merit].[61] Denis does focus on Christ's generous gift, and he restricts Christ's need to a distinctive condition experienced only in his humanity. Yet he does not dismiss Jesus's request for water or the reality of his need, even if it has been divinely chosen. In maintaining the paradoxes central to Augustine's reading of John 4, Denis thus presents a Jesus who is quite different from the "commandinge" Christ of Taylor and others.

Taylor's sermon, however, continues to emphasize Christ's lordly nature by turning to the story of Jesus's exchange with Zaccheus in Luke 19. Here he refutes the friars' insistence that "oure Iesu shulde haue beggid an hous of Zachee, whanne Crist, seynge Zachee upon þe tree, seide to him 'Zachee, hastynge come doun, for þis day I moste dwelle in þyn hous'" (20/647–50). Taylor makes the now familiar argument that Jesus spoke "as a lord commandynge and not as a nedy man begginge" (20/650–51). In a brief account of the gospel passage, the *Omnis plantacio* author similarly asserts that Jesus asked Zaccheus for housing "bi weie of comaunding as a lord, or ellis bi weie of dute and not in maner of begging" (12/236–37).

Taylor gives more detailed attention to the text and goes on to present Christ as an almsgiver, who aids the sinful Zaccheus. Taylor explains not how Christ benefits from Zaccheus's hospitality, but how Zaccheus actually benefits from being selected by God:

> And Crist þat tyme hadde about hym a greet noumbre of puple, as þe gospel seiþ, and eche of hem desiride þe presence of Crist as Zachee dide; and þei þat weren myȝty wolden haue had him to her placis, and þerfore þei grucchiden þat Crist ȝede forþ wiþ Zachee. Þanne nedide not Crist for to begge an hous. *For Zachees profiit þanne, for to turne him to þe feiþ, and not for his owne neede,* maistirfully he lymytide to himsilf Zacheis hous, and comaundide him to go doun for to receyue him into his hous. (20/651–58, my emphasis)

In Taylor's interpretation of the biblical passage, Christ does not really ask for housing at all. His presence is a gift desired by many, including the "myȝty [who] wolden haue had him to her placis." To their chagrin, Zaccheus becomes the beneficiary of Christ's attention. It is as a "lord commaundynge" that Jesus works for Zaccheus' "profit" and "maistirfully" grants him the gift of faith.

The author of *De blasphemia* also discusses Jesus's encounter with Zaccheus and similarly draws attention to Christ's lordliness; the nature of *De blasphemia's* argument, however, is slightly different from Taylor's in that the writer focuses more explicitly on the issue of Christ's dominion. In his interpretation, Jesus cannot possibly beg from Zaccheus because he is merely demanding what rightfully belongs to him. Invoking terms of political and economic hierarchy absent in the biblical text, the author argues that Jesus's request to Zaccheus is akin to a bailiff asking rent from a lord or a creditor requesting due payment of a debt: "þo freris fablen of beggynge of Crist, and seyn he beggid of ȝachee boþe meete and house. Bot here þo ydiotes faylen in discrevynge of beggynge. Ffor if a bayle aske rent to þo lord, he begges not þis rent of þo lordis tenaunte. Ne if a mon aske his dette of anoþer, he begges not þis of hym, for dyversite of title."[62] Elaborating on this "dyversite of title," the writer discusses the specific parameters of Jesus's dominion and develops another analogy that likens Christ to an earthly lord and Zaccheus to his servant: "Miche more Crist, þat was boþe God and mon, and had by state of innocense lord[ship] of al þis worlde, þof asked of his owne, as a lord shulde, þinges of his servauntis þat he had myster of and nede, he beggid not, bot nedid his servauntis thorw mercy."[63] While Taylor's Jesus actively gives charity to Zaccheus, the *De blasphemia* author asserts that Christ simply takes what is rightfully his in accordance with the dominion he possesses by virtue of his moral, social, and ontological station. Here Jesus's need is given a distinctive definition, imagined as simply those things that he requires from his servants. The poor Christ is nowhere to be found among these characterizations of Jesus as a powerful lord who commands obedience from his underlings.

The distinctiveness of these antifraternal accounts can once again be seen when compared to Denis the Carthusian's treatment of Luke 19. As in his reading of John 4, Denis accommodates the notion that Jesus could request physical lodging and material sustenance at the same time that he offered spiritual gifts. Though Denis is not interested in presenting Christ as a needy mendicant, he does not exclude the possibility that Christ did ask for housing and bodily shelter. His reading attempts to reconcile Christ's apparent supplication with his simultaneous gift of charity: "qui nondum invitatus a Zachæo, invitavit se apud eum; qui affectum ipsius cognovit, et plus illi exhibuit quam ille ausus fuit rogare, quia se ipsum præbuit illi ad commanendum et convescendum" [He who was not yet invited by Zaccheus, invited himself to his home; he (Jesus) who knew his affection and exhibited more to him, dared to beg because he offered himself to him to share housing and to eat with him].

Paradoxically, Christ dares to beg because he presents himself as a gift, and Denis goes on to emphasize how his humble request contains an inherently generous and generative nature: "quanto ardentius petitur, tanto se ipsum suaque dona copiousius impartitur" [the more ardently he begs, the more copiously he imparts himself and his gifts].[64] Like Taylor, Denis emphasizes Christ's spiritual gift to Zaccheus, but unlike Taylor he does so without entirely negating Christ's request for physical housing. Moreover, in offering such gifts, Jesus does not seem to function as the earthly lord who, as *De blasphemia* describes, orders his servants to fulfill his demands. Instead, Christ "dared to beg" out of humility and kindness in order to share his presence with Zaccheus and to share of Zaccheus's house and food.[65]

While Taylor, the *Omnis plantacio* author, and the *De blasphemia* writer are united in presenting a version of Christ incapable of receiving alms, Taylor goes on to argue that Christ actively promoted labor as a virtue that mitigates against poverty. Conforming to the newer work ethic advocated by FitzRalph, Taylor points out that Christ himself worked by following "Iosephis craft" of carpentry (21/679–81). Yet he also suggests that Christ's mission was to make others labor as well. It is at this point that Taylor makes the provocative argument that Christ healed the sick so that they could be put to work. Commenting on Mark 10:46, Luke 18:35, and John 9:8, Taylor discusses "clamorous beggeris," or lifelong mendicants who "weren nedid to sitte at ȝatis and biside weies, and crye and begge." He then recounts what he sees as Christ's categorical repudiation of this activity: "And in tokenynge þat Crist loþide sich begging, he heelide siche men not oonly in soule but also in body, þat þei myȝten gete þat hem nedide bi her bodily labour" (19/589–92). Taylor's shocking assertion implies that Christ and his miraculous works do not primarily serve as a demonstration of divine love and grace; rather, they emerge from his "loathing" and function to increase economic productivity. In this sense, Christ's role is virtually no different from the violent and coercive figure of Hunger in *Piers Plowman*: both achieve the final goal of putting the idle to work.

Taylor's interpretation of these scriptural passages once again deviates from traditional, orthodox readings of the same texts.[66] Taking John 9 as an example, we can see that Augustine does not address the issue of bodily labor at all and instead views the beggar's blindness and healing as an allegory for humanity's journey from sinfulness to faith through Christ. He thus argues that blindness is the original sin in all of mankind: "this blind man is the human race in general: for this blindness had place in the first man through sin, from whom we all draw our origin not only in respect of death, but also of unrighteousness."[67]

Exegetical discussions of Luke 18 similarly disregard the questions of labor that are central to Taylor's interpretation of the passage. Of the authorities cited by Aquinas in the *Catena Aurea,* some view the miracle of the beggar's healing as a means by which Christ affirms others' faithfulness. Gregory, for instance, argues, "Because the disciples being yet carnal were unable to receive the words of mystery, they are brought to a miracle. Before their eyes a blind man receives his sight, that by a divine work their faith might be strengthened."[68] Other commentators actually de-emphasize the question of mendicancy by highlighting the beggar's desire for Jesus's divine love rather than his desire for money or alms. Cyril notes that Christ asked the beggar what he wanted so that "those who stood by might know that he sought not money, but divine power from God"[69] (621). Gregory similarly states that "the blind man seeks from the Lord not gold but light."[70]

Denis the Carthusian's later account of the scripture gives attention to the force of the miracle that takes place. He declares that through Christ's restoration of the beggar's sight "patet potestas et magnificentia Salvatoris" [the power and magnificence of the savior are made known].[71] Denis offers perhaps the starkest contrast to Taylor's view of Christ and his treatment of the poor by commenting on Christ's charitable response to the beggar's increasingly vocal attempts to get his attention. He expounds on this point by encouraging contemporary priests and political leaders to heed the cries of the poor with sympathy and prompt support: "Denique hoc opus Christi sectari deberent prælati, principes et judices nostri . . . quum audirent aut cernerent paupers conquerentes, et vocare illos ad se, ad audiendum eorum querelas ac postulationes, ut facerent eis subventionem atque justitiam expedite" [Accordingly our prelates, princes, and judges ought to follow Christ in this work . . . when they hear and discern the bewailing poor, they ought to call them to themselves to hear their complaints and suits so that they might more readily provide assistance and justice to them].[72] While Denis's Christ advocates on behalf of the poor, Taylor's Christ loathes their cries of idleness and puts the needy to work.[73]

Clerical Corruption and the Impoverishment of the First Estate

The corresponding arguments about Jesus in *De blasphemia, Omnis plantacio,* and Taylor's sermon suggest that the Wycliffite call to return to the primitive church does not necessarily imply a wholesale return to the ideal of poverty. Rather, Taylor and the *Omnis plantacio* author effectively oppose poverty as a Christian virtue when they go on to discuss how lay society specifically fits into their vision of the apostolic model.[74] Here we see how conventional antifraternal arguments take on new force within the specifically Wycliffite program of ecclesiological reform. According to the authors, if the church is to live according to the principles of evangelical life, then the wider community is called to pursue commercial enterprises. While the church should disavow temporal possessions and extricate itself from what Taylor calls "foul wynning and marchandise" (9/179), the lay people should not similarly embrace poverty. Their involvement in the market and material production suddenly becomes a central Christian duty. Taylor, for instance, wistfully explains that if the "ordynaunce of Crist and his apostlis hadde be kept, þe comyntee of þe puple shulde haue be myȝty and sufficient in husbondderie and marchaundise to susteyne hemsilf, to paye þe lordis her rentis and oþere þingis þat ben due to hem, and to susteyne þe clergie in her office" (18/570–74). In this view, Christ *primarily* obliges the average Christian to work and make enough money to support himself, to pay his lord, and to make donations to the church.

As suggested by Christ's healing of the blind beggars, productiveness becomes a work of sanctity, and self-sufficiency is the hallmark of Christian righteousness. Taylor explains that during his own life Christ authorized the community's industriousness, "confermynge her iust labour, partynge wiþ hem of her goodis" (16/510–11). The *Omnis plantacio* writer similarly declares: "And in þe tyme of þe newe lawe Crist asignede þe temperaltees or seculer lordships to temperal lordis . . . and alowide þe comounte her liiflood gotun bi trewe marchaundise & husbondrie, for he was partener þerof" (102/2107–11). According to both authors, Christ does not call his followers to patient poverty but endorses the secular community's business ventures. Furthermore, Jesus himself willingly partakes of the profits and goods that such endeavors produce.

As Taylor and the *Omnis plantacio* author repeatedly argue, however, this model of economic productivity is woefully unattainable in contemporary medieval society because the church has deviated so fully from its apostolic roots. We have seen how the authors extend antifraternal criticism to the wider church, allowing the general lay population to serve as victims of clerical abuse. While they focus intently on the church's unjust treatment of the poor, their critique is not limited to the needy, at least when this group is understood as members of the third estate dangerously lacking in the "nidefole things" as described by Langland's Holy Churche. The Wycliffites' complaints about clerical abuse extend far beyond their concern for these poor people and involve a more central anxiety about the economic security of lay society as a whole.

Because it has covetously accumulated temporal possessions for itself, the contemporary church, according to Taylor, is at fault for making men poor, for turning able-bodied men into beggars, for draining the financial resources of the secular community. He complains that the church's divergence from Christ's policy has forced otherwise self-sufficient people into "need," generating increased demand for charitable collections:

> And if þis blessid rule, ordynaunce or pollicie of Crist and his apostlis had be kept for to now, we shulden not haue fallun into so manye inconuenyentis as we ben now, ne þer shulde not haue ben sich a grucching and rumour for vitaylis amonge þe puple vnpayed, and gaderingis or quyletis maad as we now heeren. (17/540–45)

Taylor's declaration presents an image of poverty that seems based less on dire physical need than on a notion of inconvenience and social disruption. While the "inconuenyentis" he mentions could refer to material hardship, the term also carries an association of disorder, or as the *Middle English Dictionary* cites, "impropriety" or "unfitness."[75] These latter connotations are affirmed by Taylor's further objection not just to the lack of resources per se, but to the people's complaints about such lack and their requests for more charitable collections.

After complaining, in effect, about the people's complaints, Taylor and the *Omnis plantacio* writer do, however, turn to address explicitly what they see as the community's diminishing possessions at the hands of the church. Taylor specifically deplores the fact that poverty has infiltrated all facets of society: "now, for þe wiþdrawing of þe ordynaunce and þe pollicie of Crist and his apostils, we ben fallun into so greet a defaute and into a maner wrecchidnesse þat euery astaat pleyneþ of pouerte and defaute" (18/576–79). In the *Omnis plantacio* sermon, the author similarly argues that the church's misappropriation of alms has driven the secular community into "meschevous" poverty: "al oure rewme, ȝhe, and as I suppose, ful nyȝ al cristendom [has become] ful pore and nedi and mescheuous, ouer þat it shulde haue be, if þe clergie hadde holde him apaied wiþ Cristis ordynaunce" (106/2166–69). In an extreme statement referencing all of Christendom, the author condemns a kind of need that is severe, not for its intensity in making people utterly destitute, but for its pervasiveness and infiltration into places (that is, classes) that it should not affect.

The *Omnis plantacio* author continues to deplore the realm's descent into poverty, and he explicitly criticizes the church for sinfully amassing wealth under the guise of promoting charity. While the writers gave attention to this topic in exposing the suffering of the poor, now this issue serves to expose the suffering of secular lords. Giving alms to the clergy undermines God's plan for an ordered and just society:

> if a man take þo goodis, þe whiche God in þe beste wise euene and wiþout errours haþ assigned to þe staat of seculer lordis, þe whiche he haþ appreued in his chirche, and ȝyue þo goodis to anoþer peple þat haþ no nede to hem—ȝhe to þe which peple suche goodis ben forfendid—þis shulde be callid noon almesse, but peruerting of Goddis ordynanunce or distruccioun of a staat þe which God haþ appreued in his chirche. (98–100/2062–68)

The author argues that God himself has assigned temporal wealth to lords alone. He anxiously fears that the contemporary practice of almsgiving does not just corrupt the church but more ominously threatens to destroy the entire "staat of seculer lordis." The clergy's abuse of almsgiving is not just to the detriment of the needy, who may die without the aid of charitable goods. More significantly, it is to the detriment of lay lords who face a kind of social mortality at the hands of the church.[76]

Indeed, the most strident criticism made by both the *Omnis plantacio* writer and Taylor stems from their concern that the church's accumulation of wealth threatens to undermine the integrity of the estates model and in particular the knightly class itself. The writers' anticlerical sentiment becomes even more vehement as they complain that the institution's increasing affluence has literally come at the expense of lay lords.[77] In propounding such an argument, the Wycliffites transform FitzRalph's concern for the diminishing wealth of the secular clergy into a concern for the diminishing resources of lay society and in particular the possessing classes. While FitzRalph views each gift to the friars as a theft from the beneficed church, the sermon writers view each gift to any facet of the church as a theft from lay lords. The materially poor of the third estate noticeably fade out of the picture when the writers lament that priests, monks, and friars have become virtually indistinguishable from knights and, in Taylor's words, "reioycen hem to be callid lordis and kingis in her owne" (6/110).[78]

In usurping their elite identity, the clergy have forced lay lords to live like peasants, making them unable to sustain their estate and defend the realm (Taylor, 6/111). Taylor unequivocally deplores the "poverty" of knights and declares that if society had followed Christ's rule, then "temporal lordis shulden haue be sufficient in rentis and possessiouns for to defende hemsilf and þe rewme, and for to auaunce her children." He goes on to lament that "now . . . so manye temporaltees bi þe foly ȝyuyng of temporal lordis ben ȝouun to vnprofitable puple to God and man þat vnneþe is left wherwiþ þat fortraueilid knyȝtis sones may be releeued" (17–18/545–51).[79] According to Taylor, the social order has now been dangerously reversed. In the labor legislation and *Piers Plowman,* we have witnessed the shifting identities of workers who become wasters seeking fine foods and rest. In Taylor's sermon we have an identity shift that moves in the opposite direction. The sons of knights have now become wretched laborers who are "fortraueilid" and desperately in need of sustenance.

It is true that the economic situation of lords did considerably worsen from the late fourteenth to the late fifteenth century. This deterioration was due mainly to increased wages and decreased rents following the plague—causes that the Wycliffite writers conspicuously fail to mention in blaming the church alone for all social decay.[80] The Wycliffites, however, do not just complain that the lords have fallen on hard times but argue that their collective status has been completely undermined so that knights find themselves on par with "foretravailed laborers." Despite the general decline of revenue, though, the first estate was by no means on the verge of collapse. Rather, J. L. Bolton helpfully points out that in fourteenth- and fifteenth-century England, "many great lords lived in considerable estate, built extensively, fed many retainers and indulged in that most expensive of games, politics."[81]

Nevertheless, the Wycliffite writers contend that the elite are in the direst socioeconomic straits. In a statement that echoes Taylor's concern for the "fortraueilid" knights, the *Omnis plantacio* writer asserts that lords have been reduced to poverty as a result of their ancestors' "foolish giving" to the church: "bi amortaisyng of lordships þe lordis ben vndo in grete partie, and þo þat ben yleft, bicause þat hem lackiþ her owne part þoruȝ foly ȝift of her auncetris, ben ful nedi" (106/2186–88). The *Omnis plantacio* author seems particularly preoccupied with what he sees as the fragile economic condition of knights and the compromised state of secular authority. He therefore discusses the status of lords at greater length, and his tone grows more alarmist when he declares that the clergy is quite possibly conspiring to overtake secular power entirely:

> For siþ þei han now þe more part of þe temporal lordships, and wiþ al þat þe spiritualtees and þe grete mouable tresours of þe rewme, þei mai liȝtli make a conquest upon þe toþir partie, naemli siþ þe temperal lordis ben not in noumbre, good, witt, ne manhood liik as þei han be before, and þe partie of þe clergie in alle þese poyntis encresen, and so couetousli þei ben sett upon þese goodis þat þei welden now, and mo þat þei hopen to haue, þat þei wolen not suffre her couetise to be enpungned opunli ne priueli, as fer as þei mai lette it. (46/1112–20)[82]

In the above statement, the author suggests that the power dynamics between church and state have gone terribly awry: indefatigable in its covetous desire for temporal supremacy, the church looms larger while the knights diminish in "noumbre, good, witt [and] manhood." The author is uncritical of far-reaching political regimes within the secular realm, and he expresses concern that the church has circumscribed the power of empire. In a brief discussion of the donation of Constantine, he primarily complains not that endowment has harmed the church itself, but that it has constrained imperial rule. He asks, for example, "What almesse þanne I prei þee was it to vndo þe staat of þe empire and make þe clerkis riche wiþ hise lordships?" (100/2075–76).[83]

In this context, the writers' recapitulation of traditional antifraternal arguments against Christ's mendicancy can be seen as authorizing a wider social imaginary that makes it a central mission of the apostolic church to maintain the power of temporal lords. Earlier interpretations that viewed Christ's begging as a form of commanding worked primarily to discredit the practice of fraternal mendicancy. While this is still the case with Taylor and the other writers explored in this chapter, these arguments have further implications when understood as part of the Wycliffite vision of reform. Given the writers' explicit concern for "needy" and "foretravailed" knights, Christ's masterful entitlement to the goods of the world threatens to overshadow the Christian ideals of poverty, humility, and simplicity often promoted by Wycliffites in other contexts. In this regard, Christ's lordly sanctity may not endorse a moderate form of clerical poverty so much as champion the supremacy of the lay elite.

Discriminate Charity and Ecclesiastical Reform

Seeking to rectify this decline in temporal power and avert the dissolution of lay authority altogether, Taylor and the *Omnis plantacio* author advocate a strict form of discriminate charity that would ideally withdraw temporal possessions from the church and redirect alms to those people whom they perceive as "truly needy." These individuals are ultimately not just the poor whose very survival is apparently threatened by the church's abuse of wealth. Rather, the *Omnis plantacio* author and Taylor insist that the knightly class is most urgently in "need" of alms.

In order to relieve the secular lords and affirm their political authority, the writers argue, in the words of *Omnis plantacio*, that the clergy must "remitte þis temperal swerd to lay partie" (60–62/1412–13).[84] Advocating a proposition central to Wycliffite thought, Taylor calls for the disendowment of the church:[85]

> oure clerkis, and specialy þo þat ben deed to þe world . . . shulden be redy to delyuere up into þe hondis of seculer men alle her poscessiouns and tresours . . .and on þis wise releeue þe chirche of Engelond . . . at þe ensaumple of Crist and his apostlis. (9/234–40)

Here Taylor imagines the withdrawal of temporal goods from the church as an act of charity that will reinstate the social order sanctioned by God. Speaking to his audience about the clergy, the *Omnis plantacio* writer also affirms this view:

> And ferþermor þou maist vndirstonde of þis processe þat wiþdrawyng of þese goodis fro þese ypocritis, and restoring of hem to þ[e] statis þat God hadde asigned hem to, shulde be callid not robberie of hooli chirche, as þese ypocritis seien, but raþer riȝtwise restitucioun of goodis wronge[ful]li and þeefli wiþholdun. (110/2244–49)

The author argues that the institution can be reformed through a kind of penance requiring that the clergy make restitution to the lay lords whom they have wronged.

The writers seek to ensure that temporal goods are restored to the rightful party, not only by advocating the church's disendowment but by specifying appropriate models of almsgiving. Within the larger argument refuting the clergy's claim that it rightfully possesses temporal goods by means of perpetual alms,[86] the *Omnis plantacio* author redefines alms to argue that true charity consists of giving only where there is need. In language that expands the already capacious discourse around need in the sermon, the writer now characterizes poverty as a form of "mysese" without defining the term precisely.[87] He makes Christ a proponent of discriminate charity when he declares, "if a man shulde effectueli do almesse, he most loke þat he þat shulde do almesse to were in mysese þat shulde be releued. In tokenyng wherof Crist oonli asigneþ almesse to þo in whom he markiþ mysese" (98/2051–54).

After providing this concise account of true almsgiving, the author then goes on to outline the types of donations that cannot qualify as charitable giving. The first type actually involves creating more "mysese:" "And so of þis [it] wole sue þat, if a man releeue oo wrecche and makiþ anoþer or two or mo, he doiþ noon almesse but raþer makiþ mysese." In this form of corrupt almsgiving, the donor presumably relieves the need of one person by giving her excessive amounts of aid. By failing to distribute his wealth evenly, the donor is responsible, according to the author, for propelling others into "mysese" through the denial of his gifts. He then specifies another form of corrupt charity that entails giving to those who are able to provide for themselves: "if he make riche þo þat han no nede, for as moche as þei ben sufficient to hemsilf, he doiþ noon almesse" (98/2051–58).[88] While he deplores the kind of giving that harms another or that makes an already self-sufficient person wealthy, the writer then goes on to condemn most explicitly the kind of giving that makes the clergy rich in violation of God's decrees: "and ferþermor, if he make such peple rich wiþ waast ȝyuying of hise goodis þat shulde not be riche bi þe gospel, and also ben sufficient in hemsilf, þis haþ no colour of almesse, for þis mai beter be callid a woodnesse or wasting of Goddis goodis" (99/2058–62).

Invoking a term that, as we have seen, is of critical importance to Langland, the *Omnis plantacio* author gives "wasting" a new definition. In his sermon it consistently refers to the excessive donation of alms to the church.[89] The author calls this kind of giving the "peruerting of Goddis ordynaunce" or the "distruccioun" of an estate sanctioned by God because it wastefully transfers "þo goodis, þe whiche God . . . haþ asigned to . . . seculer lordis" to "þe which peple suche goodis ben forfendid" (98/2062–66). In seeking to explain more precisely how the church has manipulated the practice of charity to its own material advantage, the *Omnis plantacio* author ultimately defines this new mode of giving not as alms, but as "al-amys," a perversion of true almsgiving. He declares: "if such almesseȝyuyng be distriyng or apeiring of ony astaat appreued of God in his chirche, it wole sue þat þe endowing of þe clergie wiþ worldli lordship ouȝte not to be callid almesse but raþer alamys, or waasting of Godis goodis, or distriyng of Goddis ordynanuce" (104/2154–58).

In order to return the perverted practice of al-amys back into the charitable activity of almsgiving so as to restore the proper social order, both Taylor and the *Omnis plantacio* author specify that only the disabled can rightfully receive alms. They follow FitzRalph's line of thought in the *Defensio Curatorum,* eliminating "the poor" as an autonomous group that should be invited to the feast described in Luke 14.[90] Taylor, for example, first quotes Christ's command from the gospel: "Whanne þou makist þe feest of pitee calle poore feble, lame and blynde and þou shalt be blessid; for þei han not wherwiþ for to rewarde þee, it shal be rewardid þee in þe rewardyng of riȝtwise men" (15/452–54). Making a similar argument, the *Omnis plantacio* writer cites Paul as an authority on almsgiving and explains that he took up collections for the poor only because they "hadden no leiser to gete hem liiflood wiþ her bodili labour, and many of þis people as it is ful licli weren pore feble, lame and blynde" (132/2753–54).[91] These interpretations of scripture generate a concrete and familiar definition of need: only the poor who are disabled should be called to the feast or rewarded with material goods.

The writers, interestingly, exhibit no concern that this strict definition of need rather conspicuously conflicts with their impassioned pleas to relieve the "impoverished" class of secular lords. Are we to presume that "nedi" knights are deserving of aid because they qualify as members of the "poore feble, lame, and blynde" who should be invited to the feast? Clearly, the answer is no, and the sermons make an exception to their policy of selective almsgiving. Able-bodied need is not a legitimate condition for members of the clergy seeking alms. But when it comes to the greatest victims of the church's misappropriations, that is, the members of the lay elite, the meaning of need changes. Physical disability gives way to the knights' socioeconomic "mysese," which can only be relieved by the "alms" they should take back from the church. These writings thus create a bizarre amalgamation of the deserving poor: an individual seems to be worthy of alms either if he is poor and disabled or if he is a lord.

While there are instances in which Taylor and the *Omnis plantacio* author seem to revere poverty as a Christian value and exhibit genuine concern for society's most needy, their overarching project of church reform clearly rejects the idealizations of poverty that can be found, for instance, at the root of Franciscan thought. The authors maintain a rigorous distinction between the church and the laity, and they sanction poverty as a way of life for the clergy alone. Even this endorsement, however, comes with the strict precaution that the church not fall into abject poverty or extreme forms of need that could lead to mendicancy. Channeling FitzRalph's antifraternalism into a plan for the reformation of the entire church, the authors reject fraternal begging and clerical ownership as sinful extremes that the contemporary institution strategically employs to bankrupt lay society. The authors thus advocate the church's return to the apostolic ideal, which in their view mandates that the clergy live in a *moderate* form of poverty; the clerics, furthermore, are not simply *given* basic provisions, but should *earn* them through their "teenful" labor in spiritual offices such as preaching and selective almsgiving.

The call to return to the apostolic life is essentially a call to preserve social distinctions, to protect the wealth and power of lords, and to restrict the presence of need within the community as a whole.[92] The Wycliffite writers conform to the major anti-poverty arguments of Fitz-Ralph's *Defensio Curatorum* which contends that the righteous Christian society follows Christ by working. Through its labor, the lay community in particular must amass enough wealth so as to support themselves and the church. Seeking to minimize the presence of poverty in society, the nonclerical population should thus be "mighty," "sufficient," and zealous in their commercial pursuits. These labors will restore the proper order of the estates model, returning secular lords to the position that has been usurped by the covetous church.

Though the writers claim that they seek to return to an originary ideal, their preferred social model does not appear to stress a traditional notion of interdependence associated with the estates structure. Rather, their vision of society promotes a sense of independence, with each estate marked by a distinct identity and an economic ideal of *self-sufficiency*. As they critique the varied forms of need that are exacerbated or caused by clerical corruption, the writers generate a subtle yet pervasive resistance to notions of vulnerability and dependence on others. While these writers reimagine society as a body united in its devotion to apostolic ideals, these very ideals entail some particularly rigid social demarcations that downplay the significance of mutual relations among all classes of people. Even the ideal church, which is dependent on the laity for support, receives that support not through charitable giving but as wages *earned* in exchange for fulfilling clerical duties.

Perhaps, though, the most obvious site of social division can be found in the tendency of Wycliffite texts to occlude the relationship between poor and rich in lay society. This was certainly an apparent omission in the *Crede*; and while Wycliffite sermons do advocate that all Christians practice almsgiving, they discuss charity mainly in the context of blaming the clergy for perverting almsgiving and increasing poverty among the laity. In criticizing the church, the texts thus find a strange alliance between knights and peasants who have both been impoverished by the institution's covetousness. However, the connection between these groups stops here. The writers give especially little consideration to the role that the lay elite play in the treatment of the poor.[93] The Wycliffite vision of community thus deemphasizes models of reciprocity, unity, and social interaction in favor of telling another story about the three estates: the sins of the institutional church have brought peasants and knights together, and the church's moral rehabilitation will finally set them apart.

CHAPTER FOUR

The Costs of Sanctity

Margery Kempe and the Franciscan Imaginary

Margery Kempe is perhaps best known for her seemingly eccentric spirituality, which entails extreme episodes of crying. Yet Kempe's religious devotion is distinctive not simply for its emotional intensity. As she undertakes her own imitation of Christ in the world, Kempe forges a path of perfection that challenges conventional standards of Christian behavior, especially for women. Acting on visions that come directly from God, Kempe is a married laywoman who commits herself to chastity; she travels extensively, visiting the site of both the apostolic church and its institutional successor; she speaks publicly about her faith; and she is not hesitant to expose the moral lapses of the contemporary clergy. In some cases, this outspokenness proves to be dangerous for Kempe, and on more than one occasion she is accused of heresy and threatened with burning. Though finally cleared of all charges, Kempe may thus share common ground with the Wycliffites of the previous chapter, for they too articulated a Christian vision that came to threaten religious orthodoxy. When it comes to the specific subject of poverty, we will ultimately find some similarity in the notions of Christian perfection developed by the Wycliffites and Kempe. Yet that similarity must be meticulously uncovered, for Kempe's imitation of Christ entails a voluntary commitment to Franciscan ideals that William Taylor and others would find deeply troubling.

Indeed, at first glance, *The Book of Margery Kempe* emerges as a rather distinctive text, for it seems to challenge the wider cultural devaluation of poverty traced in this book. While Langland, the *Crede* author, and the Wycliffite writers of the last chapter all express serious reservations about the ethical status and practical viability of voluntary poverty, the *Book* casts Kempe as a holy figure largely because she chooses a life of indigence. Kempe willingly becomes poor at Christ's command and abandons, as did Francis himself, the comforts and values of elite, urban life. When Kempe gives up the "husbondderie and marchaundise" praised so highly by Taylor, the *Book* presents this as an unequivocally sacred act.[1]

Yet, as *this* book has attempted to show, poverty proves to be a highly capacious sign generating epistemological challenges that unsettle our ability to determine not only the precise contours of material reality but also the ethical implications of different forms of life. Kempe's poverty proves to be no different, and her willing renunciation of goods raises some troubling theological and moral questions when examined with close attention to the shifting meaning of need. As we saw in chapter one, Langland is a writer who revels in the very complexity of need so as to make an ethical argument critiquing the epistemological confidence of contemporary poverty discourse. *The Book of Margery Kempe,* however, is ultimately more like the Wycliffite texts in the previous chapters; for these works, the complexity of need raises contradictions that potentially undermine their professed commitment to poverty and simplicity. In particular, Kempe's conversion to a life of poverty proves to be a highly complex act that does not simply entail replacing mercantile values with spiritual values.[2] As Sarah Beckwith explains, Kempe is not "reducible" to a "clerical or a business domain"; rather, these arenas are "mutually constructed," as demonstrated by the fact that both clerical and lay leaders in Lynn relied on mercantile pursuits in fulfilling their offices.[3] The interaction between the text's economic and spiritual concerns is indeed fraught, as Kathleen Ashley also attests; in her view, the *Book* reveals how the "bourgeois class" transforms ascetic ideals pursued by the clerical elite into a "validating ideology for their own economic and political power."[4]

Informed by these critical methodologies, this chapter explores how *The Book of Margery Kempe* highlights the intricate relations between urban, economic practices and the enduring imaginary of Christian perfection attained through poverty. Approaching mercantile and spiritual values as open to transformation and appropriation by either side, I shall explore how the text amalgamates these values so as to reshape Franciscan ideals in significant and sometimes puzzling ways. When critics have discussed the *Book*'s Franciscan connections, they have tended to focus almost exclusively on Kempe's forms of contemplation. Such work has shown how Kempe's meditations on the gospel, which place her directly into the biblical scenes themselves, resemble the Franciscan tradition of affective piety exemplified by texts such as Nicholas Love's *Mirror of the Blessed Lyf of Jesus Christ*.[5] However, as I shall show, the *Book*'s portrayal of Kempe's particular *imitatio Christi* is deeply informed by the active dimensions of Franciscanism and more particularly its view of poverty as a form of spiritual perfection.

By reading *The Book of Margery Kempe* within a Franciscan framework, we shall see how it directly participates it the late medieval debates on poverty. Specifically, the *Book* explores the ethical status of wealth, interrogates the relationship between mendicancy and dominion, and exposes the contradictions endemic to a form of voluntary poverty that confers sanctity upon its practitioner. The text approaches these issues from a unique perspective, and, compared to the other works explored thus far, the *Book* is remarkable for its lack of antifraternalism and its promotion of voluntary poverty as an ethical mode of life.[6] However, as it emphasizes the viability of Kempe's poverty, the *Book* begins to generate contradictions that complicate the text's seemingly direct endorsement of Franciscan ideology. To signal Kempe's holiness, the text consistently foregrounds her miraculous immunity to the harsh realities of material deprivation. As this happens, I argue that the *Book* reshapes Franciscan ideals of poverty into a way of life allowing Kempe to maintain financial security, the will to dominion, and an interest in economic exchange. In this sense, Kempe's poverty ironically reinforces the commercial pressures she seeks to abandon. The mercantile ideology of fifteenth-century urban society proves to be extremely pervasive as Kempe's version of saintly poverty begins to look like a means of solidifying her economic and social position—the very phenomenon that antifraternal critics so viciously condemned in their attacks on the friars.

The Book of Margery Kempe thus tries to preserve the notion that poverty is a form of perfection that even the laity should aspire to attain. However, in its attempt to preserve this sense of virtue, the text redefines poverty as a state that excludes material need and suffering. Kempe's financial security seems largely consistent throughout the work, and her poverty is ultimately reconfigured as powerlessness resulting from noneconomic factors such as her gender, age, and illiteracy. The *Book* makes its own contribution to the capacious late medieval discourse on need, as it redefines the term to locate Kempe's vulnerability not in the hunger, thirst, or invisibility frequently experienced by the involuntary poor. Rather, we find it in her status by the end of the text as a woman who seeks to travel despite her advanced years and who seeks to record her story despite her lack of clerical authority. As we shall see, however, even in these extreme circumstances Kempe's resilience emerges to complicate any straightforward view of her character as someone who is finally weak or powerful, poor or rich.

Kempe's Conversion and the Loss of Dominion

In its account of her dramatic conversion, the *Book* immediately reveals its sympathies with Franciscan ideology by describing Kempe's first steps toward Christian perfection as a rejection of worldly business and trade. Rendering the promises of urban, middle-class life as dangerous temptations, the text's provocative opening begins to suggest that moral perfection stems from poverty and the loss of dominion. When we first meet Kempe, the *Book* presents a woman who understands herself primarily in relation to her social and economic status within an identifiable town network. In recording Kempe's desire to be the best-dressed and most honored member of her community, the text portrays the world of the urban elite as a place where pride and covetousness reign. Kempe's quest for social superiority is so pronounced that her husband eventually commands Margery "to levyn hir pride."[7] Margery's reaction to this charge, however, only confirms her sense of arrogance as she denounces John's critique as a sign of his own social inferiority. Contrasting John's status with that of her politically connected father, Margery defends her claims to worldly honor by telling her husband that because "sche was comyn of worthy kenred, hym semyd nevyr . . . a weddyd hir" (24). Lest he attempt to correct her again, she also adds that "sche wold savyn the worschyp of her kynred whatsoevyr ony man seyd" (24).[8] In this characterization of Margery, the text exposes the troubling perspective of a townsperson who perceives herself primarily in terms of her social position and the advantages presumed to accompany it.[9] Kempe's status as a member of an elite, urban family defines her entire identity and shapes even her most intimate relations with others. As Kate Parker has noted, Kempe approaches her marriage from a one-sided perspective insisting that John has married into her family, without considering that she has also married into his.[10]

Resolute in her quest for material and symbolic rewards appropriate to her social position, Kempe pursues various business ventures. The text thus gives us a lens into the mercantile culture of fifteenth-century Lynn as it describes how Kempe readily takes up the trades of brewing and milling. Despite the increasingly widespread affirmation of labor in late medieval English culture, the text configures Kempe's work as yet another symptom of her desire for power and privilege. The *Book* thus declares that she pursued such trades "for pure coveytyse" and "to maynten hir pride" (24). Kempe's labor therefore proves to be quite different from the grinding work undertaken by the plowman's wife in the *Crede* or by the needy mothers described in Passus IX of *Piers Plowman*. Unlike those women struggling to provide themselves and their children with the basic necessities, Kempe labors out of no such material need.[11] We are told, rather, that her work is motivated by a deeply acquisitive spirit, by a longing for excess, by a will that "evyr desyryd mor and mor" (24).

Her business ventures are ultimately unsuccessful, and their downfall is interpreted as a divine gift rescuing Kempe from the mercantile ethos and the worldly ambition it generates.[12] Both of her trades become divinely ordained failures as the yeast in her ale inexplicably falls to the bottom and the horses procured for her mill inexplicably refuse to haul loads of corn. Hindered by this recalcitrance of nature and beast, Kempe's enterprises meet their final demise with the rebellion of her servants who eventually forsake her in shame and frustration.[13] In its discussion of Kempe's resistant subordinates, the text implicitly introduces the important subject of dominion, an issue that we know is central to the Franciscan philosophy of poverty. The *Book* makes it clear that Kempe becomes known in her community for her conspicuous lack of lordship, which the text presents as a shocking incapacity to rule others: "Anoon . . . it was noysed abowt the town of N that ther wold neythyr man ne best don servyse to the seyd creatur" (25). In this formulation, it is not the failure of Kempe's trades that catches the attention of her neighbors but rather her inability to retain even the most benign forms of power over other creatures. This type of authority is closest to Adam and Eve's prelapsarian lordship by which man naturally rules beast and master rules servant. It is thus defined as dominion of the most innocuous kind. Ockham's *Work of Ninety Days,* a text that defends Franciscan poverty against the attacks of John XXII, describes this form of dominion as a "power of reasonably ruling and directing temporal things without their violent resistance."[14] However, Kempe remains unable to exercise this natural degree of dominion over servant, beast, and nature, all of which rebel against her. The stripping away of her lordship seems to be an important step in the process of her sanctification, as she finds herself literally unable to wield the power necessary to function as a competent businesswoman.

That the text gives approval to this loss of power becomes clear if we compare this account of the servants' "rebellion" to the half-acre episode of *Piers Plowman.* Recall that the recalcitrant workers of Langland's poem transform an idealized scene of labor into one of chaos and instability, as Wastour undermines the authority of the plowman and disrupts the production of food. While the nature of Kempe's labor obviously differs from that of Piers, *The Book of Margery Kempe,* unlike Langland's poem, welcomes the dissolution of social order induced by Kempe's servants. In a move that interestingly resonates with Franciscan ideology, the text presents Kempe's loss of authority as an additional blessing marking her initial steps on the journey to Christian perfection.

Forfeiting some of her material advantages as well as the ability to control and manage those people and things beneath her, Kempe begins to relinquish her pride and covetousness. At this point, the *Book* continues to affirm the Franciscan vision of poverty as it equates Kempe's material losses with her spiritual growth. For example, after explaining that

Kempe has come to perceive her business troubles as "the skourges of owyr Lord," the *Book* explains, "*Than* sche askyd God mercy and forsoke hir pride, hir coveytyse, and desysr that sche had of the worshepys of the world" (25, my emphasis). This statement, which makes a causal connection between temporal loss and the development of virtue, becomes one of the central lessons in the opening pages of the text. Indeed, it recurs in slightly different iterations. In the preface we are told that

> [Kempe's] werldly goodys, which wer plentyuows and abundawnt at that day, in lytyl whyle after wer ful bareyn and bare. *Than* was pompe and pryde cast down and leyd on syde. Thei that beforn had worshepd her sythen ful scharply reprevyd her. . . . *Than* sche, consyderyng this wondyrful chawngyng, sekyng socowr undyr the wengys of hyr gostly modyr, Holy Cherch, went and obeyd hyr to hyr gostly fadyr, accusing hyrself of her mysdeds, and sythen ded gret bodyly penawns. (17–18, my emphasis)

Though she does not at this point renounce her "werldly goodys" voluntarily, their loss is construed as a form of sanctification. In this particular account, Kempe's deprivation and the isolation accompanying it function as powerful catalysts of virtue, eventually spurring the proud and covetous businesswoman to seek the sacrament of penance. Here it almost sounds as if our old friends Rechelesnesse and Patience could be narrating Kempe's story and teaching us that the path to Christian perfection can be found in poverty and the humility it induces. In condemning Kempe's business pursuits and calling her to poverty, the text certainly makes a powerful opening statement. It suggests, as Lynn Staley puts it, that "the world is indeed to be fled."[15]

Kempe's Radical Mendicancy

As the *Book* goes on to depict Kempe's post-conversion life and pilgrimage to the Holy Land, it further assimilates her continuing spiritual transformation to the Franciscan view of perfection by describing how Kempe embraces poverty as a holy condition. In particular, the *Book* depicts Kempe's stay in Rome as a time that is largely defined by both her response to the poor and her own experience of deprivation. Before delving into Kempe's specific experiences, however, it is important to note that the text offers an especially concentrated portrait of poverty while Kempe is in Rome. By placing Kempe's newfound commitment to poverty at the center of the Catholic Church, the *Book* perhaps makes a critique of the institution as a vastly endowed body far removed from its apostolic origins.[16] However subtle the text's ecclesiastical criticism may be, it is abundantly clear that we meet a Margery Kempe in Rome who seems quite different from the woman who originally sought worldly wealth and honor above all else. Indeed, at this point in the text, Kempe seems to have abandoned the values associated with her life as an elite citizen of Lynn, and she now associates with the neediest members of Roman society. We are told, for instance, that Kempe performs penance when she serves a poor woman for six weeks by begging food and other necessities for her. As Anthony Goodman notes, Kempe's role as a servant functions as "a very challenging and testing request to make to the daughter of an alderman of the Holy Trinity Gild at Lynn . . . to whom it was natural to order around her own servants."[17] The text indeed describes a role reversal for Kempe who now "fet hom watyr and stykkys in hir nekke for the poure woman and beggyd mete and wyn bothyn for hir." The *Book* also adds that "whan the pour womans wyn was sowr, this creatur hirself drank that sowr wyn and gaf the powr woman good wyn that sche had bowt for hir owyn selfe" (91). Kempe clearly labors on behalf of the poor woman and procures sustenance for her through begging.

Kempe also notably shares in the woman's experience of poverty as she offers her charitable assistance. The text tells us that Kempe "had no bed to lyn in ne no clothys to be cured wyth saf hir own mentyl" (90–91). It also adds that she was "ful of vermin and suffryd gret peyn therwyth" (91). Though Kempe endures such suffering, Sarah Salih finds her service problematic, viewing it not as "practical charity" but as an act that stands out more for its "gratuitous nature" than for its sincere commitment to the poor. Salih thus notes that Kempe's begging on behalf of the woman does not interfere with Kempe's ability and inclination to buy good wine for herself. She also comments on the brevity of Kempe's penitential service by noting that she abandons "the protesting old woman . . . once the spiritual exercise is complete."[18] While the acts of charity in the text are perhaps never straightforward, Salih's criticisms seem to assume that Kempe should stay permanently in Rome assisting the woman in a kind of professional service. I would argue against such assumptions to suggest that Kempe's actions here are notable because, unlike many wealthy almsgivers, she interacts directly with the poor woman, immersing herself in her world. Furthermore, it is Salih and not Kempe who crankily characterizes the old woman as someone who is "protesting" and seemingly desirable to escape. In my view, Kempe's charity is not significant as a temporary or gratuitous act; rather, it is suggestive of Franciscan ideals stipulating that the friars should "live among people considered of little value and looked down upon, among the poor and the powerless, the sick and the lepers, and the beggars by the wayside."[19] Whatever the ambiguities that may characterize Kempe's charitable act, it is important that she, like the Franciscans, attempts to inhabit the poor woman's world and shares, at least to some degree, in the woman's own suffering.

This experience perhaps prepares Kempe for the more stringent spiritual demands that God soon makes of her. Although he repeatedly tells Kempe that the best form of life entails "thynkyng, wepyng, and hy contemplacyon" (94), God also comes to insist that she relinquish all her earthly goods in order to "makyn hir bar for hys lofe" (96). When Christ directs Kempe to undertake this form of absolute poverty, the text clearly invokes the Franciscan notion of Christian perfection described in Matthew 19. Kempe thus receives a divine call urging her to become like one of Francis's holy fools, who follow Christ and seek the utmost humility in renouncing concern for temporal things.[20] Christ's command marks a major shift in the text, as the prospect of giving away her goods now constitutes for Kempe a holy action. If we return briefly to a moment much earlier in the text—to the time of Kempe's illness following her incomplete confession—we can see that renunciation has very different connotations. At one point during her sickness, Kempe asks her husband for the keys to the buttery, but "Hyr maydens and hir kepars cownseld hym he schulde delyvyr hir no keys, for thei seyd sche wold but geve awey swech good as ther was" (23).

This strangely resonant comment reveals that, within the context of the urban household, to give away one's possessions is a symptom of madness.[21] Signaling an altogether different perspective, Jesus now presents renunciation as a form of sanctity. While Kempe worries briefly about "wher sche schuld han hir levyng" once she has given away her goods (97), Christ allays Kempe's concern and encourages her in the voluntary assumption of need by recalling his own extreme hardship in sacrificing himself as a divine gift for humanity. He tells her, "Dowtyr, thu art not yet so powr as I was whan I heng nakyd on the cros for thy lofe, for thu hast clothys on thy body, and I had non" (97). Christ's words aim to put Kempe's poverty in perspective and to remind her that absolute need is a divine condition associated with his own suffering. In so doing, his speech affirms the Franciscan image of the poor Christ—an image of a being utterly lacking in the forms of dominion that the writers of the previous chapter so relentlessly attribute to Jesus.

When Christ asks Kempe to "makyn hir bar for hys lofe," some critics have focused on how his command makes her anxious about acquiring even the most basic provisions. In their view, this preoccupation works to undermine the *Book*'s conception of poverty as a freeing path of virtue. Following Delany, Roger Ladd, for example, reads Kempe's worry as a sign of her inability to reject the mercantile mindset of her class position.[22] In my view, however, the text, *at this point,* effectively contains this potential challenge to the ideal of poverty by emphasizing that Kempe's concern is fleeting. Furthermore, in subsequent chapters, the text frequently describes how gold and other possessions become a source of apprehension for her. Most significantly, Kempe's hesitation perhaps conveys not a negative view of voluntary poverty but an acknowledgement of the spiritual rigor it demands. After all, if renunciation is purely a form of freedom to be undertaken with ease, then it would not be understood as a path of perfection.

With the reassurance of Christ, Kempe overcomes her initial hesitation and seeks to live out the gospel in an unconventional fashion as a woman who chooses to remain in the world.[23] When she begins to live as a beggar, Kempe theoretically exposes herself to a form of poverty and vulnerability far more extreme than that experienced by male beggars and particularly those who practiced mendicancy voluntarily. In general, women who begged did so involuntarily, and they were subject to both real sexual danger and charges of promiscuity as they openly declared their neediness to others without the benefit of a religious network or any protection against violence. While men who were forced to beg also faced the possibility of physical violence, they were not as vulnerable as women to sexual assault or accusations of lechery.[24] Unlike the involuntary poor, men who chose a life of begging typically became friars and therefore enjoyed the advantages of membership in an official religious order. While the brothers could make use of the orders' houses, libraries, and other amenities, Kempe had no recourse to the material benefits and ecclesiastical authorization accompanying such institutionalized forms of poverty.[25] It is also important to note that even if Kempe had joined a religious order for women, her pursuit of poverty would have been confined to a convent where women were prevented from going out into the world as active mendicants.[26] For example, in contrast to their male counterparts, the Poor Clares at San Damiano lived by a rule specifying that the sisters "must live enclosed throughout their lifetime." It adds that "after they have entered the enclosure of this Order, taking the regular habit, the permission or faculty to go out may no longer be given to them, unless to plant or build that same Order."[27]

The legacy of saints and other holy women also betrays a similar hostility to the prospect of female mendicancy. For example, St. Elizabeth of Hungary, who was inspired by the Franciscans' arrival in her country, wanted to practice mendicancy, but her confessor, Master Conrad, prevented her from begging. As the record of her life explicitly indicates, after the death of her husband, Elizabeth "embraced voluntary poverty, and would have begged from door to door had not Master Conrad forbidden her."[28] In the life of Marie d'Oignies, Jacques de Vitry describes how Marie "burned with such a desire for poverty" that she planned to live as a beggar.[29] However, her attempts at mendicancy were thwarted because her friends lamented that she would leave them and because she sought to undertake a practice unsuitable for women. Marie therefore gave up her dream of mendicancy and "did what was permitted for her to do" by staying home and giving charity to others.[30] The beguine Margaret of Ypres also devoted her life to poverty and desired to practice mendicancy. While she was uncloistered and able to beg occasionally, the record of her life explains that Margaret's mendicancy was a covert activity that her spiritual director actively sought to suppress:

"Whenever she fled her mother and aunts so that she might beg, she was forced to return and remain with her mother by the often repeated command of her [spiritual] father."[31] Unlike Margaret, Francesca of Rome, whose life was recorded in the mid-fifteenth century, managed to beg without reproach; however, she perhaps feared the kind of criticism levied at Margaret and therefore restricted her begging to less traveled streets so as not to be seen by those who knew her.[32]

Perhaps it is Kempe's best known predecessor, St. Bridget of Sweden, who came closest to practicing mendicancy freely as a woman. Gregersson's life of St. Bridget describes her begging simply as a matter of fact: "Sho loued so greteli wilfull pouert þat all þat sho had, sho put it into oþir mennes handes, and when sho wald haue oght to hirselfe or to ani oþir, sho suld aske it mekeli in þe name of Iesu Criste, als it had neuir bene hir awen."[33] Here the text clearly describes Bridget's mendicancy as a testament to her deep humility. The writer, however, perhaps registers a slight sense of anxiety at her behavior by expressing a certain reluctance to imagine her entirely as a female beggar. Telling us that Bridget asks for goods as if those things "had neuir bene hir awen," the text implies her entitlement to such goods by reminding us that they were, in fact, once hers, even if she no longer exercises her rights to them. Though definitely subtle, Bridget's life arguably registers some familiar discomfort with viewing the female saint as a thoroughly destitute and vulnerable beggar. The majority of saints' lives express this concern more explicitly and encourage women to undertake domestic labor, not mendicancy, as their most sacred duty.[34] While Margaret, Francesca, and Bridget reject the limitations generally placed on women committed to poverty, their lives nonetheless feature strategies—whether rhetorical or practical—that work to restrict the reality and scope of their mendicancy. In this context, Kempe's time in Rome as an active, visible, and voluntary mendicant functions as one of the hallmarks of her nonconformity.

Before I go on to explore Kempe's unusual experience of poverty, however, I would like to turn now briefly to another source that helps illuminate the text's striking attention to female mendicancy—the manuscript of the *Book* itself. As the only surviving copy of the text, British Library MS Additional 61823 features an extensive set of annotations that offers a fascinating glimpse into how an early reader of the text interpreted Kempe's religious devotion and commitment to poverty. Written in the mid-fifteenth century by a scribe named Salthows, the manuscript was owned and annotated by the Carthusians at Mount Grace. The most elaborate commentary on the manuscript (among four different sets of annotations) is recorded in red ink. Dating from the late fifteenth or early sixteenth century, these annotations include extensive marginalia, images, and textual emendations. Critics have recently begun to explore how the red ink annotations can be understood as offering a coherent reading of the *Book* from the late medieval period.[35] Specifically, analyses of this commentary reveal how the Carthusian reader seeks to highlight the affective elements of Kempe's devotion by calling attention to her sensory apprehension of the divine, manifested perhaps most obviously in her crying and roaring. Furthermore, the red ink annotator also attempts to locate Kempe's spirituality within an identifiable mystical tradition associated with Richard Rolle and the Carthusian writers Richard Methley and John Norton.[36] While the annotator's direct allusions to these figures clearly work to associate Kempe with their affective mode of piety, critics disagree about the implications of such an association. Karma Lochrie, for instance, approaches the annotations as a legitimizing force that defines Kempe's seemingly eccentric behavior within an established mode of religious devotion.[37] Staley, however, views the commentary less benevolently. She interprets it as the reader's attempt to impose a conventional genre on the text in order to suppress the work's eclectic, fluid, and potentially subversive design.[38]

However one ultimately interprets the annotator's motivations, it becomes clear that his interest in aligning Kempe with a tradition of affective contemplation works to de-emphasize the social dimensions of her spirituality. As we have seen, Kempe's devotion extends beyond her meditative experience of Christ and includes her active practice of poverty as a form of spiritual perfection. However, the red ink annotator is conspicuously silent about Kempe's identity as a voluntarily poor woman. In general, the folios of the manuscript contain copious glosses, drawings, and points of emphasis added by the annotator; yet the folios recording the chapters that deal most explicitly with Kempe's poverty feature a remarkable lack of marginalia and images.[39] Describing her time in Rome, folios 41r–47v contain a sparse amount of commentary that simply foregrounds the work's mystical connections, while altogether ignoring the text's engagement with poverty and Kempe's interactions with the poor. Specifically, in these folios we find, for example, references to "R. hampall" and "S. bridis madyn" as well as individual drawings of a heart and flames of divine love.[40]

The annotator's lack of interest in poverty becomes further pronounced when we examine folios 44v–45v, which record the text's most dramatic engagement with issues of poverty. It is in these pages that Christ explains the importance of poverty to Kempe and orders her to give away her belongings. She then follows his command and begins living as a mendicant who must rely solely on her fellow Christians for sustenance. Curiously, none of these episodes merits the attention of the annotator, and the handwriting that customarily appears in the margins and body of the text all but disappears. The folios that come before and after these poverty-centered episodes feature images and emphatic annotations referencing Kempe's sensory experience of love, but there are absolutely no substantive comments directed at her practice of poverty. While other sections of the manuscript sometimes also feature a less densely annotated pagination, the lack of commentary in this particular segment is remarkable given the relevance of poverty to Kempe's version of spiritual perfection and to her conception of Christ as an object of devotion—topics that are consistently central to the annotator in other parts of the text.

There are certainly many possible reasons for the annotator's conspicuous silence about Kempe's poverty, and his identity as a Carthusian monk alone certainly indicates that he was not personally predisposed to the active life and the forms of poverty practiced by the Franciscans and other fraternal orders. Indeed, his refusal to comment on Kempe's poverty may function as a subtle indication of the rivalry between monastic and fraternal models of perfection.[41] However, if one follows Staley in reading his commentary as an attempt to impose convention on the *Book* and thus "to control . . . understanding of the text,"[42] then it becomes plausible to view his inattention to Kempe's poverty as a willful attempt to discount the anomalous nature of her religious practice. As we have seen, the annotator's preferred spiritual models focus almost exclusively on devotion as a form of contemplation that produces a variety of intense emotions and sensory experiences. While much of Kempe's religious devotion does conform to this model, her choice to follow Christ as an uncloistered mendicant clearly does not. Kempe's assumption of poverty and active mendicancy as a woman arguably constitutes material that cannot be readily legitimized or contained by the annotator's brand of spiritual commentary. Faced with material that resists his will to assimilate her into more theologically and institutionally acceptable terrain, the annotator simply ignores Kempe's mendicancy and professed commitment to the poor. He perhaps hopes that other readers will do the same, directing their attention instead to what he sees as the more palatable and conventional dimensions of Kempe's piety.

Poverty Without Need

In the traditions of female religious practice and in the material form of the manuscript itself, Kempe's poverty and mendicancy thus emerge as idiosyncratic forces leading Kempe down a previously untrodden path that would presumably entail great difficulty, insecurity, and danger. Despite the highly unusual circumstances of Kempe's poverty, it is quite remarkable, then, that the *Book* goes on to present her experience of utter destitution as almost entirely devoid of the suffering that would most likely accompany a life of deprivation. Most noticeably, the *Book* begins to strip Kempe's gender-bending poverty of its radicalism by reconciling the notion of absolute material need with the guarantee of a finding. This familiar idea recalls arguments made by both Nede in *Piers Plowman* and the Wycliffite writers, who sought to curb the fraternal orders' supposed covetousness by ensuring that the friars receive a basic provision of goods. However, *The Book of Margery Kempe* takes such proposals to an extreme level by describing Kempe's poverty as if it were an opportunity to acquire wealth. After Christ affirms Kempe's decision to become poor, he seeks to allay her initial concerns about "wher sche schuld han hir levyng" by telling her, "And thow hast cownseld other men to ben powr for my sake, and therfor thu must folwyn thyn owyn cownsel. But drede the not, dowtyr, for ther is gold to theward" (97). In the very moment that Christ reconfirms Kempe's commitment to poverty, he also promises to reward her with gold. In this sense, Christ's statement is fascinating in its refusal to defer the rewards of earthly poverty to the afterlife.

As we have seen in *Piers Plowman,* the figure Rechelesnesse generally invokes Franciscan ideology in his praise of voluntary poverty as a form of earthly suffering that will be transformed into heavenly bliss. He explains that for the poor "Mescheues and myshappes and many tribulacounes / Bitokeneth treuly *in tyme coming aftur* / Murthe for his mornyng and þat muche plentee" (XII.200–203, my emphasis). In the case of Margery Kempe, however, Christ literally means that her poverty will be rewarded with material wealth in the here and now. Kempe does not get sustenance and clothing as do the birds of the air and lilies of the field; rather she rises up from her meditations, goes out into the street, and meets a man who upon hearing her "good talys . . . and exhortacyonys . . . gaf her mony be the which sche was relevyd and comfortyd a good while" (97). A short time thereafter Kempe also meets an English priest who similarly supplies her with abundant funds, and the *Book* notes that his generosity "fulfilled that owr Lord seyd to hir a lityl beforn, 'Gold is to thewarde'" (101).

While voluntary poverty ostensibly offers Kempe the sacred opportunity to complete the process of fully rejecting temporal goods, it turns out that Kempe's assumption of need hardly inhibits her procurement of what are often substantial amounts of funds. The text thus seems to fulfill Bonaventure's sarcastic formulation of anti-mendicant thinking, which, in his view, perverts Christ's teaching on poverty. Ironically summarizing his opponent's perspective, Bonaventure contends, "[Christ] might also have said to the poor: 'If thou wilt be perfect, go and possess wealth.'"[43] While Kempe's poverty may not exactly lead to extravagant wealth, it does consistently afford her the opportunity to acquire material goods. There is, consequently, a problem with the *Book*'s construction of sanctity as it relates to poverty. Kempe's holiness is evident in her choice to become absolutely poor like Christ and to follow in the Franciscan tradition of Christian perfection. Yet the text also emphasizes her holiness by showing how God intervenes to provide Kempe with gifts that alleviate her need. In maintaining these two conceptions of sanctity, the text ends up redefining poverty as a state that is largely divorced from material deprivation. As it stresses Kempe's holiness, then, the text significantly complicates the value and meaning of poverty by presenting it as a condition that, at least for Kempe, readily leads to the immediate possession of material goods.

The text affirms this unusual conception of poverty by establishing a pattern in which Kempe finds that her needs as a mendicant are met with amazing consistence and regularity. Removing any concern that Kempe might experience extreme hunger or thirst in her pursuit of poverty, the text offers a detailed outline or schedule of the charity Kempe receives. First, we learn that she has the good fortune to run into a former acquaintance, Dame Margarete Florentyn, the wealthy woman who provided Kempe with transportation from Assisi to Rome. Dame Florentyn recognizes Kempe's poverty and insists that she eat with her every Sunday. Kempe's visits to the woman's house are dramatically unlike the eating experiences she shares with her fellow pilgrims. While she is typically an object of scorn shunned by her companions, she is now treated with great respect at Dame Florentyn's home. The text explains how the woman "set [Kempe] at hir owen tabil abovyn hirself and leyd hir mete with hir owyn handys" (97). Dame Florentyn's charity extends beyond her kind treatment of Kempe on Sundays, as she also supplies her with enough food and drink to last for two more days. The *Book* declares that "Whan thei had etyn, the good lady used to takyn hir an hamper wyth other stuffe that sche might makyn hir potage therwyth, as meche as wolde servyn hir for a too days mete, and filled hir botel wyth good wyn" (97–98). The text also adds that "sumtyme sche gaf hir an eight bolendinys therto" (98).

After discussing the ample provisions offered by Dame Florentyn, the *Book* goes on to describe the other charitable gifts bestowed on Kempe. For example, she is invited to dine twice a week with a man named Marcelle, who hopes that Kempe will become the godmother to his soon-to-be-born child. The text also lists an unnamed woman as another habitual almsgiver, who provides Kempe with food each Wednesday. After enumerating these occasions of her regularly scheduled charity, the text mentions that "Other days whan sche was not purveyd sche beggyd hir mete fro dore to dore" (98). This detail does remind us that Kempe is a poor woman who actively practices mendicancy. However, because this information follows the *Book*'s precise account of the charity offered to her, it does not provoke much anxiety about how Kempe will survive the poverty she has pledged.[44] Featuring such careful attention to the amounts of goods given to Kempe and the specific days on which they are given, the *Book*'s charity record makes it possible to calculate that Kempe is only required to beg one day per week.

This version of poverty which paradoxically seems to be defined by its direct alleviation raises some fascinating interpretive and theological questions. In one sense, the direct fulfillment of Kempe's needs can be seen as establishing an idealized model of charity where poverty actually inspires generosity, mercy, and compassion—virtues that are vigorously enacted within the Christian community. As Staley argues, the almsgivers' insistent acts of kindness help constitute an "alternate society." In her view, this group serves an important purpose, acting as a foil for the typical late medieval community defined by its exclusionary nature, its interest in profit, and its insistence on conformity.[45] Staley's account is certainly convincing, yet we might also ask how this idealized image of charity and social inclusion affects Kempe's practice of poverty when understood as a virtue in and of itself.

In another sense, then, Kempe's consistent reception of alms may implicitly highlight a structural problem endemic to Franciscanism. Like Langland's earlier work, the *Book* may explore the difficulty in establishing voluntary poverty as a sustainable practice. This form of poverty demands deprivation and powerlessness, yet it also paradoxically requires material support to satisfy such need and to maintain such vulnerability as a practicable Christian goal. Thus, writers like Langland, FitzRalph, and the Wycliffites criticize how voluntary poverty seems to lead to substantial wealth for the friars, who receive alms while also enjoying institutional provisions that ensure their stable existence as "needy" mendicants. To prevent the friars from acquiring wealth by claiming poverty, antifraternalists, as we have seen, propose that they should receive a basic fyndynge. *The Book of Margery Kempe* may perhaps echo this perspective, imagining Kempe's poverty as Wycliffites and others imagine evangelical poverty, understanding it as a moderate form of privation, not constituted by absolute need and vulnerability. However, we should remember that for such writers basic provisions are guaranteed "bi titil of the gospel," that is, by means of holding clerical office because the "workman is worth his mede." Kempe, though, is clearly not entitled to such provisions because she is a laywoman who becomes voluntarily poor outside of any ecclesiological office.[46] It is this lack of institutional support that makes the apparent certainty of her material assistance so striking.

If the *Book* means for its depiction of consistent charitable aid to expose the troubling contradictions of voluntary poverty, then it does so with extreme subtlety: the text registers no evident discomfort at presenting a version of poverty made possible through its very eradication. The text presents Kempe's poverty as lacking in material hardship, without criticizing this state as a form of hypocrisy or as a corruption of pure Franciscan ideals. Instead, it attempts to reshape those ideals so as to emphasize Kempe's particular sanctity. In so doing, the *Book* offers a new perspective on need, one that attempts to tailor the spiritual benefits of voluntary poverty to an agenda of economic security and social notoriety.

As it endorses a distinctive version of moderate poverty, the text thus curtails the rigors of the originary Franciscan ideal. Though the friars had recourse to their orders' houses, libraries, and other holdings, such resources were not intended to guarantee them an entirely secure supply of food and other necessities. Rather, even friars who belonged to orders that possessed some temporal goods in common should "not [have] enough for them to sustain nature unless they beg[ged] some more things."[47] While antifraternal critics sharply condemned the disparity they saw between the friars' technical definitions of poverty and their lived experiences, their sacred ideal involved creating an atmosphere of need that was not meant to be satisfied by guarantees of substantial provision. In contrast, Kempe's poverty does not seem concerned to foster the same ideal even if it proves to be finally unattainable. The *Book* thus gives new meaning to Christ's command, "Be not solicitious." Kempe hardly has to worry about "wher sche shuld han hir levyng" because her needs are met through remarkably consistent and abundant acts of almsgiving. The text has no qualms about aligning Kempe's poverty with Franciscan ideology while also accommodating that poverty to a relatively stable finding. In this sense Kempe's voluntary poverty obviates solicitude for the morrow by guaranteeing sustenance for the weeks ahead![48]

In addition to describing Kempe's steady supply of material relief, the *Book* also reveals the distinctiveness of Kempe's poverty by highlighting her newfound social acceptance as a poor person. Giving an overview of her experiences after becoming poor for Christ, the *Book* makes the concise declaration that "God gaf hir grace to have gret lofe in Rome, bothyn of men and of women, and gret favowr among the pepyl" (98). Ironically, it seems as if poverty allows Kempe to achieve the worldly worship she desired as a housewife in Lynn. The people's benevolence toward her even spreads to some of her most formidable enemies, including the administrators of the hospital of St. Thomas, who had recently ejected Kempe from their institution on grounds of her crying. While the text implicitly criticizes the fickleness of such individuals, it nonetheless describes how Kempe enjoys the benefits of their altered perspective:

> Whan the maystyr and brothyr of the hospital of Seint Thomas, wher sche was refusyd befortyme, as is wretyn beforn, herd tellyn what lofe and what favowr sche had in the cyté, they preyd hir that sche wolde come again to hem, and sche schulde be wolcomear than evyr sche was beforn, for thei weryn ryth sory that thei had put hir awey fro hem. And sche thankyd hem for her charité and dede her comawndment. And, whan sche was comyn agen to hem, thei madyn hir ryth good cher and weryn rith glad of hir coming. (98–99)

While this scene of joyful welcoming quickly shifts into an account of Kempe's humiliation upon encountering and begging from her disloyal maid, Kempe experiences hardly any other occasions of shameful suffering in her time as a mendicant.[49] Her poverty once again seems quite unusual, for as Bonventure reminds us "to suffer abuse is a sign of destitution."[50]

As the recipient of newfound social favor and copious gifts of charity, Kempe certainly emerges as a holy figure who benefits directly from God's generosity and love. However, in focusing so conspicuously on the immediate forms of God's assistance, manifested in the charitable acts of her fellow Christians, the text evades larger questions about the practicability of voluntary poverty, especially as an active pursuit for women. Does the text mollify the potential ill-effects of Kempe's mendicancy in order to combat the pervasive anti-poverty ethos? In this sense, does it avoid portraying the harsh reality of material deprivation so as to encourage other women to take up mendicancy as a hallowed form of life that rejects the morally perilous demands of getting and spending? If the *Book* indeed attempts to make this very point or one like it, I would argue that it does so at the expense of de-radicalizing Franciscan poverty to the extent that it makes Kempe's experience of "need" amenable to the elite, mercantile ideals it seeks to eschew. Furthermore, though Kempe is not sustained by nature itself and the miraculous events advocated by figures like Langland's Patience, one must question if the unusually generous charity offered to Kempe can be a sustainable model extending to other voluntarily poor women. Does the *Book* intend for Kempe to be an exemplary figure, inspiring other women to follow Christ in poverty and mendicancy? If so, could they expect to receive a similar finding from the people they encounter in foreign or unfamiliar places?

If Kempe's own stated view on almsgiving offers any indication of the text's wider perception of charity, then the prospect of receiving alms would appear to be rather bleak for an unknown beggar seeking aid. Once Kempe has left Rome and returned to England, the *Book* recounts an episode in her life that tellingly exposes her resistance to indiscriminate almsgiving. In this scene, Kempe prevents some of her fellow townsmen from giving aid to a young man who has to come to Lynn claiming that he is a priest fallen on hard times. The man initially appears before the same priest who records Kempe's story and complains to him about the "poverté and disese whech he was fallyn in be infortunyté" (64). The priest is persuaded by the man's tale of misfortune and goes on to make a charitable appeal on the man's behalf to a "worshepful" burgess and his wife, longstanding friends of the priest who have frequently assented to his prior requests for alms. Kempe happens to be present when the priest asks for their help, and she vigorously discourages them from giving charity based on the man's status as an inscrutable outsider. The text explains that

> sche was sor mevyd in hir spiryt ageyns that yong man, and seyd thei haddyn many powyr neybowrys whech thei knewyn wel anow hadyn gret need to ben holpyn and relevyd, and it was mor almes to helpyn hem that thei knewyn wel for wel dysposyd folke and her owyn neybowrys than other stawngerys whech thei knew not, for many spekyn and schewyn ful fayr owtward to the sygth of the pepyl, God knowyth what thei arn in her sowlys. (65)

Kempe seems to possess a divine awareness about the man's true intentions, yet she develops a theory of almsgiving that she recommends to fellow Christians who may lack her spiritual gifts. Thus while Kempe declares that only God ultimately knows the state of men's souls, her theory of charity does not defer to his discerning powers; rather, she actively opposes indiscriminate almsgiving because of the possibility that unfamiliar people may make fraudulent claims of need under the façade of poverty and misfortune.[51]

Espousing a model of giving that echoes *Piers Plowman*'s concern for one's needy neighbors (IX.71), Kempe successfully persuades her fellow townspeople to withhold alms from the unknown man and to direct their charity instead to "wel dysposyd folke" with whom they are familiar.[52] Kempe and her peers accept the ethical principles supporting theories of discriminate giving, and the text ultimately endorses Kempe's view by exposing the fraudulence of the strange man, who eventually takes alms from the priest himself but never returns to repay him as promised. Discriminate charity emerges here as the righteous mode of almsgiving, and in expressing familiar anxieties about unknown and possibly fraudulent beggars, Kempe, as P. H. Cullum puts it, seems to be "in concert with the 'haves' of the Lynn bourgeoisie."[53] Because Kempe maintains this position, it is worth considering if she has forgotten that she herself was once a stranger in a foreign land making appeals for charity from those who did not know her as a needy neighbor.[54] Had Kempe's fellow Christians applied her own standards of giving to their charitable activities, it is likely that Kempe would have found herself without any assistance or aid. Yet perhaps Kempe does not see herself as a typical poor person dependent on the kindness of strangers. As Kempe experiences a form of poverty eased through divine assistance, the *Book* may present her not as a model for imitation but as a saint to be wondered at and venerated.

Involuntary Poverty and the Resurgence of Kempe's Dominion

Given Kempe's declared preference for administering (but presumably not receiving) discriminate charity, we should also ask how the *Book* actually views those men and women who are recognizable as one's needy neighbors, an important question relevant to Kempe's fascinating yet troubling relationship with the humpbacked man, a subject I shall discuss below. In addition to the donor Marcelle who aids Kempe in hopes of her becoming his child's godmother, we encounter throughout the text other almsgivers who help Kempe because she prays for them or inspires them in some way. For example, the English priest, who fulfills Christ's prophecy that "gold is to theward," travels all the way to Italy to seek out Kempe because he "herd tellyn of swech a woman was at Rome the whech he longyd hyly to spekyn" (100). When he finds Kempe, he not only gives her gold but tells her that he will "no lengar suffyr hir to beggyn hir mete fro dore to dore, but prey[s] hir to eten with hym and hys felawshep, les than good men and women be the wey of charité and for gostly comfort woulde preyn hir to mete" (101). It is unlikely that the involuntary poor would often find themselves in Kempe's enviable position, as objects of competition among potential almsgivers.[55] While we have seen Kempe serving and interacting with the involuntary poor, this group of people seems to fade from the text's detailed portrait of the charity Kempe receives. We are left wondering what the community has to offer those who may not possess Kempe's gifts of crying, efficacious prayer, and good speech. Does the text think that these individuals deserve the same kind of charity so consistently bestowed on Kempe?

Kempe's relationship with the humpbacked man is an obvious place to turn for answers to these questions, and while this subject alone may not expose the text's overall view of the involuntary poor, it does open up new questions about Kempe's unusual form of poverty and the dominion she was initially shown to have lost as an unsuccessful brewer and miller. In one of the most memorable and troubling scenes of the text, Kempe, as part of her own enthusiastic assumption of poverty, gives away not only her own belongings but "swech good . . . as sche had borwyd also of the brokebakkyd man" (96). Her behavior understandably angers Richard, and the text makes his outrage clear, as it twice names Kempe's objectionable action: "Whan he wist how that sche had govyn awey hys good, he was gretly mevyd and evyl plesyd for sche gaf awey hys good, and spak ryth scharply to hir" (96). Offering the text's familiar solution to poverty, Kempe attempts to assuage his anger by telling him that his extreme need is only temporary. Without explicitly considering the immediate financial difficulties that Richard now faces, Kempe explains that she will repay him in Bristol during Whitsunweek, for, as she puts it, "I trust ryth wel that he that bad me gevyn it awey for hys lofe wil help me to payn it ageyn" (96). In this response Kempe attempts to validate her actions by telling Richard that she was merely obeying Christ when she gave away his goods, a point that implicates God himself in her sense of entitlement to items that she does not technically own. Furthermore, Christ's divine assistance has become so routine for Kempe that she confidently assures Richard that she will return his belongings in time, a promise that she indeed later fulfills.

Revealing Kempe's nonchalant response to Richard's anger, this brief but fascinating episode raises intriguing questions about the text's view of the involuntary poor. The scene first supplies the curious detail that Kempe has apparently borrowed the belongings of a man who is himself in great poverty.[56] When we are introduced to Richard a few chapters earlier, the text presents him as the quintessential figure of deserving need. Emphasizing his ragged attire, his physical disability, and his advanced age, the *Book* recounts Kempe's first encounter with Richard: "as [Kempe] lokyd on the on syde, sche sey a powyr man sittyng whech had a gret cowche on hys bake. Hys clothis wer al forclowtyd, and he semyd a man of fifty wyntyr age" (82). In their ensuing exchange, Kempe emerges as the man's potential employer, offering to pay for his labor in leading her to Rome. Richard agrees to take her in exchange for two nobles, but he eventually changes his mind, citing both his limited ability to protect her and his need to "gon on [his] purchase and beggyn [his] levyng" (83).[57] After making the extreme case of Richard's poverty clear, the text tells us that Kempe ultimately proceeds to Rome in the company of two friars and a woman. It also confirms Richard's sense of charity and loyalty, however, by noting that he serves Kempe by coming to comfort her every morning and evening.

Given the text's detailed attention to Richard's own poverty and disability, it is appropriate to question if the terms of their relationship are not somehow disturbingly reversed or at least complicated by the gender dynamics at work. Why, for example, does Kempe not serve Richard, offering him regular comfort and consolation? Furthermore, why does she borrow from his presumably paltry supply of belongings instead of providing him with whatever material items she can? Is it because Richard actually views Kempe as the one in need? Does the humpbacked man think that he should help Kempe because she is a woman traveling in a foreign country without a husband or other companions? However they view one another, Kempe's act of giving away his goods marks a troubling dimension of their relationship as the practice of voluntary poverty literally ends up exploiting the involuntary poor.[58]

Few critics have focused on Richard's plight in this episode, viewing it instead as further evidence of Kempe's commitment to poverty. Staley, for example, views Kempe's actions in this scene as constituting a "threat to a society that identifies its good with its goods."[59] Ladd similarly argues that Kempe's giving away of Richard's belongings constitutes "a thorough rejection of [her former] estate and its materialism," allowing her to become alms recipient and almsgiver at the same time.[60] In a rather confusing account of the episode, Cullum notes that Kempe seeks to practice a "spectacular" form of charity unavailable to the poor because it required "superfluity or abundance of giving."[61] Kempe thus, presumably, turns to Richard's goods in order to enact this radical type of charity. If Kempe has suddenly been transformed from alms-recipient to almsgiver, or if she embodies both of these roles at once, then one must wonder about the potential beneficiaries of her generosity. While saints like Margaret of Ypres and Bridget of Sweden begged on behalf of other people such as lepers,[62] *The Book of Margery Kempe* does not specify the recipients of Margery's and Richard's goods. Is it likely that there are many people who would be considered more deserving of Richard's belongings than the humpbacked man himself? Certainly

Lynn's elite Trinity Guild, the organization that Kempe herself would join years later, felt that such an extreme disability merited their charity. Interestingly, the guild's records feature an entry for 1373 specifying that it gave 6s. 8d. to a man with a broken back.[63]

On a more philosophical level, Kempe's decision to give away another person's possessions violates the spiritual or interior ideals of voluntary poverty, which theoretically entails the annihilation of the will to possess, claim, or manage goods—in short, the will to wield dominion. While we obviously cannot expect to hold Kempe to all the stringencies of Franciscan poverty (since she is not a Franciscan), her willing renunciation of goods, as we have seen, does have many affinities with the order's founding ideals and the religious tradition of voluntary poverty. It is therefore appropriate to turn to Franciscan sources to think about the relation between material poverty and the state of the will, a subject that has proven to be central in virtually all of the late medieval writings about poverty we have thus far explored.[64]

The Franciscan order was insistent on defining perfection as the renunciation of all material goods. Yet their writings make clear that this renunciation should facilitate a disposition that relinquishes all attachment and claims to material things. Thus, in addition to abandoning their belongings, the friars were required to give up all lordship over worldly goods, both individually and in common (except in cases of extreme necessity). *The Work of Ninety Days* explains that lordship must be surrendered if a friar hopes to annihilate the will to possess: "Those who have actually left everything, and also the will to possess, leave everything not only in respect of affection and care but also in respect of lordship and ownership, for anyone who keeps lordship and ownership does not renounce the will to possess—indeed also does not renounce the chief mode of possessing, which is to have by right of ownership and lordship."[65] As this statement indicates, lordship can be understood as the means of ownership itself but it also encompasses a range of meanings including the authority to manage, sell, give, or make claims for goods in court. By surrendering such rights, the friars can only exercise *simplex usus facti*, a form of use that "can be separated from the lordship that is a free power of selling and giving a thing and managing it at will."[66] In other words, with the permission of others who ultimately retain dominion over their belongings, the Franciscans may use items lent to them, but they do not have any rights to such goods or ownership of them, even in the case of their consumption.[67] In this vision of poverty the friars merely use goods as necessary, having surrendered all ownership and the will to manage or alienate any worldly things.

For Ockham the renunciation of individual lordship is central to a wider notion of voluntary poverty practiced within the monastic life and the other fraternal orders. While the Franciscans pursue poverty both individually and in common, these other religious take a vow of individual poverty within an order that retains some goods for the common use of its members. As Ockham explains, even in this context the surrender of individual lordship is crucial, for a person who takes a vow of poverty gives up all rights to goods that are simply held for his use. He thus declares that any such religious "is not permitted [by his own authority] to exchange, sell or give [away] a usuary thing," that is, an item designated by the order for common use.[68] In this logic, a monk or a Dominican friar, for example, could not give away or sell his particular allotment of food, clothing, or any other good since he does not hold individual lordship over such goods; rather, they are retained by the order for collective use.

While Ockham's comments obviously do not apply directly to Kempe, his defense of Franciscanism is nonetheless helpful for illustrating the point that voluntary poverty, in the most general sense, entails the renunciation of individual dominion. When read in this context, Kempe's act of giving away the humpbacked man's goods marks an aggressive and illicit claim to lordship. Significantly, her actions go far beyond those of the hypothetical monk who wrongfully seizes goods belonging to his collective; Kempe instead lays claim to property that belongs to another individual and to an involuntarily poor person at that. Though she has no authority over goods borrowed from someone else, Kempe proceeds as if she retains dominion over the humpbacked man's possessions. She therefore does not simply use the goods she has curiously borrowed from him, but instead acts as if she has the right to sell or give them away. Perhaps Bonaventure most succinctly exposes the problem with Kempe's actions in his discussion of the church's right to maintain temporal possessions. Making a comment relevant to Kempe's situation, he explains, "it is permissible to give away one's own possessions, but unlawful to waste those of another."[69]

In the very moment of giving up her own things and proclaiming her choice to follow Christ in poverty and humility, Kempe thus wields a form of dominion that theoretically undermines the rationale of the life she seeks to adopt. Kempe may literally become detached from her own material goods, but she conspicuously fails to abandon the lordship defined as the "free power of selling and giving a thing and managing it at will."[70] While denigrated in Franciscan ideology, these activities are valuable skills in the world of the urban elite. The text cannot relinquish its ideological commitments to that world, and Kempe's poverty does not seem to demand a full break from the mercantile ethos that the holy woman claims to leave behind. Indeed, in its very inception Kempe's poverty accommodates the will to exercise even illicit forms of dominion.[71]

Kempe's Poverty and the Fulfillment of Charity

Though the text seems to make the spirit of Franciscanism amenable to mercantile values, it displays no overt concern about its anomalous version of poverty, and after Kempe leaves Rome, it continues to present her as a figure sanctified by the rejection of material wealth. In its portrait of her ensuing travels throughout England, the *Book* affirms Kempe's poverty as Christ encourages her continued disdain for worldly things and accepts her good will as a legitimate substitute for charity performed in deed. While Kempe is devoted to Christ, she also wins his devotion to her because she distinguishes herself from the majority of Christians who place their business pursuits above their pursuit of God. God specifically praises Kempe because she is unlike the "holy and unholy" people who "wyl not besyn hem to love [God] as thei do to geten hem temperal goodys" (155). Unlike her fellow Christians who remain preoccupied with things of the world, Kempe seems to become increasingly concerned for her less fortunate neighbors. For example, we see her extending a newfound sympathy toward lepers, who evoke Christ's own suffering. In a moment that echoes Francis's own change of heart regarding lepers,[72] Kempe embraces the people she once held as objects of scorn:

"Now gan sche to lovyn that sche had most hatyd befor tyme, for ther was no thyng mor lothful ne mor abhomynabyl to hir while sche was in the yerys of werldly prosperité than to seen er beheldyn a lazer, whom now thorw owr Lordys mercy sche desyryd to halsyn and kyssyn for the lofe of Jhesu whan sche had tyme and place convenyent" (170–71). Though the last part of this quotation reveals how Kempe's kind treatment of lepers is limited to suitable times and places, Christ goes on to affirm that her loving attitude and thoughts themselves come to suffice as acts of charity.[73]

The *Book* makes clear that it does not see Kempe's neediness as a hindrance to charity even though we have seen that other writers worry over the relationship between charity and mendicant poverty. In *Piers Plowman*, for example, Langland eventually divorces the two concepts when Liberum Arbitrium follows Rechelesnesse and Patience's defense of poverty with the concise yet firm declaration that charity "noþer . . . beggeth ne biddeth ne borweth to ȝelde."[74] *The Book of Margery Kempe*, however, works to make Kempe's poverty compatible with charity. For example, after enumerating many of Kempe's good intentions including her desire to establish many abbeys and to donate copious alms, Christ assures Kempe that she "schalt have the same mede and reward in hyevyn for this good willys and thes good desyrys as yyf [she] haddist done hem in dede" (193). He also accepts her other charitable aspirations, telling her, "Dowtyr, I knowe alle the thowtys of thin hert that thu hast to alle maner men and women, to alle lazerys, and to alle presonerys, and as mech good as thu woldist gevyn hem be yer to serve me wyth I take it as yf it wer done in dede" (193). Articulated with quantitative specificity, Christ's view that Kempe's visions of generosity ultimately count for the acts themselves theoretically allows the text to reconcile any potential conflict between poverty and charity. As a result, Kempe can embody both virtues at the same time.

While the *Book* clearly establishes that the pursuit of poverty does not inhibit the practice of charity, it nonetheless continues to register a deep discomfort with the idea that Kempe's voluntary poverty could entail real material need or hardship. Although the text consistently makes note of the times when Kempe has no money or other resources, it continues to present such occasions as temporary anomalies immediately remedied by people who actually practice charity in deed. Just as Kempe received a steady supply of alms while in Rome, throughout her subsequent travels she benefits from divinely inspired gifts bestowed upon her almost every time that the text makes mention of her need. I rehearse the following examples to demonstrate just how consistently the *Book* works to emphasize not the reality but the alleviation of Kempe's poverty. After she returns to England, for instance, we learn that upon her arrival Kempe has "neithyr peny ne halfpenny in hir purse" (75). The very next sentence then describes how she encounters other pilgrims who give her three halfpennies. On another occasion when she is making preparations for her trip to St. James, Kempe realizes that she has "neithyr gold ne sylver to byen" the white clothing that Christ wants her to wear (105). However, he immediately tells her, "I shall ordeyn for the," and she then visits a "worshipful man" in Norwich who "bowt white cloth and dede makyn hir a gowne therof and an hood, a kyrtyl, and a cloke" (107). Not long after she receives this gift of clothing, winter sets in and Kempe, we are told, "had so meche colde that sche wist not what sche myth do, for sche was powr and had no mony, and also sche was in gret dette" (108). While Kempe asks her friends in Lynn for help and meets their initial refusal, we learn that "sodeynly cam a good man and gaf hir fowrty pens, and wyth sum therof sche bowt hir a pylche" (108–9). At this point, Christ steps in to give Kempe his customary assurance of provision. Offering a medieval version of *ne solliciti sitis*, he tells her, "Dowtyr, stody thow for no good, for I schal ordeyn for the" (109). Directly following this declaration, Christ's promise materializes before Kempe's eyes: "And aftrywarde, ther cam a woman, a good frend to this creatur, and gaf hyr seven marke for sche schulde prey for hir whan that sche come to Seynt Jamys" (109).[75]

This list of examples reveals how Christ consistently intervenes to rescue Kempe from the neediness he enjoins on her in the name of his own poverty. Paradoxically, Christ seems to make Kempe's voluntary poverty possible because he ordains for her every need. As Christ himself goes on to explain, he rewards Kempe's love in a material fashion that seems to differ only in degree from his generous treatment of the rich. He says to Kempe, "Dowtyr, thu seyst oftyn to me in thi mende that riche men han gret cawse to lovyn me wel, and thu seyst ryth soth, for thu seyst I have govyn hem meche good wherwyth thei may servyn me and lovyn me. But, good dowtyr, I prey the, love thu me wyth al thyn hert, and I schal gevyn the good anow to lovyn me wyth, for hevyn and erde schulde rathyr faylyn than I schulde faylyn the" (152–53). As he promises Kempe "good anow to lovyn [him] wyth," Christ once again offers her a finding, but in so doing, he surprisingly seems to make Kempe's love contingent on the very goods he pledges to her.[76] Furthermore, in emphasizing how Christ sustains Kempe, the text seems to move away from its earlier representation of Jesus as the naked and needy man suffering passively on the cross. Now he presents an image of himself that resonates more closely with the antifraternalists' view of Christ as a figure immune to need and incapable of renouncing all dominion.

As we have seen, the Wycliffite writers of the previous chapter interpreted the moments of Christ's supposed begging as occasions where he merely demanded goods owed to him based on his various claims to authority as the second Adam, a priest, and the Lord's son. For example, in his particular argument about Elijah "begging" from the widow of Sarapta, the *Omnis plantacio* writer explains the scope of Elijah's and thus Christ's dominion by using an analogy of earthly hierarchy. Thus when Elijah seems to beg, it is akin to a child, who "at þe commaundment of his fadir . . . biddiþ or preieþ his fadris stiward, panter or botiler or ony oþer officer of his fadris to ȝyue him mete or drynk." The giver accordingly performs no great act of charity because "such a seruaunt haþ a special maundement of his lord or maistir to mynystre suche vitails to his child, as þis woman hadde of þe hiȝ lord God to feede Helye."[77]

The Book of Margery Kempe obviously lacks the anti-mendicant focus of this Wycliffite text, yet it also interestingly invokes the image of the steward to describe Kempe's relationship with Christ. However, the *Book* deploys this image to different ends, positioning Kempe and not God himself as the lord who oversees the steward's actions. As Christ explains to Kempe, "Thu madyst me onys steward of thin howsholde and executor unto the, fulfilling of al thi wil and al thy desyr. And I schal ordeyn for the, dowtyr, as for myn owyn modyr and as for my owyn wife" (153). The steward-Christ of *The Book of Margery Kempe* pledges to fulfill Kempe's will and desire, not that of God the father as in the Wycliffite text. As a result, Kempe's Christ establishes an arrangement allowing Kempe to retain a strong sense of authority as well as the material benefits of her steward's guaranteed provisioning. While Kempe's position in this arrangement admittedly shifts among her various roles as Jesus's lord, daughter, mother, and wife, Christ's identity as Kempe's steward works to confirm the persistence of her dominion and financial resources. Despite the shifting power relations it entails, this brief episode offers an interesting twist on Wycliffite conceptions of Christ; in its particular use of the steward image, the *Book* stresses once again how Christ presents himself as a figure who ordains for Kempe's every need.

The Financial Value of Kempe's Virtue

In revealing just how well Christ ordains for Kempe, the text affirms her voluntary poverty but also ends up dissociating her from the wider population of the poor for whom need is not a temporary situation. Counteracting the brief moments when Kempe finds herself destitute are occasional references to the considerable quantities of goods she has amassed through others' charity. At the point when she arrives in Bristol, for instance, Kempe thankfully makes good on her promise to restore the money owed to the humpbacked man. However, in highlighting Kempe's good deed, the text also notably calls attention to the substantial amount of wealth that she has in her possession: "And our Lord Jhesu Crist *had so ordeyned for hir,* as sche went to Bristoweward, that *ther was govyn hir so meche mony* that sche myth wel payn the forseyd man all that sche awt him" (109, my emphasis). Kempe obviously does give away much of this money, but she continues to find herself miraculously well provisioned during almost all of her travels. The Archbishop of York certainly expresses his astonishment at the money she carries with her. After releasing Kempe for the second time, he returns her confiscated belongings to her, and as he does so, the *Book* notes that "The Erchebischop had gret merveyl wher sche had good to gon wyth abowtyn the cuntre" (133). Kempe satisfies his amazed curiosity with the rather nonchalant reply that she has received funds in exchange for the prayers she says on behalf of others. Though Kempe has abandoned the world of getting and spending, her response nonetheless indicates that she sees her spiritual practice as a form of labor entitling her to the charitable payments offered by her fellow Christians. In this sense, Kempe seems to have replaced her worldly business pursuits with spiritual activities that similarly allow her to reap material rewards.

Kempe's perspective in this instance reflects what can be seen as the text's wider attachment to the mercantile values it initially condemns. Despite its central emphasis on poverty, many critics have commented on the *Book*'s market-oriented approach to spiritual matters, noting how the text frequently commodifies Kempe's relationships with her confessors as well as the wider penitential process. They have also remarked on Kempe's evident bargaining abilities, her desire for economic autonomy, and her view of pilgrimage as a business enterprise.[78] While these dimensions of the text certainly attest to its mercantile orientation, it is also remarkable to find an interest in market relations at the very moments when Kempe explicitly disavows monetary wealth in favor of the invaluable consolations offered by Christianity.

The text features a series of paradoxical statements in which Kempe praises the nonmaterial benefits of her religious practice by conceptualizing such spiritual rewards within webs of exchange and economic calculation. For example, Kempe presents her strong desire for the spiritual nourishment of scripture in explicitly financial terms. While in contemplation she tells God, "Yyf I had gold inow, I woulde gevyn every day a nobyl for to have every day a sermown, for thi word is more worthy to me than alle the good in this werld" (140). On one level, this statement may function as an implicit critique of the quality and availability of good preachers, since Kempe can imagine a scenario of consistent preaching only as the result of her paying for such a service. But on a more obvious level, the statement reveals Kempe's continued familiarity and comfort with commercial relations and practices. While she alludes to her inability to actually pay for such preaching, she nonetheless positions herself as a consumer willing to exchange money in order to hear the word of God. Furthermore, by bringing the transcendent value of scripture into an imagined financial exchange, Kempe ultimately undermines her very point that God's word is more precious than any amount of earthly goods. Rather than affirming the scripture's immunity to worldly forms of value, Kempe inadvertently names its price as a sum that she simply cannot afford to pay. In this context, Kempe actually undermines the spirit of the notion that "man cannot live by bread alone," a declaration that imagines scripture as a nourishing force fundamentally different from material food. For Kempe, the bread of scripture becomes an item that can potentially be paid for in much the same way as one might buy a loaf of material bread.

This interest in exchange and economic appraisal appears repeatedly in the moments of the text when Kempe proclaims her attachment to the invaluable gifts bestowed by God's grace. On another occasion, the text presents a white friar loyal to Kempe who laments his superior's command that he should no longer speak or associate with her. The *Book* explains that he "had levar a lost an hundryd pownd, yyf he had an had it, than hir communicacyon, it was so gostly and fruteful" (162). Kempe also finds this enforced isolation disturbing, and she responds in kind, for as the text explains, "Sche had levar a lost any erdly good than hys comunycacyon, for it was to hir gret encres of vertu" (162). Pitting ghostly value and virtue against "an hundryd pownd" and "any erdly good," the text argues that there are transcendent gifts worth far more than any amount of money or possessions; yet by repeatedly asserting that the value of such gifts exceeds even the greatest sums of wealth, the *Book* ultimately defines these gifts within the realm of economic exchange they are meant to surpass. As a result, the text highlights the value and pervasiveness of money as much as it emphasizes the exceptional worth of Kempe's sacred gifts and relationships.

Kempe's Retreat from Poverty

Book 2 goes on to make Kempe's attachment to mercantile values more obvious by presenting her as a figure who is ultimately disconnected from the poor, as someone who more readily employs the needy than identifies with them. At first, the opening of Book 2 seems to counteract the text's persistent preoccupation with market dynamics. It recalls Kempe's earlier decision to "forsakyn the occupasyon of the world" (207), and it then recounts how she attempts to prompt a similar conversion in her son who makes his living "usyng marchawndyse and seylyng ovyr the see" (207). Describing how his mother encourages him to "fle the perellys of this world," the *Book* seeks to reaffirm its portrait of Kempe as a woman detached from the culture and values of the urban elite.[79] As she makes her way to Germany following her son's successful conversion and subsequent death, however, Kempe is more often presented as a member of an elite class. She ultimately emerges as someone who disdains the company of the poor unless they serve her as a reliable source of labor.

Before exploring this characterization of Kempe, however, it is important to acknowledge that there are times on her travels to Germany when she does experience poverty. The text, though, makes clear that it is largely the same kind of temporary poverty she encounters throughout the first book. For example, Kempe initially hesitates to take the trip to Germany because, as she explains to her daughter-in-law, she is "not purveyd of gold ne of sylver sufficiently for to gon with as [she] awt to be" (212). In a familiar move, Christ reassures Kempe with the promise that he will "purveyn for [her] and getyn [her] frendys to helpyn [her]" (212). Not surprisingly, after Kempe boards the ship to Germany we learn that the captain "ordeynd for hir mete and drynke and al that was necessary unto hir" (215).

After spending several weeks in Germany, Kempe's return journey proceeds rather differently, and she consorts with the poor only as a last resort after finding herself without any appointed traveling companion or fellowship. While we have seen Kempe at times aiding the poor and sick, at this point the text makes it clear that she associates with such needy people only because she has no other option. She approaches her company with a glaring lack of charity, and the text works quite explicitly to emphasize the ways in which Kempe is dissociated from her temporary traveling companions. For example, the *Book* supplies the detail that when Kempe and her group arrived at any town, Kempe "bowte hir mete," while "hir felaschep went on beggyng" (221). Kempe has clearly abandoned her practice of mendicancy at this point in the text, and she seems content to see to her own needs without any overt concern for her companions' lack of food.

In addition to distinguishing Kempe from those forced to beg for their food, the text also conveys a rather clear sense of her embarrassment at having to consort with people whose clothing is infested with vermin. While her companions remove their clothes to pick out the insects, Kempe finds such behavior unacceptable and remains fully dressed only to develop a more severe case of lice: "Thys creatur was abavyd to putte of hir clothis as hyr felawys dedyn, and therfor sche thorw hir comowyng had part of her vermin and was betyn and stongyn ful evyl bothe day and nyght tyl God sent hir other felaschep" (221). In contrast to her companions, this description presents Kempe as upholding a higher standard of modesty and courtesy; the actions of her fellow travelers are apparently too loathsome for Kempe to take up herself.

In her reading of this episode, Staley remarks on the recurrence of the term "felaschep" and the use of the word "commonwyng" to emphasize Kempe's solidarity with her destitute companions. Arguing that the episode exposes "other forms that community might take," Staley declares that Kempe's time with these people enables her to recognize that "we can be bound together by more than law." She adds that "We can find ourselves forced, like our fellows, to sit naked on the grass, picking lice from our clothes while others ride by, well-fed and amply clothed."[80] While Staley wants to see a radical reconceptualization of community in this episode, her reading is not altogether valid because Kempe does not actually seem to be one of the underfed folks who sits naked and picks lice. The terms "felaschep and comownyng" do not, in my view, indicate Kempe's solidarity with the poor but instead function as a rather thin attempt to mask the text's more overt and sympathetic portrayal of Kempe's detachment from such pitiable creatures. Discussing the vermin that plagues both Kempe and her companions, the text betrays a tacit sense of disdain for her company as it attributes Kempe's extreme suffering to her "comowyng" or interaction with these poor people, not to her refusal to adopt their remedy for such suffering, however humiliating it might be.[81] Kempe's only relief comes with God's decision to "sen[d] hir other felaschep," that is, a form of companionship more suited to the standards of life to which Kempe is accustomed (221).[82] In providing her with other company, the divine presence at this point in the text differs markedly from the needy, naked, and suffering Christ, whose image goes unrecognized in the poor people whom Kempe seeks to escape.

The text makes Kempe's implicit hostility toward her poor companions more clear by emphasizing that her involuntary association with them costs her both precious time and money. In a move that begins the process of redefining need as a nonmaterial condition, the text insists that Kempe would never travel with such creatures by choice: "Nede compellyd hir to abydyn hem and prolongyn hir jurné and ben at meche mor cost than sche shculde ellys a ben" (221). Here, need seems to refer to Kempe's social isolation and vulnerability, not to her economic status, for as we are told, her time with the poor pilgrims ends up costing her more money than she otherwise would have spent. In this remarkable comment, which distances Kempe from the perspective of the poor, the text asserts that her expenses have been increased because of her enforced association with poor people—people who we should remember are so needy that they, unlike Kempe, must beg for food. Furthermore, while Kempe up to this point has repeatedly been the object of scorn because she travels too slowly, the above quotation subjects Kempe's poor companions to the same criticism, complaining that they are responsible for prolonging her journey.

Such comments demonstrate how the text's view of this group marks a radical departure from its previous approbation of poverty as a sacred and relatively benign condition. At this point, Kempe seems more concerned to uphold values commonly associated with the urban elite as she desires to travel efficiently, minimize her expenses, and find more appropriately dignified company. Perhaps Kempe speaks here from a position that represents her status late in life as a member of Lynn's exclusive and powerful guild of the Holy Trinity. While the guild certainly aided the poor in significant ways, its members did not likely identify them as equals or view them as welcome companions, for such figures were certainly excluded from membership in the guild.[83] Kempe's recollections perhaps function as a kind of distancing mechanism that seeks to prevent her past experiences with the poor from defining her present and future status as an influential woman of Lynn. Thus, in Kempe's recollections, her time with this particular group of poor people is not one of compassion or solidarity; rather, a sense of embarrassment, annoyance, and dissociation emerges to distinguish her social status from theirs.

In the latter part of her journey back to England, Kempe becomes more clearly identified with the employing classes as she seeks out the poor not strictly for their companionship or for any charitable activity but as a source of labor that makes her travels possible. Finding herself repeatedly abandoned by her fellow travelers, Kempe manages to get assistance by paying others for their services as her guides and protectors. For example, after leaving Aachen, Kempe cannot keep up with the group of pilgrims she meets, so she asks for help from a friar, whom she learns has recently been robbed. Identifying him as someone in need of money, Kempe asks for his assistance, appealing not so much to his sense of charitable obligation as to his need for earthly rewards: "Than sche spak wyth the powr frer . . . proferyng to aqwityn hys costys tyl he come at Caleys, yf he wolde abydyn wyth hir and latyn hir gon wyth hym tyl thei comyn ther, and yet gevyn hym reward besyden for hys labowr" (222).

The text features other similar instances in which Kempe emerges as a seemingly well-provisioned employer seeking needy people who can facilitate her journey home to Lynn. For instance, once she arrives in England, she proceeds to the house of a poor man and knocks on his door early in the morning. After he appears "hogelyd in hys clothys unsperd and unbotenyd," Kempe requests his assistance "prey[ing] hym, yf he had any hors, that he wolde helpyn hir to Cawntyrbury, and sche schulde aqwityn his labowr" (225).[84] She is also finally able to return to Lynn after convincing the hermit who first led her out of town to accompany her on the return. Despite his initial resistance, Kempe convinces him to accompany her by "profery[ng] hym to aqwityn hys costys be the wey homeward" (230). These examples work to dissociate Kempe from the poor by presenting her not as their equal but as their master or employer.

Another particular account describing Kempe's arrival in London similarly signals her desire to inhabit a position of socioeconomic authority. Kempe's return to London finds her notably self-conscious about her shabby clothing. Her commitment to poverty once again gives way to embarrassment as she disguises herself until she "myth a made sum chefsyawns," allowing her to obtain clothing she deems more appropriate to her social status. The text's choice of terminology here is especially illuminating since the word "chefsyawns" is defined as the act of borrowing money, "especially on security or/and at interest."[85] In his sermon, Taylor interestingly calls attention to this very term, declaring that "amonge marchauntis is a new deuelrie . . . þat is called þe newe cheuyshaunce." Defining the term essentially as usury, Taylor denounces "chefsyawns" as a form of avarice condemned by Christ himself.[86] While Kempe is not the lender practicing usury at this moment in the *Book*, the text's casual use of the term is striking compared with Taylor's anger at its moral implications. Taylor spends over twenty lines condemning "chefsyawns," but Kempe has no reservations about participating in a commercial activity that potentially opposes the virtues of poverty and charity she strived to cultivate earlier in the text. Her negotiations are apparently successful, as Kempe soon finds the things she needs among some "worschepful" women in London. These people appear to be a welcome change of "felaschep" from the poor folk with whom Kempe was forced to travel in Germany. She now finds herself being entertained at feasts where she associates with prominent figures including men "of the cardenalys hows" (227).

Kempe's Distinctive Need

While Kempe, as I have argued, becomes less readily associated with the poor and at times almost disdainful of their suffering, the *Book* nonetheless manages to convey a real sense of Kempe's vulnerability and need, especially in its account of her final return to England. This sense of her weakness results from the text's redefinition of need as a condition determined not primarily by economic factors but by Kempe's status as a woman of advanced years. As we have seen, Kempe has ample financial resources to pay for others' assistance along her journey. It is clear, though, that she resorts to employing others because of her own limited physical abilities, and the text repeatedly calls attention to the difficulties Kempe experiences as she tries to keep up with younger and faster pilgrims. Her attempts to follow her guide on the way to Wilsnak, for instance, cause her "gret labour and gret disese" (217). Her struggles only increase on this leg of the journey, and Kempe's suffering does not provoke her guide's sympathy but rather increases his ire and frustration. The text reveals the extreme hardship she experiences by emphasizing the discrepancy between the abilities of Kempe and her guide: "Sche myth not enduryn so gret jurneys as the man myth, and he had no compassion of hir ne not wolde abydyn for hir. And thefor sche labowryd as long as sche myth tyl that sche fel in sekenes and myth no ferther" (218). The guide's ill treatment of Kempe becomes so pronounced that it prompts the outrage of local women, who "having compassyon, seydyn many tymys to the foreseyd man that he was worthy gret blame for he labowryd hir so sor" (218). However, their concern goes unheeded by the guide, who seeks to make Kempe suffer in hopes that she will forsake his company: "He, desiryng to be delyveryd of hir, chargyd not what thei seydyn ne nevyr sparyd hir the mor" (218).

Adding to this portrait of suffering, the text offers more details about Kempe's distress as a woman "to agyd and to weyke to holdyn foot" with the other pilgrims she meets. In addition to facing her own physical limitations, Kempe also encounters the threat of sexual violence as she comes across priests who speak "many lewyd wordys unto hir, schewyng unclenly cher and cuntenawns, proferyng to ledyn hir abowtyn if sche wolde" (220). In recounting such scenes the *Book* makes Kempe's vulnerability almost palpable.[87] In spite of her sufficient financial resources, Kempe nonetheless emerges as a figure of need, dependent on the compassion and physical assistance of others. Her ability to pay for help does not then ultimately grant Kempe a powerful sense of authority, allowing her to benefit effortlessly from the fruits of others' labor. Rather, her money seems to function as a rather desperate remedy for the community's lapse of charity. The end of the *Book* thus records the failures of Christian fellowship, failures in which Kempe herself is at times complicit. While the text may exhibit a certain resistance to the ideal of absolute poverty and the suffering of the involuntary poor, it nonetheless refuses to present Kempe's financial resources as the perfect solution to the problems she faces. Kempe must resort to offering money in exchange for being treated with kindness.

It is perhaps the final stage of Kempe's life that most clearly demonstrates her paradoxical position as a woman of means utterly dependent on the labor and good will of those whom she employs. The events concerning the *Book*'s inception are worth considering in some detail because they illuminate how the text presents Kempe not simply as a female visionary but as an employer who struggles to find a reliable laborer for her spiritual enterprise. As Ashley notes, the production of a readable object is the quintessential goal for Kempe: "Margery may invoke ineffability topoi in claming inability to describe her mystical experiences, but the materiality of the written document is crucial to the personal validation of her life; she must produce a hagiographic text to record her mystical visions and substantiate her claims to sanctity."[88] The famous proem of the *Book* recounts the numerous difficulties that Kempe first encounters when she attempts to record her life twenty years after her first vision of Christ.[89] Many critics have commented on this section of the work, often discussing the complex relations that develop between Kempe and her scribe.[90] These relations are significant, for as Felicity Riddy explains, they constitute the *Book* itself: "texts are embedded in the processes of getting on with other people, getting them to do what we want, and doing things together with them; indeed, texts are themselves a mode of social interchange."[91] Focusing on the "interchange" between Kempe and scribes, I want to consider the opening scene as a distinctive representation of a conflict that has by now become familiar to us in texts ranging from *Piers Plowman* and fourteenth-century labor legislation to the antifraternal polemic of Wycliffite writers.

In many ways, the opening of the *Book* describes an ongoing dispute between an employer and her laborers. In this case, the lines of conflict are not drawn strictly along class markers but rather reflect gender divisions as an illiterate woman seeks out the authorizing voice of a trained cleric. The opening increases our appreciation for the forthcoming text as it reveals how the *Book* was almost never written due partly to uncontrollable events but mainly to the recalcitrance and ineptitude of the scribes Kempe employs.[92] While, as we have seen, the text values the resistant workers who forestall Kempe's earlier attempts at brewing and milling, the *Book* goes on to generate a sense of alarm as it painstakingly describes the reluctance and failures of Kempe's spiritual laborers. After the death of the first scribe, an Englishman who spent much of his life in Germany, Kempe solicits the help of a priest who finds the text incomprehensible.[93] He nonetheless promises to try to read it again at another time, but he ultimately abandons his work. We learn that his refusal to work stems not from idleness, the sin that *Piers Plowman* attributes to its wasters and that the *Crede* attributes to its fraternal drones. Rather, the priest's resistance is a result of his "cowardyse" at succumbing to the "evel spekyng of this creatur and of hir wepyng" (19). The *Book* gives us a sense of Kempe's displeasure and frustration at the priest's refusal to labor, when it mentions his obstinacy, "notwythstandyng the creatur cryed often on hym therfor" (19). Unlike Piers who calls Hunger to his aid, Kempe has no means of compelling the priest to labor, and, after a four-year interval, he finally declares his inability to work for Kempe, telling her that "he cowd not redyn [the book], whefor he wold not do it" (19). Viewing his service to her as a form of "perel" (20), the priest eventually refers Kempe to another man familiar with the language and writing of the first scribe.

As she seeks the assistance of this latest candidate, Kempe entices him with the promise of generous payment, offering him "a grett summe of good for hys labowr" (20). This scribe, however, also finds the task impossible, and Kempe is left with no laborer until the priest finds himself so "vexyd in his consciens" that he agrees to fulfill his original promise to try reading the book once again.[94] The proem concludes by describing how Kempe's prayers help transform the priest into a competent scribe who miraculously finds reading the book "mych mor esy . . . than it was beforntym" (20). The text's production, however, is not without additional troubles. Using the same term that denotes in Taylor's sermon the physical disability that prevents people from laboring, the priest begins to write, but finds himself incapacitated because his eyes became "myssyd so that he might not se to make hys lettyr ne might not se to mend hys penne" (20). After he puts on glasses that make his vision worse, Kempe ultimately dismisses his failing eyesight as the work of the devil. She uses her spiritual insight to encourage the priest in his labor, and he returns to his task to find that "he myth se as wel . . . as evyr he dede befor be day lyth and be candel light bothe" (20).

In outlining these events, the text plays with the typical power dynamics of the employer-laborer relationship by emphasizing Kempe's complete dependence on her scribe to undertake a task that her illiteracy prevents her from performing herself. Ironically, despite her substantial financial resources, she is powerless in securing a laborer who has both the physical and spiritual competence to record her life. She nonetheless retains great need of a scribe not simply to write down her words but to authorize the text as a legitimate spiritual work. Arguing that the scribe might be a strategic fiction of the text, Staley explains his importance: "Lacking a scribe, we would be left with one woman of forty-something (that age thought of as post-menopausal and thus less 'female,' in which so many medieval women say they began to write), who sits down to record a series of visions and adventures that occurred some years before. How would we class such a work? Would it be picaresque narrative? Satire?"[95] As Staley describes it, Kempe must rely on the presence of a male scribe, whether actual or imaginary, to make her story truly legible within the contexts of late medieval religious culture. The power of the scribe's authorizing role becomes especially apparent in chapter 24 as he describes a time when he refused to continue writing without some evidence of Kempe's gift of prophecy. Recognizing the authority of the scribe, Kempe, we learn, "sumdel for drede that he wold ellys not a folwyd hir entent for to wryten this boke, *compellyd*, dede as he preyd hir and telde hym hir felngys what schuld befallyn in swech materys as he askyd hir" (64, my emphasis). Here, Kempe does not seem to occupy the position of an authoritative employer; rather she seems closer to figures like Piers's workers who are compelled to labor because of Hunger's violent threats.

Yet, despite this sense of powerlessness, Kempe also emerges as an authoritative figure who tests her scribe's ability to discern the sanctity of her story. It is Kempe's special grace that transforms her worker's disability and reluctance into a virtuous industriousness that, in turn, allows others to become witnesses to her holiness. In this sense, she perhaps can be seen not as a passive woman compelled by her scribe's threats, but as an employer who compels her scribe to labor through the miraculous power of prayer. Commenting on Kempe's agency as the motivating force behind the written text, Lochrie discusses how the scribe's ability to read and write results from Kempe's "interdiction," an act that she defines as Kempe's "insertion of her own voice between text and reader." Lochrie explains that "This interdiction becomes [Kempe's] authorizing practice, which not only inaugurates the book but resurfaces in the text whenever the scribe (or reader) loses faith in her authority."[96] Kempe actually benefits from the scribe's reluctance and doubt, for she transforms these modes of resistance into an affirmation of her sanctity and the labor she both requests and demands.[97] Overall, Kempe proves to be irreducible to any one position or role. She is an illiterate woman dependent on a male scribe for her story to be told. And she is also a powerful visionary who captures what remains elusive for Langland in the plowing of the half-acre—she inspires others to labor with love and faith.

Kempe's liminal position at the beginning of the *Book* is relevant to her paradoxical status throughout the text as a woman who experiences a form of poverty that does not minimize her access to material goods or her acceptance of temporal power. She claims to reject the mercantile ideals central to urban life, but her attempt to live out a radical social gospel ends up reproducing the very socioeconomic pressures she seeks to renounce. In this sense, the *Book*'s claims of poverty reveal the intricacies of ideological change with particular acuteness. Unwilling to reject the benefits of Franciscan piety in an explicit fashion, the text seeks to hold onto a powerful spiritual tradition that still retains ethical force in late medieval England. Indeed, the *Book* seems anxious about the commercial practices, worldly ambitions, and material rewards that define the life of the elite in Lynn. Yet the demands and appeals of that life exert an equally powerful hold on the text. In describing her post-conversion activities, the *Book* writes approvingly of Kempe's consistently successful attempts to attain financial security and wield temporal authority—goals that she was also said to pursue as a sinful businesswoman.

The *Book* attempts to reconcile these competing ideologies by making the demands of evangelical poverty more palatable to Kempe's identity as a bourgeois woman in fifteenth-century Lynn. As a result, the text generates competing claims about poverty's role as a force of sanctification. Kempe is rendered holy through her willful acceptance of Christlike destitution. Yet she is also rendered holy through her favored status as a recipient of miraculous gifts that protect her from the very poverty she claims to suffer. Given this economic security, Kempe's greatest need comes in other forms of hardship that reveal the difficulties of her life as an aged and illiterate woman. But even in these arenas, Kempe's identity is far from straightforward, and she continues to inhabit a number of competing roles. It is perhaps this sense of fluidity that ultimately defines Kempe as a radical religious figure. The path of perfection that she undertakes and the forms of sanctity she claims to embody require her to fulfill seemingly impossible duties in serving as both mendicant and almsgiver, mystic and merchant, laborer and employer.

CHAPTER FIVE

Communal Identities

Performing Poverty, Charity, and Labor in York's Corpus Christi Theater

York's Corpus Christi drama, as it re-creates the whole of biblical history, explores theological material central to the late medieval debates about poverty, charity, and labor. Yet the York cycle is especially intriguing not simply for its discussion of such issues, but because the plays are immediately implicated in these issues, existing as cultural productions undertaken by the city's labor guilds. York's Corpus Christi drama is therefore a crucial resource for understanding late medieval conceptions of poverty: the plays' exploration of this issue is simultaneously a performance of community fully subject to the economic pressures and social tensions that define it.[1] Like *The Book of Margery Kempe,* the plays illuminate the socioeconomic concerns particular to late medieval urban culture. And again, like Margery's text, they call attention to their status as works manufactured by physical and spiritual labor.

In highlighting the material conditions of their production, however, the plays go beyond any written work because they are at once artistic, economic, and theological endeavors carried out within the physical and political domain of the city. As we have seen in the previous chapters, the rhetorical strategies of anticlericalism and the generic pressures of hagiography can produce writing about poverty that occludes certain realities or modes of social relation. The most significant of these occlusions can be found not only in the Wycliffite tendency to sideline the relationship between the lay elite and the involuntary poor but also in *The Book of Margery Kempe*'s efforts to describe Kempe's miraculous immunity to extreme deprivation. In contrast to these works, dramatic performance entails different strategies of representation that make it difficult to downplay material realities and modes of interaction. To perform poverty is to give presence to absence, conferring substance on the notoriously flexible language of lack and deprivation.[2] As it locates poverty in the bodies, faces, and voices of actors, the theater makes it visible, allowing the image of the poor to occupy a central place in the city, moving through its streets, permeating its public spaces. Moreover, in the world of the theater, actors communicate with other actors, actors communicate with audience members, and audience members communicate with one another. Constituted by these simultaneous interactions and opportunities for meaning, the plays anatomize social relations with the utmost intricacy. The pageant texts' insights are compounded and sometimes challenged by the theater's own dramatic resources in representing poverty. Furthermore, as productions that in themselves are potentially labor-intensive, impoverishing, and motivated by charity, the York plays can be understood as the embodiment of the very issues they explore.

This chapter examines York's Corpus Christi drama as a theatrical and economic production fully implicated in the city's labor regimes and political networks. Discussing three pageants that pay special attention to labor, charity, and need, I will argue that the York plays uniquely crystallize the wider cultural conflicts around poverty in late medieval England. By staging poverty and giving dramatic life to the poor themselves, the plays offer a forceful critique of many ideas central to the anti-poverty ethos that the Wycliffites and Margery Kempe ultimately adopt. Though they use the distinctive resources of theater, the plays recall *Piers Plowman* in some ways by exposing the occlusions and omissions that frequently characterize polemical discussions of need. The plays' critique thus offers a strand of continuity with an earlier era, but it also exposes a significant change, revealing distinctive preoccupations central to the urban economy of fifteenth-century York. While the city should not be seen as a unique site of protocapitalist advancement but rather as a place that shares continuities with the socioeconomic order of rural England, York did possess a particular political system that institutionalized and regulated labor in very specific ways.[3] When compared to the guild records relevant to York's Corpus Christi theater, the pageants' perspective looks increasingly anomalous, for the city's official documents generate a competing discourse of poverty, charity, and social unity.

The plays thus work against the dominant ideology as they literally animate unpopular notions such as the legitimate reality of the able-bodied poor and the ethical imperatives of indiscriminate almsgiving. Their powerful lessons, though, are perhaps best taken by audiences as personal advice not applicable to the wider principles structuring the civic body and informing its socioeconomic practices. The political regimes of York operated according to a different set of standards, revealing how the economic concerns of urban society affirmed the basic tenets of the anti-poverty ethos. The plays offer a radical call for indiscriminate charity and civic unity, but, as the very mechanism of the guild-based theater suggests, these ideals have no institutional viability within a civic structure committed primarily to social differentiation and the promotion of labor.

Before turning to the plays themselves, I would like to give a brief overview of York's civic government, focusing specifically on how the city's Corpus Christi theater served to facilitate the political goals of the ruling elite. The city of York was led by a mercantile oligarchy, which consisted of the mayor, the council of twelve, and the council of twenty-four. The governmental body also included the council of forty-eight, a group of artisans representing "the commons." This group, however, had little power beyond formally affirming the decisions of the mercantile elite. As an indication of their lesser status in the government hierarchy, the forty-eight were fined for failing to convene for meetings regarding annual elections and the pageants.[4] As this detail suggests, the mercantile oligarchy was effectively in control of the city government.

This group not only manipulated access to the freedom of the city, but also relied on a rigidly divided labor force and the plays themselves in order to secure their own power and financial interests.[5] The guild system in York and the labor statute of 1363 created an artificial division of labor mandating that craftsmen focus on a single, narrowly defined pursuit. Heather Swanson interprets this statute as part of the wider body of post-plague legislation that "tried to control the rapidly changing labor market." Within the guild-based economy of York, the law's effects were quickly felt, as documented by the city's Freemen's Register, where, as Swanson explains, "men taking up the freedom were increasingly described by a specific occupation."[6]

While membership as a laborer in a particular guild may have seemed to preserve a group's monopoly on a trade, the guild system had some distinct disadvantages and impracticalities for workers. First, the notion of restricting one person to a single craft opposed the real life situation of many urban laborers. Work tended to be multi-occupational, as men and women practiced different trades within their households.[7] Second, occupations were defined so rigidly that there was inevitable conflict among guilds practicing related trades.[8] As a central responsibility of the guilds, the Corpus Christi plays were directly implicated in these labor conflicts. If the searchers discovered one guild infringing on another's trade, it was fined, with half of the money going to the pageant of the wronged guild and the other half going to the city itself. In this way, the labor system and the plays themselves served the interests of the mercantile elite. As Sarah Beckwith explains, "it was in the interests of the town government to proliferate artificial divisions between the guilds: the more guilds, the more searchers, the more searchers, the more fines."[9] The city and the plays were also financed in part by fines generated from faulty labor. The searchers penalized substandard labor with the imposition of fines that were once again split between the guild's pageant costs and the city. While Corpus Christi drama may very well celebrate Christ's body as an image of unity, the plays emerged from this wider social body constituted by fractured units of craftsmen and a larger split between artisan laborers and the mercantile oligarchy.

Christ's Entry and the Meaning of Community

Given that the artisan guilds and the plays functioned, at least in part, to enforce a rigid socioeconomic order, it seems appropriate to begin with the pageant most often hailed as a celebration of civic unity.[10] The

Entry into Jerusalem offers a detailed representation of community as it portrays the world of Jesus, his apostles, and ordinary people seeking Christ's attention. This pageant is particularly significant because it features Christ's procurement of the ass, his healing of the blind man, and his exchange with Zaccheus. These gospel events, as we saw in chapter 3, are central to the debates about Christ's mendicancy. While it does not engage directly with these conflicts, the play makes an important ideological statement in rejecting some of the central tenets of antifraternal discourse. The *Entry* notably refuses to present the apostolic community as a static ideal that ultimately exposes the moral flaws of medieval society.[11] It develops a notion of community that emerges from social interaction often characterized by tension, conflict, and misunderstanding. The evangelical world of this play thus differs from that of the Wycliffite writings because it becomes a means of exploring and critiquing the similarly fraught interactions that constitute medieval society. The play is also distinctive for its sympathetic portrayal of all types of needy people including the able-bodied poor. And, finally, in staging the social relations that take place around Christ, the play exposes an issue largely deemphasized by both the Wycliffites and *The Book of Margery Kempe*. As Christ is greeted by the lay elite and by the involuntarily poor men who seek his aid, the *Entry* anatomizes the troubling distance between these groups of people even as they occupy the very same "stage."

In its opening scene, the play expands on the biblical account of Christ's request for the ass before he enters Jerusalem. Its extensive treatment of this episode raises familiar questions relevant to Franciscanism: Did Christ and the apostles beg for the necessities of life having renounced all dominion? Or did they exercise lordship in taking goods to which they were entitled? The pageant does not take a clear position: in contrast to standard antifraternal arguments concerning Christ's mendicancy, the *Entry* makes the nature of Christ's need and lordship a source of conflict within the apostolic community itself. When he first addresses the apostles, Jesus tells them simply to go and fetch an ass from a nearby castle. His statements initially evoke antifraternal sentiment because they characterize his request explicitly as a command. He tells the apostles, "Gois with gud hart and tarie noȝt, / My comaundement to do be ȝe bayne."[12] While alluding to the image of a commanding and masterful

Christ, the play soon complicates this view, for Christ himself goes on to consider how his "command" might not be interpreted as such by the owner of the ass. Jesus recognizes that meaning emerges through acts of reception and exchange, and he anticipates that the apostles' attempt to procure the ass is likely to provoke suspicion or conflict. Christ therefore acknowledges the contentious nature of his command and tells Phillip and Peter how to respond if someone objects to their taking the beast:

> Yf any man will ȝou gaynesaye,
> Say þat youre lorde has nede of þam
> And schall restore þame þis same day
> Vnto what man will þam clayme. . . .
> (29–32)

Christ's answer here invokes the tricky term "nede" without specifying how he exactly understands it. Does Jesus, as the antifraternalists suggest, need the ass in the same way that a lord simply requires something from his servants? Or does Jesus, as the Franciscans suggest, need the ass because he is in a state of extreme poverty possessing nothing and claiming nothing as his own? The play also offers another possibility as it describes Christ's need in different terms, presenting it as a condition that stems from his obligation to fulfill prophecy, a word that dominates the pageant's discourse. In this sense, Christ needs to sit on the ass "so þe prophicy clere menyng / May be fulfillid here in þis place" (24–25).[13] Jesus then spells out the prophecy itself, declaring: "Doghtyr Syon, / Loo, þi lorde comys rydand an asse / Þe to opon" (26–28). While Christ aims to clarify the words of the prophecy, he leaves the precise nature of his need obscure.

This obscurity remains evident as the play progresses, for when Peter and Phillip go to fetch the animal, they express divergent views on the nature of the task at hand. Peter approaches their task within a seemingly Franciscan framework, insisting that they must ask for permission to take the animal. He thinks, in short, that they must beg for it because neither Christ nor the apostles has dominion over the beast. Referring to the ass's rightful owner (or his servant), Peter tells Phillip, "Go we to hym þat þame gan bynde, / And aske mekely" (55–56). Phillip, however, immediately objects to Peter's proposal and maintains that they need not beg for the beast because it is "common." In his view, it is unnecessary to make even a superficial request for the animal because it is free for their use:

> The beestis are comen, wele I knawe,
> Therefore vs nedis to aske less leue;
> And oure maistir kepis þe lawe
> We may þame take tyter, I preue.
> (57–60)

Phillip here makes an argument that the antifraternalists would be likely to support in their case against the Franciscan theory of poverty. While he does not reference Christ's dominion explicitly, he seems to have a comparable idea in mind when he asserts that Jesus has a right to the ass because he "keeps the law." Phillip perhaps suggests that Jesus has access to the town's privileges because he willingly submits himself to its civil laws and customs. Or perhaps he refers to the law of the gospel, viewing Christ, in line with antifraternal arguments, as a priest who is entitled to the common goods he needs.

In any case, Phillip gets the last word, and the apostles proceed on his assumption. It quickly proves faulty, however, because it opposes the porter's theory of commonality. After they try to take the ass, the porter accuses Phillip and Peter of exercising illicit dominion: "Saie, what are ȝe þat makis here maistrie, / To loose þes bestis withoute leverie?" (64–65). The porter challenges Phillip's theory of lordship and commonality, and his resistance forces the apostles to revert to Peter's original plan of mendicancy. They beg for the animal with humility: "Sir, with þi leue, hartely we praye / Þis beste þat we might haue" (72–73). The porter eventually grants the apostles their wish because he has heard of Jesus the prophet (85). Yet he does so only after questioning the audacity of their master's claim to the ass, "What man is þat ȝe maistir call / Swilke priuelege dare to hym clayme?" (78–79).

Extrapolated from a single line in the gospel, this fraught exchange is significant for its refusal not only to present Christ's need as a settled issue but to depict the apostolic community as an exemplar of social harmony. In regard to this first issue, the play reveals the complexity of need as a subject that Christ, Peter, Phillip, and the porter all interpret differently. Like *Piers Plowman,* the *Entry* exposes problems with any rigid or predetermined conception of the term. Traditional theories pitting Christ's mendicancy against his dominion have little efficacy in this exchange. Even if Philip is right in assuming that Jesus is entitled to the beast, the porter, who has control of the animal, does not adhere to this same view. Though the porter expects the apostles to beg for the ass, he eventually grants their request based not so much on Christ's neediness as on Jesus's particular status as a prophet with whom he is familiar.

In sidelining the major preoccupations of antifraternal discourse, the pageant also highlights how Peter and Phillip's exchange with the town's gatekeeper becomes a quest for consensus between conflicting domains of apostolic and civic authority. Ruth Nissé reads this episode as an idealized representation of civic government as enacted through processes of interpretation and conciliation. She explains, "The idea of common property here provides an occasion for the ideal community to demonstrate its mechanisms of sound rule by negotiation." She goes on to explain that this process takes place as the porter "weighs the apostles' lack of city livery against their 'intente' (73), or account of Jesus as 'God and man withouten blame' (83), and decides by 'gode resoune' (75) to give them the ass."[14] This view is compelling as it describes how the porter and the apostles ultimately achieve resolution, yet it does not consider the implications of disputing notions of commonality in the first place.

If we explore such implications, it seems as though the gatekeeper's objection and eventual concession reveal the limitations that undermine any idealization of civic unity. Perceiving Peter and Phillip as unknown outsiders, the porter initially declares that they cannot have the beast because they are "without livery." While the porter never denies that the ass is common, his reference to livery suggests that the animal is available only to individuals bearing some visible claim to its use. Beadle and King gloss the term "livery" as "permission," and the *Middle English Dictionary* defines it more specifically as "a document authorizing the release of animals," citing the above line from the pageant as the only example of this sense. However, in listing the more conventional definition of livery as "the official garb of a guild" or "the membership of a guild or company," the *MED* may offer another meaning relevant to the play.[15]

If we apply this sense of the term to the *Entry,* then the pageant configures the town as a place where only those marked with authorizing signs of membership are readily welcomed and entitled to "common" goods.

This situation is suggestive of the exclusionary labor practices operating within medieval York itself. The artisan guilds were insistent on restricting their commercial pursuits and privileges only to those individuals who were official members of the organization. The guild records betray a particular anxiety about "foreigners," a term that could apply not only to people from other nations or towns, but also to anyone who was not a member of a guild.[16] With respect to the former group, the city in 1419 enacted a law preventing foreigners from holding civic office: "nulli Scoti nec aliqui alii alienigene, habitantes . . . libertatem civitatis hujus . . . occupent officia scrutatorum, constabulariorum aut aliqua alia officia civitatis" [no Scots or any other alien, holding . . . the freedom of this city . . . should occupy the office of searchers, constables or any other office of the city].[17] Viewing such people as a threat to the common good, the law adds that "nec intrabunt nec venient in aulam communem vel aliqua alia loca civitatis, sub pena imprisonamenti xl dierum, ad videndum vel audiendum secreta consilia vel negocia hujus civitatis" [neither will they enter or come into the common court or any other place of the city, under pain of imprisonment for forty days lest they might see or hear the secret plans or business of this city].[18] In this case York's political space is made inaccessible to those who lack "livery" as native citizens of England. These people should not be privy to the secrets of the governmental elite.

The ordinances of the walkers and glasiers impose a different kind of civic restriction as they seek primarily to prevent non-guild members from practicing their trade. Understanding the term "foreign" with regard to guild membership, the ordinances of the walkers (1463/4) stipulate that

> it is this day ordeyned, establisshed and by common assent agreed, that no man of this citee delyvere any clothe within the fraunchesse therof to any foreyn walker to full or to wirk, nor noo clothe fulled or wroght by any foreyne walker of any mannes of this citee risseyue within the fraunchesse o payne of ij s., to be forfaite als oft tymez as any suche persone doo the contrarie.[19]

The glasiers' ordinances of the same year similarly mandate that "no maister of the said craft supporte any maner of foreyner within this citee or without ayeinst any other maister in any point concerning the wele, worship and proffecte of the same craft, opayne of leisyng of xiij s. iiij d."[20] This legislation clearly attempts to protect the interests of craftsmen who work within the guild system and seek to retain a monopoly on their trade. However, it offers economic benefits to these workers at the expense of others. As legislation for artisans who comprise the commons of the city, such ordinances notably demarcate the precise boundaries of commonality, limiting specific occupations, spaces, and materials to specific types of people whose "livery" grants them access to such things.

While it does not present exactly the same scenario, the debate about the ass in the *Entry* similarly exposes the exclusionary posture of the town. It also reveals how conflicting claims to commonality potentially undermine the very meaning of the term. As we have seen, Peter and Phillip have different views of the "common" goods they seek. The porter complicates things further by initially treating the apostles as foreigners, who do not have access to goods that are available to recognized members of the town. The porter's reluctance is thus an indication that notions of commonality are often constrained by the community's endorsement of socially divisive policies. While, as Nissé explains, the porter is eventually persuaded to hand over the beast, it is Jesus's status as a prophet that goes a long way toward convincing him to do so. How might the process of civic rule by negotiation take place if it were a truly ordinary person who claimed need of the common goods? Jesus's triumphant entry, which ostensibly provokes civic unity and collective affirmations of his authority, is made possible only after an extended dispute that exposes the instability of these very concepts. The play thus shows how forms of commonality, community, and collectivity are ultimately defined by social and hermeneutic conflict.

The *Entry* makes this observation about community more apparent as it turns to explore the social relations between the rich and the poor, the politically prominent and the socially marginal. The porter declares his intention to proclaim Christ's coming to everyone, "ȝonge and olde in ilke a state" (107). However, he directs his subsequent announcement solely to the chief citizens, to the "lordyngis gaily dight" in the kind of sumptuous clothing that was likely to have been produced by the Skinners (115). The porter courteously addresses the lords by asking God to "kepe [them] in [their] semelyté / And all honoure" (116–17). While his greeting is certainly conventional, it significantly calls attention to the burgesses' elevated status. As they affably discuss their knowledge of Jesus and related tales of his miraculous acts, a sense of cohesion evolves among the chief citizens.

Their conversation develops into a form of civic discourse that further shapes the individual burgesses into a collectivity. They establish a common understanding of Christ's identity and develop a fitting response to his arrival. In so doing, the burgesses go from recognizing Christ as a prophet to naming him as their sovereign (127–88). Their individual statements are thus transformed into a covenant that establishes their common assent to "meete Christ as [their] own kyng, / And kyng him call" (172–73). As Nissé's careful reading of this episode shows, the "burgesses' will is figured as a form of mutual persuasion, a disavowal of any factions in favor of perfect hermeneutic clarity."[21] It is indeed striking to see how easily they reach consensus on an issue as important as kingship, especially when the king teaches "agaynste [their] lawis [they] used so lang" (144). In contrast to the play's earlier episode, the burgesses offer a model of political accord founded on absolute hermeneutic transparency.

As they stand gathered awaiting Jesus, the action shifts to his procession into the city. When he enters York/Jerusalem, however, Christ encounters a form of community that appears to be very different from the unified civic body that has just been constructed. At this point the play presents a world inhabited by socially marginal figures, and in so doing it relocates the gospel setting, placing events that happened in Jericho within the city of Jerusalem. The *Entry* goes on to recount gospel episodes that are central to both William Taylor's promotion of labor and the wider theory of discriminate almsgiving.[22] The play thus describes how Christ heals the blind man and the lame man, but it notably also expands on the gospel stories to include a poor man in its list of characters.[23] While this inclusion may not seem especially notable, it is significant in the context of late medieval poverty debates and antifraternal readings of Luke 14. Recall that such readings consistently exclude the poor as a discrete category of deserving need, stipulating that alms should be given only to the poor who are also lame and blind. By including a poor man who is entirely separate from the lame and blind characters, the *Entry* acknowledges the reality of able-bodied need and thus refuses to accept the assumptions of antifraternal discourse and post-plague labor legislation. The resources of theater powerfully give a human form and a living presence to a category of poverty that is repeatedly occluded in these discursive arenas. With a poor character standing before the audience and other actors, the representational strategies of theater ensure that the man's need cannot be denied just because there are lame and blind characters in the scene as well.

While the actor's physical presence alone conveys the reality of able-bodied need, it does not ensure the sympathetic portrayal of such a figure. For instance, if the antifraternal writers of chapter three were to stage this pageant, their representation of an able-bodied poor man would undoubtedly seek to expose the character's fraudulence and illegitimacy.[24] The *Entry*, however, is not concerned with disproving the validity of the poor man's need or associating his poverty with moral corruption. Indeed, the pageant is striking for emphasizing the poor man's decided lack of sinfulness. His dramatic performance consists of the charitable work he undertakes in helping the blind man get Christ's attention. When he observes the blind man's confusion about the noise and gathering crowd, the poor man immediately approaches him and asks, "Man, what ayles þe to crye? / Where wolde þou be? Þou say me here" (295–96). He continues to assist the blind man, advising him on Christ's precise location and coaching him on the best way to make himself known: "Loo, [Jesus] is here at þis same place. / Crye faste on hym, loke þou be bolde, / With voyce right high" (318–20). As he aids the blind man, the poor man also functions as a foil for Peter and Phillip who react to the man's crying with annoyance and disdain (330–33). The poor man becomes recognizable as a figure for Christ since he, like Jesus himself, ministers to the blind beggar with love and mercy. The poor character is not interested in wheedling gold or alms from Jesus, but rather serves as an interpreter and advocate for the blind man. His assistance proves to be instrumental in enabling him to win Christ's attention and healing touch.

It is perhaps troubling, however, that the poor man does not have his own personal encounter with Christ. The pageant text shows Jesus interacting with the blind and lame, yet he does not speak directly to the poor man. This lack of explicit interaction could potentially be interpreted as Christ's disregard or even his disdain for the able-bodied poor. Yet the play also allows for this lack of interrelation to be viewed in a more favorable light. In this sense, Christ's failure to interact with the poor man suggests that poverty is not a condition or defect that requires divine healing. This notion would certainly oppose Taylor's arguments that Jesus healed the blind and lame beggars in order to put them to work.[25]

The resources of dramatic representation also allow for the possibility that Christ does respond favorably to the poor man. Indeed, the costumes of both characters, if made to be similar, could signal a telling identification between the son of God and the average poor person who gets no special treatment in daily life. Furthermore, Christ might signal his affection for the poor man through nonverbal signs. Within the performance, a telling look, a quick embrace, or even the touch of a hand might affirm the play's seemingly sympathetic portrayal of this character. Overall, what remains important is that the *Entry* does not display anxiety about the poor man's legitimacy or productive value. Rather, the character confirms a discrete category of able-bodied poverty, he charitably serves to enable one of Jesus's miracles, and he demonstrates that Christ's mission extends beyond the eradication of need.

The miraculous healing of the lame and the blind gives way to Christ's exchange with Zaccheus and the play's final representation of the city's burgesses. This shift in concentration, on the one hand, emphasizes Christ's unifying power as he extends his attention and blessing to the wealthy sector of society including the rich tax collector and the chief citizens of the city. On the other hand, this shift in focus is so extreme that it creates an image of society radically divided into exclusive spheres of rich and poor. This polarized representation restricts notions of consensus and harmony to discrete arenas and thus undermines any sense of a truly unified social body within the world of the play.

In presenting Christ's exchange with Zaccheus, the play continues to focus on gospel passages central to Franciscanism and wider debates about fraternal mendicancy. The *Entry,* though, more conspicuously distances itself from the most controversial issues as it omits Christ's fraught request or command to stay in Zaccheus's house. Given this omission,

Christ's protracted conversation with Zaccheus more readily accords with traditional commentaries on the gospel story that emphasize the conversion Zaccheus experiences.[26] Nevertheless, his transformation still significantly keeps the subject of poverty at the forefront of the play. The tax collector's dramatic movement toward penitence entails material satisfaction, and Zaccheus announces that he will make restitution for his sins by giving half of his goods to the poor and repaying the people whom he has cheated (449–53).

Zaccheus's promise to give so generously to the needy is certainly praiseworthy, but, in the performance of this particular pageant, his pledge contains some potentially disturbing undertones. Because the audience would have just seen an actual poor character helping the blind man, Zaccheus's promise of almsgiving may come across as somewhat empty, for it is directed at a seemingly theoretical contingent of the poor. At the moment when the tax collector proclaims his charitable intentions and calls to mind the suffering of the needy, the play would seem to highlight the absence of these very people. While the scripture similarly de-emphasizes any direct connection between Zaccheus and the poor, the audience watching the play might be inclined to wonder where the socially marginal figures from the previous scene have gone. Have they left the performance area to make way for the wealthy figures of the pageant? Do they stand at the margins of the "stage" as silent observers to the action taking place? If the latter possibility is the case, does Zaccheus have any awareness of the poor man's presence and his need? Would he perhaps gesture to the poor man to come with him, or would the tax collector ignore this particular individual in order to give alms at a later time to other people, perhaps focusing personally on those he has wronged?

As these questions suggest, the staging allows for possibilities that either affirm or mitigate against the rigid social division that structures the pageant as a whole. Thus, the staging potential could make Zaccheus's promise into a merely theoretical profession of charity or an actual act of giving to one's needy neighbors. However it might have been staged, what remains clear is that the poor man and the other marginal figures do not regain a voice in the play; rather, as both performance and text, the *Entry* becomes much more interested in presenting the civic recognition of Christ as king and exploring how that recognition takes place in the sphere of wealth and political power inhabited solely by the burgesses.

The last section of the *Entry* marks the play's progression fully into the arena of wealth and prominence associated with the burgesses and their elite form of government. Significantly, the historical evolution of the pageant text also generates this movement into the world of wealth and power. In its account of the play, the 1415 *Ordo Paginarum* lists that six rich men and six poor men should play the citizens gathered to welcome Christ.[27] The extant manuscript, however, alters this original list of characters by removing the poor men and including only eight rich citizens. As Nissé states, the original cast featuring both rich and poor men "leaves us with a tantalizing trace of a play that took all strata of the urban community into account as public figures, allowing for at least the rhetorical representation of poor artists and possibly for even poorer unemployed or homeless people." In contrast the later play text "presents the mercantile class as fully in charge of public discourse."[28] Indeed, the play concludes with a powerful representation of unity and collectively authorizing speech, but it confines these only to the wealthy citizens who each hail Christ in acknowledgement of his role as king, healer, and savior.

The significance of this final episode has been debated by critics who find that it offers potentially different political implications. Considering the role of the burgesses in relation to the governmental structure of York, Martin Stevens views this triumphant ending as a flattering affirmation of the oligarchs' power and rhetorical skill.[29] Nissé, however, argues that the burgesses' speech has subversive connotations. She views the artisans' portrayal of these elite figures as a potential appropriation of their governmental roles. The craftsmen, Nissé argues, "claim [their rhetorical and political] skills for themselves" by performing as effective civic leaders. This form of representation consequently "strains[s] the play's implicit ideological division between imagined and practiced rule."[30] Nissé's reading usefully complicates previous interpretations of the play, but the *Entry* is perhaps less radical than she suggests in destabilizing the political hierarchy. This becomes evident if we consider power dynamics beyond the artisan/merchant relationship. While artisans were undoubtedly excluded from the city's elite governmental body, they too belonged to a restrictive guild system that excluded women, unskilled workers, itinerant laborers, and the poor. These groups, which were denied guild membership, were not an insignificant sector of York's population. According to Swanson, "The majority of town dwellers were poor. Right at the bottom of the social pile was a broad category including the sick and elderly, vagrants and beggars, prostitutes, widows and underemployed or unemployed laborers."[31]

Whether one sees the burgesses of the *Entry* strictly as a flattering representation of the governmental elite or as the artisans' subversive appropriation of authority, we would do well to remember that neither of these perspectives acknowledges the reality of the poor.[32] This is the case because the guild structure renders this category of people entirely invisible as it "comprehends only skilled manufacturing by men."[33] The guilds, furthermore, "overwhelmingly catered for the respectable and excluded the very poor."[34] Indeed, the members of such societies, in the words of Gervase Rosser, "strove to dissociate themselves from the permanent marginals, the terminally poor. . . . [A]pprehension about this gloomy world (of poverty) was, indeed, one of the circumstances which gave such weight to the value of guild membership."[35] While the guilds thus offered a means of separating its members from society's most marginal figures, the *Entry* pageant brings such people to the center of the city's streets in an official celebration of Christ's body. In the play, the poor, blind, and lame men are just as integral to Christ's entry as are the burgesses who ultimately name him as king.

However, the pageant implicitly critiques the social divisions between these groups by dividing the play into disconnected spheres of poverty/social marginality and wealth/political power. As we have seen, the *Entry* provocatively calls attention to an often overlooked contingent of the needy by including a poor character who is distinct from his blind and lame companions. But the pageant stops there, allowing the figure to disappear from the text. Just as the opening scene reveals the conflicts and tensions that define the apostolic community, the play as a whole offers a deeply fragmented portrait of society. In its overall structure, Christ's exchange with socially marginal figures is sandwiched between the burgesses' formal declarations of his authority. Without any interaction between these sets of characters, the pageant's configuration emphasizes how certain voices are excluded from official regimes of power and wealth.[36] At the triumphant end of the play, it is again worth asking, where is the poor man? Why does he not speak words of welcome and authorization to Christ? How can we understand the unifying social ideal of Corpus Christi when Christ enters a city that seems more like two distinct places inhabited by separate classes of citizens divided into rich and poor?

The Labor of Crucifixion

Marking the liturgical and dramatic beginning of the passion, the *Entry* leads to the plays' subtle exploration of the legal, political, and social processes by which Christ comes to be crucified. For this reason, the *Entry* is often seen as the pinnacle of a form of social unity that immediately begins to unravel in the following pageants. Stevens, for instance, describes the passion plays as "an urban nightmare of . . . utter disorder."[37] Nissé similarly argues that the *Entry*'s "consensus disintegrates into political and hermeneutic tyranny."[38] While the passion plays certainly depict the horrific consequences of misrule, the *Crucifixion* offers a remarkable, if surprising, image of social cohesiveness formed around the naked, needy, and suffering Christ. Turning now to this pageant, I shall explore how the *Crucifixion* critiques the cultural idealization of labor associated with the anti-poverty ethos traced in this book. While the late medieval discourses of poverty often present labor as a panacea for all social and moral ills, the *Crucifixion* ironically locates an industrious solidarity among workers in the very moment that they perform Christianity's most violent act.

The *Crucifixion* has been troublesome to critics seeking to understand the precise relationship between a guild's sponsorship of a pageant and the content of the pageant itself. Considering the "trade symbolism" of the play, many critics have noted that the pinners are not really affirmed or applauded for performing the work of crucifixion. Stevens remarks that "the trade symbolism does not elevate" the public perception or status of the pinners.[39] Kathleen Ashley also comments that in the *Crucifixion* "the very skills claimed by the producing guilds are shown . . . in a negative light."[40] Because such gruesome labor does not confirm the purity or goodness of the pinners' trade, critics have largely understood the guild's role in the play as a catalyst for penance. J.W. Robinson has raised the possibility that "the sinful craftsmen were publicly acknowledging their sin" in the performance of the play.[41] Other critics such as Stevens argue that this awareness of sin extends not only to the guild members but to the audience as well, so that all people must acknowledge "human culpability in the death of Christ."[42]

In foregrounding the action of the soldiers, the pageant does deliberately work to create an identification between the audience and those who crucify Christ (rather than a connection between the audience and Christ himself).[43] But the above readings perhaps oversimplify that relation and work from a reductive understanding of penance. In their view the single enactment of crucifixion seems to impel contrition for a specific group of people. Rejecting such cause and effect readings, Ashley points out that "the issue of where the producers or audience members found their subject positions in this play cannot be resolved so simply and constructively."[44] In their attempts to view the play's labor as somehow productive, sanctifying, or worthy, critics have tended to close off other interpretative possibilities for the pageant. Ashley's reading of the play offers a notable exception in concentrating on "its workplace politics and its ethic of diligence and ingenuity." Developing aspects of her view that the pageant actually scrutinizes "the work ethic itself,"[45] I want to explore in some detail how the play exposes problems within the contemporary labor system and particularly reveals that there are dangers inherent in seeing labor as an unquestionably moral act. The *Crucifixion* exposes that there are liabilities associated with industrious, hierarchically minded labor; it demonstrates how a divided and fully compliant work force might come at the expense of other values emphasizing the meaning and ethical implications of one's occupation.

The opening scene of the *Crucifixion* offers an idealized account of workers seeking to fulfill the demands of their lords as efficiently and thoroughly as possible. In the very first lines of the play, a soldier urges his companions to begin the task commanded to them by their superiors. Speaking as a kind of anti-waster—as a person who seems desperately eager to get to work—he says:

Sir knyghtis, take heede hydir in hye
This dede on dergh we may noght drawe.
Зee woote youreselffe als wele as I
Howe lordis and leders of owre lawe
Has geven dome þat þis doote schall dye.
(1–5)

The play conveys an immediate sense of the soldiers' place in the political hierarchy; and it begins with an urgent call not to waste any time in performing the labor of crucifixion. The other soldiers respond in a remarkable spirit of cooperation: each voices his assent and readiness to obey the "lordis and leders of [their] lawe."

The opening of the *Crucifixion* goes on to parallel the idealized scene of labor that initiates the half-acre episode in *Piers Plowman*. This becomes especially clear when the second soldier echoes the language of Langland's text in proposing that they divide the work equally among themselves: "Sir, alle þare counsaile wele we knawe. / Sen we are comen to Caluarie / Latte ilke man helpe now as hym awe" (6–8).[46] The other soldiers affirm this industrious spirit and proclaim their desire to get to work at once:

III Miles: We are alle redy, loo,
Þat forward to fullfille.
IV Miles: Late here howe we schall doo,
And go we tyte þertille.
(9–12)

Within the imaginary of antifraternal discourse and post-plague labor legislation, the soldiers function as ideal laborers. They express both a will to work and a clear awareness of their place in the social order. These laborers would thus be very likely to earn the approval of their guild masters, or perhaps win praise from other familiar figures including Pierce the Ploughman, Richard FitzRalph, and William Taylor.

After this initial speech, the play verges on hyperbole as it continues to portray the soldiers as incredibly eager and industrious laborers. They repeatedly call attention to the immediacy of their work and how its fulfillment will earn them honor and praise from their lords, symbolic rewards that seem to suffice for wages or any other material compensation. These men are clearly not the type of late medieval workers who threatened their employers' financial interests by seeking excessive wages or feigning poverty so as to acquire alms. The repetition of the soldiers' compliant speech demonstrates how persistently the play develops their characters as ideal laborers. The first soldier declares, "It may noȝt helpe her for to hone / If we schall any worshippe wynne" (13–14). And in the dialogue that follows, each of the other soldiers speaks his turn once again, giving his verbal assent to undertake the project of crucifixion. In a parody of the consensus reached by the burgesses of the *Entry*, the soldiers establish the importance and urgency of their labor. They declare,

> II Miles: He muste be dead nedelyngis by none.
> III Miles: Þanne is goode tyme þat we begynne.
> (15–16)

Several lines later, they add:

> I Miles: Thanne to þis werke vs muste take heede,
> So þat oure wirkyng be noght wronge.
> II Miles: None other noote to neven is nede
> But latte vs haste hym for to hange.
> (25–28)

The fourth soldier sums up their enthusiasm, exclaiming, "Commes on, late kill þis traitoure strange" (32).

The soldiers' dialogue may perhaps seem ironic since they talk about the immediacy of their work instead of just getting on with it. But any irony is short-lived as they agree to put an end to their conversation and direct their attention to the project at hand. A flurry of activity then ensues when the third soldier states that he has already "gone for gere goode speede, / Bothe hammeres and nayles large and lange" (29–30). Making sure that everything has been prepared as efficiently as possible, they seek to perform their labor with skill. The soldiers thus proclaim, "Sen ilke a thyng es right arrayed, / The wiselier nowe wirke may we"

(37–38). And later, as they begin their task, the first soldier announces, "now work we wele" (48).

After the soldiers make such fervent proclamations of their ability and eagerness to work, the play evolves into a detailed and myopic exploration of the mechanical labor of crucifixion. With Christ giving only two brief speeches in the entire play, the *Crucifixion* focuses almost wholly on the issue of work. As Beckwith puts it, the *Crucifixion* "is famously a pageant about making: the making of the central icon of late medieval Christianity, the body of Christ."[47] As the soldiers obsessively attempt to fulfill the commands of their masters, they exhibit a spirit of partnership and amicable industriousness. Parodying the notion of the community as Corpus Christi, the soldiers come together at the site of Christ's body to lay him on the cross. Working interdependently, each takes responsibility for securing a different part of his body:

> II Miles: Nowe, certis, I schall noȝt fyne
> Or His right hande be feste.
> III Miles: Þe lefte hande þanne is myne—
> Late see who beres hym beste.
> IV Miles: Hys lymmys on lenghe þan schalle I lede,
> And even vnto þe bore þame bringe.
> I Miles: Vnto his heede I schall take hede,
> And with myne hande helpe hym to hyng.
> (81–88)

The divisive and horrific action of Christ's crucifixion begins here with the unity and cooperation of the soldiers performing their civic duty. As they work congenially to secure Christ to the cross, the soldiers create what Beckwith has aptly termed "a perverted community of effort and action."[48]

It is important to acknowledge that the soldiers' work of crucifixion is theologically necessary, ensuring Christ's ultimate redemption of humanity. The play cannot, then, blame the soldiers for following their orders; nor can it expect them to rebel against their leaders, somehow anticipating the consequences of their labor before divine history could make such effects apparent. While it accepts these theological mandates, the play nonetheless acknowledges the horrors of Christ's crucifixion however necessary or ultimately beneficial to humankind. Just as the trial plays examine the flawed legal procedures that produce Christ's eventual condemnation, the *Crucifixion* questions the means by which human beings become capable of acting on such a verdict. In re-creating Christ's life, persecution, and death, the plays cannot help but ask, if Jesus came to the city of York today, would we condemn him all over again?

As we have seen, the primary way that the play imagines the most significant act in Christian history is to render it as an idealized form of labor, an ideal that is also central to the late medieval period's antipoverty ethos. The soldiers perform this portentous and deeply violent act because it is work ordered by their masters whom they serve with utmost obedience. In portraying this scenario, the *Crucifixion* evokes contemporary labor practices within York itself. Emphasizing their unity and their narrowly focused work, the pageant presents the soldiers as if they were members of a medieval guild specializing in the work of crucifixion. Like the city's craftsmen, the soldiers work under the supervision of masters; as the play emphasizes the hierarchical nature of their labor, it replicates a social order based on the vertical ties binding craftsmen, searchers, and the governmental elite. While it bears repeating that the work of crucifixion is necessary, it is perhaps the one form of labor that might licitly be performed with reluctance or resistance. But the soldiers, as we have seen, approach their work eagerly and industriously with little awareness of its implications and potential effects. The play thus exposes a problem relevant to the contemporary labor system: the extremely narrow focus on a single occupation occludes the wider significance of the work itself and obfuscates forms of social unity not bound by strictly hierarchical relations between laborers and their masters. Like the *Entry* pageant, then, the *Crucifixion* entails a striking social divide: the laborers are in no way aware that the poor man they are charged with crucifying might be a human being at the very least worthy of their consideration and recognition as such.

In treating the horrific action of crucifixion as if it were routine labor,[49] the soldiers refuse to acknowledge their work in personal or human terms. When they first attempt to nail Christ to the cross, they are subsumed with practical concerns about effectively completing their task. They initially realize, for example, that the holes in the cross have been measured incorrectly. As the third soldier acknowledges that the cross "was ouer-skantely scored," he does not accept blame for the inaccurate measurements but implicitly suggests that someone else has provided them with faulty materials (111). The soldiers do not give up their work in anger or frustration, but use their ingenuity to continue laboring productively and cooperatively. If the holes do not fit Christ's body, then they decide to make Christ's body fit the holes. Viewing Jesus both as a kind of prop in their labor and as the raw material,[50] the first soldier devises a plan to fasten Christ to the cross. He says to the others, "Why carpe ȝe so? Faste on a corde / And tugge hym to, by toppe and taile" (113–14). They continue to work together stretching Christ's hands into the right position. After they accomplish this task, the fourth soldier logically suggests, "Go we all foure thanne to his feete, / So schall oure space be spedely spende" (123–24). As he proposes an order for their labor, the soldier notably figures the work of crucifixion as a productive activity, as a way to "spend their space" usefully so as to prevent any kind of wasting.

As the soldiers begin to nail Jesus to the cross, they make it clear that they seek to manufacture a product that will meet the expectations and standards of their lords.[51] While stretching Jesus to make his feet meet the bores, the first soldier urgently says, "Haue done, dryue in þat nayle, / *So þat no faute be foune*" (141–42, my emphasis). In a statement that recalls the practice of searching a guild's manufactured goods, the soldier insists on producing "quality" work with no identifiable imperfections. The Carpenters' ordinances (1482) provide useful examples of the punitive laws regarding the searchers' discovery of faulty work:

> yf ony wyrk ony wark within this cite, libertes and precintes of the same, ony thing pertenyng to the said occupacion of wryghtes, that is unsuffciently, unabill, and unwarkmanly wrought, that the sersours of the said occupacion at the desyr of the awner of the same wark shall serch it, and yf it be foundyn unsufficiently wroght be the syght of the said sersowrs, he or tha that heryn be foundyn defective shall as oft tyms as tha be foundyn defective forfate vj s. viij d., in the form abovesaid to be payd and devydyd; and ouer this, he that is so defective shall make sufficient amendes to the pairte tharby grevyd or hurt.[52]

The ordinances also stipulate that faulty work must be reported to the mayor:

> yf the sersowrs of the said occupacion fynd a defaute in the said occupacion and present it not to the mair and the chamberlayns for the tym being, that the sersour shall for hys consillment as oft tyms as he thar in is foundyn defective forfate to the wele of the communalte oft hys cite xl d.[53]

As these ordinances demonstrate, labor practices in York were carefully scrutinized and monitored by the searchers and the governmental body itself. Faulty work would not go unpunished, and the culpable laborer was required to make financial and material restitution to both the city and the individuals he wronged. The searchers as well were subject to the authority of the mayor and chamberlains, who sought to ensure that they would consistently enforce the city's labor regulations.

Significantly, the soldiers in the *Crucifixion* do not seem bothered by the regulatory practice of searching; rather, they actively seek approval from their lords for their industrious labor. After nailing Christ to the cross, the fourth soldier is so eager to show the end-product to their sovereigns that he forgets that they have yet to elevate the cross. Desperate to prove their loyalty and to display their accomplishment, he exclaims, "I wille goo saie to oure souueraynes / Of all þis werkis howe we haue wrought" (151–52). This hyper-industrious work ethic seems to preclude the need for searchers altogether.[54]

Because they are concerned primarily with the opinions of their lords, the soldiers do not really consider their work in any moral or social terms beyond showing obedience to their sovereigns. It is perhaps unfair to expect them to recognize their own culpability in the death of a man who would ultimately prove to be their savior; yet it is also striking to see how the play eradicates the soldiers' potential empathy for Christ as a poor man subject to a gruesome punishment. Any hope for compassion is consistently subsumed within the soldiers' desire to flaunt their obedience and industriousness by manufacturing a crucified body.

The play thus shows how the focus on work functions as a distancing mechanism that allows the soldiers to separate themselves from the ethical reality of Jesus's death. In her reading of the *Crucifixion* and other plays depicting Christ's bodily suffering, Claire Sponsler comments on the concrete and explicit nature of the soldiers' violent treatment of Christ: "To a striking degree the violence against Christ is personalized, staged as the actions of individual agents, not as an anonymous exercise in abstract power, an emphasis that again calls attention to the operations of power embodied in real individuals."[55] While the *Crucifixion* does present personalized forms of violence, it also foregrounds work and hierarchical obedience as means of abstracting the soldiers and audience from the extreme brutality that is enacted. In performing their work, the soldiers, as we have seen, consistently construe horrific acts of torture as elements of routine labor. For instance, as they attempt to nail Jesus to the cross, the second soldier focuses only on the mechanical aspects of his work: "here is a stubbe will stiffely stande, / Thurgh bones and senous it schall be soght— / This werke is wele, I will warande" (102–4). Essentially, the soldier is focused on the process of crucifixion as a craft, not as an act of violence per se. Praising the durability of his tools, he perceives the mechanical attachment of flesh to wood as good work done in the service of his lords. While they sometimes revel in increasing Christ's pain, they generally show little awareness of Christ as a suffering human being. Seeking to attach a body to a cross, they labor under the assumption that "It is no force how felle he feele" (135).

The soldiers' narrow-minded regard for the details and outcome of their labor reaches its peak when they elevate Christ's body. This moment represents the height of the symbolic and moral significance of the crucifixion; it also invokes an image of Christ as an utterly needy being. In *Piers Plowman,* for example, Nede locates Christ's most extreme destitution at the moment of crucifixion: "he þat wrouhte al þe worlde was willefolliche nedy, / Ne neuere noen so nedy ne porore deyede" (XX.49–50). Similarly, in *The Book of Margery Kempe,* recall that Christ reassures Kempe in her own poverty by referring to the greater severity of his neediness at the time of his death: "Dowtyr, thu art not yet so powr as I was whan I heng nakyd on the cros for thy lofe, for thu hast clothys on thy body, and I had non" (97). While the Jesus of York's *Crucifixion* pageant is also naked and utterly destitute, the soldiers remain oblivious to his neediness and suffering.[56] This is made clear as the pageant ironically focuses on the soldiers' hardship in attempting to raise the cross.[57] Although they are initially worried that they will be unable to lift the object, the soldiers decide not to ask for help and proudly undertake the project on their own (169–75). As if they alone are skilled practitioners in the "art" of crucifixion, the soldiers maintain their cooperative work ethic and position themselves at the four ends of the cross so as to bear the weight equally (174–84). In a darkly comic scene, the play then presents a drawn-out account of the soldiers' suffering and complaints:

> I Miles: For-grete harme haue I hente,
> My schuldir is in soundre.
> II Miles: And sertis I am nere schente,
> So lange haue I borne vndir.
> III Miles: This crosse and I in twoo muste twynne,
> Ellis brekis my bake in sondre sone.
> (189–94)

The play highlights the soldiers' total insensitivity as their histrionic complaints stand in stark contrast to Jesus's silent suffering.

Outraged at the difficulty of their labor, the soldiers blame Christ for casting a spell to inhibit their strength. Once they are able to lift him, they retaliate against Jesus by allowing the cross to fall forcefully into the mortise "so all his bones / Are asoundre nowe on sides sere" (223–24). As this incident shows, when the soldiers finally give any consideration to Christ, they do so only with the purpose of increasing his suffering. Even this brutal attention, however, is short-lived, and the soldiers quickly turn away from Christ to focus on the mechanics of their labor. Faced once again with defective materials for which they claim no responsibility, the soldiers notice that the hole is too large to support the cross (229–32). As they seek to stabilize it by hammering in wedges, the play presents yet another occasion of the soldiers' cooperative labor and thereby postpones the climatic recognition that Christ has actually been crucified.

After the soldiers finish their "job," they taunt Christ by asking if he approves of their work. His powerful response functions as the climax of the play by calling both the soldiers and the entire audience to recognize the grave implications of the labor that has been so earnestly performed throughout the pageant. As Beckwith remarks, "The action is belatedly separated from the perception of its effect, increasing the emphasis on what has been done."[58] Demanding the public's attention, Christ commands "al men þat walkis by waye or strete" to stop (253). In the performance of the *Crucifixion,* one can imagine the actor's words powerfully capturing the attention of various people in York who might be selling food and drink or moving among the various pageant stations. The crucified Christ of the York plays offers a contrast to the relentlessly productive version of Jesus in antifraternal discourse.[59] He seeks to interrupt the people's busy comings and goings to insist that they look at his needy and naked body in order to acknowledge both his suffering and their implication in it. Christ puns on the notion of "travail" as a form of both suffering and work, when he commands, "Takes tente ȝe schalle no trauayle tyne" (254). In one sense, Christ insists that the audience pay attention so that they will not disregard his travail or suffering. In another sense, however, Christ also demands that they pay attention so that they will not neglect the spiritual travail or the penitential work of recognizing for themselves the crucifixion's significance.[60]

Jesus then commands "all men" to consider his suffering body. He tells them:

> Byholdes myn heede, myn handis, and my feete,
> And fully feele nowe, or ȝe fyne,
> Yf any mournyng may be meete,
> Or myscheue measured vnto myne.
>
> (255–58)

Urging the spectators to see his exposed body, Christ commands the attention and compassion that he has been denied throughout the laborious process of crucifixion. At this moment he is not simply a commodity or the product of the soldiers' work. Rather, he is a speaking and suffering subject. He asks the people not only to think about the magnitude of his suffering but also to consider their involvement in it. As he names the individual parts of his body, Christ implicitly calls out to the different facets of the community. His speech, which evokes 1 Corinthians 12, reminds the audience members that they are a single body connected to one another through Christ's sacrifice and love. This familiar idea finds expression in Thomas Wimbledon's 1388 sermon which declares that "al mankynde is oo body whos kyndely heete is charite, þat is loue to oure God and to oure neyȝebore."[61] Indeed, Christ's powerful speech works to remind the busy passersby that they constitute one body and that "if one member [of the body] suffer any thing, all the members suffer with it."[62]

This message has particular relevance for the soldiers who perceive themselves as dutifully fulfilling their lords' commands by crucifying Christ. Their whole-hearted deference to the hierarchical order generates a narrow sense of community preserved by the soldiers' common labor in destroying a perceived source of social disruption. This notion of community, it should be noted, is not particularly unusual in medieval culture, given the reality of legally sanctioned practices such as the burning of heretics.[63] While the play does not seek to abolish hierarchical regimes or exclusionary measures, it does emphasize the troubling consequences of such models. The soldiers understand community in a restricted form—only as it applies to themselves and their relation to their superiors. The poor and suffering recede from their social and moral consciousness.

In this sense, the play dramatizes one of the major effects of the labor regime in York. As we have seen, artisans labored in a rigidly hierarchical system designed to minimize collective or collaborative interactions among members of different guilds. In establishing a labor structure that fostered division and competition among workers, "the authorities effectively undermined the corporate identity which might develop amongst the artisans as a whole."[64] While the play does not strictly represent the soldiers as contemporary craftsmen victimized by a repressive labor system, it does reveal how their hyper-industrious work ethic fuels an almost compulsive commitment to hierarchy at the expense of even perceiving other relational forms. Given the soldiers' blindness to Christ's poverty and suffering, this play offers no hint at the possibility of corporate identity forming between the artisan laborers and the lower ranks of society. The soldiers instead focus almost exclusively on pleasing their superiors through the labor of crucifixion. The play thus highlights how the soldiers' obsessive attention to the details of work and the production of a satisfactory "commodity" overshadows any examination of the larger motives or consequences of their labor. What finally remains most troubling, then, is not so much the fulfillment of their civic obligations, but the eager narrow-mindedness with which they perform their duty. When Christ asks God to forgive the soldiers because "What þei wirke wotte þai noght" (261), he states what is perhaps the most important lesson of the play. Indeed, the soldiers never fully understand the nature and implications of their work.[65] While they are able to perform the mechanical labor of nailing Christ to the cross and raising his crucified body, their narrow attention to the physical details of work precludes even the slightest awareness of their "craft's" wider significance.

Social Unity and the *Last Judgment*

The York cycle's skepticism concerning idealized views of labor becomes more significant in its final pageant. As the culmination of both the day's events and the whole of cosmological history, the *Last Judgment* offers perhaps the most forceful challenge to the major tenets of the antipoverty ethos explored throughout this book. The play reveals the catastrophic costs of social division and advocates a rigorous form of indiscriminate almsgiving that divorces need from the all important issue of labor. The final pageant builds on the ethical commitments of the *Entry* and the *Crucifixion* as it recognizes the able-bodied poor, calls for the merciful treatment of all needy people, and insists on the absolute interdependence of all Christians. Yet the play's radical perspective on these topics proves to be fascinatingly complicated as it is articulated by the mercers, the wealthiest and most powerful guild in York.[66] Exploring the socioeconomic practices of this group and the wider guild system, we shall see how the play's forceful call to social unity emerges as an anomalous ethical vision that opposes the guilds' own discourses of poverty and charity as these emerge from legal documents pertaining to the production of the plays.

Of all the pageants in the York cycle, the *Last Judgment* places the greatest stress on the significance of almsgiving by enacting the final salvation or damnation of souls based on their charitable deeds. Locating Christ's discussion of the works of mercy (Matthew 25) within the actual moment of the last judgment, the pageant places special emphasis on the absolute importance of aiding the hungry, sick, and naked who make appeals for help. The *Last Judgment* thus shows that the criteria for salvation center around one's response to poverty and need. It makes a direct link to the *Crucifixion* pageant as the crucified Christ reappears in this pageant, displaying his wounded and needy body. The social implications of his sacrifice are made clear in this final play as his body becomes a symbol for the poor as well as the wider community to which they belong. Christ draws attention to the suffering he has endured for humanity. Questioning the community's commitment to charity, he asks his people: How have you sacrificed for me? How have you sacrificed for one another? These questions become especially powerful since the play begins by invoking the *memento mori* tradition in order to remind the audience members of their own impending death (49–56). In this context, the play's ensuing discussion of charity becomes a palpably relevant lesson to the citizens of York gathered to watch the play.[67]

As the play outlines the process of judgment, it espouses a form of charity that is thoroughly generous and quite different from the discriminate forms of charity with which we have become familiar. After selecting and welcoming to heaven the souls who are saved, Christ describes how they consistently and devotedly helped the poor, who as he later explains bear his own identity in their suffering. Recapitulating Matthew 25, Jesus describes their charitable dispositions: "Whenne I was hungery, ȝe me fedde, / To slake my thirste youre harte was free" (285–86). He goes on to recount their charitable actions in greater detail and reveals the seemingly limitless love and generosity impelling their acts of almsgiving. Christ explains that these souls were always ready to give aid under any circumstance:

> When any þat nede hadde, nyght or day,
> Askid ȝou helpe and hadde it sone.
> Youre fre hartis saide þem neuere nay,
> Erely ne late, mydday ne none,

But als ofte-sithis as þe wolde praye,
Þame thurte but bide and haue þer bone.
(311–16)

As he recalls the souls' charitable actions, Christ's language stresses their radically free and open spirit; he explains that they were *always* willing to give to *any* person, at *any* time, in *any* place, however often they were asked. This extreme version of generosity opposes the kind of painstaking concern that drives theories of discriminate almsgiving. In Christ's account, what matters most is the willingness to give, not the discerning impulse to withhold alms from those who may not appear to be truly worthy.

As the souls respond to their designated fates, the play affirms nonselective modes of almsgiving because it presents both groups as completely ignorant of their achievements or failures in charity. Neither group accepts praise or blame for having helped or denied Christ; rather, the play emphasizes the utter incapacity of humans to recognize the Christlike suffering of the poor.[68] Indeed, the play works against a totalizing power of judgment by emphasizing the souls' own ignorance of their deeds. The good souls, for example, question how they acquired the resources to nourish Christ when his power and grace are actually the source of all their possessions and goods (301–4). Another soul then directly asks Jesus when exactly they helped him,

Whanne waste þat we þe clothes brought,
Or visite þe in any nede,
Or in þi sikenes we þe sought?
Lorde, when did we þe þis dede?
(305–8)

Despite their fundamental differences, the damned souls follow the good souls in acknowledging their ignorance about their own response to suffering. They put the following questions to Christ:

I Anima Mala: Whan had þou . . .
Hungir or thirste . . . ?
Whan was þat þou in prisoune was?

> Whan was þou naked or herberles?
> II Anima Mala: Whan was it we sawe þe seke, allas?
> Whan kid we þe þis vnkyndinesse?
> Werie or wette to late þe passe,
> When did we þe þis wikkidnesse?
>
> (349–56)

The bad souls are not cognizant of how their actions affected Christ, and their questions accordingly expose the extreme limitations of human discernment.

In addition to highlighting the souls' incapacity to recognize the "worthiness" of alms recipients, the play does not seek to define meritorious forms of discriminate charity. As he recounts the deeds of the souls, Christ, to be sure, consistently refers to the need of the hungry, sick, and naked who originally asked them for help. However, he does not elaborate or fixate on the precise conditions or causes of their neediness. This perspective obviously contrasts with the writers explored in chapter 3, who acknowledge need only as a consequence of physical disability. Taylor specifically reveals the play's ideological distance from his own view of Matthew 25. After explaining that those who give alms will be rewarded with everlasting life, he names the recipients as "men in prisoun" or those who are "siik wiþ ony of þese þre maner siiknessis specified before."[69] Following the standard gloss of Luke 14, Taylor's allusion to the three types of sickness refers back to the feebleness, lameness, or blindness that prevent men from working and thereby entitle them to take alms.[70] Unlike Taylor's sermon, the *Last Judgment* refuses to stipulate that the hungry, naked, and sick are legitimately needy because they cannot work. It does not confine need to physical disability, nor does it scrutinize the poor people's claim to charity. Rather, the pageant is remarkable in its insistence that the most meritorious form of giving is the most nondiscerning—granting aid at any time or any place to any person who asks.

While the *Last Judgment* recalls the *Crucifixion* in highlighting Christ's body as a site of neediness and suffering, it also recalls the *Entry* in drawing attention to the issue of dominion as applied to Christ's poverty. It is the bad souls who allude to the mendicancy controversies in questioning the legitimacy of Christ's need. Specifically, they express disbelief that Christ could suffer poverty either for himself or in the guise of others. As he asks the following question, one of the bad souls implies that Christ's expansive lordship precludes his experience of poverty: "Whan had þou, lorde þat all thing has, / Hungir or thirste, sen þou God is?" (349–50). The damned soul suggests that need is a condition fundamentally antithetical to Christ's divinity. He therefore proceeds on the assumption that he could not have denied Christ because Christ could not have been needy. The good souls similarly question Christ, but they do not quibble over the reality of his need (301–4). While they indeed perceive Jesus as all powerful, as the source of all their goods and belongings, the good souls convey a feeling of gratitude for his gifts, not a sense of incredulity at his professed poverty. The bad souls, however, articulate a different perception of Christ. Viewing him as all-possessing, they assume that Christ's entitlement to the goods of the world nullifies his experience of need. They seek to defend their lapse in almsgiving with an argument familiar from anti-mendicant discourse that denies their charitable obligation in the first place.

As he sits in judgment Christ rejects the bad souls' attempts to justify their behavior. He enumerates precisely how they failed in charity and presents a stark picture of their consistent rejection and isolation of the poor. Just as the good souls unfailingly gave aid, the bad souls repeatedly ignored or denounced the cries of the needy. Christ exposes how the bad souls, who "wer sette as sirs on benke" chased the poor from their gate so that they "stode þeroute, werie and wette" (327–28). He also exposes their disdain for the underprivileged, common members of the community by stating that the rich neglected to visit him when he was sick, "for [he] was poure" (334). He similarly recalls that when he needed rest and housing, they "with dyntes draffe [him] fro [their] dore" (338). In all, Christ explains how the bad souls witnessed his "mischeffe . . . manyfolde" but always rejected him (345).

In enumerating their consistent denials of almsgiving, Christ implicitly characterizes how a charitable community should function. In place of scrutiny, denial, and isolation, the play imagines a community where the rich are directly aware of the poor and treat them with mercy. The boundaries that keep the needy outside of the rich men's gates, houses, and daily lives must be dissolved. In Christ's vision of community, his sacrifice binds the poor and rich together.[71] While the play does not ultimately seek to abolish forms of hierarchical relation and eradicate the ills of poverty, it nonetheless promotes social unity in demanding the formation of a communal body defined by consistent and concerned interaction between rich and poor.[72] The Christ of the *Last Judgment* urges the audience in York to remedy the social ruptures that characterized his entry into Jerusalem and that led to his crucifixion—events that the Corpus Christi plays make present again and again in the world of performance.

In its compassionate representation of extreme material poverty and in its call for indiscriminate charity, the *Last Judgment* is certainly radical in and of itself, but the pageant becomes even more so when compared to the treatment of poverty and charity in documents pertaining to the merchant and artisan guilds in York. These documents present varied conceptions of poverty and charity that emerge from the main divisions and demands generated by the wider labor system in York. Perhaps most relevant to this study are the documents of the mercers, the guild that performed the *Last Judgment*. This particular guild can be readily differentiated from the other guilds performing the plays since its members comprised the elite mercantile oligarchy that oversaw the regulation of artisan labor. Given their powerful economic and political position, the mercers' commercial practices and the circumstances of the pageant's production offer a fascinating counterpart to the *Last Judgment*'s sympathetic treatment of poverty and its call to charity and social unity.

As critics have pointed out, the mercers performed "the most expensive and elaborate play of all."[73] As the most prosperous guild, they were perhaps the only group who had sufficient financial resources for producing such a lavish play. Highlighting the vast expenses involved in its production, Simon Shepherd and Peter Womack have argued that the play's "apotheosis of the underprivileged needs to be read alongside the surviving props list for the play."[74] In the long list of the guild's costumes, props, and scenery, there are several particularly spectacular objects mentioned including, "ij paire Aungell Wynges with Iren in þe endes"; "A brandreth [?*frame*] of Iren þat god sall sitte vppon when he sall sty [*ascend*] vppe to heuen"; "A heuen of Iren With a naffe of tre [*wooden pulley*]"; "ij peces of rede cloudes & sternes [*stars*] of gold langing to heuen"; "ij peces of blue cloudes payntid on bothe sides"; "iij peces of rede cloudes With sunne bemes of golde & sternes for þe heist of heuen."[75] Featuring sophisticated mechanical apparatuses for God's ascension and an elaborate representation of heaven replete with gold stars and red and blue clouds, the *Last Judgment*'s props list shows that the mercers spared no expense in creating an atmosphere of divine magnificence.[76] This "extravagance," according to Shepherd and Womack, "shows how much the York mercers were prepared to spend on their privileged situation at the top of the Corpus Christi bill."[77]

Focusing on more symbolic reasons for the mercers' assignment to the *Last Judgment* pageant, Stevens argues that this elite guild performed the final play because "the end of a procession was, in fact, the place of greatest honor."[78] A consideration of the play in the larger context of its production by the mercers reveals that the *Last Judgment* functions, at least in part, to display the merchant guild's material wealth and affirm their sense of honor. What does it mean, then, to plead the case of the poor, hungry, and naked through such an elaborate production financed by an elite group of merchants who seek, at least in part, to affirm their own prosperity and reputation?

This question merits further attention and becomes more complicated in light of the mercers' trading practices and the guild's perception of poverty and charity in relation to their business dealings. In his article on the "trade symbolism" of the York cycle, Alan Justice posits a link between the commercial practices of the mercers and the action of the *Last Judgment* pageant. Focusing on the mercers' use of weights in their trade, Justice argues that

> The association of the mercers with the play of judgment appears to be derived from the characteristic tools of the mercer, his weights, which were subject to examination by the searchers of the craft to guarantee the honesty of his dealings. The mercer weighed various goods against his standard weights to determine their value. The action of the Judgment is the weighing of human souls against the standard established by Christ sitting in judgment.[79]

By highlighting the centrality of the weights both in the mercers' trade and the pageant itself, Justice makes an analogy likening the evaluative work of the mercers to that of Christ. Given this implicit parallel, it seems reasonable to question the mercers' authority to judge, their perception of poverty, and their enactment of charity within medieval York. The records in the *York Memorandum Book* for the year 1366 indicate at least one instance in which a mercer refused to allow the searchers to measure the accuracy of his weights, suggesting their fraudulent alteration.[80] As this occasion reminds us, the mercers' acts of judgment, unlike God's, were not infallible, but took place in a quest for profit and political authority.

Indeed, we can see that the mercers' business practices played a central role in the government of York. The city's central governing body was dominated by the mercers, and for much of the time when the plays were performed the major civic offices were virtually shut off to the artisan class. As Swanson explains,

> The mayoralty and the aldermanic bench were packed by merchants who had acquired their administrative experience by dominating the major civic offices, those of sheriff and chamberlain. The power of this mercantile elite could not be challenged by craft groups. On rare occasions a spectacularly successful individual artisan left his own craft to join the merchants and it was as a merchant he then had access to power.[81]

Even Richard Homan, for all of his idealization of Corpus Christi's unifying power, is forced to acknowledge the political dominance of the mercers: "The distribution of political power among the guilds and groups of guilds is balanced to suggest representation of all, but in fact to concentrate power in the hands of the mercers."[82]

The mercers controlled international trade and the wholesale distribution of goods that were needed by the craftsmen, and they consolidated their commercial strength throughout the late fourteenth to mid-fifteenth centuries.[83] While the power balance between merchants and artisans began to shift in the late fifteenth century, the mercers were the predominant economic and political force in late medieval York.[84] Indeed, Dobson concludes that

The York Corpus Christi plays, no doubt like the feast of Corpus Christi itself, were deliberately made to appeal to every sector of English urban and rural society; but in this world their greatest rewards were enjoyed by the mercantile elite of the city. From the late fourteenth century onwards the latter are so unlikely to have been unaware of those rewards that they must surely hold first place as the most influential sponsors, and even initiators, of the greatest annual feat of corporate ritual within their city.[85]

Given the powerful status of the mercers, it is interesting that the guild's charter (1430) complains that they have been afflicted with poverty.[86] This document sheds light on the central functions of the mercers' professional organization. Similar to the guilds of craftsmen, the mercers' guild had two purposes: "the one mercantile and industrial, the other religious and social; the one devoted to fostering the worldly advantage of its members, the other interested mainly in their spiritual welfare."[87] The mercers thus were also known as the fraternity of the Holy Trinity, and, as their account rolls demonstrate, these two aspects of the guild were "entirely interdependent."[88] As it generates a distinctive discourse of poverty and charity, the mercers' charter provides a fascinating example of how the guild's commercial and charitable goals have become amalgamated.

In the document, the mercers seek to acquire substantial lands and rents under the professed claim of dire poverty and the need to establish a charitable refuge for their underprivileged brothers. The charter presents a tale of material loss and misfortune:

> Sciatis quod cum quamplures homines mistere mercerie civitatis nostre Ebor,' abundantes pro tempore et multum locupletes tam in mercibus quam in aliis rebus secularibus, postmodum, per maris infortunium aliosque casus fortuitos, ad tantam devenerint miseriam et inopiam, quod parum aut nichil habuerunt, unde vivere aut se ipsos possent sustinere, nisi elemosina, ope et relevamine Christi fidelium et Deo devotorum. Unde diverse valide et potentes persone mistere predicte ejusdem civitatis, zelo caritatis fervide et accense, id pie intuentes, et ab egestate et miseria hominum predictorum sua viscera non claudentes, terras, tenementa, et redditus infra civitatem

> predictam et suburbia ejusdem seu alibi infra regnum Anglie, ad honorem Dei et in auxilium et relevamen pauperum et indigencium mistere predicte . . . licentia nostra mediante, adquiere proponant ut accepimus.
>
> [Know that whereas many men of the mystery of mercers of our city of York, plentiful for a time and very rich in merchandise as in other worldly things, afterwards, through the misfortune of the sea and other accidents, have come to such misery and want that they have little or nothing from which they might live or sustain themselves, unless by alms, help, and relief of those faithful of Christ and devoted to God. Whence diverse, strong, and powerful people of the said mystery of the same city, inflamed by the zeal of charity, dutifully considering it, and not closing their hearts from the poverty and misery of the said men, propose to acquire that we receive, through our license, lands, tenements, and rents within the said city and the same suburbs or others within the kingdom of England . . . to the honor of God in help and relief of the poor and indigent of the said mystery.][89]

In its declarations of indigence, the charter employs a discourse of poverty that understands need in terms that are very different from the representation of Christ's hunger and thirst in the *Last Judgment.* Here, property acquisition is coded as an act of zealous charity aimed at easing the hardship of the neediest of men. Their alleviation comes not in the *Last Judgment*'s forms of alms, that is, in food, drink, and clothing, but in "lands, tenements, and rents." While positing justificatory causes of its poverty, the guild's claims of need did not necessarily reflect the mercers' actual financial and political situation at the time of this declaration. Sellers exposes the nature of this discrepancy:

> As the mystery had a large membership, it naturally included both the successful and unsuccessful trader, but this exaggerated picture of abject poverty is at variance with the account roll of the society for 1432, which tells a tale of prosperity and expansion. . . . The real state of affairs seems to have been that the mercers of York,

> a flourishing community of merchants carrying on both home and foreign trade, wished to consolidate their financial position.[90]

As Sellers goes on to explain, their expression of poverty is not simply evidence of the mercers' hypocrisy, but a rhetorical strategy central to civic discourse. Just as Wycliffite complaints about needy knights fueled their critique of the church, here the mercers' professed need provides a rationale for the guild's acquisition of additional resources. The guild wished to create an illusion of impoverishment because "if they approached the government, who did not favor the concentration of wealth in the hands of an immortal trading community, with a simple statement of their wishes possible refusal loomed before them. But the amassing of wealth for charitable purposes was not regarded with so much suspicion."[91]

While the disparity between the guild's economic position and their profession of dire need is a conventional element of medieval civic rhetoric,[92] one wonders how this document should be understood in relation to the pageant performed by the mercers. In the context of the guild's business negotiations, the *Last Judgment*'s language of dire need and misery takes on a new meaning that seems quite removed from Christ's oration in Matthew 25. Putting these divergent views of poverty together, we can see how, at the very least, the pageant's call to aid the most marginal members of society exposes the mercers' more restricted arena of professional concern for the advancement of their own communal body.[93] But it is perhaps unfair to note the guild's extremely fluid understanding of poverty without acknowledging that the mercers' production of the play can itself be understood as an act of charity dependent on the guild's wealth and maintenance. After all, regardless of any particular financial agenda pursued by the mercers in their business dealings, their pageant does call attention to people burdened by forms of poverty that were probably quite different from the guild's documentary claims of need. One wonders how medieval audiences might respond to the play's passionate concern for the needy when that concern is articulated by elite civic leaders who oversee a wider socioeconomic system largely at odds with the *Last Judgment*'s daring social vision.

Indeed, the play's conception of poverty, almsgiving, and community remains distinctive when explored in relation to the artisan guilds whose ordinances offer yet another perspective on these issues. The language of poverty and charity becomes even more expansive as the artisan guilds offer their own proclamations of need and pleas for charitable assistance. The records of such guilds present conceptions of poverty and charity that differ from both the mercers' treatment of these subjects and the *Last Judgment*'s enactment of them. In the artisans' unique deployment of these terms, poverty and charity become the troubling consequences of enforced labor divisions and conflicts among craftsmen. The records, then, ultimately reveal how the labor structure in York organizes artisans in such a way as to make the *Last Judgment*'s conceptions of charity and unity unworkable as widespread civic ideals. Before turning to these wider implications, however, it is necessary to show how the artisan guilds generate a distinctive discourse of poverty by presenting the term almost exclusively as the craftsmen's inability to finance a pageant.

This professed financial hardship exposes some of the tensions endemic to Corpus Christi theater and its reliance on rigid divisions among the craft guilds. The artisans' claims of poverty stem at least in part from the city's requirement that individual guilds must sponsor and solely bear the expense of performing an annual pageant. Rife with complaints of indigence, the ordinances of the artisan guilds, as Swanson notes, do not so much reveal the craftsmen's interest in "maintaining a monopoly" but expose their anxiety over "raising adequate funds to pay for the increasingly onerous burden of the pageants."[94] Indeed, over the course of the later fifteenth century and the whole of the sixteenth century, the cost of the plays would have been "increasingly onerous" for most guilds, given what historians have seen as the city's economic collapse.[95] This severe recession was caused in large part by York's loss of prominence in the cloth trade and in shipping.[96] Yet in the examples that follow, we find guild records predating York's economic decline that feature the guilds' consistent expression of poverty in regard to the production of the pageants. While some documents I cite are not dated, my aim here is not so much to identify the precise cause of a guild's poverty as it is to explore how the guilds' documentary expressions of need invoke the Corpus Christi plays and generate a discourse with implications for the plays' conceptions of poverty and charity.

The coopers were one guild that sought to make their neediness clear to the civic government. In a petition to the city, the coopers begin by engaging in a figurative form of begging:

> A lour treshonurable & tresreuerent seignour Meir de la Citee deuerwyk Suppliont treshumblement voz poures conciteinz les Coupers deuerwyk . . . come ils ount tresgraund charge a lours poures estates pur sustiner & mateigner lour pagyne & Iue de y ceste iour de copore christi. (*REED: York,* 2:620)[97]
>
> [To their very honorable and very reverent lord mayor of the city of York, your poor concitizens the coopers of York, entreat very humbly . . . as they have a very great charge against their impoverished state to sustain and maintain their pageant and play of this day of Corpus Christi.](*REED: York,* 2:843–44)

In this explicit declaration of need, the coopers conspicuously name their pageant as a burden that exacerbates their already impoverished status. They continue to elaborate on their indigence and cite as a cause of their poverty their separation from the joiners, a guild that had previously shared with them responsibility for the play. After explaining that "lour artifice & eux mesmes sont trespoures gentz si bien destate come dauoir" [their guild and they themselves are very poor people, so very distressed as to possessions], the coopers also note that "auxint les Iunours qestoient ouesqez eux pur sustiner la dit pagyne sont oustez de eux" [the joiners who were with them to maintain the said pageant have been separated from them] (*REED: York,* 2:620; 2:843–44). The specific complaint about being separated from the joiners gives us a glimpse into the negative consequences of the more widespread divisions among the craft guilds. This instance alone demonstrates how even a single division between two guilds results in increased financial hardship for groups responsible for putting on a pageant.

The craftsmen's experience of poverty is not limited to the coopers, and other guilds similarly create visions of their fallen prosperity compounded by their obligations to York's Corpus Christi theater. The curriers, for instance, describe themselves as "pluis pousez gentz & poures qils soleient ester auaunt ces hures" [people weaker and poorer than they used to be before these times] (*REED: York*, 2:619; 2:843), and they go on to cite their pageant as a cause of further impoverishment.[98] They humbly entreat the mayor "consider le poure estate del artifice des Couuereours . . . coment ils sount chargez ouesqez vne pagyne a tres graundes costages & Importables" [to consider the poor situation of the said guild of the curriers . . . how they are charged with a pageant of very great costs and too grievous to be borne] (*REED: York*, 2:619; 2:843). Even the goldsmiths, one of the wealthiest artisan guilds, find the demands of Corpus Christi theater overwhelming.[99] While they were assigned two pageants, the goldsmiths seek financial support or release from one of their plays by similarly declaring that they have fallen into an impoverished state (1468):

> aurifabri hujus civitatis Ebor' annis preteritis onus grave et expensas excessivas pro duabus paginis suis in ludo Corporis Christi portabant; jamque mundus alteratus est super ipsos, et ipsi plus solito in bonis pauperiores sunt effecti . . . .[et] sectam fecerunt frequentem maioribus et consilio camere pro subsidio habendo in hac parte in suorum importabilium onerum relevamen; vel alias, quod exonerarentur de una paginarum suarum cum causantibus expensis, que ea occasione indies excrescunt, onus utrarumque paginarum suarum non potuerunt sine nimio eorum incommodo diucius sustinere.
>
> [the goldsmiths of the city of York in years past have borne heavy burden and excessive expenses for their two pageants in the Play of Corpus Christi. And now times have changed for them and they have been made poorer in goods than usual . . . and made frequent suit to mayors and the council of the chamber for having aid either as relief of their unsupportable burdens or else that they be relieved of one of their pageants, since, as costs which grow daily on this account explain, they have not been able to sustain the burden of both their pageants any longer undue hardship.][100]

In addition to these bald professions of poverty, there are many other examples of artisan guilds begging the city for relief from the "nowne powere and insufficience" that they claim prohibits their continued sponsorship of a pageant.[101]

Seeking relief from their economic hardship, the guilds that complain of poverty also appeal for an unusual form of charity: they ask the city to command other laborers to contribute money to their pageant. These requests take various forms as guilds seek revenue from a number of sources—from newly installed members of their own guild, from artisans in other guilds infringing on their trade, or from foreigners and non-guild members who similarly encroach on their particular industry. The coopers offer an example of a guild that views its newly advanced members as a potential source of aid. The coopers propose a remedy for their impoverishment by asking,

> Qe please a votre tresbountinouse seignourie en amendment de lour dit artifice ordeigner & suffrer estre registre deuaunt vous qe qiconqez qi desormes fait leuer nouelle shoppe & comence doccupier come mestre en la dite Citee paia a son comencement vj s. viiij d. . . . . pur sustiner lour pagyne auauntdite & ceo en complisement de charitee. (*REED: York,* 2:620)

> [May it please your very bounteous lordship to make amendment of their said guild to ordain and allow to be registered before you that whoever henceforth has raised a new shop and first takes an engagement as master in the said city, will pay at his entry 6 s. 8 d. . . . to maintain their aforementioned pageant, and this as an act of charity.] (*REED: York,* 2:843–44)

Presenting their request explicitly as an act of charity, the guild asks, in effect, that new masters and shopkeepers be taxed in contribution to the increasingly onerous expense of their pageant. While such revenue may have indeed felt like charitable relief to those coopers who were long-established in their trade, it is perhaps unlikely that new masters or shopkeepers would have viewed a mandatory fee with such a spirit of generosity.

In many other cases, charity ironically emerges as the result of conflicts among the artisan guilds, especially those practicing related trades. As we have seen, the divisions that the mercantile oligarchy imposed on craftsmen were highly artificial, and such rigid classifications fostered competition and labor disputes among artisan workers.[102] In these disputes, one guild would typically complain about a group of craftsmen encroaching on its trade, and to resolve such conflicts the mercantile oligarchy would offer "charity" to the wronged guild by imposing a fine on the offending craftsmen.

While the documents recording such guild conflicts are significant in many ways, they remarkably work to redefine the concept of charity by transforming the alms of the *Last Judgment* into a system of fines imposed by the city on certain guilds. Just as poverty takes on distinctive connotations in these records, charity becomes the mercantile oligarchy's decision to order other craftsmen to contribute pageant funds to the guild upon whose trade they have infringed. This form of charity, then, as we shall see, opposes the models of giving in the *Last Judgment* since it actually emerges from the enforced dissolution of communal bonds among artisans.

The records contain numerous instances of pleas for charity resulting from inter-guild conflicts.[103] For example, the carpenters and tilers appeared before the city in 1425 disputing which guild was entitled to produce draught louvers. While each guild had been constructing the louvers and thus earning profits from them, the city determined that "capitalis factura lodiourm . . . pertinuit & pertinet principaliter ad carpentarios" [the chief manufacture of the louvers . . . belonged and belongs principally to the carpenters]. As a result the city government mandated that any tilers making and selling louvers "sint contributorij ad paginam carpentariorum annuatim ad unum denarium tantam primo termino solucionis" [should be contributors yearly to the carpenters' pageant of one penny from the first pageant term]. The records also stipulate that regardless of who originally made the louvers, the tilers should hang all of them without further "murmure vel contradiccione" [murmur or contradiction]. As this last condition begins to suggest, the city's rulings in these kinds of disputes do not only serve to manage economic disparities caused by the artificial division of labor and the guilds' mandatory production of a pageant. Rather, the city's determinations seek, however successfully or ironically, to enforce a sense of charity and fraternity among competing guilds.

The pageant fines, then, become the mechanism that restores harmonious relations between feuding craftsmen. The record concerning the tilers and the carpenters makes the charitable dimensions of the city's intervention clear, as it notes that the oligarchy also requires the disputing guildsmen to offer one another a sign of peace and love. The ordinance states that the mayor and councilors "considerabant quod omnes homines vtrarumque arcium predictarum sint adinuicem amici boni & quod in signum amicicie inter eos firmande isti artifices hic presentes simul oscularentur & sic factum est" [decided that all the men of both of the aforesaid crafts should be good friends to one another, and that in token of the friendship to be forged among them, those craftsmen here present should exchange a kiss, and so it was done] (*REED: York*, 1:41; 2:726–27).

As this case shows, the city's insistence on charity ironically emerges from the conflicts created by its own requirement that artisans be divided into artificially rigid labor classifications. Rather than encouraging artisans to recognize their common interests and work collectively, the guild system split the body of craftsmen into competing parts. The resultant disputes, as we have seen, demand a version of charity in which the mercantile oligarchy steps in to "resolve" the very conflicts it creates. It restores the broken bonds among craftsmen by administering a form of charity that requires one guild to pay money toward another's pageant as a "meene of soccour and supportacion."[104] In this particular context, the language of charity once again differs from that of the *Last Judgment* pageant, where food, drink, and clothing constitute the primary means of relief voluntarily given by one individual to another. Here, charity becomes a part of business negotiations, and it functions as the oligarchic body's attempt to mediate the conflicts it creates and depends on within the body of artisan workers.

The artisans' proclamations of poverty and their requests for charity make it clear that the craft guilds were certainly oppressed by the policies and practices of the mercantile oligarchy. Despite the economic and political inequalities separating these two groups,[105] it is important to recognize that merchants and artisans are nonetheless allied in freely employing the rhetoric of poverty and in asking for charitable assistance. In the dimension of Corpus Christi theater portrayed in the guild records, we find that poverty, in its many forms, permeates all levels of the civic institutions involved in producing the plays. The claims of need articulated within each stratum of the social hierarchy allow the guilds to assert various causes, whether that cause is buying land, as in the case of the mercers, or seeking pageant money, as in the case of the craftsmen. In highlighting the rhetorical flexibility of poverty, my point here is not to dismiss the possibility that the guilds did actually experience financial hardship, especially in the wake of the city's economic decline beginning in the later fifteenth century. However, the reality of the guilds' neediness does not change its particularity as a form of poverty that emerges from specific conditions and results in specific forms of hardship.

If the guilds' poverty is to be considered a consequence of the city's overall economic decline, then we should acknowledge how that decline exacerbated economic problems endemic to the guild system. Furthermore, in cases where the city's recession may be the primary cause of the guilds' proclaimed impoverishment, then the guilds' poverty would still be different in degree and kind from the indigence experienced by the city's neediest people, those consistently made visible by pageants such as the *Entry* and the *Last Judgment.* This sector of the urban population was also affected by larger economic trends that would have intensified their already significant poverty.[106] The claims of need that penetrate all levels of the city and its Corpus Christi drama are thus hardly uniform or attributable to a single source. The language of poverty and charity, so important to ethical thought in the Middle Ages, emerges in York's theater as a deeply intricate terrain where neediness unites the mercantile elite, artisan laborers, and the hungry, thirsty, and naked of the *Last Judgment.*

In contrast to the forms of social unity that the *Entry,* the *Crucifixion,* and the *Last Judgment* encourage, the guild system also relies on an exclusionary structure that becomes especially evident if we consider the groups' view of charity, not when sought as a remedy for a guild's collective poverty, but when distributed as social aid for its individual members. Not surprisingly, the ordinances of the artisan guilds, and particularly those of carpenters, develop a conception of charity that revises the extreme generosity preached by Jesus in the *Last Judgment.* To be sure, the carpenters' version of almsgiving seeks to help its members who have fallen on hard times, but its generosity, as officially recorded in the civic documents, does not extend beyond the community of its own brotherhood. While the *Last Judgment* advocates a radically indiscriminate form of giving, the carpenters develop a program of charity primarily suited to the institutional demands of the guild system. Informed by the discourse of discriminate charity, the ordinances betray a deep suspicion about the legitimacy of those seeking aid, and the guild seems primarily concerned with protecting its charitable system from abuse or exploitation.

As they emphasize the split between the "fraternity" or religious aspects of the guild and its dimensions as an "occupation" or mystery, the carpenters' ordinances (1482) articulate a program of almsgiving for its own members.[107] The concern for one's fellow brothers speaks to a charitable sense of cohesion within the guild but it also highlights the larger system's emphasis on division, as their view of social support does not extend beyond the guild's own members.[108] Envisioning community as a rather narrowly defined body, the guild offered to support its members who had fallen into poverty:

> it is ordeynd that if ony of the said fraternitie fall to povert so that tha may not wyrk, or happyn to be blynd, or to leis thar gudes by unhap of the world, then the forsaid bredyrhode to gyffe tham iiijd. every weke, as lon as tha liff, by way of almusse.[109]

In accord with the teaching of the *Last Judgment,* the ordinance acknowledges the brothers' charitable obligations to one another. However, the document diverges from the pageant in displaying anxiety about aiding only those individuals legitimately entitled to alms. While the carpenters recognize that forces beyond one's control ("unhap") can lead to poverty, they also follow contemporary trends in citing the inability to work as the major precondition for receiving alms. In this sense, the document refuses to recognize a category of able-bodied poverty that may persist even when an individual works consistently. This reality may not have been unknown to carpenters attempting to provide for themselves and their families in the difficult times of the city's economic decline. While the *Last Judgment* does not scrutinize the worthiness of alms recipients, the carpenters make it clear that to be deserving of the guild's support, one of their own must be lame, blind, or suddenly impoverished by some uncontrollable event.

The guild makes its anxiety about valid forms of need even more apparent when the ordinances go on to specify additional requirements for receiving charity from the fraternity. Invoking concerns about fraudulent and idle living, the document continues,

> Also, it is ordenyd that what a brodir shall to be admittyd to take almous, shalbe sworn a pon a buke that he shall trewly lyffe apon hys allmous and hys awn gude, without wast or gyffyng away of tham, and what so ewyr he levys at his dying that longys to hum self, hys dettes payd and hys beriall reasonably done, shall remayn to the said fraternite as thar own proper gudes.[110]

The ordinance exhibits fear that the guild's alms may be wasted or given away. It thus attempts to ensure the proper use of charity by mandating that the recipient live rightfully and honestly off of the economic assistance he has received.[111] In addition to specifying the proper use of its alms, the "brotherhood" also seeks a return on its charitable investment by mandating that any remaining wealth after the recipient's death, burial, and payment of debts, should revert back to the guild. While it may seem to oppose the spirit of generous giving in the *Last Judgment*, such a return is presumably designed to maintain the carpenters' viability as a financially stable guild with adequate resources for the future needs of its members. Their motivation in this case demonstrates how the carpenters ensure that the ideal of charity conforms to the guild's central role as an enduring business organization. In contrast to the ethos of the pageant, the group of craftsmen develops an official system of charity most noticeably concerned with minimizing its use and maintaining the guild's financial resources.

It is not surprising, then, that following these anxious proclamations of charity, the ordinances turn their attention to the importance of work as a strategy necessary to prevent poverty. The carpenters initiate what Sellers terms as "an embryo labor exchange" by articulating a plan that seeks to keep its members actively working:[112]

> Also it is ordenyd that yf ony of the said bredir have nede to a workman at ony tym, and a nodir of hys bredir is owt of wark and has no wark to doo, that the said brodir, that has neid of a warkman, shall

> rather take in to wark hys brodir of the said fraternite then ony odyr that is not brodyr, yf he will wyrk as he may deserif, apon the payn of forfatour of xx d. to be payd by hym that doos the contrary, the sum xx d. to be devydid as is above said.[113]

The guild seeks to limit the number of its members who cannot support themselves through work by demanding that the carpenters turn to their brothers first and foremost as a labor resource. The ordinance thus requires that carpenters in need of a workman employ other carpenters in need of work. This ambitious plan obviously demands a supervisory regime, and the ordinances provide for a kind of overseer to keep track of the whole operation:

> Also it is ordenyd that thar shalbe every yer a brodir chosyn and assigned of the said fratnernite, to whom every broodier that is owt of wark shall make knawlege that he is owt of wark, so that he that would have a warkman may have knawlege of hym that is owt of wark.[114]

Seeking to prevent carpenters from employing outsiders or from allowing their own members to go any length of time without working, the ordinances establish a fairly elaborate system of labor notification and regulation.

This system demonstrates that when the ideal of charity is implemented in the labor structure of York, the radically free mode of almsgiving espoused in the Corpus Christi play gives way to a model of discriminate charity concerned with promoting labor. On one level, the insistence on the productivity of the guild's own members can be seen as a charitable attempt to prevent poverty—a goal that the *Last Judgment* play does not explicitly seem to share. However, in positing labor as the ultimate solution to indigence, the guild records become another discursive arena that fails to acknowledge the possible existence of the working poor. Along with the *Entry*, the *Last Judgment* implicitly recognizes this category since it does not scrutinize the legitimacy of the Christlike poor, elaborate on the causes of their poverty, or insist that only the disabled can be truly needy. Along with the *Crucifixion*, the *Last Judgment* also promotes a wider social vision opposing the guilds' more particular concerns as stated in the guild records. Entire segments of the city's inhabitants including itinerant laborers and the working poor remain excluded from the guilds' official documentation of the responsibility they bear to the members of Christ's body.

In seeking to fulfill their charitable obligations within a system demanding labor and profit, or at least financial stability, the guild records reveal the virtual impossibility of living out the *Last Judgment*'s teachings at an institutional level. Despite its forceful lessons, the play's radical conception of charity and community ultimately has no place in York's civic regimes, for these rely on social division, and they generate a competing ethical discourse. In this way, the urban economy of late medieval York ultimately constrains the force of the pageant's challenge to its most central values. To enact the pageant's lessons in their fullest sense as a corporate practice would entail a massive restructuring of corporate identity. Indeed, if lived out within the guild system, the ethical imperatives of the *Last Judgment* would undermine that very system, rendering its modes of exchange impracticable and its conceptions of morality obsolete.

Yet perhaps this argument overstates the case in finding such an extreme disconnect between the ethos of the guilds and the ethos of the *Last Judgment* pageant. After all, it begs the question of why the mercers would perform a play promoting conceptions of poverty and charity at odds with the institutional system they oversaw. This question deserves serious consideration, and it is indeed tempting to seek a conclusive answer. One might be inclined, for example, to resolve the contradictions endemic to the mercers' pageant by arguing, in the first place, that there are really no contradictions to be resolved.[115] Perhaps for the mercers themselves it sufficed to practice indiscriminate charity on a voluntary basis in their personal lives, not as an official practice mandated by the guild.[116] Or perhaps the mercers thought that the charitable activities of their guild, especially in its auspices as the fraternity of the Holy Trinity, satisfied the play's ethical demands.[117] Indeed, historians have pointed out how such associations often helped the poor by, for example, inviting them to annual feasts held in honor of the group's religious patron.[118] The mercers might have seen such occasions as indiscriminate acts of generosity performed collectively in fulfillment of the play's moral vision.

This scenario therefore might have allayed the moral anxieties of some guild members; however, the play would seem to challenge the very idea that Christians can compartmentalize the works of mercy, limiting the performance of charity to particular circumstances. The very possibility of salvation, as the *Last Judgment* makes clear, depends on taking seriously the absolute interdependence of all people. Recall the pageant's dramatic account of the necessary *relentlessness* of charity that offers aid at every time in every place to every person. This charitable work is constituted by relations among people in all facets of life. In this sense, the pageant's lessons could not be fulfilled by individual acts of charity or even by the occasional collective act of charity, for the play's moral demands remain applicable to guildsmen in their business activities. The *Last Judgment,* then, challenges mechanisms of social separation allowing Christians to imagine only specific roles, times, or places as suitable for helping the poor. Such mechanisms obfuscate the unity that the play urges among all people who are bound within Christ's body by mutual responsibility.

Consequently, some mercers may have found the play's lessons impossible to fulfill in belonging to a guild that, in spite of its charitable activities, nonetheless excluded the poor from its membership and benefited to some degree from schemes of social division. In recognizing this disjunction, the mercers might have performed the *Last Judgment* out of a penitential spirit. Their pageant would be seen in this context as a compensatory gesture seeking to acknowledge the distance between their commercial activities and the play's extreme version of generosity. For the mercers, then, to perform the *Last Judgment* would be, essentially, to ask for forgiveness in ascribing to an ethical ideal that their socioeconomic practices prevented them from fulfilling.

Yet penitence may not be the answer, for one could also argue that the mercers might have seen the play's moral lessons as little more than an artifact from some distant time. Rather than taking the pageant's forceful ethic literally—an act that would have effectively led to the guild's dissolution—the mercers might have viewed the *Last Judgment*'s warnings as an extreme and outmoded example of moral guidance. Given the increasing dominance of the anti-poverty ethos, the play's perspective might have indeed seemed antiquated long before the Reformation would doom the entire cycle as such. The *Last Judgment* play, when viewed from this angle, becomes, then, a mere exercise in nostalgia.[119] Its performance would allow the mercers to recall some idealized past when it was still possible to pursue indiscriminate charity—a well-intentioned practice, but one with no real application in the more sophisticated socio-economic regimes of the day.

But there too are problems with this possibility, and the sheer intricacy of theatrical representation makes it impossible, I think, to uncover the mercers' intention in performing a play with such radical conceptions of charity and poverty. While the guild ordinances tend to reflect the economic interests of rather clearly defined parties, the motivations of those involved in the theater are potentially diverse and are thus much harder to judge. In the world of dramatic performance, skinners, pinners, and mercers alike occupy a liminal space in that they both retain and relinquish their identities as guildsmen within the city of York. Their varied interactions with their fellow actors, their varied conceptions of the particular characters they play, and their varied connections with the spectators all generate dynamic possibilities for meaning. These preclude any singular account explaining, for example, precisely how the skinners would have understood the *Entry*, or exactly why the mercers performed the *Last Judgment*. Ashley's comment about the *Crucifixion* pageant bears repeating in this context: "the issue of where the producers . . . found their subject positions . . . cannot be resolved so simply and constructively."[120]

Indeed, attempting to provide a single rationale for a guild's production of a highly complex pageant proves to be very tricky business especially when it comes to the issue of poverty. Given the limits to what we can know about a guild's motivations, what remains most compelling about the plays in relationship to the guild records is their commitment to portraying an extremely wide social arena. The performance of York's Corpus Christi plays makes visible a range of poor and needy people often excluded in late medieval poverty polemic and civic discourse, which feature a telling obsession with the "deserving" poor. The theater is distinctive for anatomizing the intricacy of social relations: it makes the able-bodied poor stand beside the lame and blind, and it makes the needy occupy the very same space inhabited by the rich. In contrast, the guild records, like much Wycliffite writing and like *The*

Book of Margery Kempe, exploit the capacious rhetoric of poverty to advance a particular financial interest or class position. In so doing, they occlude certain forms of economic reality and deemphasize specific models of social relation. The material signs of York's theater, however, consistently affirm the realities of material deprivation among the omnipresent claims of need found within the civic records.

The poor man of the *Entry* pageant, Jesus's crucified body, and the needy Christ of Matthew 25 all come alive in York's Corpus Christi drama to make claims on the consciences of performers and audience members alike. They perform important ethical work by highlighting the reality of able-bodied poverty, by exposing the social and moral costs of highly regulated labor, and by revealing the difficulty of discerning Christ-like need. These poor figures thus ultimately emerge as visible, but endangered, reminders of what York's labor system and the wider anti-poverty ethos seek to deny. Perhaps we as audience and community members in the present age still have need for such reminders, for the lessons of these plays also seem glaringly absent in modern discourses of poverty, a subject to which I now turn in the epilogue.

EPILOGUE

Nickel and Dimed

Poverty Polemic Medieval and Modern

In late medieval England, writers interrogated the meaning of poverty with great urgency. In many ways, their dynamic and intricate writings reveal how increasing anxiety about poverty was a matter of historical specificity marked by a radically different post-plague economy, a flourishing ideology of antifraternalism, and a growing concern with the regulation of agricultural and urban labor. Yet, the literature of this period also speaks to many modern anxieties about poverty—an issue that, in its continued presence, signals a connection to the medieval past, disproving familiar narratives of modern progress and enlightenment. In addition to transgressing vast historical boundaries as a persistent economic reality, poverty also still provokes epistemological and ethical challenges that were operative more than five hundred years ago. As a subject of literary inquiry poverty continues to transform the work of writing and reading into a fundamentally ethical practice. It remains true that how readers interpret the signs of poverty and discern the presence of need are crucial acts that have power to influence a community's charitable practices, its definition of justice, and its conception of itself as a social body.

It may seem surprising to argue that there are similarities in medieval and modern approaches to poverty given the massive economic, political, and social transformations that have come to make the medieval past at times seem almost illegible to readers and students of the twenty-first century. Indeed, we live in an enormously different world born out of the death of feudalism, the triumph of capitalism, and the legacy of the Reformation—to name only a few examples of cultural change. Despite these highly significant transformations, one can nonetheless find haunting continuities in the ways that poverty captures our ethical imagination and forces us to consider our relationships to other human beings. In the pages that follow, I want to pursue some of these continuities by offering a reading of Barbara Ehrenreich's recent work, *Nickel and Dimed: On (Not) Getting by in America*. When placed in dialogue with texts from late medieval England, Ehrenreich's book can be seen in a new light, emerging as a text that reveals how poverty provokes enduring cultural anxieties even in the face of great historical change. Before exploring these substantive connections, however, it is important to give a brief overview of the book and to describe its notoriety in a much more recent past.

In *Nickel and Dimed*, Ehrenreich leaves behind her life as a writer and attempts to make a living as a low-wage laborer. Over the course of three months, she lives in three different cities, working as a waitress, a maid, a nursing home assistant (on weekends), and a retail clerk. In each case, it proves impossible for Ehrenreich to cover her expenses, and she repeatedly finds herself beset by poverty. Written as a personal account that seeks to translate the genuine experience of need into an entertaining and compelling narrative, *Nickel and Dimed* is arguably one of the most important texts discussing poverty in twentieth-century America. As a winner of various awards, *Nickel and Dimed* has spent more than one hundred weeks on the *New York Times* best-seller list since its initial publication in 2001.[1] It has also garnered fame as a popular choice for university-sponsored summer reading programs.[2] The text, furthermore, was adapted into a play that toured nationally in 2003, winning a Los Angeles Drama Critics' Circle Award.

While Ehrenreich's book has garnered a great deal of praise, it has also prompted a great deal of conflict, yet neither the book's critics nor its champions have recognized how *Nickel and Dimed* participates in a long legacy of debates about the moral and interpretive problems endemic to poverty. When read in light of the issues and texts discussed in the previous chapters of this book, *Nickel and Dimed* becomes an exploration of familiar, enduring questions: How is poverty defined? For whom can it be a legitimate experience? Which people are deserving of aid? In raising these questions, the book—and the controversy it provoked—engage with other more specific issues central to medieval conflicts about poverty. For example, when Ehrenreich herself descends into the low-wage workforce, her text exposes the continued appeal of voluntary poverty, a phenomenon that many might dismiss as irrelevant to modern economic concerns. Ehrenreich's work joins earlier texts such as the *Life of St. Francis* or *The Book of Margery Kempe* in featuring an elite and sophisticated figure who willingly claims an authentic experience of poverty in the name of some greater theological, philosophical, or political purpose.[3] As we shall see, this willful claim of neediness generates a familiar anxiety for both Ehrenreich and her critics who raise questions about the authenticity and implications of the chosen poverty that forms the very basis of the book.

Furthermore, as *Nickel and Dimed* attempts to show how working people regularly find themselves in need, the book harkens back to medieval labor laws and antifraternal discourse by revealing continued resistance to the notion of a legitimate form of able-bodied poverty. Though Ehrenreich's book responds to an altogether different economic situation in which workers consistently find themselves forced into poverty, *Nickel and Dimed* seeks to unravel the assumption that those capable of labor cannot be truly poor—a profound myth that has flourished in our cultural imagination thanks in no small part to the legacy of medieval poverty polemic. And finally, as Ehrenreich reflects on the relationship between Christian ethics and economic practice, her book sparks a familiar and impassioned debate about the status of poverty. The question remains, is poverty a hallmark of Christ-like sanctity or an obstacle to the central aims of a Christian community?

Ehrenreich revisits debates about the nature of poverty, the ethical practice of charity, and the legitimate meaning of need within the context of national welfare reform. Specifically, she seeks to investigate the effects of the Personal Responsibility and Work Opportunity Reconciliation Act. Passed in 1996, this law called for a major overhaul of the welfare system, and it marked the first time in American history that significant welfare entitlement benefits were revoked.[4] While the very existence of a national welfare system marks a key difference from the largely deinstitutionalized acts of charity in the Middle Ages, modern welfare legislation takes advantage of ideological innovations found in medieval labor law. The fourteenth-century statutes, as we have seen, marked an attempt to keep wages down by describing workers as able-bodied idlers. Though the twentieth-century welfare reform act has the different goal of getting people off of welfare, the modern law nonetheless makes use of the rhetorical strategies found in medieval labor legislation. The result is that both sets of laws overtly make the same claims, broadcasting anxiety about the dangers of what they see as an illegitimate form of poverty. The medieval labor laws and the modern welfare reform act are thus aligned in their explicit preoccupation with putting able-bodied people to work.

In a summary of the 1996 law developed by the House of Representatives Committee on Ways and Means, we can find a telling rationale for this unprecedented welfare legislation. As the document argues, this new law is needed to disrupt a disturbing trend in social aid policy. To use medieval terminology, the government, it explains, originally implemented a system of discriminate charity but then lapsed into indiscriminate giving, offering aid to people who could support themselves through work: "Since creation of the first Federal welfare entitlements in 1935 to help States aid the needy who were aged, blind, or children, the Federal Government had gradually expanded the entitlement concept. As a result, the Nation's welfare system now provides millions of families headed by able-bodied adults with a package of guaranteed benefits." Seeking to revise this system, the law proposes to return to an earlier time, when only the truly needy could receive guaranteed federal assistance. In a phrase that evokes antifraternal glosses on Luke 14, the law develops a category of the deserving poor that includes children as well as the "needy" who are "aged" or "blind." It contrasts these people with those who should not be guaranteed federal assistance, that is, the undeserving "able-bodied adults."

While the government declares that it seeks to maintain the welfare system as a "safety net for families experiencing temporary financial problems," the law makes a familiar ideological move in proposing that work is the primary antidote to poverty. The law thus imagines itself as an effective means of "attacking dependency," and it stipulates that "All able-bodied adults who have been on welfare for two years must participate in some activity designed to help them become self-supporting."[5] While we have seen from Wille's apologia in *Piers Plowman* that it can be difficult to identify legitimate and productive forms of labor, the welfare reform act attempts to avoid any such ambiguity. It therefore goes on to set "strict work standards" and enumerates a series of "tightly defined" "work activities."[6]

In *Nickel and Dimed* Ehrenreich seeks to test the efficacy of this legislation. Her book questions and ultimately disproves the assumption that "a job was the ticket out of poverty and that the only thing holding back welfare recipients was their reluctance to go out and get one."[7] Lurking beneath this assumption one finds familiar stereotypes about the poor along with the foundational premise that neediness is legitimate only for the "lame, feeble, and blind." The power of this idea becomes evident when we see that anxiety about discerning "true" need extends beyond Ehrenreich's primary argument that able-bodied workers cannot in fact escape poverty. Rather, concerns about the validity of need permeate the book's overall rationale and methodology. These ultimately expose the ambiguities inherent in Ehrenreich's own claims of poverty as a writer turned low-wage laborer.[8] Both critics of the book and, to a certain extent, Ehrenreich herself wrestle with her status as a needy person, for it is her experience of poverty that supports the book's wider claims about the insufficiency of wages. Turning first to Ehrenreich herself, we can see that although she initially attempts to cast her project as an objective, scientific investigation, she reveals the complexities of her authorial identity as someone who is potentially either a legitimate member of the working poor or an elite imposter. Strategically employing both identities at various times, Erhenreich unwittingly raises questions about the authenticity and ethical status of voluntary poverty in the modern era.

In the introduction to *Nickel and Dimed,* Ehrenreich explains the premise of the book by describing it as a research project performed in a spirit of scientific inquiry. Instead of "sitting at a desk and fiddling with numbers," Ehrenreich, a former biologist, wants to "plunge into the chaos of nature" by getting out into the real world (3). She undertakes this project with careful deliberation and develops a series of rules meant to guarantee the experiment's validity. While not as rigorous as Francis's earlier rule, Ehrenreich's obligations stipulate that she will not "fall back on any skills derived from [her] education or usual work"; she will take the best paying jobs she can get; and she will perform them diligently. She will also stay in the least expensive housing possible, allowing for minimum standards of "safety and privacy" (4). Ehrenreich also sets herself some "reassuring limits." Considering both her transportation needs and her authorial obligations, she will always allow herself a car partly because "a story about waiting for buses would not be very interesting to read" (4). She also refuses to subject herself to any extreme forms of poverty, seeking instead to ensure that her basic needs for food and shelter are consistently met (5). Specifying these parameters, Ehrenreich attempts to characterize her experiment as a rational and balanced way of getting information about life in the lower classes.

It quickly becomes clear, however, that making claims about poverty is a far more complicated business. Ehrenreich's allusions to science and objectivity cannot resolve the complexities of her project, and she goes on to raise questions about the ethical liabilities and epistemological limits of her own methodology. She cultivates a capacious social mobility, presenting herself alternately as an authentic member of the working poor and as a mere imposter who cannot presume to know the nature of their genuine experiences. Implicitly acknowledging the interpretive ambiguity inherent to poverty, Ehrenreich engages in a subtle process of negotiation in an attempt to ensure the ethical status of her project as a book that ultimately seeks justice for the involuntary poor.

When Ehrenreich initially describes the origin of the idea for her project, she establishes her identity as a member of the intellectual elite. Calling attention to the material circumstances of her life as a writer, she explicitly acknowledges that she is far removed from the world that would become the object of her study. The work's opening sentence reads, "The idea that led to this book arose in comparatively sumptuous circumstances" (1). Ehrenreich goes on to describe how the project first took shape while she enjoyed a thirty-dollar lunch with her editor (1). Ehrenreich repeatedly refers to this dimension of her identity as she continues to detail the nature of her experiment. Acknowledging that she was poor only while performing research for the book, she explains that she was not an authentic low-wage worker because she "was only visiting a world that others inhabit full-time, often for most of their lives" (6). The temporary nature of her experiment ensures that Ehrenreich remains attached to the world of privilege that she eventually plans to rejoin. She explains that "With all the real-life assets I've built up in middle age—bank account, IRA, health insurance, multi-room home—waiting indulgently in the background, there was no way I was going to 'experience poverty' or find out how it 'really feels' to be a long-term low-wage worker" (6). Here, Ehrenreich implicitly suggests that a defining factor of poverty is insecurity and vulnerability. As someone who possesses a wide safety net of resources, Ehrenreich insists that she cannot fundamentally know what it means to experience true need.

Indeed, the very nature of Ehrenreich's project prevents her from fully abandoning her previous life because it demands that she remain a writer, reporting on her own activities and encounters in the low-wage workforce. Ehrenreich explains how her role as an author marks her experience of poverty as an act of deception: "There was always, of course, the difference that only I knew—that I wasn't working for the money, I was doing research for an article and later a book. . . . This deception, symbolized by the laptop that provided a link to my past and future, bothered me, at least in the case of people I cared about and wanted to know better" (8). With material and symbolic connections to a professional identity in another life, Ehrenreich emphasizes her alienation from low-wage workers who inhabit an utterly different world.

Yet Ehrenreich also downplays this distant and detached persona, and at other moments in the introduction she claims to identify directly with the people she temporarily joins. Ehrenreich thus cultivates a counter-identity to her role as an elite writer by asserting that her descent into poverty is a fundamentally authentic act. She tells us that she has always been familiar with poverty—it is a form of life from which she has never been far removed:

> In my own family, the low-wage way of life had never been many degrees of separation away; it was close enough, in any case, to make

> me treasure the gloriously autonomous, if not always well-paid writing life. My sister had been through one low-paid job after another—phone company rep, factory worker, receptionist—constantly struggling against what she calls "the hopelessness of being a wage slave." My husband and companion of seventeen years was a $4.50 an hour warehouse worker when I fell in with him. . . . My father had been a copper miner; uncles and grandfathers worked in the mines or for the Union Pacific. (2)

Ehrenreich now presents her life as a writer as if it were an anomalous moment of privilege in an otherwise poverty-stricken existence. Though she admits that her experimental descent into poverty is temporary, she also makes her life as a writer seem somehow temporary—it is an unexpected diversion on a preordained trajectory of low-wage work. Ehrenreich goes on to explain that her research for *Nickel and Dimed* does not therefore constitute a fully voluntary or potentially voyeuristic trip into poverty. She has "had enough unchosen encounters with poverty in [her] lifetime to know it's not a place you would want to visit for touristic purposes; it just smells too much like fear" (6). Ehrenreich is now a person all too familiar with the place she revisits so as to write *Nickel and Dimed*. She does not revel in an exotic underworld of poverty that she can readily escape. Rather, she returns to face an originary self—reverting to the way of life she has known most deeply.

Ehrenreich makes her most explicit claim of authenticity by declaring that she was in fact a low-wage worker during the research phase of her book. Though she has previously admitted that she does not ultimately need the income she earns, Ehrenreich declares that she was "exaggerating the extent of the 'deception'" she perpetrated as a low-wage worker (9). She explains, "There's no way . . . to pretend to be a waitress: the food either gets to the table or not. People knew me as a waitress, a cleaning person, a nursing home aide, or a retail clerk not because I acted like one but because that's what I was, at least for the time I was with them" (9). In this framework, Ehrenreich claims that her journey into working poverty is entirely valid. The potential for fraud is mitigated by the actual performance of labor, not by one's dependence on the wages that labor produces.

In the introduction, then, Ehrenreich is sometimes the sophisticated and sensitive writer attempting to bridge a socioeconomic distance that she admits cannot be fully overcome. At other times, she is an authentic member of the working poor, who performs the hard labor for which she was originally destined having grown up as part of a working-class family.[9] Though she develops social and authorial roles that are clearly oppositional, they are united by a coherent ethical pretense that reveals continued anxiety about the practice of voluntary poverty. Each persona allows Ehrenreich to justify this practice from a unique perspective. In acknowledging how her identity remains rooted in a life altogether separate from the world of working poverty, Ehrenreich reveals her psychic distance from the involuntary poor. Though she thus exposes the epistemological limits of her experiment, Ehrenreich employs a rhetorical strategy that allows her to emerge as a knowledgeable writer precisely because she does not feign omniscience. This acknowledgement also functions as an ethical justification for the book: it reveals that Ehrenreich refuses to present the complex lives and diverse experiences of the working poor as transparent material that she can readily appropriate. However, in creating a counter-persona, Ehrenreich is able to posit an epistemological and ethical rationale altogether different from the one described above. As a member of a working class family who actually performs low-wage labor in the course of her research, Ehrenreich does not have to tiptoe respectfully around the objects of her study who inhabit another realm of existence. Rather, she can write both knowledgeably and justly abut the experiences of the working poor because these are fundamentally her experiences as well.

Ehrenreich also characterizes her research methodology as a dualistic enterprise shaped by the contradictory perspectives of the sophisticated writer and the ordinary worker. On the one hand, Ehrenreich acknowledges the complexities of poverty as a subject that necessitates special research methods; on the other hand, she describes the book as a matter of simple economic calculation—as a veritable list of income and expenses—that requires no special methodology whatsoever. Speaking as the detached and erudite writer, Ehrenreich first makes a surprising admission that potentially undermines the entire purpose of her book. When it comes to the prospect of making a living on minimum wage, she tells us that even before she started the project she knew that it was simply not possible: "if the question was whether a single mother leaving welfare could survive without government assistance in the form of food stamps, Medicaid, and housing and child care subsidies, the answer was well known before I ever left the comforts of home." After quoting earnings and housing statistics, Ehrenreich explains that in 1998 "the odds against a typical welfare recipient's landing a job at . . . a 'living wage' were about 97 to 1." So, she asks, "Why should I bother to confirm these unpleasant facts?" (3).

Ehrenreich's question indicates that her book is not intended to prove an argument about the inadequacy of minimum wage and the reality of working poverty. Because the numbers already establish these facts, she goes on to list other reasons for going forward with the project. Ehrenreich knows that poverty is a subjective experience that extends beyond numerical quantifications. She acknowledges that "surprises lurk in the most mundane measurements," and she plans to seek these out (3). For example, Ehrenreich suspects that the working poor might have undocumented means of survival. Speaking as the removed intellectual, she wants to expose these unknown entities, perhaps "discover[ing] some hidden economies in the world of the low-wage workers" (3). She also tells us that she might discover symbolic economies offering the poor psychic and emotional benefits. In this regard, Ehrenreich wants to test the allegedly restorative potential of hard work, and with obvious irony she hypothesizes, "Maybe I would detect in myself the bracing psychological effects of getting out of the house, as promised by the wonks who brought us welfare reform" (4). Yet Ehrenreich also knows that labor and poverty can make claims on the poor, and she therefore surmises that she might find "unexpected costs—physical, financial, emotional—to throw off all [her] calculations" (4). In this framework, Ehrenreich must necessarily become poor herself because she is investigating a world that is hidden and unknown to all but its true inhabitants. She understands the complexities of poverty as force that exceeds economic formulas; low-wage work might offer "hidden economies" as well as psychic and symbolic rewards, or it might entail adverse effects not readily quantifiable through statistics.

Ehrenreich's status as an investigative reporter who understands the theoretical intricacies of poverty, but not its realities, positions her once again as an outsider. She counters this perspective by offering a competing methodology for her book—one that opposes her earlier statements about the work's predictable outcome if poverty were approached strictly as a numbers game. Near the end of the introduction, Ehrenreich adopts a voice of earnest simplicity, claiming that her goal as a writer is "straightforward and objective." Put simply, she tells us that she becomes a low-wage worker because she "just [wanted] to see whether [she] could match income to expenses, as the truly poor attempt to do every day" (6). While Ehrenreich in this statement marks herself as different from the "truly poor," she also attempts to align herself with these very same people by claiming that her project is simple, straightforward, and ultimately just a question of basic math. Her earlier acknowledgements about the predictability of income and expense equations are now conspicuously absent as are her previous explanations about the unquantifiable aspects of poverty. In their place we have the very opposite account of the book's methodology—it is an ordinary attempt to make ends meet—an activity that she performs along with the working poor themselves.

These twists and turns in perspective permeate Ehrenreich's entire characterization of her project. When she goes on finally to discuss the implications of her experiment, the familiar pattern once again emerges. The detached writer fearful of exploiting the poor declares that her own foray into poverty was purely personal: "I make no claims for the relevance of my experiences to anyone else's, because there is nothing typical about my story" (9). But, of course, Ehrenreich transforms her personal experience into a written account ultimately valuable for its exemplarity. Later in the introduction her personal experiment is thus generalized, functioning as the "best-case scenario" for anyone attempting to make a living as a low-wage worker (10). The writer's supposedly atypical and individual experience becomes a moral lesson meant to educate readers not about Ehrenreich herself but about the difficult reality experienced every day by working people across America.

While the book seeks to uncover the reality and hardships of working poverty, its readers have not been entirely sympathetic to Ehrenreich's intended message. In describing their objections to *Nickel and Dimed,* critics from across the political spectrum tend to focus on Ehrenreich's voluntary poverty, for the book's broader claims depend on its legitimacy. What Ehrenreich purports to know about poverty is based on her genuine experience of this condition and her association with people for whom it is not a matter of choice. For this reason, reviewers' assessments of *Nickel and Dimed* often function as diagnostic acts attempting to discern if Ehrenreich herself is truly needy—if her claims of poverty are indeed authentic. The judgments rendered by critics in turn offer themselves up for judgment because they reveal larger assumptions about the nature of community in modern America. Critics' charges of fraud, their accusations of elitism, and their assurances about the true experience of poverty anchor a wider social vision predicated on particular conceptions of justice, dignity, and human relations.

In their assessments of the book, reviewers attest to the provocative nature of *Nickel and Dimed* as they repeatedly engage in acts of discernment. For example, in a review for the leftist publication *Z Magazine*, Cara Spindler declares that "The unanswered, but always present, question in *Nickel and Dimed* is how valid is [Ehrenreich's] method of research." Spindler goes on to explain that "My friends and I were divided over whether her month long stint as a house-cleaner, and then later as a waitress, was or was not valid."[10] Unlike Spindler, some critics have clearly been persuaded by Ehrenreich's selective disclaimers about the legitimacy of her poverty, and they therefore assume that the question of validity is irrelevant. Linda Brebner, for instance, approvingly cites Ehrenreich's "understanding that she could not possibly replicate the 'real life' of the working poor."[11] Yet, as we have seen, Ehrenreich does at times claim her poverty as authentic, and many critics object to this notion, viewing *Nickel and Dimed* as a woefully inadequate account of what the true poor experience every day. Spindler's review is a good example of this skepticism toward Ehrenreich's assertions of authenticity: "She could leave at any moment. She didn't tell her co-workers that they were being observed, written about, and exampled. Her slightly-indignant attitude towards the management and the work showed the ever present high-low split in our culture, and where she thought she fit on that scale." For Spindler, Ehrenreich's temporary stint as a "slightly-indignant" laborer fails to permeate a rigid, class-based boundary.[12]

In viewing Ehrenreich's poverty as "temporary" and "incomplete," critics point to what they see as the book's epistemological and ethical failures. Perhaps John Cook conveys this perspective most clearly when he suggests that Ehrenreich's research method is "the journalistic equivalent of learning what it's like to be blind by closing your eyes."[13] In epistemological terms, Cook's comment implicitly asks how Ehnrenreich can write authoritatively about a subject she cannot really understand; and, moreover, in ethical terms, it casts suspicion on Ehrenreich's motives as a writer who claims to know what the critic has shown she cannot. Voluntary poverty is once again interpreted primarily as an act of fraud. Ehrenreich's work becomes an unsuccessful attempt to conceal her elite identity and claim association with the involuntary poor.

Many reviewers thus take it upon themselves to expose the nature of Ehrenreich's deception and describe its harmful effects on the working poor. In so doing they argue that Ehrenreich's attitude of superiority functions to disparage working people and misrepresent the positive aspects of their lives as laborers. In making such assertions, critics often focus on moments in the text when Ehrenreich makes frank admissions about the frustrations involved in performing low-wage work. For example, in her time spent working at a Wal-Mart in Minnesota, Ehrenreich finds herself growing more hostile toward the customers—people who are also potentially low-wage workers struggling to make ends meet. At one point she watches with growing anger as a child proceeds to pull pieces of clothing off of the racks. In a clearly ironic tone, she notes that "the thought that abortion is wasted on the unborn must show on my face, because [the child's] mother finally tells him to stop." In another moment, Ehrenreich describes how she begins to "hat[e] the customers for extraneous reasons, such as, in the case of the native Caucasians, their size." She elaborates, "I don't mean just bellies and butts, but huge bulges in completely exotic locations, like the backs of the neck and knees" (165). In some ways, these painfully honest comments might be reassuring to readers because they can make Ehrenreich seem more human and because they prove her very point about the hardships of low-wage labor. She is someone whose spirit and ordinary generosity have been negatively affected by the reality of performing work that garners little respect.[14] Yet—and perhaps unsurprisingly—other critics read comments like the ones above as evidence that Ehrenreich "at times . . . appears insensitive to the very individuals she writes about."[15]

Irony is lost on many critics who see Ehrenreich's remarks about overweight shoppers or annoying children as a sign of disdain that affirms Ehrenreich's superiority above all else.

Given that many critics find a pervasive sense of condescension in the book, they view its ostensible call for justice much as they view Ehrenreich's poverty: it is a thin veneer that unsuccessfully masks an elitist attitude detrimental to the poor themselves. From the outset, as the book's premise makes clear, Ehrenreich claims to support the working poor, advocating for both higher wages and better work environments. Describing how some employment practices eviscerate workers' political agency, Ehrenreich writes tellingly of the ways in which low-wage employees can be made to feel like criminals as they are routinely subjected to drug tests, personality tests, and other means of surveillance.[16] At times, she expresses outrage that her co-workers themselves are not outraged by such treatment. Yet in criticizing the degradation of the poor and their lack of political will, Ehrenreich, according to some mostly conservative critics, troublingly confers these very qualities on them. For example, after warning that *Nickel and Dimed* is a book beloved by "leftist professors," Steven Malanga argues that Ehrenreich "turns on the very people with whom she's trying to sympathize, imagining that they can only accept their terrible exploitation because they've become psychologically incapable of resisting."[17] As a result, the working classes emerge in her narrative as shadowy and hapless victims doomed to an empty existence. A review of the book in *FrontPage,* David Horowitz's on-line magazine, similarly calls *Nickel and Dimed* a series of "victim caricatures," "Soviet realism poster symbols," or "stick-figure women."[18]

These accusations entail a sharp ethical critique, for they insist that Ehrenreich actually reproduces traditional stereotypes of the poor. Her plea for the dignified treatment of workers backfires, critics argue, because the book itself fails to treat such people with dignity. Instead, *Nickel and Dimed* suggests that the working poor are incompetent and perhaps even lazy—at least in political terms—without Ehrenreich's savvy insights. The critics, then, need to step in to show readers the true face of low-wage workers. Mark D. Fefer thus explains that "Some of the people Ehrenreich encounters are trying to take pride in their seemingly dismal jobs." He notes, however, that "their effort [to do so] typically elicits from [Ehrenreich] only scorn or impatience."[19] Another reviewer declares that Ehrenreich gets it wrong for failing to realize that "most . . . [low-wage workers] seem proud to be working, proud of their work, and proud of the companies for which they work."[20]

These arguments derive their ethical force from a familiar epistemological claim. The critics assert that they know how the poor really live, and so the critics are the ones who can best protect their interests against the false claims of someone like Ehrenreich—someone who has chosen poverty voluntarily. The hostile reviewer thus works to recover what Ehrenreich has taken away; he redeems a sense of value and significance in the lives of the working poor. Another review in *FrontPage Magazine* offers perhaps the best example of this approach. Michael Tremoglie first cites one of Ehrenreich's most candid declarations about what she ultimately learned from her experiment: "no job, no matter how lowly, is truly unskilled" (193). Tremoglie then uses this comment as evidence not of Ehrenreich's advocacy of laborers but of her fundamental elitism. In response to her conclusion about the difficulty of low-wage work, he asks a rhetorical question: "Barbara Ehrenreich is just realizing this now?"[21]

While critics from across the political spectrum all invoke the moral high ground in criticizing *Nickel and Dimed,* the conservative reviewers in particular make ethical claims that feature some telling absences. First, many of these critics are confident in their knowledge about the true nature of the working poor, who, they allege, are only sketchily presented in the text: unlike Ehrenreich, the critics have known all along about the difficult reality of low-wage work; and, again, unlike Ehrenreich, they somehow have had access to the innermost thoughts of her co-workers, assuring us about their true feelings of pride and self-respect. Furthermore, such critiques often fail to engage with Ehrenreich's primary argument in the book about the inadequacy of wages. It is remarkable how seldom such hostile reviews turn to economic theories or market analysis to disprove Ehrenreich's claims. Rather, the critics insist that the work of waitresses, salespeople, and maids is valuable primarily in symbolic terms. Such workers, they claim, are satisfied with their lives and deservingly proud of their jobs. Though these critics find fault with Ehrenreich for denying the productive contributions made by low-wage workers, they do not consider the relationship between symbolic and material rewards. If such work confers pride, dignity, and symbolic value on its practitioners, then should it not be compensated sufficiently? In failing to address this question, critics make a familiar ideological move by presenting work as a panacea for social ills. If it does not offer people living wages, then at least it grants them a sense of pride—a level of dignity that Ehrenreich allegedly denies them in her call for sustainable income and improved working conditions.

In addition to questioning Ehrenreich's ethical position in relationship to the involuntary poor, critics also explicitly debate the book's relationship to Christianity. Once again, Ehrenreich's personal status becomes the focus for both criticism and praise of *Nickel and Dimed*. Though she is a self-proclaimed Marxist and atheist, Ehrenreich follows in a long tradition of medieval writers who consider how Christian ethics are bound into discussions of poverty and work. Ehrenreich explicitly makes comments about Christianity on two occasions in the book, and, in so doing, she offers differing perspectives on religion that reveal once again the hermeneutic and ethical complexity of poverty. Ehrenreich first turns to consider Christian ethics after she attends a church revival one evening while she is working in Maine. She finds the event uninspiring and remarks that "It would be nice if someone would read this sad-eyed crowd the Sermon on the Mount, accompanied by a rousing commentary on income inequality and the need for a hike in the minimum wage." Ehrenreich laments that the contemporary church has excluded economic issues from its arena of moral concern. Objecting to its ethical vision, she complains that the institution has willfully obfuscated Christ's role as a politically radical figure: "Jesus makes his appearance here only as a corpse; the living man, the wine-guzzling vagrant and precocious socialist, is never once mentioned, nor anything he ever had to say. Christ crucified rules, and it may be that the true business of modern Christianity is to crucify him again and again so that he can never get a word out of his mouth" (68–69). Criticizing an undifferentiated notion of "modern Christianity," Ehrenreich promotes an evangelical vision that features a "vagrant" Christ opposed to the interests of the wealthy. For Ehrenreich, belief in Christ should entail a challenge to the current socioeconomic situation; Jesus stresses the importance of the needy by calling for the rich to give up their copious possessions in assistance to the poor.

While Ehrenreich finds reformist potential in Christianity, she clearly finds fault with modern churches for failing to harness that potential. This skepticism about religion becomes more prominent in other sections of the book; and Ehrenreich shifts into the traditional Marxist perspective as she goes on to criticize the political implications of religious values such as humility, simplicity, and patience. While working as a maid, for example, Ehrenreich lapses into a moment of fantasy in which she develops an imagined spiritual motivation for her labor. Drawing from Christianity and other religious traditions, she tries envisioning her work as if it were a holy vocation dedicated to humility and simplicity: "while scrubbing and Windexing and buffing, I cobble together a philosophy of glorious nonattachment. I draw on the Jesus . . . who said that the last shall be first and that, if someone asks for your cloak, give him your robe as well. I throw in a dab of secondhand Buddhism remembered from a friend's account of a monastery in northern California where rich people pay to spend their weekends meditating and doing various menial chores, housework included" (108). As Ehrenreich continues to shape this elaborate vision, she presents religious faith as a fantasy that sustains her work as a low-wage laborer. Religion makes her work a higher pursuit in spiritual terms, but it has the material effect of keeping workers passive and complacent. In this mentality, both her efforts and the suffering of Holly, a co-worker recently injured on the job, become blessed gifts. She tells us, "I am not working for a maid service; rather, I have joined a mystic order dedicated to performing the most despised of tasks, cheerfully and virtually for free—grateful, in fact, for this chance to earn grace through submission and toil. Holly can bleed to death in my presence if she likes, and I will just consider her to be specially favored by an inscrutable God, more or less as Jesus was" (108).

In Ehrenreich's fantasy, spiritual motivation and religious belief function as a means of tolerating and therefore perpetuating injustice. Jesus's praise for humility and peace seems to lose all political force in this imaginary, and the physical suffering of Ehrenreich's co-workers becomes a testament to their presumed sanctity, not to their exploitation at the hands of business owners in a capitalist economy. Ehrenreich delivers this narrative diversion with irony, for it undermines the basic premise of the book as an argument for higher wages and better working conditions. Predictably, her "exalted mood lasts [only] for about a day." While Ehrenreich offers different models of Christianity, positing it as a force that on the one hand promises political revolution and that on the other hand preserves the status quo, these opposing perspectives are aligned, for they present Christianity as a religion that essentially values poverty and simplicity. Ehrenreich questions the implications of promoting such virtues, as she imagines them as a force with the potential either to improve the lives of the poor or to perpetuate their misery.

Critics of the book have been drawn to Ehrenreich's comments on Christianity, and here too we find opposing arguments about her treatment of the subject. What has garnered most attention from critics, however, is the very idea uniting Ehrenreich's conflicting comments about religion—that Christian faith entails a commitment to poverty, humility, and simplicity. When the University of North Carolina at Chapel Hill assigned *Nickel and Dimed* as required reading for all incoming freshmen in 2003, a group of politically conservative students and politicians protested. Following on the heels of the previous year's controversial book, the Koran, the university's choice of *Nickel and Dimed* was seen by Republican State Senator Austin M. Allran as "part of a larger pattern . . . about being anti-Christian."[22] An alliance of students and state legislators took out a full-page ad in the Raleigh *News & Observer* claiming that *Nickel and Dimed* "mounts an all-out assault on Christians, conservatives, and capitalism."[23] Positing what can perhaps be seen as a new kind of trinity, the ad assumes that these three entities somehow form a seamless and organic whole, with Christianity, conservatism, and capitalism all advancing the goals of one another. Indeed, for Senator Allran, it was nothing less than an insult to hear Christ described as a "wine-guzzling vagrant" who espoused a potentially leftist form of politics. Allran told the media, "I am offended because I am a Christian and [Ehrenreich] is an atheist. . . . I don't like the disparaging remarks she made about Jesus. If I was [at the University of North Carolina], I would sue the school for religious discrimination, and, in fact, I think that someone needs to."[24] While Senator Allran's comments derive from a politically conservative strain of modern evangelical Christianity, they raise the specter of antifraternal ideology in the Middle Ages.

The senator's objections to *Nickel and Dimed* fascinatingly reproduce debates pitting a destitute, vagrant Christ against his business-minded counterpart. Allran would very likely approve of William Taylor's Christ who encourages not poverty, but labor, self-sufficiency, and the benefits of "husbondderie and marchaundise."[25]

Yet other critics disagree with accusations that *Nickel and Dimed* marks an attack on Christianity, and some reviewers see the book as a powerful call to Christian ethics. Joni Scott, for example, finds this call all the more remarkable because it has been articulated by someone outside of the Christian tradition. She argues that "it seems to have taken an atheist to do a Christian's job."[26] Indeed, other reviewers think that the book is powerful because it helps reveal what it means to be a Christian by educating readers about the cardinal virtue of justice. Thus, for Frederic and Mary Ann Brussat, Ehrenreich exemplifies one of Aquinas's lessons on sanctity: "Thomas Aquinas once wrote: 'Saints have a heart full of justice.' On these terms alone, Barbara Ehrenreich is a modern day saint crying in the wilderness that the poor and the vulnerable be treated fairly."[27] Jimmy Dorrell articulates a similar conception of justice in his review of *Nickel and Dimed,* and he remarks that "defending the poor and oppressed is inextricably connected to our faith." He goes on to criticize the mainstream evangelical church for concentrating on "a single issue, such as abortion," while ignoring "other injustices" that include poverty and hunger. Dorrell reveals his ideological distance from critics like Senator Allran by arguing that the church's myopia promotes a "privatized, self-protecting, non-biblical version of Christianity." For critics like Dorrell, *Nickel and Dimed* exposes an essential dimension of Christian morality that is all too often ignored in modern religious practice. He laments that "the average businessman or woman sitting in Sunday school class sees no connection with faith and justice in the public sector."[28]

Despite the potential ambiguities to be found in the book's conception of Christianity, its treatment of voluntary poverty, and its epistemological reach, what remains clear from *Nickel and Dimed* is that it seeks to make a powerful claim on the consciences of its readers. Though Ehrenreich does not write from a Christian perspective, she ultimately offers *Nickel and Dimed* in the hope that it will serve as a catalyst for penitence. After recapitulating how low-wage labor so often fails to offer workers self-sufficiency and a sense of dignity, Ehrenreich questions how readers should finally respond to this socioeconomic reality. Her answer is unequivocal, and she says that "the appropriate emotion is shame—shame at our own dependency . . . on the underpaid labor of others" (221). Here, Ehrenreich appeals to an emotion with powerful moral consequences. As Langland writes, "Ther smyt no thyng so smerte, ne smelleth so foule / As Shame."[29] Yet Ehrenreich's invocation of shame recalls Langland in another way, reminding us of his insistent use of the phrase *redde quod debes.* In this sense, Ehrenreich goes on to present the work of the lower class as a precious gift that greatly exceeds any compensation or wages they may earn. Using the second person to highlight the relationship between the reader and the typical low-wage worker, Ehrenreich explains that "When someone works for less pay than she can live on—when, for example, she goes hungry so that you can eat more cheaply and conveniently—then she has made a great sacrifice for you, she has made you a gift of some part of her abilities, her health, and her life" (221).

Ehrenreich turns the tables on traditional stereotypes that present the poor as fundamentally lazy people dependent on the generosity and assistance of others. Rather, the poor are first and foremost people who work, and their underpaid labor emerges as a gift generated by a deep-seated spirit of charity. This gift has made its beneficiaries indebted to the working poor, and Ehrenreich calls on the middle and upper classes to render what they owe to their fellow people. She claims that "The 'working poor,' as they are approvingly termed, are in fact the major philanthropists of our society. They neglect their own children so that the children of others will be cared for; they live in substandard housing so that other homes will be shiny and perfect; they endure privation so that inflation will be low and stock prices high. To be a member of the working poor is to be an anonymous donor, a nameless benefactor, to everyone else" (221). These powerful words are evocative of York's *Last Judgment* play or Langland's Passus IX, for they insist that the needy are the true givers of charity. Such generosity, however, entails troubling consequences—it not only compromises the material and psychological welfare of the givers, but endangers the moral welfare of the recipients as well.

Nickel and Dimed's contentious portrait of poverty as something that is at once performed and endured—as a condition that is both material and spiritual, heroic and wretched—reminds us that medieval conceptions of poverty continue to inform modern discussions of the issue in powerful, if implicit, ways. For all of the subject's intricacies in both medieval and modern times, what remains perhaps most clear is that poverty still functions as a force that makes powerful claims on human beings. Ehrenreich's work attests to this singular attribute of poverty, for the book's arguments provoke a range of charged reactions. Whether hostile or positive, the responses to *Nickel and Dimed* share a level of intensity, revealing how poverty has the power to prick at the conscience. Even if the book's account of poverty does not generate the shamefulness demanded by Ehrenreich, it still touches a nerve with readers, provoking some critics to articulate rationales that seek (however successfully) to justify wider ethical commitments and forms of social relation. Ehrenreich's representation of poverty demands a response, and like their medieval predecessors, modern critics and writers harness the issue's epistemological ambiguity for different political and ethical ends. As *Nickel and Dimed* continues to show how poverty impinges on questions of labor, representation, and Christian ethics, the book taps into enduring cultural anxieties. Though performed in a modern, secular context, Ehrenreich's own claims of poverty generate a familiar urgency once again revealing the hermeneutic challenges and ethical stakes involved in any attempt to discern poverty's presence.

NOTES

Introduction

1. *Francis of Assisi: Early Documents,* ed. and trans. Regis J. Armstrong, J. Wayne Hellmann, and William J. Short, 3 vols. (Hyde Park, NY: New City Press, 1999–2001), 1:193.

2. On the Franciscan order, its philosophy of poverty, and early antifraternal conflicts, see the earlier and later rules of St. Francis, in *Francis of Assisi: Early Documents,* 1:63–86, 99–106; Malcolm Lambert, *Franciscan Poverty: The Doctrine of the Absolute Poverty of Christ and the Apostles in the Franciscan Order, 1210–1323* (St. Bonaventure, NY: Franciscan Institute, 1998), 221–69; Gordon Leff, *Heresy in the Later Middle Ages,* 2 vols. (Manchester: Manchester University Press, 1967), 1:51–167; Janet Coleman, "Property and Poverty," in *The Cambridge History of Medieval Political Thought,* ed. J. H. Burns, 607–48 (Cambridge: Cambridge University Press, 1988), 630; James Doyne Dawson, "William of Saint-Amour and the Apostolic Tradition," *Medieval Studies* 70 (1978): 223–38; Penn R. Szittya, *The Antifraternal Tradition in Medieval Literature* (Princeton: Princeton University Press, 1986), 11–61; and Takashi Shogimen, *Ockham and Political Discourse in the Late Middle Ages* (Cambridge: Cambridge University Press, 2007), chap. 1, which offers the helpful reminder that the Franciscan theory of poverty was not "monolithic and immutable" (38).

3. Kenneth Baxter Wolf, *The Poverty of Riches* (Oxford: Oxford University Press, 2003), 4.

4. Michael Hardt and Antonio Negri, *Empire* (Cambridge, MA: Harvard University Press, 2000), 413. Bruce Holsinger and Ethan Knapp, "The Marxist Premodern," *Journal of Medieval and Early Modern Studies* 34, no. 3 (2004): 463–71, at 470n6, remark that this tribute to Francis is perhaps surprising given the other influential perspective that Francis's poverty worked to endorse a protocapitalist ideology. See, for example, Lester Little, *Religious Poverty and the Profit Economy in Medieval Europe* (Ithaca: Cornell University Press, 1978). Kellie Robertson, *The Laborer's Two Bodies: Labor and the "Work" of the Text in Medieval Britain, 1350–1500* (New York: Palgrave Macmillan, 2006), 190–93, also briefly discusses the problems with Hardt and Negri's nostalgia for the medieval past.

5. On changing conceptions of poverty in relation to antifraternal discourse or the labor statutes, see David Aers, *Community, Gender, and Individual Identity: English Writing, 1360–1430* (London: Routledge, 1988), chap. 1; Christopher Dyer, *Making a Living in the Middle Ages: The People of Britain, 850–1520* (New Haven: Yale University Press, 2002), 282–85, 290, 315, 319; Anne Middleton, "Acts of Vagrancy: The C-Version Autobiography and the Statute of 1388," in *Written Work: Langland, Labor, and Authorship,* ed. Stephen Justice and Kathryn Kerby-Fulton, 208–317 (Philadelphia: University of Pennsylvania Press, 1997); Maria Moisa, "Fourteenth-Century Preachers' Views of the Poor: Class or Status Group?" in *Culture, Ideology and Politics,* ed. Ralph Samuel and Gareth Stedman Jones, 160–75 (London: Routledge and Kegan Paul, 1982); Bertha Putnam, *The Enforcement of the Statute of Laborers during the First Decade after the Black Death* (New York: Columbia University Press, 1908); Frank Rexroth, *Deviance and Power in Late Medieval London,* trans. Pamela E. Selwyn (Cambridge: Cambridge University Press, 2007), chap. 1; Miri Rubin, *Charity and Community in Medieval Cambridge* (Cambridge: Cambridge University Press, 1987), 31–33, 71–72; and Wendy Scase, *Piers Plowman and the New Anticlericalism* (Cambridge: Cambridge University Press, 1987), chap. 3.

6. These are terms employed respectively by Moisa, "Fourteenth-Century Preachers' Views," 166, and Aers, *Community, Gender, and Individual Identity,* 35. See also Catharina Lis and Hugo Soly, *Poverty and Capitalism in Pre-Industrial Europe,* trans. James Coonan (Atlantic Highlands, NJ: Humanities Press, 1979), 52. George Ovitt, *The Restoration of Perfection: Labor and Technology in Medieval Culture* (New Brunswick: Rutgers University Press, 1986), chap. 5, sees seeds of this changing attitude toward labor in the thirteenth century when the church began to "secularize" labor, "creating for [its] practitioners a separate identity within Christian culture" (138). On new conceptions of sloth as a sin opposed to labor, see Nicola Masciandaro, *The Voice of the Hammer: The Meaning of Work in Middle English Literature* (Notre Dame, IN: University of Notre Dame Press, 2007), 117–20.

7. Louise Fradenburg, "Needful Things," in *Medieval Crime and Social Control,* ed. Barbara A. Hanawalt and David Wallace, 49–67 (Minneapolis: University of Minnesota Press, 1999), 57. On poverty as a representational sign in *Piers Plowman,* see David Aers, *Sanctifying Signs: Making Christian Tradition in Late Medieval England* (Notre Dame, IN: University of Notre Dame Press, 2004), chap. 5.

8. "Claim," *v., Oxford English Dictionary,* 2.a.

9. "The Later Rule," in *Francis of Assisi: Early Documents,* 1:103.

10. These particular points, which derive from William's *Collectiones,* are treated in Szittya, *The Antifraternal Tradition,* 48. For an account of William's role in the mendicant controversy at the University of Paris, see Dawson, "William

of Saint-Amour and the Apostolic Tradition," and Szittya, *The Antifraternal Tradition,* 11–61.

11. John also undermined the Franciscan theory of poverty by withdrawing papal ownership of the order's goods and property and by denying the Franciscan distinction between use and dominion. See *Ad conditorem canonum* (1322) and *Cum inter nonnullos* (1323) as well as *Quia quorumdam mentes* (1324) and *Quia vir reprobus* (1329) in *Bullarium Franciscanum,* ed. Conrad Eubel (Rome: Typis Vaticanis, 1898), vol. 5, no. 486, 233–47; no. 518, 256–59; no. 554, 271–80; and no. 820, 408–49, respectively. For a discussion of these conflicts and their effects on the Franciscan idealization of poverty, see Leff, *Heresy in the Later Middle Ages,* 1:51–167; Lambert, *Franciscan Poverty,* 221–69; Rubin, *Charity and Community,* 71–72; and Aers, *Community, Gender, and Individual Identity,* 23–25.

12. Richard FitzRalph, *Defensio Curatorum,* in *Trevisa's Dialogus,* ed. John Perry, EETS o.s. 167 (Cambridge: Cambridge University Press, 1925), 80. I discuss FitzRalph and his role in the mendicancy conflicts in chapter three.

13. On the demographic and economic changes resulting from the plague, see John Hatcher and Edward Miller, *Medieval England: Rural Society and Economic Change, 1086–1348* (London: Longman, 1978), 29; M. M. Postan, *The Medieval Economy and Society: An Economic History of Britain in the Middle Ages* (London: Weidenfeld and Nicolson, 1972), 27–39; Dyer, *Making a Living,* 268, 271–72, 357–58; J. L. Bolton, *The Medieval English Economy, 1150–1500* (London: J. M. Dent, 1980), 214–15, 238–41; E. B. Fryde, *Peasants and Landlords in Later Medieval England* (New York: St. Martin's Press, 1996), 114; and Brian Tierney, *Medieval Poor Law: A Sketch of Canonical Theory and Its Application in England* (Berkeley: University of California Press, 1959), 112.

14. "Claim," *v., Oxford English Dictionary,* 4. See also "claimen," (v.), *Middle English Dictionary,* 1.(a). Such an idea certainly seems to inform the practices of "clamerous beggars," who outraged the Wycliffite preacher William Taylor. See William Taylor, "Sermon of William Taylor," in *Two Wycliffite Texts,* ed. Anne Hudson, EETS o.s. 301 (Oxford: Oxford University Press, 1993), 21/673. On the etymology of "claim" and "clamorous," which stem from the Latin verb "clamare," see the entries for each word in the *Oxford English Dictionary.*

15. For discussions of the labor statutes and their investment in protecting the interests of elite employers, see Aers, *Community, Gender, and Individual Identity,* chap. 1; Dyer, *Making a Living,* 282–85, 290, 315, 319; Middleton, "Acts of Vagrancy"; Rubin, *Charity and Community,* 31–33; and K. Robertson, *The Laborer's Two Bodies,* chap. 1.

16. *Statutes of the Realm,* ed. A Luders et al. (London: 1810–28), 23 EDW, III. c.1–4, 1:307.

17. Marjorie McIntosh, *Controlling Misbehavior in England, 1370–1600* (Cambridge: Cambridge University Press, 1998), 130, helpfully describes the

difference between the ideology of the labor laws and social reality in the late fourteenth century: "[In a time] marked in most regions by secondary plague outbursts occurring on average every ten years or so, newcomers were probably welcomed to the community if they were willing to work at all, not hurried out as vagabonds. Even the idlers were less of a problem than in more densely populated periods: empty housing was abundant, and because real wages were high those who chose not to seek regular employment could get by with only a limited amount of daily or harvest time labor." See also Aers, *Community, Gender, and Individual Identity,* chap. 1 and Christopher Dyer, *Standards of Living in the Later Middle Ages: Social Change in England, c. 1200–1520* (Cambridge: Cambridge University Press, 1989), 253–54.

18. *Statutes of the Realm,* 23 EDW, III. c.5–7, 1:308.

19. See also the 1351 Statute of Laborers, which accuses servants of pursuing "ease" and "covetise" to the "great damage of great men, and impoverishing of all the said Commonalty"; *Statutes of the Realm,* 25 EDW, III. c.1–2, 1:311. I discuss below the constructions of poverty found in other labor laws and petitions.

20. See, "claim," *n., Oxford English Dictionary,* 2.

21. On medieval debates about the practice of charity, see Michel Mollat, *The Poor in the Middle Ages,* trans. Arthur Goldhammer (New Haven: Yale University Press, 1986), 134; Rubin, *Charity and Community,* 68–74; Aers, *Community, Gender, and Individual Identity,* 23–24; Tierney, *Medieval Poor Law,* 54–64; Tierney, "The Decretalists and the 'Deserving Poor,'" *Comparative Studies in Society and History* 1, no. 4 (1959): 360–73; McIntosh, *Controlling Misbehavior,* 91; and Barbara Hanawalt, "Reading the Lives of the Illiterate: London's Poor," *Speculum* 80 (2005), 1068.

22. Cited in Aers, *Community, Gender, and Individual Identity,* 24. See also Mollat, *The Poor in the Middle Ages,* 134. For the continued relevance of debates about charity in antifraternal conflicts of late medieval England, see, for example, Richard of Maidstone's *Protectorium Pauperis, Carmelus* 5 (1958), 141.

23. This particular phrase is taken from the 1376 Commons' Petition against Vagrants (*The Parliament Rolls of Medieval England,* ed. C. Given-Wilson et al. [Woodbridge: Boydell, 2005], 5: 338; also available on CD-ROM [Leicester: Scholarly Digital Editions, 2005], Edward III 1376 April, Membrane 15). However, laws as early as the 1349 ordinance criminalize indiscriminate charity, stipulating that no one "upon the said Pain of Imprisonment shall, under the colour of Piety or Alms, give any thing to such, which may labour" (*Statutes of the Realm,* 23 EDW, III. c.5–7, 1:308).

24. Middleton, "Acts of Vagrancy," 238–41, helpfully discusses the nature of this anxiety.

25. *The Parliament Rolls of Medieval England,* 5: 338; or CD-ROM, Edward III 1376 April, Membrane 15. I use the translation in R. B. Dobson, ed., *The Peasants' Revolt of 1381* (London: Macmillan, 1983), 74. On the connections

between poverty and vagrancy, see Middleton, "Acts of Vagrancy," and Barbara Hanawalt, "Reading the Lives of the Illiterate," 1084; see also Rexroth, *Deviance and Power in Late Medieval London,* 86–96.

26. For the 1388 Cambridge Statute, see *Statutes of the Realm,* 12 RICH. II, c. 7, or *English Economic History: Select Documents,* ed. A. E. Bland, P. A. Brown, and R. H. Tawney (London: G. Bell and Sons, 1915), 173. The innovations of this law can also be observed in its post-1381 perception of workers as a potential source of violence and disruption. It thus stipulated that workers were not allowed to carry weapons or participate in certain games on Sundays. The law is also unique in making agricultural labor compulsory for any kind of worker whose services might be needed during the harvest. Furthermore, it proclaims that children aged twelve and up, who have been habitually accustomed to agricultural labor, must remain in that occupation. On this statute and its novel measures, see Middleton, "Acts of Vagrancy"; McIntosh, *Controlling Misbehavior,* 98; and K. Robertson, *The Laborer's Two Bodies,* 18, 159–60, 186–87. Relevant to the statute's attempts to stabilize social identity is an earlier law (1361), which stipulated that wandering laborers were to be returned to their community of origin to face not only imprisonment but also the possibility of being branded on the forehead with an "F" signaling falsity. See *Statutes of the Realm,* 34 EDW, III. c.10, 2:367. Noting that there is no evidence that this law was actually enforced, K. Robertson, *The Laborer's Two Bodies,* 17–19, discusses how it is nonetheless important because it imagines a new way of making the identities of laborers meaningfully visible by attempting to transform their bodies into texts.

27. On the improved conditions for peasants and the declining economic circumstances for lords after the plague, see, for example, Bolton, *The Medieval English Economy,* 214–15, 238–41; Dyer, *Making a Living,* 268, 274–94, 357–58; and Fryde, *Peasants and Landlords,* 114.

28. From the late fourteenth to the early fifteenth centuries, there were periods of declining wage rates and instances of famine, events that could certainly force working people into poverty. Moreover, in the second half of the fifteenth century, the economic situation began to shift, and many places in England suffered from an overall financial decline. Bolton, *The Medieval English Economy,* 241, offers a helpful reminder that "the prosperity of all classes of the peasantry must not be exaggerated." On brief periods of declining wage rates, see Dyer, *Standards of Living,* 219. On the famine of 1437–40, see Fryde, *Peasants and Landlords,* 116. And for discussions of what McIntosh calls the "rather different [economic] situation of the fifteenth century," see her *Controlling Misbehavior,* 192; Bolton, *The Medieval English Economy,* chap. 8; Dyer, *Making a Living,* 268; and Fryde, *Peasants and Landlords,* 115, 145–47.

29. On the varied causes of poverty affecting young people, householders, and the elderly, see Judith Bennett, "Conviviality and Charity in Medieval and Early Modern England," *Past and Present* 134 (1992): 19–41, at 40. Hanawalt, "Reading the Lives of the Illiterate," 1075, gives concrete examples of the flexible

meanings of poverty as she studies London wills that define, without any explicit rationale, some people as "beggars," some as "paupers," and others as simply "poor people." Given the capacious conceptions of poverty in the Middle Ages, my own terminology of poverty in this book is often deliberately unspecified, though I attempt throughout to call attention to the range of meanings that are possible in approaching poverty as a material, social, political, and spiritual condition.

30. The obligation to give alms selectively to the "truly needy" can be observed in certain forms of charitable practice in late medieval England. For example, wills routinely named the deserving poor as beneficiaries, the foundations of almshouses specified standards of eligibility, and the membership ordinances of religious guilds denied assistance to members who begged publicly. See, for example, Dyer, *Standards of Living,* 244–51; Hanawalt, "Reading the Lives of the Illiterate," 1082–83; P. H. Cullum and P. J. P. Goldberg, "Charitable Provision in Late Medieval York: 'To the Praise of God and the Use of the Poor,'" *Northern History* 29 (1993): 24–39; Ben McRee, "Charity and Gild Solidarity in Late Medieval England," *Journal of British Studies* 32, no. 3 (1993): 195–225, at 210–11; and Rexroth, *Deviance and Power in Late Medieval London,* chap. 6.

31. My exploration of the literature of poverty is by no means meant to be exhaustive. Given the widespread presence of poverty in medieval literature, this book is also a provocation encouraging others to examine additional texts so as to flesh out the cultural picture more fully.

32. My commitment to the close reading of texts is informed by the tenets of New Formalism, which seeks to enrich historical and cultural criticism by foregrounding the formal dimensions of texts. Close reading is clearly essential to this practice as Marjorie Levinson describes, "Reading, understood in traditional terms as multilayered and integrative responsiveness to every element of the textual dimension, quite simply produces the basic materials that form the subject matter of even the most historical of investigations. Absent this, we are reading something of our own untrammeled invention, inevitably less complex than the products of reading"; "What is New Formalism?" *PMLA* 122, no. 2 (2007): 558–69, at 560.

33. Barbara Ehrenreich, *Nickel and Dimed: On (Not) Getting by in America* (New York: Henry Holt, 2001), 216.

Chapter One

1. Luke 16:26, *The Douai-Rheims Bible.*

2. For readings of the parable emphasizing Dives's failure in mercy and charity, see Thomas Aquinas, *Catena Aurea,* ed. and trans. John Henry Newman, 4 vols. (Southampton: St. Austin Press, 1997), 3:562–64; Denis the Carthusian, *Opera Omnia,* 42 vols. (Monstrolii: Typis Cartusiae S. M. De Pratis, 1896),

12:127; Anne Hudson and Pamela Gradon, eds., *English Wycliffite Sermons,* 5 vols. (Oxford: Oxford University Press, 1983–96), sermon 1, esp. lines 70–72; William Taylor, "The Sermon of William Taylor," in *Two Wycliffite Texts,* ed. Anne Hudson, EETS o.s. 301 (Oxford: Oxford University Press, 1993), 12, lines 349–56; *Omnis plantacio,* in Anne Hudson, ed., *The Works of a Lollard Preacher,* EETS 317 (Oxford; Oxford University Press, 2001), 28, lines 727–32.

3. Here I refer to Hunger (VIII.277–81), Patience (XV.299–300), Abraham (XVIII.274–85), and the Samaritan (XIX.233–46) in William Langland, *Piers Plowman: The C-Version; Will's Visions of Piers Plowman, Do-Well, Do-Better, and Do-Best,* ed. George Russell and George Kane (London: Athlone Press, 1997). All subsequent references to *Piers Plowman* will be cited parenthetically by Passus and line number.

4. The first phrase is spoken by Holy Churche at I.172 and by Repentance at VII.103; the second phrase is spoken by Study at XI.70; and the third phrase is spoken by the Samaritan at XIX.223. See also IX.70–281, a passage explicitly directed to potential almsgivers.

5. Anne Scott, *Piers Plowman and the Poor* (Dublin: Four Courts Press, 2004), 64, takes this point as a major premise of her book, arguing that "Langland has a direct, practical and ongoing concern for the material relief of the poor which he regards as fundamental to any individual's pursuit of salvation." Her work, however, largely dismisses the hermeneutic complexities associated with almsgiving and tends to suggest that Langland favors indiscriminate charity. D. Vance Smith, *Arts of Possession* (Minneapolis: University of Minnesota Press, 2003), 112, observes other difficulties in the poem's call to charity regarding especially how the text does not distinguish "between what is to be disposed of and what is to be retained."

6. The most relevant studies concerning poverty and *Piers Plowman* include Robert Adams, "The Nature of Need in *Piers Plowman* XX," *Traditio* 34 (1978): 273–302; David Aers, "*Piers Plowman* and Problems in the Perception of Poverty: A Culture in Transition," *Leeds Studies in English* 14 (1983): 5–25; David Aers, *Community, Gender, and Individual Identity: English Writing 1360–1430* (London: Routledge, 1988), chap. 1; David Aers, *Sanctifying Signs: Making Christian Tradition in Late Medieval England* (Notre Dame, IN: University of Notre Dame Press, 2004), chap. 5; Lawrence Clopper, *Songes of Rechelesnesse: Langland and the Franciscans* (Ann Arbor: University of Michigan Press, 1997); Louise Fradenburg, "Needful Things," in *Medieval Crime and Social Control,* ed. Barbara A. Hanawalt and David Wallace, 49–67 (Minneapolis: University of Minnesota Press, 1997); Kathleen Hewett-Smith, "Allegory on the Half-Acre: The Demands of History," *Yearbook of Langland Studies* 10 (1996): 1–22; Kathleen Hewett-Smith, "'Lo, here lyflode ynow, yf oure beleue be trewe': Poverty and the Transfiguration of History in the Central Visions of *Piers Plowman,*" *Chaucer Yearbook* 5 (1998): 139–61; Kathleen Hewett-Smith, "'Nede

Hath No Lawe': Poverty and the De-stabilization of Allegory in the Final Visions of *Piers Plowman*," in *William Langland's Piers Plowman: A Book of Essays*, ed. Kathleen Hewett-Smith, 233–53 (New York: Routledge, 2001); Margaret Kim, "Hunger, Need, and the Politics of Poverty in *Piers Plowman*," *Yearbook of Langland Studies* 16 (2003): 131–68; Jill Mann, "The Nature of Need Revisited," *Yearbook of Langland Studies* 18 (2004): 3–29; Anne Middleton, "Acts of Vagrancy: The C-Version Autobiography and the Statute of 1388," in *Written Work: Langland, Labor, and Authorship*, ed. Stephen Justice and Kathryn Kerby-Fulton, 208–317 (Philadelphia: University of Pennsylvania Press, 1997); Derek Pearsall, "Poverty and Poor People in *Piers Plowman*," in *Medieval English Studies Presented to George Kane*, ed. E. D. Kennedy, R. Waldron, and J. S. Wittig, 167–85 (Woodbridge: Boydell and Brewer, 1988); Derek Pearsall, "Lunatyk Lollares in *Piers Plowman*," in *Religion in the Poetry and Drama of the Late Middle Ages*, ed. Piero Boitani and Anna Torti, 163–78 (Cambridge: Cambridge University Press, 1989); Wendy Scase, *Piers Plowman and the New Anticlericalism* (Cambridge: Cambridge University Press, 1989), chaps. 3–4; Anne M. Scott, *Piers Plowman and the Poor*; Geoffrey Shepherd, "Poverty in *Piers Plowman*," in *Social Relations and Ideas*, ed. T. H. Aston, P. R. Cross, and C. Dyer, 169–89 (Cambridge: Cambridge University Press, 1983); and Penn R. Szittya, *The Antifraternal Tradition in Medieval Literature* (Princeton: Princeton University Press, 1986), chap. 7.

7. Scott, *Piers Plowman and the Poor*, 114. See also Nicolette Zeeman, *Piers Plowman and the Medieval Discourse of Desire* (Cambridge: Cambridge University Press, 2006), for the argument that poverty or lack has a spiritually generative function in *Piers Plowman*. Approaching poverty primarily in terms of kynde, Zeeman explains that lack is beneficial for it "characterize[s] the revelatory lessons of the natural order" (215).

8. Clopper, *Songes of Rechelesnesse*. In arguing for the influence of Joachite thought on *Piers Plowman*, Kathryn Kerby-Fulton, *Books Under Suspicion: Censorship and Tolerance of Revelatory Writing in Late Medieval England* (Notre Dame, IN: University of Notre Dame Press, 2006), 158, also suggests that Langland has "empathies with rigorist Franciscan ideals."

9. Aers, *Sanctifying Signs*, chap. 5.

10. On *Piers Plowman* and labor legislation, see Aers, *Community, Gender, and Individual Identity*, chap. 1; Clopper, "Need Men and Women Labor?: Langland's Wanderer and the Labor Ordinances," in *Chaucer's England: Literature in Historical Context*, ed. Barbara Hanawalt, 110–29 (Minneapolis: University of Minnesota Press, 1992); Middleton, "Acts of Vagrancy"; Steven Justice, *Writing and Rebellion: England in 1381* (Berkeley: University of California Press, 1996), chap. 3; and Kellie Robertson, *The Laborer's Two Bodies: Labor and the "Work" of the Text in Medieval Britain, 1350–1500* (New York: Palgrave Macmillan, 2006), 45–50. On the antifraternal and anticlerical dimensions of

Piers Plowman, see Robert W. Frank, "The Conclusion of *Piers Plowman,*" *Journal of English and Germanic Philology* 49 (1950): 309–16; Szittya, *The Antifraternal Tradition,* chap. 7; T. P. Dolan, "Langland and FitzRalph: Two Solutions to the Mendicant Problem," *The Yearbook of Langland Studies* 2 (1988): 35–45; and Scase, *Piers Plowman and the New Anticlericalism.* Kathryn Kerby-Fulton suggests that Langland's poem participates not in a "new anticlericalism," but in enduring interclerical conflicts; see her "*Piers Plowman,*" in *The Cambridge History of Medieval English Literature,* ed. David Wallace, 513–38 (Cambridge: Cambridge University Press, 1999), esp. 529–32.

11. For a relevant approach to *Piers Plowman,* see William Rogers, *Interpretation in Piers Plowman* (Washington DC: Catholic University of America Press, 2002), which argues that "what the poem *does* is to cause its reader to reflect on the activity of interpretation itself" (6).

12. Maureen Quilligan, *The Language of Allegory* (Ithaca: Cornell University Press, 1979), 33. Hewett-Smith, in "Allegory on the Half-Acre," "Lo, here lyflude ynow," and "Nede Hath No Lawe," explores the relationship between poverty and allegory in *Piers Plowman.* Her work, however, approaches allegory strictly as an interpretive hierarchy that seeks to move from literal to allegorical signification. In her reading of the poem, the material reality of poverty consistently frustrates or complicates this process. While the literal level of allegory is certainly relevant to material forms of poverty that cannot be transcended, I am primarily interested in the personifications of Langland's allegory and the dynamic shifts that develop among them. Elizabeth Salter's early work offers a more flexible approach to Langland's allegory, which remains helpful to my understanding of the poem. She describes how *Piers Plowman* "proceeds by a succession of different allegorical modes, working changeably, sometimes rapidly, with local and global applications"; *Piers Plowman: An Introduction* (Cambridge, MA: Harvard University Press, 1962), 66. See also, Sarah Tolmie, "Langland, Wittgenstein, and the End of Language," *Yearbook of Langland Studies* 20 (2006): 115–39, which helpfully warns against "pre-understanding" Langland's personifications whose meaning is generated "in the real-time of the poem, from moment to moment" (120).

13. For the argument that Wille's apologia in C.V.1–104 was Langland's last addition to the poem, see Middleton, "Acts of Vagrancy." Before publication of the C-text, the catalog of beggars in C. IX.70–161 circulated in two distinct and less developed forms found in Huntington MS HM 114 and the Ilchester manuscript. See Wendy Scase, "Two *Piers Plowman* C-text Interpolations: Evidence for a Second Textual Tradition," *Notes and Queries* 232 (1987): 456–63. Kathryn Kerby-Fulton notes that the C.V and C. IX interpolations bear "an intimate relation" to one another; "Langland and the Bibliographic Ego," in *Written Work,* 86. On this basis, she argues against Middleton for an earlier composition date of C.V. For the purposes of this chapter, the precise date of origin

for each interpolation is less important than the thematic connection between the passages and their placement together as distinctive additions to the received version of the C-text.

14. Rogers, *Interpretation in Piers Plowman,* 109.

15. On the inevitable connection between need and excess, see Fradenburg, "Needful Things," esp. 50–52, which discusses this issue from a psychoanalytic perspective.

16. For a different perspective on the relationship between need and desire, see Zeeman, *Piers Plowman and the Medieval Discourse of Desire,* 189–95, which traces the development of a "negatively revelatory" view of nature in Christian theology. In this tradition, need and the patient suffering of lack have a spiritual function, generating a positive sense of desire for the divine. In Holy Churche's discourse, however, need seems to produce a different form of desire, one that does not lead explicitly to the divine but to excess within a decidedly material realm.

17. Holy Churche's warnings about the human tendency toward excess perhaps become clearer when one compares her lines to the similar lesson articulated by Mercy in the late medieval play *Mankind.* Mercy tells Mankind: "'Mesure is tresure'; I forbide yow not the use. / Mesure yowrsylf ever. Beware of excesse. / The superfluouse guise I will that ye refuse; / When nature is suffisyde, anon that ye sese"; *Mankind,* in David Bevington, ed., *Medieval Drama* (Boston: Houghton Mifflin, 1975), ll. 236–40. Unlike Holy Churche's teaching, Mercy's speech offers no statements that emphasize the difficulty in living out such lessons.

18. See the note to I.136 in William Langland, *Piers Plowman: An Edition of the C-text,* ed. Derek Pearsall, York Medieval Texts, 2d series (Exeter: University of Exeter Press, 1994). For other discussions of the moral dimensions of "kynde knowing," see Hugh White, *Nature and Salvation in Piers Plowman* (Cambridge: Cambridge University Press, 1988), chap. 2; Britton J. Harwood, *Piers Plowman and the Problem of Belief* (Toronto: University of Toronto Press, 1992), 9–10, 14–19; and Zeeman, *Piers Plowman and the Medieval Discourse of Desire,* 7, 102, 161.

19. Fradenburg, "Needful Things," 51.

20. For a relevant discussion of Holy Churche's particular view of Christ and the figure's wider arguments, see Aers, *Sanctifying Signs,* 100–102.

21. Nor does she quote Jesus's statement in the same gospel passage to "give to everyone who asketh thee."

22. Douce 104 is the only known illustrated manuscript of *Piers Plowman.* Produced in 1427 for an unknown patron, the manuscript contains a Hiberno-English translation of the C-text. Though it features seventy-four illustrations, the manuscript is by no means a luxury volume but seems to have been produced with an eye toward economy. On the Douce manuscript see, Langland,

Piers Plowman: The C Version, 3–4; Derek Pearsall and Kathleen Scott, eds., *Piers Plowman: A Facsimile of Bodleian Library, Oxford, MS Douce 104* (Cambridge: D. S. Brewer, 1992); and Kathryn Kerby-Fulton and Denise Despres, *Iconography and the Professional Reader* (Minneapolis: University of Minnesota Press, 1999).

23. Kerby-Fulton and Despres, *Iconography and the Professional Reader,* 106.

24. Aers, *Community, Gender, and Individual Identity,* chap. 1, has most fully pursued how this section of the poem engages with fourteenth-century labor legislation and post-plague socioeconomic problems.

25. On the shifting nature of Hunger's definitions of hunger, see Kim, "Hunger, Need, and the Politics of Poverty," 152–58.

26. Aers, *Community, Gender, and Individual Identity,* 35–49.

27. Ibid., 43–44. On the 1388 Statute, see Middleton, "Acts of Vagrancy."

28. Aers, *Community, Gender, and Individual Identity,* 47.

29. Aers, "*Piers Plowman* and Problems in the Perception of Poverty," 12.

30. The illustrator of the Douce manuscript recognizes a problem with Hunger's lack of discrimination as a violent force, a subject I discuss below in greater detail. While the text states in this particular moment that Hunger caused hermits to dig, the illustrator is aware that Hunger, as an extreme condition, compels all people (not just wasters or hermits) to work. Accordingly, he presents a digger too "well-dressed for the task he undertakes"; Kerby-Fulton and Despres, *Iconography and the Professional Reader,* 65.

31. Kim, "Hunger, Need, and the Politics of Poverty," 153.

32. On the absence of a spiritual impetus for the workers' labor, see Hewett-Smith, "Allegory on the Half-Acre," 13–14.

33. Pearsall, "Poverty and Poor People in *Piers Plowman,*" 175–76.

34. Kim, "Hunger, Need, and the Politics of Poverty," 156.

35. Kim, "Hunger, Need, and the Politics of Poverty" 155, puts the same problem in different terms: "The allegorical character begins by selling himself as the cure to human malaise and ends up characterizing himself as a deadly killer to the very needy."

36. The death of Lazarus by hunger certainly problematizes R. E. Kaske's view that Hunger represents, in part, "biblical 'hunger and thirst after justice'" (190). See his "The Character Hunger in *Piers Plowman,*" in *Medieval English Studies Presented to George Kane,* ed. Kennedy, Waldron, and Wittig, 187–97.

37. Kim, "Hunger, Need, and the Politics of Poverty," 154.

38. It seems as if Hunger himself understands these troubling dimensions of his identity, when he too advocates the need for moderation in consuming food; see VIII.270–77.

39. For a discussion of *Piers Plowman* in relation to famine and other causes of diminished food supply in fourteenth-century England, see Robert W. Frank, "The 'Hungry Gap,' Crop Failure, and Famine: The Fourteenth-Century Agricultural Crisis and *Piers Plowman,*" *Yearbook of Langland Studies* 4 (1990): 97–104.

40. On the discourse of Rechelesnesse and Patience in this section of the poem as it relates to Franciscan conceptions of poverty, see E. Talbot Donaldson, *Piers Plowman: The C-text and Its Poet* (New Haven: Yale University Press, 1949), 169–80, and Clopper, *Songes of Rechelesnesse,* 80–82, 87–93, and chap. 6. On Patience and Franciscanism specifically, see Guy Bourquin, *Piers Plowman,* 2 vols. (Paris: Champion, 1978), 404–41, 693–736; Pearsall, "Poverty and Poor People in *Piers Plowman,*" 182–85; Aers, *Community, Gender, and Individual Identity,* 60–62; Aers, *Sanctifying Signs,* 120–33; and Clopper, *Songes of Rechelesnesse,* 238–44.

41. On the different connotations of Rechelesnesse, see Donaldson, *Piers Plowman: The C-text and Its Poet,* 171–72, and Clopper, *Songes of Rechelesnesse,* 225.

42. Hewett-Smith, "Lo, here lyflode ynow," 158–59.

43. On Abraham's wealth, see, for example, Hervaeus Natalis, *The Poverty of Christ and the Apostles* (Toronto: Pontifical Institute of Medieval Studies, 1999), 26, which gives the Dominican perspective that Abraham "was most perfect, and yet . . . had great wealth."

44. Shepherd, "Poverty in *Piers Plowman,*" 182, remarks that Langland's sympathetic view of Rechelesnesse "changes to wariness." While Clopper, *Songes of Rechelesnesse,* 223, acknowledges problems with the figure's teaching, the poem, in his view, ultimately supports the Franciscan ideal of recklessness that Rechelesnesse himself has failed to perfect. Zeeman, *Piers Plowman and the Medieval Discourse of Desire,* remarks that the figure promotes "arguments for moral inaction" (217), though presumably such wrong turning, according to her wider thesis, can be ultimately channeled toward the will's spiritual growth.

45. Pearsall, "Poverty and Poor People in *Piers Plowman,*" 182.

46. Clopper, *Songes of Rechelesnesse,* 213.

47. Aers, *Sanctifying Signs,* 120–21.

48. Clopper, *Songes of Rechelesnesse,* 238–45.

49. See Aers, *Sanctifying Signs,* 123–24.

50. The Dominican Hervaeus Natalis makes an objection to the Franciscan ideas espoused by Patience when he explains that "If one refers to the . . . manna that was given to the children of Israel, then it must be said that the privilege of a few does not make a common rule" (*The Poverty of Christ and the Apostles,* 73).

51. Aers, *Sanctifying Signs,* 126–28, remarks that Patience's sudden insistence on moderation is problematic because it demands an acceptance of the things he has thoroughly rejected in his attachment to Franciscan ideals: the material realm and the actual food provided by Actyf.

52. See Aers, *Sanctifying Signs,* 129–30, for the argument that Patience's view of the sins contrasts with their allegorical representation in Passus VI and VII.

53. See, for example, Prudentius, "*Psychomachia,*" in *Prudentius,* ed. and trans. H. J. Thomson, vol. 1 (Cambridge, MA: Harvard University Press, 1949; repr. 1969); Siegfried Wenzel, ed., *Summa virtutum de remediis anime* (Athens:

University of Georgia Press, 1984); and Siegfried Wenzel, ed., *Fasciculus Morum* (University Park: Pennsylvania State University Press, 1989).

54. Clopper, *Songes of Rechelesnesse,* 274.

55. Scott, *Piers Plowman and the Poor,* 114.

56. Aers, *Sanctifying Signs,* 131.

57. Scase, *Piers Plowman and the New Anticlericalism,* 76.

58. Discussing Anima in the B-text, Szittya, *The Antifraternal Tradition,* 261, explains that begging opposes the fundamentally important doctrines of restitution and charity in the poem. Aers, *Sanctifying Signs,* 136, suggests that Liberum Arbitrium's remark constitutes a "supersession of the Franciscanizing sign of poverty."

59. On Liberum Arbitrium, see Harwood, *Piers Plowman and the Problem of Belief,* 103–12, and Paul Sheneman, "Grace Abounding: Justification in Passus 16 of *Piers Plowman,*" *Papers on Language and Literature* 34 (1998): 162–78. Contrary to my view, Clopper, *Songes of Rechelesnesse,* 262–72, reads Anima in the B-text as another figure associated with radical Franciscanism.

60. On the importance of charity in *Piers Plowman* as a virtue and remedy that exceeds the power of poverty and inheres in different economic states, see Salter, *Piers Plowman: An Introduction,* 87; Szittya, *The Antifraternal Tradition,* 260–61; Scase, *Piers Plowman and the New Anticlericalism,* chap. 4; and Aers, *Sanctifying Signs,* 135.

61. Traugott Lawler, "Harlot's Holiness: The System of Absolution for Miswinning in the C Version of *Piers Plowman,*" *Yearbook of Langland Studies* 20 (2006): 141–89, suggests that this line refers specifically to the secular clergy (148). It should be noted that Liberum Arbitrium's anticlericalism is also targeted at "freres and monkes" who take "luyther wynnynges in all here lyf tyme" (XVII.35–36).

62. On charity, familial responsibility, and inheritance, see Brian Tierney, "The Decretists and the 'Deserving Poor,'" *Comparative Studies in Society and History* 1, no. 4 (1959): 360–73, and Scase, *Piers Plowman and the New Anticlericalism,* 84, 103–5.

63. On the notion that the church holds goods only on behalf of the poor, see Scase, *Piers Plowman and the New Anticlericalism,* chaps. 3 and 4.

64. Jacobus de Voragine, *The Golden Legend,* trans. William Granger Ryan, 2 vols. (Princeton: Princeton University Press, 1993), 2:65.

65. For discussion of this quotation, see Aers, *Sanctifying Signs,* 129–33.

66. On Wycliffism and disendowment, see, "The Lollard Disendowment Bill," in Anne Hudson, ed., *Selections from English Wycliffite Writings* (Toronto: University of Toronto Press, 1997), 135, and Anne Hudson, *The Premature Reformation: Wycliffite Texts and Lollard History* (Oxford: Clarendon Press, 1988), 114–16, 337–42. For disendowment as a reformist issue predating Wycliffism, see Kathryn Kerby-Fulton, *Books Under Suspicion,* 4–5 and 136–39, though

Kerby-Fulton acknowledges that "by the time of the C-text, Wycliffite disendowment cries are raging" (144).

67. Aers, *Sanctifying Signs,* 145.

68. In his edition of the C-text, Pearsall takes "adoun" to be "anoen." Such a reading would further emphasize the immediacy of the Samaritan's aid.

69. Clopper, *Songes of Rechelesnesse,* 224.

70. On the social dimensions of the mass and sacraments, see John Bossy, "The Mass as a Social Institution 1200–1700," *Past and Present* 100 (1983): 29–61, and Sarah Beckwith, *Signifying God: Social Relations and Symbolic Act in the York Corpus Christi Plays* (Chicago: University of Chicago Press, 2001).

71. My argument stresses the relationship between the active work of charity and the sacraments, yet it does not advocate a Pelagian or semi-Pelagian understanding of the poem. While characters such as Trajan may encourage such readings, the poem's evolving process arguably disrupts the efficacy of Pelagian theology when Liberum Arbitrium emphasizes the need for almsgivers to participate in penance; when the charitable figure of Abraham describes the suffering he experiences along with Lazarus; and when Langland describes *semyuief*'s utter incapacity to heal himself from the ravages of sin. Aers puts it well in relation to this last example: "In Luke's gospel the Samaritan . . . enacts the perfection of love to which the divine precepts call their followers: 'Go and do now in like manner.' But the narrative of the Samaritan and s*emyuief* together with Christ's elaborate commentary in *Piers Plowman* make it clear that no one can even begin to hear this precept, let alone fulfill it perfectly, without having been placed in the church, where Christ has left the essential sacraments" (*Sanctifying Signs,* 148). For the longstanding critical view that *Piers Plowman* reflects Pelagian tendencies or a "liberal" approach to the salvation of the heathen deemphasizing the sacraments, see, Janet Coleman, *Piers Plowman and the Moderni* (Rome: Edizioni di storia e letteratura, 1981); Adams, "Piers's Pardon and Langland's Semi-Pelagianism," *Traditio* 39 (1983): 367–418; Pamela Gradon, "Trajanus Redivivus: Another Look at Trajan in *Piers Plowman,*" in *Middle English Studies Presented to Norman Davis in Honor of his Seventieth Birthday,* ed. Douglas Gray and E. G. Stanley, 93–114 (Oxford: Clarendon Press, 1983); Gordon Whatley, "*Piers Plowman* B 12.277–94: Notes on Language, Text, Theology," *Modern Philology* 82 (1984): 1–12; Frank Grady, *Representing Righteous Heathens in Late Medieval England* (New York: Palgrave Macmillan, 2005), 22–35; and Kerby-Fulton, *Books Under Suspicion,* 375–91.

72. See also Aers, *Sanctifying Signs,* 146.

73. On the semantic and moral ambiguity of Nede, see Szittya, *The Antifraternal Tradition,* 268, and Fradenburg, "Needful Things."

74. There is a longstanding critical debate regarding the precise nature and moral character of Nede. Generally sympathetic readings of the figure can be found in D.W. Robertson and Bernard F. Huppé, *Piers Plowman and Scriptural*

Tradition (Princeton: Princeton University Press, 1951), 227–28, 231; Morton W. Bloomfield, *Piers Plowman as a Fourteenth-Century Apocalypse* (New Brunswick: Rutgers University Press, 1961), 135–52; Aers, *Community, Gender, and Individual Identity,* 63–65; Kathryn Kerby-Fulton, *Reformist Apocalypticism and Piers Plowman* (Cambridge: Cambridge University Press, 1990), 146–49; Hewett-Smith, "Nede Hath no Lawe," 244; Clopper, *Songes of Rechelesnesse,* 93–97; Mann, "The Nature of Need Revisited"; and Rogers, *Intepretation in Piers Plowman,* 143–64. For views of Nede emphasizing his more sinister aspects and connections with antichrist, see Frank, "The Conclusion of *Piers Plowman,*" 311; Adams, "The Nature of Need"; Szittya, *The Antifraternal Tradition,* 247–87; White, *Nature and Salvation,* 90–91; Scase, *Piers Plowman and the New Anticlericalism,* 65–68; James Simpson, *Piers Plowman: An Introduction to the B-text* (New York: Longman, 1990), 232–34; and Harwood, *Piers Plowman and the Problem of Belief,* 133–35. Other critics have remained more neutral, focusing on the complexities, ambiguities, and divisions of Nede and the poem's versions of neediness. See, for example, Middleton, "Acts of Vagrancy," 271; Fradenburg, "Needful Things"; Kim, "Hunger, Need, and the Politics of Poverty," 162; and Aers, *Sanctifying Signs,* 150–56.

75. Kim, "Hunger, Need, and the Politics of Poverty," 165. On the relationship between the allegorical figure of Nede and the presence of need throughout the poem, see Mann, "The Nature of Need Revisited," 13–14.

76. Fradenburg, "Needful Things," 55.

77. On the relations between Nede's and Holy Churche's teachings, see Adams, "The Nature of Need," 275; Mann, "The Nature of Need Revisited," 15–17; and Zeeman, *Piers Plowman and the Medieval Discourse of Desire,* 280.

78. On the theologically troubling dimensions of Nede's argument, see Frank, "The Conclusion of *Piers Plowman,*" 311, and Aers, *Sanctifying Signs,* 151.

79. On need and the issue of a fraternal "fyndynge," see Robert W. Frank, *Piers Plowman and the Scheme of Salvation* (New Haven: Yale University Press, 1957), 116–17; Bloomfield, *Piers Plowman as a Fourteenth-Century Apocalypse,* 147–48; Szittya, *The Antifraternal Tradition,* 286–88; Dolan, "Langland and FitzRalph," 40; Clopper, *Songes of Rechelesnesse,* 293–96; and Aers, *Sanctifying Signs,* 152–53.

80. See Liberum Arbitrium's representation of the different forms that charity can take (XVII.6–24). On love as Wille's craft, see Szittya, *The Antifraternal Tradition,* 278–80.

81. On Langland's use of the term "lollar," see Pearsall, "Lunatyk Lollares"; Scase, *Piers Plowman and the New Anticlericalism,* 147, 149–60; Middleton, "Acts of Vagrancy," 276–88; Andrew Cole, "Langland and the Invention of Lollardy," in *Lollards and Their Influence in Late Medieval England,* ed. Fiona Somerset, Jill C. Havens, and Derek G. Pitard, 37–58 (Woodbridge: Boydell, 2003); Derek Pearsall, "Langland and Lollardy: from B to C," *Yearbook of Langland Studies,* 17 (2003): 7–24, at 11–12; Andrew Cole, "William Langland's Lol-

lardy," *Yearbook of Langland Studies* 17 (2003): 25–54; and Anne Hudson, "Langland and Lollardy?" *Yearbook of Langland Studies* 17 (2003): 94–105.

82. Middleton, "Acts of Vagrancy," 241. On Langland's view of false mendicancy as an obvious sign of "social disease," see Shepherd "Poverty in *Piers Plowman*," 170–71.

83. Hewett-Smith, "Lo, here lyflode ynow," 148.

84. William Langland, *Piers Plowman: The B Version,* rev. ed., ed. George Kane and E. Talbot Donaldson (London: Athlone Press, 1988), VII.75–76. Langland cites the full quote from Gregory in the following line, "*Non eligas cui miserearis ne forte pretereas illum qui meretur accipere, / Quia incertum est pro quo deo magis placeas.*"

85. Aers, in *Sanctifying Signs,* 107, discusses another set of interpretive problems endemic to this section of the poem when he notes that the text specifies that the pardon is comprised of only two lines. This passage, then, presumably functions as a massive gloss on the pardon, and it is delivered by an unnamed speaker.

86. Pearsall, "Poverty and Poor People in *Piers Plowman,*" 179.

87. Neville Coghill, "The Character of Piers Plowman Considered from the B-text," *Medium Ævum* 2 (1933): 108–35, at 128.

88. While Russell and Kane offer the term "lo[rell]es" in line 101, I follow Pearsall in designating the term as "lollares," a label confirmed by the reference to "lollares lyf" in line 103.

89. On the treatment of hermits in *Piers Plowman,* see Edward Jones, "Langland and Hermits," *Yearbook of Langland Studies* 11 (1997): 67–86, and Ralph Hanna, "Will's Work," in *Written Work,* 48–53.

90. The interpretive difficulties posed by the structure of this passage can also be revealed by comparing it to other interpolations of this material in the Ilchester manuscript and Huntington Library HM 114. Describing the "second textual tradition" of Langland's classification of beggars, Scase notes that "the structure of [this] shorter version is simpler and clearer. . . . Here are treated sequentially the true poor, then false beggars and holy hermits." Furthermore, she notes that "the absence of the phrase 'lunatic loller' . . . means that here lunatics more clearly belong in the category of the true poor" (*Piers Plowman and the New Anticlericalism,* 150, 158–59).

91. For discussions of the "lunatyk lollar," see Pearsall, "Lunatyk Lollares," and Scase, *Piers Plowman and the New Anticlericalism,* 136–37. Clopper, *Songes of Rechelesnesse,* chap. 5 and Kerby-Fulton, *Books Under Suspicion,* 232, contend that the lunatic lollars are holy figures associated with Franciscan poverty, while Aers, *Sanctifying Signs,* 111–15, and Cole, "William Langland's Lollardy," 25–55, offer compelling arguments against such a reading.

92. The Douce illustrator makes an intervention into Langland's taxonomy and seeks to distinguish the figure of the "lunatyk lollar" visually by presenting him with innocently waving hands as if unthreateningly dismissing any human

authority. The figure is furthermore layered with a light gold dust, which, according to Kerby-Fulton and Despres, functions as a sign of dignity and sanctity (*Iconography and the Professional Reader,* 31, 138).

93. David Lawton, "English Poetry and English Society" in *The Radical Reader,* ed. Stephen Knight and Michael Wilding, 145–68 (Sydney: Wild and Woolley, 1977), 152.

94. On the hermeneutic challenges posed particularly by the "lunatyk lollares," see Aers, *Sanctifying Signs,* 115.

95. Scase, *Piers Plowman and the New Anticlericalism,* 151–52; Middleton, "Acts of Vagrancy," 282.

96. Middleton, "Acts of Vagrancy," 282.

97. Scase, *Piers Plowman and the New Anticlericalism,* 155; see also 125–26, 133–38.

98. Middleton, "Acts of Vagrancy," 284–85. See also Scase, *Piers Plowman and the New Anticlericalism,* 157.

99. Cole, "Langland and the Invention of Lollardy," 40.

100. Ibid., 47.

101. Ibid., 57. In a very brief discussion of C. IX, Kerby-Fulton, in *Books Under Suspicion,* 232, argues, like Cole, that Langland de-emphasizes the Wycliffite meaning of the word "lollar." However, unlike Cole, she argues that he does this through his discussion of the "lunatic lollars," material that she sees as revelatory in its associations with spiritual Franciscanism. By including this material, Langland, according to Kerby-Fulton, reclaims the term "lollar" from Wycliffism, a movement that came to "repulse" him for its "cultural narrowness" and antirevelatory literalism.

102. Cole, in "William Langland's Lollardy," 34, comes closest to addressing this question when he recognizes that "lollar" works as a form of classification in *Piers Plowman* and other texts. Yet he stops short of pursuing potential problems with the term's use as a means of specification, especially within the ethically and epistemologically treacherous terrain of almsgiving.

103. See Cole, "William Langland and the Invention of Lollardy."

104. John Bowers, *Chaucer and Langland: The Antagonistic Tradition* (Notre Dame, IN: University of Notre Dame Press, 2007), 121, helpfully remarks that "Langland's . . . wrestling with the word *lollare* in his C-text provoked more problems than it dispelled."

105. Shepherd, "Poverty in *Piers Plowman,*" 175.

106. Kim, "Hunger, Need, and the Politics of Poverty," 158.

107. Middleton argues that "this waking interlude is the last major revision Langland made in his poem, and that it serves to organize, formally and thematically, many of the distinctive concerns of the C-revision" ("Acts of Vagrancy," 209). Whether or not this material was definitely Langland's final addition to the poem, for the purposes of this chapter it seems fitting to see it as a

kind of culminating episode reflecting simultaneously on the issues under discussion here—poverty, sacramentality, and the opacity of need.

108. On the ambiguity of Wille's moral identity and occupation, see Donaldson, *Piers Plowman: The C-text and Its Poet,* 223–24; John Bowers, *The Crisis of Will in Piers Plowman* (Washington, DC: Catholic University of America Press, 1986), 103–4, 167–68, and chap. 7; Lawrence Clopper, "The Life of the Dreamer, the Dreams of the Wanderer in *Piers Plowman,*" *Studies in Philology* 86 (1989): 276–79; Middleton, "Acts of Vagrancy"; and D. Vance Smith, *The Book of the Incipit* (Minneapolis: University of Minnesota Press, 2001), chap. 4, "Thema."

109. See Donaldson, *Piers Plowman: The C-text and Its Poet,* 199–226; Hanna, "Will's Work"; and Middleton, "Acts of Vagrancy."

110. Middleton, "Acts of Vagrancy," 254, 260.

111. Ibid., 215.

112. Here I use Pearsall's edition, which in my view keeps to the spirit of the previous lines focusing on how Wille serves the wider community.

113. Scase, *Piers Plowman and the New Anticlericalism,* 139. Outlining the history of gyrovague satire, Scase also notes that it was a "satire based on classification" (133).

114. On the impossible fantasy of making social identity textually legible—whether in the passports legislated by the 1388 Cambridge Statute or in Langland's poem itself—see Middleton, "Acts of Vagrancy," 216.

115. On the interior dimensions of the allegory in this episode, see Rogers, *Interpretation in Piers Plowman,* 145, and Aers, review of *The Laborer's Two Bodies,* by Kellie Robertson, *Yearbook of Langland Studies* 19 (2005): 226–36.

116. On the uncertainty and interpretive difficulty of moral self-examination, see Richard Newhauser, "On Ambiguity in Moral Theology: When the Vices Masquerade as Virtues," trans. Andrea Nemeth-Newhauser, in *Sin: Essays on the Moral Tradition in the Western Middle Ages,* Variorum Collected Studies Series, essay I (Aldershot: Ashgate, 2007).

117. Middleton, "Acts of Vagrancy." Nicola Masciandaro attests to the validity of Wille's ambiguous labor, noting that this episode of the poem "insists that an individual's work may elude objective, rational justification and yet be known subjectively, through conscience, to be both licit and necessary"; Nicola Masciandaro, *The Voice of the Hammer: The Meaning of Work in Middle English Literature* (Notre Dame, IN: University of Notre Dame Press, 2007), 123.

118. Scase, *Piers Plowman and the New Anticlericalism,* 173, does not acknowledge the change that takes place in Wille but argues that "The poet never does remove the gyrovague's mask."

119. On the relations between the economic language of Wille's apologia and the parable of the pearl of great price (Matthew 13:45–46), see Kathryn Kerby-Fulton, "Langland and the Bibliographic Ego," 90–93. Offering a contrary view, Smith reads Wille's speech not as a metaphor but as an economic

practice associated with the discourse of mercantilism. See D. Vance Smith, *Arts of Possession*, 108–10, 115–16, 135–38, 146–47, 152–53.

120. Scott, *Piers Plowman and the Poor*, 174, offers helpful comments about Wille's penance and self-examination: "In moving from the debate immediately to the Church to make his confession, Will asserts the liturgically repeatable power of the sacrament to justify and renew his intention." Ultimately, however, I disagree with Scott's final point that it is Wille's apostolic poverty that gives his life justification.

Chapter Two

1. The year 1393 is a *terminus a quo* for the *Crede* based on its reference to Walter Brut's prosecution in lines 657–62. Helen Barr considers 1401 a *terminus ad quem* for the poem because it makes no mention of the burning of Wycliffites despite its explicit outrage at the persecution of Brut and Wyclif himself. See the introduction to *Pierce the Ploughman's Crede* in Helen Barr, ed., *The Piers Plowman Tradition* (London: J. M Dent, 1993), 9–10.

2. On the role of the *Crede* within an identifiable "Piers Plowman Tradition," see Derek Pearsall "The Piers Plowman Group," in *Old English and Middle English Poetry* (London: Routledge and Kegan Paul, 1977), 182–83; David Lawton, "Lollardy and The Piers Plowman Tradition," *Modern Language Review* 76 (1981): 780–93; Barr, *The Piers Plowman Tradition*, 1–14; and Helen Barr, *Signes and Sothe* (Cambridge: D. S. Brewer, 1994), 1–9.

3. For readings of *Piers Plowman* and Wycliffite writings that emphasize shared thematic content, see Derek Pearsall, "Langland and Lollardy: From B to C," *Yearbook of Langland Studies* 17 (2003): 7–24; Anne Hudson, "Langland and Lollardy?" *Yearbook of Langland Studies* 17 (2003): 94–105; and Andrew Cole, "William Langland's Lollardy," *Yearbook of Langland Studies* 17 (2003): 25–54.

4. Fiona Somerset, "Expanding the Langlandian Canon: Radical Latin and the Stylistics of Reform," *Yearbook of Langland Studies* 19 (2003): 73–92; Shannon Gayk, "'As Plouȝmen Han Preued': The Alliterative Work of a Set of Lollard Sermons," *Yearbook of Langland Studies* 20 (2006): 42–65. See also John Bowers, "*Piers Plowman* and the Police: Notes Toward a History of the Wycliffite Langland," *Yearbook of Langland Studies* 6 (1992): 1–50. For readings that explore potential affinities between *Piers Plowman* and Wycliffite belief, but ultimately find a more general spirit of reform in *Piers Plowman*, see Pamela Gradon, "Langland and the Ideology of Dissent," *Proceedings of the British Academy* 66 (1980): 179–205; David Lawton, "Lollardy and the Piers Plowman Tradition"; and Anne Hudson, "Epilogue: The Legacy of *Piers Plowman*," in *A Companion to Piers Plowman*, ed. John Alford, 251–66 (Berkeley: University of California Press, 1988).

5. See also Christina Von Nolcken, "*Piers Plowman*, the Wycliffites and *Pierce the Ploughman's Crede*," *Yearbook of Langland Studies* 2 (1988): 71–102; David Aers, "John Wyclif: Poverty and the Poor, *Yearbook of Langland Studies* 17 (2003): 55–72; and James Simpson, *Reform and Cultural Revolution* (Oxford: Oxford University Press, 2002), 374–78.

6. Simpson, *Reform and Cultural Revolution*, 378, similarly notes that the *Crede* "marks a radical narrowing of the project of *Piers Plowman* in the simplicity of its polemical message, and a reversal of *Piers* in its ecclesiological exclusivity." See also Hudson, "Epilogue: The Legacy of *Piers Plowman*," 255–56. On the antifraternalism of the *Crede*, see Penn Syzitta, *The Antifraternal Tradition in Medieval Literature* (Princeton: Princeton University Press, 1986), 197–211.

7. Katherine Little, *Confession and Resistance: Defining the Self in Late Medieval England* (Notre Dame, IN: University of Notre Dame Press, 2006), 29–47, finds a similar phenomenon in her study of sin within the Wycliffite sermon cycle.

8. On the ambiguities and difficulties of Wyclif's ecclesiology, see Aers, *Faith, Ethics, and Church: Writing in England, 1360–1409* (Cambridge: D. S. Brewer, 2000), 119–48.

9. See, for example, Bruce Holsinger, "Lollard Eckphrasis: Situated Aesthetics and Literary History," *Journal of Medieval and Early Modern Studies* 35, no. 1 (2005): 67–89, and Gayk, "As Plouȝmen Han Preued." In contrast, Steven Justice remarks that Lollardy was "programmatically prosaic . . . and positively suspicious of aesthetic pleasures"; see his "Lollardy," in the *Cambridge History of Medieval English Literature*, ed. David Wallace, 662–89 (Cambridge: Cambridge University Press, 2002), 679.

10. Holsinger, "Lollard Eckprhasis," 80.

11. Ibid., 80–86.

12. James Simpson, *Burning to Read: English Fundamentalism and Its Reformation Opponents* (Cambridge, MA: Harvard University Press, 2007), 132.

13. This is the opening scene of Passus VIII in the B-text and Passus X in the C-text. Because of the *Crede*'s post-1393 composition date, it is difficult to surmise if the *Crede* author drew from the B-text or the C-text of *Piers Plowman*. This is a fascinating intertextual question, but because this study is concerned primarily with the overarching differences between Langland's work and the Wycliffite poem, it is not necessary to make a precise determination about the version used by the *Crede* author. In spite of the changes that Langland makes from the B-text to the C-text concerning poverty, his larger epistemological, hermeneutical, and ecclesiological models remain largely consistent. For the sake of consistency in this project, all of my own references to *Piers Plowman* in this chapter will refer to the C-version.

14. I will discuss the ramifications of this change in later sections of this chapter.

15. See the introduction to *Piers the Plowman's Crede,* in James Dean, ed., *Six Ecclesiastaical Satires* (Kalamazoo: Medieval Institute Publications, 1991), 3.

16. "*Pierce the Ploughman's Crede,*" in Barr, *The Piers Plowman Tradition,* l.123, l.325, and l.396 respectively. All subsequent quotations will be cited parenthetically by line number. I cite only three alms requests because the narrator becomes so disgusted with the pride of the Dominican friar that he leaves presumably before the friar can ask for alms (265).

17. See Jill Mann, *Chaucer and Medieval Estates Satire* (Cambridge: Cambridge University Press, 1973) for traditional characterizations of the friar.

18. See A. I. Doyle, "An Unrecognized Piece of *Pierce the Ploughman's Crede* and Other Work by Its Scribe," *Speculum* 34 (1959): 428–36, at 434.

19. On the 1382 Blackfriars Council, see Anne Hudson, *The Premature Reformation: Wycliffite Texts and Lollard History* (Oxford: Clarendon University Press, 1988), 70–75. The *Crede* itself references the council at 531–32.

20. *Pierce the Ploughman's Crede,* in Barr, *The Piers Plowman Tradition,* 231, note to lines 506–14.

21. On the aesthetic quality of this passage as an example of eckphrasis, see Holsinger, "Lollard Eckphrasis," 80–86.

22. *Pierce the Ploughman's Crede,* in Barr, *The Piers Plowman Tradition,* 220, note to line 165. The poem's use of the term "pryuytie" is also relevant to the standard Wycliffite critique of monks, canons, and friars as forming private religions or sects cut off from the commonality of worship in Christ. For a discussion of this view in Wyclif, see, for example, Szittya, *The Antifraternal Tradition,* 165–66, 181–82; for this idea in Wycliffite writings, see Anne Hudson, *Premature Reformation,* 342–51.

23. The *Crede* reserves its most heavily alliterative language for descriptions of the friars' landscape. Barr, *Signes and Sothe,* 41, notes that "as a whole, however, *Crede* refuses the validity of sumptuous expression both in its statements and its alliterative practice."

24. Holsinger, "Lollard Eckphrasis," 83, discusses these comparisons as working within the eckphrastic passage to "instill a critical awareness of clerical wealth and the idolatry of visual culture."

25. Unlike donations to the friars, financial contributions to the parish church were not voluntary. On the severe penalties levied on those who failed to pay their tithes to the parish church, see Eamon Duffy, *The Stripping of the Altars: Traditional Religion in England, 1400–1580* (New Haven: Yale University Press, 1992), 356–57.

26. For the argument in Wycliffite writings that attention to images detracts from aiding the poor, who are the true images of God, see, for instance, Anne Hudson, ed., *Selections from English Wycliffite Writings* (Toronto: University of Toronto Press, 1997), 83, 117.

27. On tax rates in late medieval England, see Christopher Dyer, *Making a Living in the Middle Ages: the People of Britain, 850–1250* (New Haven: Yale

University Press, 2002), 269. For the argument that clerical wealth increases the tax burden of the laity, see also Nicholas Hereford, "Nicholas Hereford's Ascension Day Sermon, 1382," ed. Simon Forde, *Medieval Studies* 51 (1989): 205–41.

28. *The Middle English Dictionary* includes the following relevant definitions for "clene" as an adjective: "morally clean, righteous, pure, innocent, guiltless" (2.a) and "splendid; elegant" (5.a). As an adverb, it defines "clene" as "handsomely, neatly, properly;" "well made, finely finished" (2.a). All of these senses are at play in the three lines of the *Crede* describing the friar's cope.

29. In describing the elaborate clothing of the friars, the *Crede* author conforms to traditional representations of friars in medieval estates satire. See Mann, *Chaucer and Medieval Estates Satire*, 37–54.

30. In this sense the poem works against what Mann, in *Chaucer and Medieval Estates Satire*, 21, sees as the rhetorical strategies of Chaucer's General Prologue, which prevent readers from responding to the work's satirical portraits in a spirit of "simple moral disapproval." She argues that Chaucer's friar is described in ambivalent language that resists any attempt to denounce him strictly as a hypocrite (53–54).

31. On the centrality of deception as a theme in traditional anticlerical satire, see Wendy Scase, *Piers Plowman and the New Anticlericalism* (Cambridge: Cambridge University Press, 1989), 120–21.

32. Sarah Beckwith, *Signifying God: Social Relation and Symbolic Act in the York Corpus Christi Plays* (Chicago: University of Chicago Press, 2001), 154–55. For a discussion of hypocrisy in reference to the *Summoner's Tale*, pastoral manuals, and some Wycliffite writings, see Fiona Somerset, "'Mark Him Wel for He is On of þo': Training the 'Lewed' Gaze to Discern Hypocrisy," *English Language History* 68 (2001): 315–34.

33. Beckwith, *Signifying God*, 152.

34. See also lines 694–98 where Pierce elaborates on how the friars' clothing marks a concealment of pride and a rejection of penitence.

35. In this sense the *Crede* can be understood as part of the larger concern with discerning hypocrites as discussed in Somerset, "Mark Him Wel." However, given the poem's disregard for interiority (an issue I discuss later in this chapter), the *Crede* departs from the texts that, in Somerset's terms, turn the discerning eye inward, "toward the often difficult project of discerning one's own motives and character" (329).

36. For a discussion of this satiric strategy see Helen Barr, "Wycliffite Representations of the Third Estate," in *Lollards and Their Influence*," ed. Fiona Somerset, Jill C. Havens, and Derrick G. Pitard, 197–216 (Woodbridge: Boydell, 2003), 213.

37. This methodology, however, also potentially implicates the narrator himself who provokes the friars' hostile commentary about the other orders. Specifically, he initiates each conversation with the declaration that he has just been

with another type of friar, who claims moral perfection and advanced spiritual knowledge. See, for example, lines 38–39, 239–40, 276–79, 348–49.

38. See lines 279–89 and 245–49.

39. "The Rule and Testament of St. Francis," in F. D. Matthew, ed., *The English Works of Wyclif,* EETS o.s. 74 (London: Kegan Paul, 1980), 42.

40. The friar's invocation of Francis as a mediatory figure touches on the Wycliffite objection to intercessionary prayer. The Wycliffites asserted that prayer should be directed to God alone because only he has the power to respond. For a concise account of this idea, see Hudson, *Premature Reformation,* 302–3.

41. While Wycliffites frequently denied the efficacy of auricular confession, here the emphasis, as in *Piers Plowman,* falls on the friars' exploitation of the sacrament for profit. On Wycliffite views of confession, see Hudson, *Premature Reformation,* 294–99, and Little, *Confession and Resistance,* 38–39, 49–50, 58–74.

42. The closest we get to any such moment comes when the narrator abruptly parts ways with the Dominican, saying, "And therefore frere, fare well; here fynde y but pride" (266). In his meeting with the Franciscan and the Austin, the narrator denounces the orders' sinfulness, but speaks only to himself (138, 335).

43. See, for example, Langland, *Piers Plowman: The C Version,* ed. Russell and Kane, V.109, XI.166.

44. See Little, *Confession and Resistance,* 29–47.

45. Beckwith, *Signifying God,* 140.

46. Kellie Robertson, *The Laborer's Two Bodies: Labor and the "Work" of the Text in Medieval Britain, 1350–1500* (New York: Palgrave Macmillan, 2006), 26.

47. Somerset, "Mark Him Wel," 317, makes the following comment about the limits of hypocrisy: "The surface appearance of the body cannot be fully subjected to conscious control. Instead that body's dispositions and practices leave marks on its surface: traces of past actions, present thoughts, and persistent habits that conflict with the image its person—or the person whose it is—would like to project." The *Crede*'s plowman would seem to be an extreme example of this case, suggesting a fundamental aversion to or incapacity for hypocrisy.

48. Terry Eagleton, *After Theory* (New York: Basic Books, 2003), 2. Eagleton makes this remark while also critiquing what he sees as the "trivialization of sexuality" within modern cultural theory (3).

49. Taking the literal representation of Pierce's wife to the level of abstraction, David Lampe notes that "An ardent Lollard might even argue that Peres's wife is Dame Poverty who, with her three children, is shown to be fruitful and not sterile like the abandoned bride of the false Franciscans"; see his "The Satiric Strategy of *Peres the Ploughman's Crede,*" in *The Alliterative Tradition in the Fourteenth Century,* ed. Paul E. Szarmach and Bernard S. Levey, 69–80 (Kent: Kent State University Press, 1981), 75. I discuss the hermeneutical implications of reading Pierce's wife as an allegorical expression later in this chapter.

50. Eagleton, *After Theory,* 42.

51. The text's emphasis on Pierce's poverty, labor, and generosity accords with what Mann sees as the traditional figure of the plowman in medieval estates satire. Mann, in *Chaucer and Medieval Estates Satire,* 67–73, describes how this figure, which is based on *Piers Plowman* and other literary sources, fuses priestly ideals with industriousness, generosity, and humility. Against Mann's view of the plowman in estates satire, Elizabeth Kirk, in "Langland's Plowman and the Recreation of Fourteenth Century Religious Metaphor," *Yearbook of Langland Studies* 2 (1988): 1–21, argues that Langland recuperates the plowman figure from a tradition that is particularly hostile to plowmen and manual laborers. Barr concurs with Kirk and notes that Wycliffite texts diverge from the generally negative treatment of the plowman to present the figure as "an exemplar of poverty, simplicity, honesty, and necessary social labor in contrast to . . . the second estate"; Barr, "Wycliffite Representations of the Third Estate," 208.

52. On the Wycliffite notion of the priesthood of all believers, see Hudson, *Premature Reformation,* 325–27.

53. Margaret Aston discusses the importance of the division between the able-bodied and the lame, sick, or blind poor in Wycliffite writing against the friars; see her "'Caim's Castles': Poverty, Politics, and Disendowment," in *The Church, Politics, and Patronage in the Fifteenth Century,* ed. Barrie Dobson, 45–81 (New York: St. Martin's Press, 1984), 49. The following chapter gives a full account of this distinction among beggars and the gospel text from which it derives.

54. This image derives from Virgil's *Georgics,* book 4, and is later invoked by thinkers such as Aquinas and Giles of Rome. See Barr, *The Piers Plowman Tradition,* 336, note to line 987.

55. Szittya, *The Antifraternal Tradition,* 153, discusses how Wyclif's antifraternalism, as part of his larger anticlericalism, distinctively promotes the destruction of the fraternal orders, not simply their reform. See also Hudson, *Premature Reformation,* 348–51.

56. For a reading of *Mum and the Sothsegger* (and this scene particularly) in reference to the political circumstances of "Lancastrian usurpation," see Frank Grady, "The Generation of 1399," in *The Letter of the Law: Legal Practice and Literary Production in Medieval England,* ed. Emily Steiner and Candace Barrington, 202–29 (Ithaca: Cornell University Press, 2002).

57. On Wyclif's support of the lay elite, See David Aers, *Faith, Ethics, and Church,* 119–48, and his "John Wyclif: Poverty and the Poor."

58. Sam Norwood makes this point and offers an illuminating reading of this passage in his "Wandering 'Wastours': Medieval and Early Modern Portrayals of Itinerant Laborers, Minstrels, Merchants, and Thieves" (M.A. thesis, Lehigh University, 2006).

59. See Barr, *Signes and Sothe,* 23.

60. Ibid., 48.

61. See, for example, lines 325–27, which describe how the Austins use texts as objects to be exchanged for alms, not as sources of religious and moral instruction. John Scattergood discusses this phenomenon in his "*Pierce the Ploughman's Crede*: Lollardy and Texts," in *Lollardy and the Gentry in the Later Middle Ages,* ed. Margaret Aston and Colin Richmond, 77–94 (New York: St. Martin's Press, 1997), 84.

62. Barr, *Signes and Sothe,* 84. Barr adds that the friars "reverse the senses of signs, making financial substitution of the spiritual meaning" (85).

63. Barr, *Signes and Sothe,* 85, notes that in this line "the rhetorical device of anaphora calls attention to the friars' vice of inverting the true meanings of words."

64. Scattergood, "*Pierce the Ploughman's Crede*: Lollardy and Texts," 80.

65. Kantik Ghosh, *The Wycliffite Heresy: Authority and the Interpretation of Texts* (Cambridge: Cambridge University Press, 2002), discusses the "sola scriptura" dimensions of Wycliffism. In his study, Ghosh notes that this influential idea constituted only a part of Wycliffite hermeneutics, which, at least in the case of Wyclif himself, nonetheless relied on the interpretive tools, categories, and practices it rejected. Ghosh's larger project seeks to explore a range of hermeneutic practices advocated and enacted by Wyclif and his followers. For other discussions of Wycliffite interpretive practices and the terminology of "grounded" texts, see Hudson, *Premature Reformation,* 273–77, 280–81, 375–78, and Anne Hudson, "A Lollard Sect Vocabulary?" in *Lollards and Their Books,* ed. Anne Hudson, 165–80 (London: The Hambledon Press, 1985). For the view that the *Crede* develops an "anti-intellectual" perspective, see Scattergood, "*Pierce the Ploughman's Crede*: Lollardy and Texts," 90.

66. Hudson, *Premature Reformation,* 269–77, discusses similar Wycliffite attitudes toward evangelical preaching.

67. On the reading practices central to sixteenth-century reformers, see Simpson, *Burning to Read,* chaps. 3–6.

68. See, for instance, Barr, *Signes and Sothe,* 48–49; George Kane, "Some Fourteenth-Century 'Political' Poems," in *Medieval English and Ethical Literature: Essays in Honor of G.H. Russell,* ed. G. Kratzmann and J. Simpson, 82–91 (Cambridge: Cambridge University Press, 1986); and Lampe, "The Satiric Strategy of *Peres the Ploughman's Crede,*" 77–78.

69. Barr, *Signes and Sothe,* 48–49.

70. Kane, "Some Fourteenth-Century 'Political' Poems," 89.

71. Lampe, "The Satiric Strategy of *Peres the Ploughman's Crede,*" 77–78.

72. See J. L. Austin, *How to Do Things with Words,* ed. J. O. Urmson and Marina Sbisa (Cambridge, MA: Harvard University Press, 1962).

73. Wilfred Cantwell Smith, *Faith and Belief: The Difference Between Them* (Oxford: Oneworld Publications, 1998), 78.

74. Ibid., 114–15.

75. In many ways Ghosh's arguments concerning a "distinctive" Wycliffite hermeneutic appear very similar to the methods of scriptural interpretation discussed by Augustine in *On Christian Doctrine.* While I outline Ghosh's points more fully below, it is important to note that Augustine also links virtuous modes of living with the right interpretation of scripture. For instance, he argues that biblical interpretation should lead to charity and thus to the cultivation of love for God and neighbor (book 3, XV). However, in order to grasp a text's full meaning and the significance of charity, a reader must approach scripture already possessing charity and humility. He explains, "when the reader has been prepared by this instruction . . . with a meek and humble heart, subjected easily to Christ with a burden that is light, established, rooted, and built up in charity so that knowledge cannot puff him up, let him turn next to the examination and consideration of ambiguous signs in the Scriptures" (book 2, XLII). Later in the text, after remarking on the role of the Holy Spirit in teaching, Augustine adds, "no one rightly learns those things which pertain to life with God unless he is made by God docile to God"; Augustine, *On Christian Doctrine,* trans. D.W. Robertson (Upper Saddle River, NJ: Prentice-Hall, 1958), book 4, XVI. Despite the correspondences between Augustine and the writers cited by Ghosh, I have chosen to consider the *Crede*'s hermeneutic teaching primarily in light of Ghosh's analysis because I find that his work offers a concise summary of a similar hermeneutic model at work in Wycliffite texts, whether or not such a model can be distinctively associated with Wycliffism, as Ghosh claims.

76. Ghosh, *The Wycliffite Heresy,* 43.

77. Ibid., 60.

78. Describing the connection between righteous Christian behavior and the power of language, Barr, in *Signes and Sothe,* 93, explains that the *Crede* "advocates a model of language in which persuasive rhetoric is matched by the sanctity of living."

79. Ghosh, *The Wycliffite Heresy,* 60.

80. The pilgrim's more narrow quest for knowledge bears on a notion of teaching and learning that is fundamentally different from that of *Piers Plowman.* In the *Crede,* the narrator seeks the words of a single prayer; he wishes to be taught the prayer, that is, to receive it, not to say it, enact it, or perform it for himself. This model of learning, which opposes Wille's struggle to do well, possibly reduces the narrator's own culpability, agency, and need for self-awareness in his spiritual questioning.

81. As many critics have pointed out, the poem blames the friars and not Wyclif for disputing the nature of the Eucharist. See, for example, Barr, *Signes and Sothe,* 116, and Scattergood, "*Pierce the Ploughman's Crede*: Lollardy and Texts," 91.

82. Pierce claims that Christ's words alone are necessary for comprehending the nature of the Eucharist. In Pierce's arguments, as Scattergood notes, "all difficulties tend to disappear, even in relation to something as intellectually tricky

and contentious as the sacrament of the altar. . . . Because Christ said, 'Hoc est corpus meum' all philosophical and doctrinal problems disappear"; "*Pierce the Ploughman's Crede*: Lollardy and Texts," 91.

83. Aers, "Walter Brut's Theology of the Sacrament of the Altar," in *Lollards and Their Influence,* ed. Somerset, Havens, and Pitard, 115–26, at 120.

84. For the praise of Brut, see lines 657–61.

85. Aers, in *Faith, Ethics, and Church,* 40–47, discusses how the church becomes a dramatically diminished force in Wyclif's ecclesiology, given its submission to a secular regime not required to uphold the clergy's commitment to poverty and pacifism. Aers also shows how Wyclif, much like the *Crede* author, employs a scapegoating mechanism that enables him to disregard the details and problems of his ecclesiology in favor of condemning the contemporary clergy (146–47).

86. Remarking on the de-institutionalized status of the Creed, Barr, in *Signes and Sothe,* 48–49, explains that "it is placed neither in the comparatively innocent context of preaching conversion, nor in the examination of a parishioner's understanding of basic Christian texts, nor in a liturgical setting. Instead it forms the conclusion of an alliterative poem whose basic premise questions the adequacy of discourses sanctioned by the church." While the Creed thus stands in to remedy the church's inadequate discourses, its emergence outside of any formal context, including those suggested by Barr, raises difficulties for how the Creed can be fixed as an accessible, comprehensible, and central component of spirituality.

87. On the importance of preaching in Wycliffism, see Hudson, *Premature Reformation,* 196–97, 363–56.

88. See lines 661–68, for the *Crede*'s criticism of the church's persecutory practices.

89. Scattergood, "*Pierce the Ploughman's Crede*: Lollardy and Texts," 92.

90. Barr, *Signes and Sothe,* 54.

91. Holsinger, "Lollard Eckprhasis," 80–86.

92. Von Nolcken, "*Piers Plowman,* the Wycliffites, and *Pierce the Ploughman's Crede,*" 92–93.

93. On the particular complexity of Langland's dream vision, see A. C. Spearing, *Medieval Dream-Poetry* (Cambridge: Cambridge University Press, 1976), 141.

94. See Aers, *Piers Plowman and Christian Allegory* (New York: St. Martin's Press, 1975), 88–109, for a cogent analysis of the allegorical operations at this point in the poem.

95. Spearing, *Medieval Dream-Poetry,* 159.

96. Ibid., 159–60.

97. Lampe, "The Satiric Strategy of *Peres the Ploughman's Crede,*" 75.

98. On the archetypical nature of the *Crede,* see Von Nolcken, "*Piers Plowman,* the Wycliffites, and *Pierce the Ploughman's Crede,*" 88.

99. Ibid., 89.

100. Barr, *Signes and Sothe,* 49.

101. This is not to say that there are never static modes and nonallegorical forms of representation in *Piers Plowman.* To the contrary, Elizabeth Salter, *Piers Plowman: An Introduction* (Cambridge: Cambridge University Press, 1989), 74, describes some of these static modes by explaining, for instance, that allegory can at times take on a "diagrammatic" character associated with "schematized drawings" of images such as the tree of charity. However, as Salter herself and Aers, *Piers Plowman and Christian Allegory,* 88–109, have shown, this static image can shift into a dynamic relation among different levels of temporality and signification.

102. Discussing Wycliffite writing more generally, Pearsall, "Langland and Lollardy," 23, offers a comment relevant to the *Crede,* which asserts truth against the fraudulent friars without ever attempting to integrate these separate spheres: "There is never in Langland the hammering persistence, the obsessive 'party-line' repetitions of coded words and phrases, the certainty of being right . . . that characterize hard-line Lollard writing. Like the partisan writing of any group committed to political action, it can admit of no doubt or demur. But Langland, who is a poet, is not certain he is right: he gropes, circles, qualifies, returns again and again to difficult questions, seeks always after truth."

103. Barr, *Signes and Sothe,* 49, notes the fusion of voices at the end and also cites the following lines.

Chapter Three

1. "The Twelve Conclusions of the Lollards," in Anne Hudson, ed., *Selections from English Wycliffite Writings* (Toronto: University of Toronto Press, 1997), 24.

2. On the use of the term "pore men" in Wycliffite writing, see Hudson, *Selections from English Wycliffite Writings,* 151, note to line 1; Helen Barr, "Wycliffite Representations of the Third Estate," in *Lollards and their Influence in Late Medieval England,* ed. Fiona Somerset, Jill C. Havens, and Derek G. Pitard, 197–216 (Woodbridge: Boydell, 2003); and Wendy Scase, *Literature and Complaint in England, 1272–1553* (Oxford: Oxford University Press, 2007), 88–90.

3. Michel Mollat, *The Poor in the Middle Ages,* trans. Arthur Goldhammer (New Haven: Yale University Press, 1986), 260.

4. Margaret Aston, "'Caim's Castles': Poverty, Politics, and Disendowment," in *The Church, Politics, and Patronage in the Fifteenth Century,* ed. Barrie Dobson, 45–81 (New York: St. Martin's Press, 1984), 67.

5. Barr, "Wycliffite Representations of the Third Estate," 212, 215. For further discussion of poverty in Wycliffite thought, see Anne Hudson, "Poor Preachers, Poor Men: Views of Poverty in Wyclif and his Followers," in *Haresie*

und vorzeitige Reformation im Spatmittelalter, ed. Frantisek Smahel, 41–54 (Munchen: R. Oldenbourg Verlag, 1998).

6. This is not to say that Wycliffite prose does not retain some of the stylized elments found in poetry. For example, see Shannon Gayk's essay, "'As Plouȝmen Han Preued': The Alliterative Work of a Set of Lollard Sermons," *Yearbook of Langland Studies* 20 (2006), 42–65.

7. For studies of Wyclif that similarly find a marginalization of poverty within his larger program of ecclesiological reform, see David Aers, *Faith, Ethics, and Church: Writing in England, 1360–1409* (Cambridge: D. S. Brewer, 2000), 119–48, and "John Wyclif: Poverty and the Poor," *Yearbook of Langland Studies* 17 (2003): 55–72. For historical evidence that Wycliffism appealed not to lower-level artisans and the poor, but to more wealthy and upwardly mobile members of society, see also Maureen Jurkowski, "Lollardy and Social Status in East Anglia," *Speculum* 82 (2007): 120–52; Robert Lutton, *Lollardy and Orthodox Religion in Pre-Reformation England* (Woodbridge: Boydell and Brewer, 2006), chap. 5; Derek Plumb, "The Social and Economic Spread of Rural Lollardy: A Reappraisal," *Studies in Church History* 23 (1986): 111–29; and Derek Plumb, "The Social and Economic Status of the Later Lollards," in *The World of Rural Dissenters,* ed. Margaret Spufford, 103–31 (Cambridge: Cambridge University Press, 1995).

8. On the events surrounding FitzRalph's appearance at the papal court in Avignon, see Katherine Walsh, *A Fourteenth-century Scholar and Primate: Richard FitzRalph in Oxford, Avignon, and Armagh* (Oxford: Clarendon Press, 1981), 406–45, and Penn R. Szittya, *The Antifraternal Tradition in Medieval Literature* (Princeton: Princeton University Press, 1986), 123–31. On FitzRalph's life and his role in the mendicancy conflicts, see James Doyne Dawson, "Richard FitzRalph and Fourteenth-Century Poverty Controversies," *Journal of Ecclesiastical History* 34 (1983): 315–44; Aubrey Gwynn, "The Sermon Diary of Richard FitzRalph," *Proceedings of the Royal Irish Academy* 44 (1937): 1–57; and Wendy Scase, *Piers Plowman and the New Anticlericalism* (Cambridge: Cambridge University Press, 1989), chaps. 1–3.

9. For information about the occasion of Taylor's sermon, the controversy it generated, and his career more generally, see the introduction to Anne Hudson, ed., *Two Wycliffite Texts,* EETS 301 (Oxford: Oxford University Press, 1993), xiii–xv. According to the *St. Alban's Chronicle,* Master Richard Alkerton preached at St. Paul's Cross the day after Taylor's sermon in order to rebut all his arguments. Alkerton's response was one of many conflicts that marked Taylor's entire career. As Hudson notes, there is no extant copy of Alkerton's sermon.

10. Hudson, *Two Wycliffite Texts,* xxiv.

11. Hudson dates the *Omnis plantacio* sermon between 1407 and 1413. For further background, see the introduction to Anne Hudson, ed., *The Works of a Lollard Preacher,* EETS 317 (Oxford: Oxford University Press, 2001), xlviii–lxi. Hudson herself has remarked on the complementary nature of these

works, noting their related content, "overlap" in the authorities cited, and "similarity" in vocabulary (lvii–lviii). She initially suggests that Taylor may have authored *Omnis plantacio,* but then dismisses the possibility based on the author's seemingly heretical view of the Eucharist—an issue conspicuously absent in the heresy investigations of Taylor (lviii). The anonymous writer of *Omnis plantacio* discusses the Eucharist briefly in the sermon and in a later tract, *De oblacione jugis sacrificii*. After dismissing other Wycliffites as possible candidates for authorship, Hudson concludes that *Omnis plantacio* remains an anonymous text, composed by a traveling preacher, who was likely to have received academic training.

12. The arguments against fraternal mendicancy have a long history beginning in the 1250s in Paris and extending to the late medieval period in England. The most influential arguments against the friars can be found in writings by William of St.-Amour, John XXII, Richard FitzRalph, and John Wyclif. For arguments defending the fraternal position, see, for example, writings by Bonaventure, Thomas Aquinas, William of Ockham, Richard Maidstone, and William Woodford. There is a substantial critical literature on this controversy, and I have found the following works helpful in describing the nature and scope of the fraternal debates: Aubrey Gwynn, *The English Austin Friars in the Time of Wyclif* (London: Oxford University Press, 1940), 211–69; Gordon Leff, *Heresy in the Later Middle Ages,* 2 vols. (Manchester: Manchester University Press, 1967), 1:51–238, 2:546–48; Dawson, "Richard FitzRalph and Fourteenth-Century Poverty Controversies"; Szittya, *The Antifraternal Tradition,* chaps. 1–4; Janet Coleman, "Property and Poverty," in *The Cambridge History of Medieval Political Thought,* ed. J. H. Burns, 607–48 (Cambridge: Cambridge University Press, 1988); Scase, *Piers Plowman and the New Anticlericalism,* 15–22, 47–78; Brian Tierney, *The Idea of Natural Rights: Studies on Natural Rights, Natural Law and Church Law, 1150–1625* (Atlanta: Scholars Press, 1997), chaps. 4–8; Malcolm Lambert, *Franciscan Poverty: The Doctrine of the Absolute Poverty of Christ and the Apostles in the Franciscan Order, 1210–1323* (St. Bonaventure, NY: Franciscan Institute, 1998), 221–70; Fiona Somerset, *Clerical Discourse and Lay Audience in Late Medieval England* (Cambridge: Cambridge University Press, 1998), chap. 5; and Takashi Shogimen, *Ockham and Political Discourse in the Late Middle Ages* (Cambridge: Cambridge University Press, 2007), chap. 1.

13. Walsh, *A Fourteenth-century Scholar,* 469, 413, notes that the *Defensio Curatorum* exists in eighty-four different manuscripts, and she states that "manuscript circulation and early printings reveal [the *Defensio Curatorum*] to have been the most influential piece of anti-mendicant polemic published during the later middle ages."

14. On Trevisa's career, his interest in translation, and his possible associations with Wycliffism, see David C. Fowler, *The Life and Times of John Trevisa, Medieval Scholar* (Seattle: University of Washington Press, 1995), 118–234, esp. 182.

15. On the relationship between FitzRalph's writings and Wyclif/Wycliffism, see John Wyclif, *De domino divino,* ed. R. L. Poole (London: Wyclif Society, 1890); Walsh, *A Fourteenth-century Scholar,* 453; Leff, *Heresy in the Later Middle Ages,* 2:546–47; Gwynn, *English Austin Friars,* 59–73; Michael Wilks, "Predestination, Property, and Power: Wyclif's Theory of Dominion and Grace," *Studies in Church History* 2 (1965): 220–36, rprt. in *Wyclif: Political Ideas and Practice,* 16–32 (Oxford: Oxbow Books, 2000); and Stephen Lahey, *Philosophy and Politics in the Thought of John Wyclif* (Cambridge: Cambridge University Press, 2003), 1–23, 49–63. For a study of dominion in Wycliffite thought, see Howard Kaminsky, "Wycliffism as Ideology of Revolution," *Church History* 33 (1963): 57–74.

16. See too Scase, *Piers Plowman and the New Anticlericalism,* 56–57, 62, 71, 100, 109–10.

17. These appellations are listed in Walsh, *A Fourteenth-century Scholar,* 457n20, and they can be found in Wyclif, *De civili dominio,* ed. Reginald Poole, (London: Wyclif Society, 1890), vol. 3; Wyclif, *De blasphemia,* ed. Michael Dziewicki (London: Wyclif Society, 1893), 232; and *Opus arduum,* cited in Anne Hudson, "A Neglected Wycliffite Text," *Journal of Ecclesiastical History* 29 (1978): 257–79, at 265. For other examples of Wycliffites' praise of FitzRalph, see Nicholas Hereford, "Nicholas of Hereford's Ascension Day Sermon, 1382," ed. Simon Forde, *Medieval Studies* 51 (1989): 205–41, and *De blasphemia contra fratres* in Thomas Arnold, ed., *Select English Works of John Wyclif,* 3 vols. (Oxford: Clarendon Press, 1869–71), 3:412.

18. See Nicholas III, *Exiit qui seminat* and *Liber Sextus* in Emil Friedburg, ed., *Corpus Iuris Canonici,* 2 vols. (Leipzig: Tauchnitz, 1879), vol. 2, cols. 1108–21. On this bull see, Leff, *Heresy in the Later Middle Ages,* 1:83–100; Lambert, *Franciscan Poverty,* 132–56; and Dawson, "Richard FitzRalph and Fourteenth-Century Poverty Controversies," 316–28.

19. John XXII's legislation concerning Franciscan poverty can be found in *Bullarium Franciscanum,* ed. Conrad Eubel (Rome: Typis Vaticanis, 1898), vol. 5. Specifically, *Ad contidorem canonum* (no. 486, 233–47) rejected Franciscan distinctions between natural and civil law as well as the order's theory of *simplex usus facti,* or simple use—a condition without any legal rights. *Cum inter nunullos* (no. 518, 256–59) declared heretical the doctrine of Christ's absolute poverty and the related notion that Jesus and the apostles did not possess any right of use over temporal goods. *Quia vir reprobus* (no. 820, 408–49) established that Adam held from God dominion over the goods in Eden and that he originally held this dominion not in common but individually before the creation of Eve. On this papal legislation, see Leff, *Heresy in the Later Middle Ages,* 1:157–66; Lambert, *Franciscan Poverty,* 245–69; and Dawson, "FitzRalph and Fourteenth-Century Poverty Controversies," 324–29. Also relevant as a source of John XXII's arguments against the Franciscans is the work of the Dominican

Hervaeus Natalis, *The Poverty of Christ and the Apostles,* trans. John D. Jones (Toronto: Pontifical Institute of Medieval Studies, 1999).

20. As John Kilcullen and John Scott note, "John's decretals on Franciscan poverty seem to have had little effect on the thinking of the Franciscan Order—even those who submitted to John's authority found ways of salvaging the traditional theory of Franciscan poverty"; Willam of Ockham, *Work of Ninety Days,* trans. John Kilcullen and John Scott, 2 vols. (Lewiston: Edwin Mellen, 2001), 1:40. See also Malcolm Lambert, "The Franciscan Crisis under John XXII," *Franciscan Studies* 32 (1972): 123–43, at 139–40.

21. Scase, *Piers Plowman and the New Anticlericalism,* 52. For FitzRalph's particular attention to the Franciscans in his attacks on the friars, see Walsh, *A Fourteenth-century Scholar,* 373.

22. On the distinctiveness of this argument when compared to traditional arguments against the friars made by the secular clergy, see Scase, *Piers Plowman and the New Anticlericalism,* 18–19, 47–56.

23. Dawson, "Richard FitzRalph and Fourteenth-Century Poverty Controversies," and Scase, *Piers Plowman and the New Anticlericalism,* chaps. 1 and 3.

24. See FitzRalph, *De pauperie salvatoris,* Book VI. Poole prints the first four books of *De pauperie salvatoris* as well as a table of contents for the last three books in Wyclif, *De domino divino,* 264–72, 273–476. The rest of the work can be found in, Russell Oliver Brock, "An Edition of Richard FitzRalph's *De pauperie salvatoris*: Books V, VI, and VII" (Ph.D. diss., University of Colorado, 1953). The following accounts have helpfully informed my discussion of FitzRalph's view of dominion: Dawson, "Richard FitzRalph and Fourteenth-Century Poverty Controversies"; Scase, *Piers Plowman and the New Anticlericalism,* 18–19, 51–54; and Somerset, *Clerical Discourse and Lay Audience,* 168–69.

25. According to the notion of dominion by grace, one wields authority over other humans and lower creatures by virtue of righteousness, living in a state of grace. See FitzRalph, *De pauperie salvatoris,* 2:1–9; Wyclif, *De civili dominio,* vol. 1; and Wyclif, *De domino divino.* For discussion of this idea, see Gwynn, *English Austin Friars,* 59–73; Leff, *Heresy in the Later Middle Ages,* 3:546–49; Wilks, "Wyclif's Theory of Dominion and Grace"; and Lahey, *Philosophy and Politics,* 39, 40, 43, 116, 154. I treat the view of dominion by grace later in this chapter.

26. Richard FitzRalph, *Defensio Curatorum,* in *Trevisa's Dialogus,* ed. John Perry, EETS o.s. 167 (Oxford: Oxford University Press, 1925), 61. Hereafter cited parenthetically by page number.

27. Szittya, *Antifraternal Tradition,* 141, makes this comment in reference to the same passage from FitzRalph.

28. The implicit anticlerical appeal of FitzRalph's thought is apparent in this statement, which potentially restricts all clerics to possessing only the basic necessities. See Scase, *Piers Plowman and the New Anticlericalism,* 56–57.

29. My use of the term "right" belies a complex debate about the meaning of *ius* in relation to Franciscan conceptions of poverty. While the intricacies of this conflict are too involved to pursue here, it is worth presenting some brief guidelines outlining how FitzRalph's point differs from the canon law position that any person had a right to necessities in case of extreme need. FitzRalph's argument about the rights conferred on the clergy would seem to accord with the notion of a positive right established by human law as opposed to a natural right guaranteed by the law of heaven. The Francisicans claimed to renounce all positive rights and civil dominion, retaining a natural right to the goods of others only in moments of extreme necessity. See, for example, Ockham, *Work of Ninety Days,* chap. 61. FitzRalph's argument suggests that the friars' clerical activities grant them the very rights that they claim to renounce. Furthermore, FitzRalph would not see the friars' claims of poverty as indicating extreme need given their able-bodiedness and their involvement in pastoral work. This idea resonates with Hervaeus's point that Christ and the apostles retained the necessities of life by right because these were owed to them by the people in exchange for their preaching. He thus views Christ as a laborer who "has a right to what is owed him by reason of his work"; Hervaeus Natalis, *The Poverty of Christ and the Apostles,* 48. On the complex and varied meanings of *ius* in the context of debates about Franciscan poverty, see Tierney, *The Idea of Natural Rights,* chaps. 5 and 6. For a discussion of rights of use in Ockham's *Work of Ninety Days,* see Shogimen, *Ockham and Political Discourse,* 68–71.

30. Scase, *Piers Plowman and the New Anticlericalism,* 67.

31. Szittya, *The Antifraternal Tradition,* 140.

32. Scase, *Piers Plowman and the New Anticlericalism,* 51. Scase also explains that property resulted from Adam's fall since the loss of natural dominion necessitated the creation of civil dominion and private property to be managed by human laws. While this constitutes a traditional argument concerning the fall, FitzRalph most readily associates poverty (not property) with original sin.

33. David Aers, *Community, Gender, and Individual Identity: English Writing, 1360–1430* (London: Routledge, 1988), 25.

34. On the importance of this gospel passage in Wycliffite writings, see Aston, "Caim's Castles," 49. On its relevance to late medieval poverty conflicts more generally, see Scase, *Piers Plowman and the New Anticlericalism,* 63–64.

35. Scase, *Piers Plowman and the New Anticlericalism,* chaps. 1–3.

36. "The Sermon of William Taylor," in Hudson, *Two Wycliffite Texts,* 13, lines 366–37. Hereafter cited parenthetically by page and line number.

37. *Omnis plantacio,* in Hudson, *The Works of a Lollard Preacher,* 28, lines 733–35. Hereafter cited parenthetically by page and line number.

38. Another Wycliffite sermon on Luke 16 makes the dangers of wealth clear: "Crist telluth in this parable how richessus ben perilows, for liȝtly wole a riche man vsen hem in to myche lust"; Anne Hudson and Pamela Gradon, eds.,

English Wycliffite Sermons, 5 vols. (Oxford: Oxford University Press, 2001–2006), 1:1/1.

39. Barr, "Wycliffite Representations of the Third Estate," 199, describes how Wycliffite writers favor poor labors by redirecting anti-peasant discourse at the clergy.

40. See Hudson and Gradon, *English Wycliffite Sermons,* 1:1, for a reading of Luke 16 that does not apply the same anticlerical lesson to Dives. This marks a relatively rare instance when a Wycliffite writer considers how the lay elite may harm the poor. However, in the sermon cycle the treatment of Luke 12 follows the more standard line when the sermon explicitly applies the moral lesson to the clergy: "þis gospel telliþ by a parable hou men shulden fle aueriss, and speciali prestis of Crist"(3:220/1–2).

41. For other complaints that the church consumes the alms of the poor and harms them through avarice, see, for example, F. D. Matthew, ed., *The English Works of Wyclif,* EETS o.s. 74 (London: Trübner, 1880), 173, 233; Arnold, *Selected English Works of Wyclif,* 3:372/14–18, 3:383/4, 3:415/26; "The Testimony of William Thorpe," in Hudson, *Two Wycliffite Texts,* 67/1426 ff.; and Hudson and Gradon, *English Wycliffite Sermons,* 1:48/34, 1:E23/55, 1:E12/77.

42. Aston, "Caim's Castles," 67.

43. In emphasizing the notion of common goods, the authors here implicitly refer to original or natural dominion by which Christ and the apostles jointly shared in the goods of the world. While this original lordship was diminished by Adam's sin, Christ restored it through grace, allowing common access to necessary goods. See *Omnis plantacio* (68/1553–62) for a brief discussion of "þe lordship þat riȝtwise men han upon þe goodis of þis world, bi titil of grace or riȝtwisnesse." The author does not spell out which people live in "riȝtwiseness" and grace—a problematic omission making it seemingly impossible to identify members of this sanctified group. On the unknowability of the predestinate in Wyclif's thought, see Leff, *Heresy in the Later Middle Ages,* 2:549; Aers, *Faith, Ethics, and Church,* 131–32; and Wilks, "Wyclif's Theory of Dominion and Grace." If those who possess lordship by grace are not necessarily the predestinate but those who live righteously through their daily acts and behaviors, then this model also occludes how one recognizes righteousness among shifting practices and contingent circumstances.

44. In his mention of "customable" beggars, Taylor alludes to a larger taxonomy of begging that runs throughout the sermon. Customable beggars are those who habitually beg in order to make a living. Associated with these are "clamorous" beggars whose livelihood similarly consists of active and permanent begging. Opposed to these related categories, is the "constreyned" beggar, who is forced into mendicancy only by circumstantial factors. See Hudson, *Two Wycliffite Texts,* 103, note to line 672. This basic taxonomic model can be found in *Omnis plantacio* (26/675) and other Wycliffite texts. For a brief discussion

of this taxonomy and its relevance to Wycliffite writing, see Aston, "Caim's Castles," 56. See also Hudson and Gradon, *English Wycliffite Sermons,* 4:142n114, for references to Wyclif's treatment of "clamorous" begging.

45. On the notion of evangelical poverty as a moderate form of indigence, see Scase, *Piers Plowman and the New Anticlericalism,* 58.

46. The clear attack on mendicancy as a legitimate practice and the idealization of the church as a fiscally sound institution challenge Lawrence Clopper's argument that some seemingly antifraternal texts ascribed to Wycliffites were actually written by reformist Franciscans. See his analysis of the Wycliffite translation of the Franciscan Rule and Testament, "Of the Leaven of Pharisees," and "Fifty Heresies and Errors of the Friars," in "Franciscans, Lollards, and Reform," in *Lollards and Their Influence,* 177–96.

47. See also Hervaeus's account of Christ's dual nature, which elaborates on "the right owed to Christ" in both his human and divine forms (*The Poverty of Christ and the Apostles,* 96–97).

48. For Wyclif's similar discussion of the titles of Christ, see *De domino divino,* 10–12, and *De civili dominio,* 1:38–42, as noted in Hudson, *Works of a Lollard Preacher,* 260, note to line 221.

49. As an example of the friars' defense against such arguments, see Ockham, *Work of Ninety Days,* 2:661–63. Arguing against John XXII's *Quia vir reprobus,* the text insists that "Christ observed a poverty that existed through lack of lordship." He notes that Christ lacked "the lordship that is ownership" even in the state of innocence because no ownership existed in this state and because he willingly took on the defects of poverty for our benefit.

50. Christ's procurement of the ass before entering Jerusalem is also a relevant text, though it is not addressed in Taylor's sermon, *Omnis plantacio,* or Hudson and Gradon, *English Wycliffite Sermons.* For a brief reference to the three gospel passages invoked to prove or disprove Christ's mendicancy, see *Upland's Rejoinder,* 330–41, in *Jack Upland, Friar Daw's Reply, and Upland's Rejoinder,* ed. P. L. Heyworth (London: Oxford University Press, 1968). See also Hudson and Gradon, *English Wycliffite Sermons,* 4:142nn114 and 116 for references to these passages in Wyclif's sermons. On the role of these gospel texts in fraternal debates on Christ's mendicancy, see Somerset, *Clerical Discourse and Lay Audience,* 167–79.

51. Another Wycliffite sermon implicitly emphasizes Jesus's dominion, saying, "Crist was lord of al þis worlde. And ȝif þe lord axe drynke of his seruaunt, who seye þat he beggide of hym?"(Hudson and Gradon, *English Wycliffite Sermons,* 3:163/13–15).

52. In making this argument, Taylor goes on to discuss how Christ's words should be understood based on his intention to turn the woman from adultery. For a different yet related discussion of intention as it relates to FitzRalph's notion of "excitative speech," see Fiona Somerset, "Excitative Speech: Theories of

Emotive Response from Richard FitzRalph to Margery Kempe," in *The Vernacular Spirit: Essays on Medieval Religious Culture*, ed. Renate Bumenfeld-Kosinski, Duncan Robertson, and Nancy Bradley Warren, 59–82 (New York: Palgrave, 2002).

53. Although the *Omnis plantacio* author does not employ Taylor's argument in his discussion of the woman of Samaria, he does use the same logic in his commentary on Elijah's exchange with the widow of Sarapta. He explains that Elijah did not beg in asking water and bread from the widow because God "commandide" her "to feede Helye, not al for Helies nede or profit, but cheefli for þe nede and profit of þat widue" (129–30/2685–87).

54. *De blasphemia contra fratres*, in Arnold, *Select English Works of John Wyclif*, 3:413–14.

55. Augustine, "Homilies on the Gospel of St. John," in *Nicene and Post Nicene Fathers*, ed. Philip Schaf, 10 vols. (Grand Rapids, MI: William B. Eerdmans, 1956), 7:100. He adds that "The strength of Christ created thee, the weakness of Christ created thee anew. The strength of Christ caused that to be which was not; the weakness of Christ caused that what was should not perish. He fashioned us by his strength, He sought us by His weakness."

56. Augustine, "Homilies," 7:100. He then interprets Christ's trip into Samaria as a figure for the incarnation so that "His journey is the flesh assumed for us."

57. Ibid., 7:101.

58. Ibid., 7:102.

59. Denis the Carthusian, *Opera Omnia*, 42 vols. (Monstrolii: Typis Cartusiae S. M. De Pratis, 1896), 12:346, Art.XL.6; translation mine. Denis's point is reminiscent of arguments made in defense of the friars that acknowledge his lordship as a divine being and legitimate his mendicancy as a human being. For a helpful account of these arguments as articulated by Hardeby in particular, see, Somerset, *Clerical Discourse and Lay Audience*, 166, 175–77.

60. Denis the Carthusian, *Opera Omnia*, 12:346, Art. XL.6. This particular idea would certainly find sympathy in the rigorous endorsement of work featured in fourteenth-century labor legislation and the discourse of literary figures such as the *Crede*'s plowman.

61. Ibid., 12:347, Art. XI.8; translation mine.

62. Arnold, *Select English Works of John Wyclif*, 1:414.

63. Ibid. The *Omnis plantacio* author makes a similar argument about 1 Kings 17. He refutes the claim that Elijah begged water and bread from the widow because he argues that Elijah was merely following God's command to go into Sarapta and to find a woman who would feed him. The author explains that "Helye beggide no more of þis woman þan a child beggiþ whanne, at þe commaundment of his fadir, he biddiþ or preieþ his fadris stiward, panter or botiler or ony oþer officer of his fadris to ȝyue him mete or drynk, and namely

þere as such a seruaunt haþ a special maundement of his lord or maistir to mynystre suche vitails to his child, as þis woman hadde of þe hiȝ lord God to feede Helye" (130/2689–2694). See also Hervaeus, *The Poverty of Christ and the Apostles,* 43.

64. Denis the Carthusian, *Opera Omnia,* 12:158, Art. XLII.5; translation mine.

65. In the exegesis of Luke 19:1–10 found in the *Catena Aurea,* the authorities do not emphasize Christ's lordly and commanding spirit. Overall, they tend to focus on Zaccheus's movement from sin to grace, and they allegorize Christ's coming to the man's home as his coming to the Gentile people. See, for example, Bede's commentary on the passage; *Catena Aurea,* 4 vols. (Oxford: J. H. Parker, 1841–45), 3:628.

66. In the case of Luke 18:35, Taylor's reading also differs from that of Hudson and Gradon, *English Wycliffite Sermons,* 1:39/62–64, which takes Jesus's healing of the blind man as an example that "we schulden wende by Ierycho and speke wiþ þis blynde man, and do werkys of mercy to hym goostly as Crist dide."

67. Augustine, "Homilies," 7:245.

68. Aquinas, *Catena Aurea,* 2:619.

69. Ibid., 2:621.

70. Ibid., 2:623. This reading is also given in the *Glossa Ordinaria*: "non petit caecus aurum vel aliquid temporale . . . sed lucem eterne visionis"; *Biblia Latina cum glossa ordinaria,* 4 vols. (Brepols: Turnhout, 1992), 4:204.

71. Denis the Carthusian, *Opera Omnia,* 12:155, Art. XLI.43; translation mine.

72. Ibid., 154–55, Art. XLI.40; translation mine. While Taylor would certainly argue that his Christ does act with charity and justice toward the poor, his version of these virtues accords with what might be termed a "conservative" ideology that has affiliation with vagrancy legislation, Hunger's repressive strategies, and the *Crede*-plowman's complaints about fraternal drones. Denis's argument that the clergy and political leaders should be responsive to the problems of the poor stems from a perspective that does not presume poverty to be associated with sloth or sin. Ministering to the poor with justice, then, would not necessarily mean simply putting them to work but would entail a range of charitable duties aimed at alleviating their suffering.

73. In commenting on Luke 18, the numerous authorities cited by Aquinas accord with the examples I have quoted above in disregarding questions of labor and mendicancy. There is one exceptional commentary which associates the miracle with productivity. Theophyl writes, "And to show that our Lord did not even walk without doing good, He performed a miracle on the way, giving His disciples this example, that we should be profitable in all things, and that nothing in us should be in vain" (*Catena Aurea,* 3:619). In this instance, however, Jesus's productivity is evident by example, not by his insistence that the healed must now labor.

74. As we saw in the last chapter on the *Crede,* it is often difficult to get a precise sense of how the church and lay society are defined in Wycliffite thought. Taylor's sermon and the *Omnis plantacio* writer present the church as a discrete institution that is separate from the lay population. Their theory that clerics held dominion by "titil of gospel" seems to entail a conception of the priesthood as a distinct office. This vision of the church and its relation to lay society contrasts with the idealized two estate structure that Barr finds in Wycliffite writing that overtly privileges the priesthood of all believers; see her "Wycliffite Representations of the Third Estate," 205. Taylor's and the *Omnis plantacio* writer's version of the church does resonate with Wyclif's ecclesiology; see Aers, *Faith, Ethics, and Church,* 130–48.

75. "Inconvenience" (b). The term also signifies unspecified and therefore possibily immaterial "harm, damage, misfortune or affliction" (a).

76. Such arguments for restoring the former glory of knights perhaps offer an important qualification to Barr's view that there is a "radical potential" and "dissident energy" in Wycliffite writings that describe the third estate ("Wycliffite Representations of the Third Estate," 198, 215). While Barr acknowledges that such dissidence is not directed at secular lords, it is worth recognizing that in Taylor's and the *Omnis plantacio* sermon, any "radical" concern for the value of the third estate accompanies a wider social model that seeks to bolster the power of the lay elite.

77. Hudson briefly discusses similar complaints in Wycliffite writing concerning the church's impoverishment of lay lords; see her "Poor Preachers," 52–53.

78. As the *Omnis plantacio* author complains about the clergy's and particularly the monks' and canons' excessive wealth, he refutes the argument that such groups do not actually possess temporal lordship since they hold their goods in common, through original lordship, as Christ and the apostles did. The author specifically argues that: (1) such clergy engage in secular duties on their estates in the same way that knights do in their own domains; (2) such clergy own and manage lands in conjunction with secular lords; (3) such clergy claim jurisdiction over the non-clerical population and even determine, in some cases, whether people should live or die; and (4) even if such clergy hold this lordship in common, it is nonetheless sinful because it is secular. The writer concludes this battery of arguments by insisting that if the clerics truly possessed lordship in common through grace, they would not constantly engage in lawsuits and seek to protect their original lordship through the irrelevant means of civil law.

79. As we have seen in *Piers Plowman,* Liberum Arbitrium cautions lay lords against donating their goods to the church, thereby depriving their heirs of inheritance. Yet his warnings clearly stop short of proclaiming the general impoverishment of knights. His more restrained speech offers a contrast to the vigorous anticlericalism of the Wycliffite sermon.

80. On the status of the lay elite, see Christopher Dyer, *Making a Living in the Middle Ages: The People of Britain, 850–1520* (New Haven: Yale University Press, 2002), 330–40, and J. L. Bolton, *The Medieval English Economy, 1150–1500* (London: J. M. Dent, 1980), 207–34. In blaming the church for the economic problems affecting the lords, the Wycliffite writers interestingly obscure the fact that the late fourteenth and the fifteenth centuries were also an economically difficult time for monasteries and ecclesiastical lords, some of whom went bankrupt. See, for example, Christopher Dyer, *Standards of Living: Social Change in England, c. 1200–1520* (Cambridge: Cambridge University Press, 1989), 101, and Dyer, *Making a Living*, 337.

81. Bolton, *The Medieval English Economy*, 220.

82. On the "notion of a clerical conspiracy" in writings by Wyclif and the Wyclifittes, see Hudson, *The Works of a Lollard Preacher*, 272, notes to lines 1100–1120.

83. Taylor's emphasis on the laity's commercial obligations also corresponds with what Aers sees as Wyclif's inadvertent prioritization of temporal activities and lay power; see Aers, *Faith, Ethics, and Church*, 130–48. See also Barr, "Wycliffite Representations of the Third Estate," 202, for a discussion of the Wycliffite view that the clergy undermines civil authority.

84. Luke 22:30; Matt 26:52.

85. See, for instance, the "Lollard Disendowment Bill" in Hudson, *Selections from English Wycliffite Writing*. For further discussion of disendowment in Wycliffite thought, see Anne Hudson, *The Premature Reformation: Wycliffite Texts and Lollard History* (Oxford: Oxford University Press, 1988), 337–42, and Aston, "Caim's Castles."

86. Hudson, in *The Works of a Lollard Preacher*, 185, notes to lines 1929–31, notes that the idea of perpetual alms refers to "the gift of property by a secular person to a . . . [religious] community." Thus, "*lordship* does not descend through inheritance as is the case in normal medieval secular society, but accrues by virtue of the original gift of alms to the house or community."

87. According to the *MED*, "mysese" can signify "physical or mental discomfort: pain, suffering, misery, distress" (1a). It can also refer to "a particular form or source of physical or mental discomfort" such as "need, hardship, poverty, want of food, hunger, starvation, physical affliction or infirmity, weakness" (2a–b).

88. Cf. Scase, *Piers Plowman and the New Anticlericalism*, 72–76.

89. Taylor makes reference to the clergy "waastynge" the alms of poor men "in worldly vanytees," but does not define or elaborate on the term as the *Omnis plantacio* author does.

90. Like late medieval labor legislation, the sermons' approach to selective almsgiving is more rigorous than that of the canonists. This is because their theory of deserving poverty appears to stem from fears about the abuse of charity—a motivation that opposes what Brian Tierney sees as the generally more munifi-

cent intentions behind the canonists' preferential orders of alms recipients; see his *Medieval Poor Law: A Sketch of Canonical Theory and Its Application in England* (Berkeley: University of California Press, 1959), 60–62.

91. For the same reading of Luke 14, see also Hudson and Gradon, *English Wycliffite Sermons,* 1:2/68–69, 76–79.

92. In Taylor's sermon, the commitment to the lay elite becomes especially striking when he sanctions the temporary begging of knights returning from war. This acceptance is surprising given the sermon's overall hostility to able-bodied begging and given Wycliffite objections to war and crusading. See 2/675 ff., as well as Hudson's note on these lines.

93. An exception to this occlusion can be found in the tract entitled "Of Servants and Lords," in Matthew, *The English Works of Wyclif,* 226–43. However, in their introduction to *English Wycliffite Sermons,* Hudson and Gradon similarly remark on the shadowy treatment of the relations between knights and lower ranks. They also note that the potential faults of the lay elite are "little elaborated" (4:152–53).

Chapter Four

1. "The Sermon of William Taylor," in Anne Hudson, ed., *Two Wycliffite Texts,* EETS o.s. 301 (Oxford: Oxford University Press, 1993), 18/572.

2. There is a substantial amount of critical literature discussing various manifestations of the tension between the text's commitment to spiritual or clerical values and its attachment to a bourgeois or mercantile ideology. See, for example, David Aers, *Community, Gender, and Individual Identity: English Writing, 1360–1430* (London: Routledge, 1988), 80–87, 120–40; Kathleen Ashley, "Historicizing Margery: *The Book of Margery Kempe* as Social Text," *Journal of Medieval and Early Modern Studies* 28, no. 2 (Spring 1998): 371–88; Sarah Beckwith, *Christ's Body: Identity, Culture, and Society in Late Medieval Writings* (London: Routledge, 1993), 98–110; Sheila Delany, "Sexual Economics, Chaucer's Wife of Bath, and *The Book of Margery Kempe,*" in *Writing Woman: Women Writers and Women in Literature Medieval to Modern,* ed. Sheila Delany, 76–92 (New York: Schoken Books, 1983); Brian W. Gastle, "Breaking the Stained-Glass Ceiling: Mercantile Authority, Margaret Paston, and Margery Kempe," *Studies in the Literary Imagination* 36, no. 1 (2003): 123–47; Roger A. Ladd, "Margery Kempe and her Mercantile Mysticism," *Fifteenth-Century Studies* 26 (2001): 121–41; and Lynn Staley, *Margery Kempe's Dissenting Fictions* (University Park: Pennsylvania State University Press, 1994).

3. Beckwith, *Christ's Body,* 102.

4. Ashley, "Historicizing Margery," 382.

5. On *The Book of Margery Kempe* and the Franciscan tradition of affective contemplation, see Denise Despres, "Margery Kempe and Visual Meditation,"

Fourteenth Century English Mystics Newsletter 11, no. 1 (1985): 12–18; Brad Herzog, "The Augustinian Subject, Franciscan Piety, and *The Book of Margery Kempe*: an Affective Appropriation and Subversion of Authority," *Philological Review* 30, no. 2 (2004): 67–88; and David Wallace, "Mystics and Followers in Siena and East Anglia: A Study in Taxonomy, Class, and Cultural Mediation," in *The Medieval Mystical Tradition in England*, ed. Marion Glasscoe, 169–91 (Exeter: University of Exeter Press, 1982).

6. *The Book of Margery Kempe* clearly lacks the deep-rooted spirit of antifraternalism found in the Wycliffite sermons. However, there are moments in the text that offer hints of antifraternal criticism, though these are not aimed at the friars' abuse of poverty. For example, the most notorious of these moments occurs when a new friar, known for his preaching, comes to Lynn and bars Kempe from his masses due to her excessive weeping. For discussions of the text's implicit antifraternalism, see Staley, *Margery Kempe's Dissenting Fictions*, 106–7.

7. Margery Kempe, *The Book of Margery Kempe*, ed. Lynn Staley (Kalamazoo: Western Michigan University, Medieval Institute Publications, 1996), 24. Hereafter cited parenthetically by page number.

8. Kempe's father was one of Lynn's most influential citizens who served as mayor five times and held other prominent offices including the position of alderman of the Holy Trinity guild. For discussions of Kempe's family background and the connections between the Trinity guild and the town government, see Anthony Goodman, *Margery Kempe and Her World* (London: Longman, 2002), chap. 2; Beckwith, *Christ's Body*, 98; Deborah Ellis, "Margery Kempe and King's Lynn," in *Margery Kempe: A Book of Essays*, ed. Sandra J. McEntire, 139–63 (New York: Garland, 1992); and Ladd, "Mercantile Mysticism," 122–23.

9. For the argument that the *Book* criticizes medieval urban culture as materialistic and profit oriented, see Staley, *Margery Kempe's Dissenting Fictions*, esp. chap. 2 and Ladd, "Mercantile Mysticism."

10. Kate Parker, "Lynn and the Making of a Mystic," in *A Companion to The Book of Margery Kempe*, ed. John H. Arnold and Katherine J. Lewis, 55–73 (Cambridge: D. S. Brewer, 2004), 56.

11. On the unnecessary nature of Kempe's work, see, Aers, *Community, Gender, and Individual Identity*, 87.

12. For the view that the *Book* criticizes Kempe's entrepreneurial practices without condemning commercial activity more generally, see Aers, *Community, Gender, and Individual Identity*, 77.

13. Ladd, "Mercantile Mysticism," 126–28, discusses how the defiance of Kempe's servants inaugurates a larger pattern of abandonment in the *Book*.

14. William of Ockham, *Work of Ninety Days*, trans. John Kilcullen and John Scott, 2 vols. (Lewiston: Edwin Mellen, 2001), 1:234. While Ockham explains that human beings no longer possess Adam and Eve's prelapsarian forms of dominion, he does note that its closest counterpart comes in seemingly natural forms of rulership involving, for instance, a man's control of an animal: "the

'lordship' [mastery] by which a boy or servant is said to dominate his lord's horse, because he can rule it as he pleases, and generally every violent power which cannot be resisted, is, in respect of certain non-moral conditions, more like the lordship of our first parents than is the lordship anyone has over temporal things from human agreement, beyond natural lordship" (237). On Ockham's treatment of Adam and Eve's lordship, see Takashi Shogimen, *Ockham and Political Discourse in the Late Middle Ages* (Cambridge: Cambridge University Press, 2007), 61–62.

15. Staley, *Margery Kempe's Dissenting Fictions,* 48.

16. Ibid., 121.

17. Goodman, *Margery Kempe and Her World,* 200.

18. Sarah Salih, "Margery's Bodies: Piety, Work and Penance," in *A Companion to The Book of Margery Kempe,* 172.

19. "The Earlier Rule," in *Francis of Assisi: Early Documents,* ed. and trans. Regis J. Armstrong, J. Wayne Hellman, and William J. Short, 3 vols. (New York: New City Press, 1999), 1:70, IX.2.

20. For a discussion of the connections between Kempe and the Franciscan tradition of the holy fool, see Karma Lochrie, *Margery Kempe and Translations of the Flesh* (Philadelphia: University of Pennsylvania Press, 1991), 158–60.

21. Describing the "extravagant almsgiving gestures" undertaken by Elizabeth of Hungary and Francesca of Rome, P. H. Cullum similarly remarks that Kempe's giving away of the goods in the buttery would prompt her servants to see her not as a holy figure but as a mad woman. See Cullum's "'Yf lak of charyte be not ower hynderawnce': Margery Kempe, Lynn, and the Practice of the Spiritual and Bodily Works of Mercy" in *A Companion to The Book of Margery Kempe,* 186.

22. Ladd, "Mercantile Mysticism," 130. See also Delany, "Sexual Economics." It is also worth mentioning that, according to William of Ockham, *Work of Ninety Days,* 1:210, 224, the voluntary renunciation of possessions entails only the renunciation of *excessive* solicitude, which goes beyond concern for the basic necessities of life.

23. On Kempe's unconventional practice of mendicancy as an example of how Kempe resists "conformity with conventional female life," see Aers, *Community, Gender, and Individual Identity,* 99.

24. Citing criminal records from late medieval Europe, Sharon Farmer explains that poor women and, especially those who were single, were more frequently victims of sexual violence than elite women; see her *Surviving Poverty in Medieval Paris: Gender, Ideology, and the Daily Lives of the Poor* (Ithaca: Cornell University Press, 2002), 37. This unfortunate reality perhaps contributes to Kempe's fears about the threat of rape during her solitary travels. Farmer also discusses how the "sexual modesty" of beggars was called into question when the beggars were women (126).

25. For brief discussions of Kempe's poverty as entailing a more radical and extreme form of need than the institutionalized poverty of the Franciscan

friars, see Lochrie, *Margery Kempe and Translations of the Flesh,* 160, and Staley, *Margery Kempe's Dissenting Fictions,* 121.

26. Despres and Lochrie briefly comment on how Kempe's imitation of the gospel challenges the religious practices that were institutionally sanctioned for women. See Despres, "Margery Kempe and Visual Meditation," 16, and Lochrie, *Margery Kempe and Translations of the Flesh,* 160.

27. Regis J. Armstrong and Ignatius C. Brady, eds., *Francis and Clare: The Complete Works* (Mahwah, NJ: Paulist Press, 1982), 212n6.

28. Jacobus de Voragine, *The Golden Legend,* trans. William Granger Ryan, 2 vols. (Princeton: Princeton University Press, 1993), 2:309.

29. Jacques de Vitry, "The Life of Marie d'Oignies," in *Two Lives of Marie d'Oignies,* trans. Margot H. King (Toronto: Peregrina, 1998), 89.

30. Ibid.

31. Thomas de Cantimpré, *The Life of Margaret of Ypres,* trans. Margot H. King (Toronto: Peregrina, 1990), 37.

32. See Guy Boanas and Lyndal Roper, "Feminine Piety in Fifteenth-Century Rome: Santa Romana," in *Disciplines of Faith: Studies in Religion, Politics, and Patriarchy,* ed. Jim Obelkevich, Lyndal Roper, and Raphael Smith, 177–93 (London: Routlege and Kegan Paul, 1987), 181–82.

33. Bridget of Sweden, *The Liber Celestis of St. Bridget of Sweden,* vol. 1, ed. Roger Ellis, EETS o.s. 291 (Oxford: Oxford University Press, 1987), 4.

34. Discussing the examples of Clare, Elizabeth, Margaret, and Mary of Oignies, Sharon Farmer, in *Surviving Poverty in Medieval Paris,* 126–27, helpfully explores the clerical approbation of manual labor as an alternative to female mendicancy. For individual accounts of the conflicts pertaining to these women, see Albert Huyskens, ed., "The Letter of Conrad of Marburg," *Quellenstudien zur Geschichte der hl. Elizabeth Langräfin von Thüringen* (Marburg: N. G. Elwert, 1908), 158; Thomas de Cantimpré, *The Life of Margaret of Ypres,* 57; John Moorman, *A History of the Franciscan Order from Its Origins to the Year 1517* (Oxford: Oxford University Press, 1968), 32–39, 207; and Jacques de Vitry, "The Life of Marie d'Oignies," 3, all cited in Farmer.

35. For various accounts of the annotations' overall meaning and effect, see Kelly Parsons, "The Red Ink Annotator of *The Book of Margery Kempe* and his Lay Audience," in *The Medieval Professional Reader at Work: Evidence from Manuscripts of Chaucer, Langland, Kempe, and Gower,* ed. Kathryn Kerby-Fulton and Maidie Hilmo, 143–216 (University of Victoria, 2001). See also Lochrie, *Margery Kempe and Translations of the Flesh,* 120–22, 206–19, and Staley, *Margery Kempe's Dissenting Fictions,* 96–99.

36. See, for example, folio 33v (chapter 28) and folio 51v (chapter 44). For a brief discussion of Methley's and Norton's mystical writings, see A. G. Dickens, *The English Reformation* (University Park: Pennsylvania State University Press, 1989), 40–42. Regarding the manuscript of *The Book of Margery Kempe,*

Parsons offers a helpful appendix enumerating the manuscript's annotations and coordinating these with chapter number and the page/line number of the EETS edition of the *Book*. My comments here and below are aided by Parsons's work as well as my own examination of the manuscript, which I am grateful to the British Library for making available to me.

37. See Lochrie, *Margery Kempe and Translations of the Flesh,* 25, 122, 208–28.

38. See Staley, *Margery Kempe's Dissenting Fictions,* 99.

39. Folios 41r–47v record chapters 34–40, which recount Kempe's time in Rome where she initially commits herself to poverty.

40. See folios 43v, 44v, and 46v.

41. The Carthusian Customs reveals the distinctiveness of the order's perspective when it comes to the subject of poverty. Emphasizing their fundamental disinterest in urban society and worldly concerns, the document declares, "To the poor people of this world we give bread or anything else that our will or our means suggest, but rarely do we take one of them in under our roof; instead we send them into town. For after all, we have taken refuge in the isolation of this hermitage not in order to take worldly care of other people's physical needs but for the eternal welfare of our own souls." *Consuetudines* xx.1, *Patrologia Latina,* CLIII, 673–74. Quoted in Lester Little, *Religious Poverty and the Profit Economy* (Ithaca: Cornell University Press, 1978), 87.

42. Staley, *Margery Kempe's Dissenting Fictions,* 96.

43. Bonaventure, "The Defense of the Mendicants," in *The Works of Bonaventure,* trans. José de Vinck, 5 vols (Patterson, NJ: St. Anthony Guild Press, 1966), IX.9, 4:188.

44. Deborah Ellis, "The Merchant's Wife's Tale: Language, Sex, and Commerce in Margery Kempe and in Chaucer," *Exemplaria* 2 (1990): 595–626, at 612, explicitly rejects the legitimacy of Kempe's poverty without fully considering its paradoxes or implications. She argues that Kempe "pretends to a poverty that in reality she never approaches, financing her pilgrimages with loans rather than true begging and feeding herself by arrangement rather than charity." In his critique of Franciscian poverty, Kenneth Baxter Wolf argues that Francis himself did not experience "authentic destitution" because his needs were consistently fulfilled by "some unexpected, timely act of charity"; *The Poverty of Riches* (Oxford: Oxford University Press, 2003), 21.

45. Staley, *Margery Kempe's Dissenting Fictions,* 64–65.

46. On evangelical poverty and the forms of dominion guaranteed by clerical office, see chap. 3.

47. William of Ockham, *Work of Ninety Days,* 211.

48. Goodman, *Margery Kempe and Her World,* 201, remarks on Kempe's success as a beggar and views it as evidence of the surplus wealth in Rome, not as a potentially problematic component of her poverty.

49. Goodman, *Margery Kempe and Her World,* 201, notes how Kempe's time as a mendicant in Rome is one characterized by ease: the only anxieties expressed are about bad weather.

50. Bonaventure, "Defense of the Mendicants," IX.24, 211.

51. Ladd, "Mercantile Mysticism," 128, draws a connection between Kempe's emphasis on local almsgiving and the charitable practices of Lynn's Holy Trinity guild, which customarily distributed aid to the needy citizens of the town. Ladd acknowledges that in favoring this mode of almsgiving, Kempe "remains within the charitable ideology of her original estate position." Deborah Ellis sees Kempe's suspicion of strangers as "a function of her strong identification with Lynn"; "Margery Kempe and Kings Lynn," 151. In this part of the text, Kempe's view regarding charity might challenge Staley's view of Kempe as a force who dissolves boundaries structuring conventional communities.

52. It is perhaps not surprising that Kempe's fellow townspeople are so readily convinced to withhold alms, given that the St. Albans Chronicle records how beggars kidnapped three children from Lynn in 1417 and mutilated them so as to get more alms. For a discussion of this record, see Goodman, *Margery Kempe and Her World,* 18.

53. Cullum, "Yf lak of charyte," 188.

54. Susan Dickman describes how Kempe's own experience of poverty is confined primarily to Rome, "limited in time and space and carefully insulated from life in Lynn." For these reasons, she suggests that Kempe's poverty may have been "conceived as an experiment" rather than as a consistent way of life; see Susan Dickman, "Margery Kempe and the Continental Tradition of the Pious Woman," in *The Medieval Mystical Tradition in England,* ed. Marion Glasscoe, 150–68 (Cambridge: D. S. Brewer, 1984), 163.

55. Staley, *Margery Kempe's Dissenting Fictions,* 64–65, views Kempe's benefactors as offering a model of charity that critiques the social division of medieval society. Yet it is important to acknowledge that this model does not explicitly account for the place of the involuntary poor within its system of giving. We see instances when Kempe serves such people, but we do not really witness people of means helping the involuntary poor who shadow the text.

56. Goodman, *Margery Kempe and Her World,* 200, ignores this curious detail and Richard's own potential poverty by describing him as a "well-heeled beggar," who happens to be "flush" when he encounters Kempe.

57. In describing Richard's preference for begging, the text might be seen as implicitly criticizing him for rejecting gainful employment. However, this reading is discouraged when the *Book* emphasizes his limited capacity to help her and his charitable behavior toward her.

58. For an explicitly critical reading of Franciscanism as a movement that directly injured the involuntary poor, see Wolf, *The Poverty of Riches.* Kempe's donation of the humpbacked man's goods as well as her status as a popular alms

recipient may offer a peculiarly concrete example of the injustice that, according to Wolf, defines the relations between the voluntary and involuntary poor.

59. Staley, *Margery Kempe's Dissenting Fictions*, 71.

60. Ladd, "Mercantile Mysticism," 129.

61. Cullum, "Yf lak of charyte," 191.

62. See Thomas de Cantimpré, *The Life of Margaret of Ypres*, 37, and Bridget of Sweden, *The Liber Celestis of St. Bridget of Sweden*, 4.

63. Cited in Ben R. McRee, "Charity and Gild Solidarity in Late Medieval England," *Journal of British Studies* 32, no. 3 (1993):195–225, at 215.

64. It is worth noting that *The Work of Ninety Days* declares that the apostles became poor in order to serve as examples for their fellow human beings: "it was fitting and necessary that the apostles as the original founders (after Christ) of the new church . . . should *invite* others to the most perfect contempt of the world not only by their teaching but also by their life" (1:269, my emphasis). Elsewhere we also find a similar point, "After the apostles were proclaimers of gospel poverty, it was in no way permissible for them to do anything that could turn hearers away from gospel poverty, because they were obliged to lead their hearers to gospel poverty *by teaching and example*" (2:791, my emphasis). The apostles' promotion of poverty could in no way be construed as a call to enforce it on others, as Margery does to Richard.

65. Ibid., 1:200.

66. Ibid., 1:276.

67. Ibid., 1:77, explains this point: "in all the things they use the Friars Minor have simple use of fact and nothing of right. The Friars Minor say that this should be understood to mean that they use things consumable by use (and things not consumable by use) by the permission or grace of the granter, without any human right by which they could litigate in court for the thing or for use of the thing."

68. Ibid., 2:522.

69. Bonaventure, "Defense of the Mendicants," VIII.23, 188.

70. Ockham, *Work of Ninety Days*, 1:53.

71. In chapter 43, Kempe perhaps exhibits a similar will to dominion when she plans to offer alms received from pilgrims to the shrine of the trinity in Norwich, rather than using such alms for her needs. It is not long after this episode that Kempe's friends in Lynn refuse to lend her more money because she has given away her own goods as well as those of other men (108). Their objections may expose a familiar hostility to voluntary poverty as a form of financial irresponsibility placing a burden on those who work for a living. Their criticisms might also be relevant to the argument outlined above as they protest against Kempe's paradoxically willful act of giving away other people's goods. Fearful that she might give away their own hard-earned donations, her neighbors are likely unpersuaded by Kempe's claims of poverty. Her actions up to this point

have offered them little assurance that she might actually use their alms to alleviate her need.

72. See, for example, Thomas of Celano, "The Life of Saint Francis," in *Francis of Assisi: Early Documents,* 1:195.

73. Staley, *Margery Kempe's Dissenting Fictions,* 99, notes how Kempe's kind treatment of lepers is limited by gender expectations, as she kisses female lepers. Thus, while Kempe's actions allow her to reach out to marginal people excluded from everyday society, her radical religious practice, like that of St. Clare, "is explicitly circumscribed by society's sensitivity to gender categories."

74. William Langland, *Piers Plowman: The C Version; Will's Vision of Piers Plowman, Do-Well, Do-Better, Do-Best,* ed. George Russell and George Kane (Berkeley: University of California Press, 1997), XVI.372.

75. The gifts Kempe receives are incredibly generous when compared to regular standards of charitable giving in late medieval England. Christopher Dyer, *Standards of Living in the Middle Ages: Social Change in England, c. 1200–1520* (Cambridge: Cambridge University Press, 1989), 253, notes that the absolute minimum given to indigent tenants and prisoners was ¼ d., the cost of a loaf of bread weighing approximately two pounds. Guild members in need of aid and those living in almshouses typically received 1d. per day.

76. Ladd, "Mercantile Mysticism," 133, notes that the text's reference to "good" can mean either physical goods or grace, and he interprets the quote in a way that allows for both possible meanings.

77. Anne Hudson, ed., *The Works of a Lollard Preacher,* EETS 317 (Oxford: Oxford University Press, 2001), 130/2689–94.

78. Noting Kempe's place in a "mercantile late medieval religious culture," Nicholas Watson, for instance, remarks that Kempe uses "quantitative reckoning" in order to "understand, explain, and influence the divine"; see his "The Making of the *Book of Margery Kempe,*" in *Voices in Dialogue: Reading Women in the Middle Ages,* ed. Linda Olson and Kathryn Kerby-Fulton, 395–434 (Notre Dame, IN: University of Notre Dame Press, 2005), 418. Clarissa Atkinson describes the text's version of God as a "great banker or merchant prince" in her *Mystic and Pilgrim: The Book and World of Margery Kempe* (Ithaca: Cornell University Press, 1983), 60. Gastle, in "Breaking the Stained-Glass Ceiling," 130–33, discusses Kempe's tendency to track her expenses on pilgrimage, and he describes some of the economic dimensions of Kempe's spirituality. Ladd, "Mercantile Mysticism," 191, comments on how pilgrimage functions as a business "eased by [Kempe's] ability to pay." Staley, *Margery Kempe's Dissenting Fictions,* 79–83, discusses how the text and its version of Jesus promote models of salvation, pardon, and absolution that are fully consonant with market relations and objectives.

79. Ladd, "Mercantile Mysticism," 134, initially worries over Kempe's less than stringent response to her son's mercantile pursuits by advising him not to give up these occupations completely. Rather, she tells him that he should "not

settyn hys stody ne hys besynes so mech thereupon [his trade] as he did" (207). Ladd ultimately reads Kempe's lukewarm statement here as "an improvement of his earlier state of sin," and he views the second book more broadly as confirming Kempe's rejection of the mercantile ideology—an argument that I question below.

80. Staley, *Margery Kempe's Dissenting Fictions,* 75.

81. Calling Kempe both "fastidious and modest," Goodman, *Margery Kempe and Her World,* 54–55, notes Kempe's annoyance at having contracted vermin and goes on to assert that she had "high consumption standards and valued courtliness."

82. Staley sees Kempe's trip to and from Aachen as presenting "an image of fifteenth-century society whose fundamental disorder is the manifestation of its factionalization" (*Margery Kempe's Dissenting Fictions,* 192). Staley's point here is apt, especially if one takes into account the possible ways in which Kempe herself might be complicit in the fracturing of community.

83. On Lynn's Holy Trinity Guild see, McRee, "Charity and Gild Solidarity" and Ladd, "Mercantile Mysticism."

84. Staley, *Margery Kempe's Dissenting Fictions,* 167, argues that Kempe's travels in England at this point in the text resonate with Christ's entry into Jerusalem. While Staley makes a provocative analogy, it is nonetheless problematic due to the fact that Kempe summons the poor at all hours and pays them to assist her on her journey much as an employer might. These actions arguably dissociate her from Christ, who is himself so poor that he must borrow a donkey, not pay for the use of one. If the text does seek to link Kempe with Christ entering Jerusalem, then perhaps this discrepancy works to criticize the contemporary community and its forms of hierarchy, which cannot imagine a truly poor woman benefiting from the generosity of strangers.

85. See "chevisaunce," in the *Middle English Dictionary,* 6(b).

86. Hudson, *Two Wycliffite Texts,* 14/416–18.

87. Staley notes that in many of her travels, Kempe "dramatizes a more incipient violence that is only partially checked by the social contracts that serve as the basis of community" (*Margery Kempe's Dissenting Fictions,* 67).

88. Ashley, "Historicizing Margery," 375.

89. Discussing how Kempe ignores the premature urgings of others to write her book, Ashley notes that the text "emphasizes her independence from clerical writers and her response to the mandates of God" ("Historicizing Margery," 377). Such independence is, however, fleeting as Kempe must solicit clerical aid when she deems it time to record her story.

90. See Ashley, "Historicizing Margery," 375–77; Beckwith, *Christ's Body,* 95; Lochrie, *Margery Kempe and Translations of the Flesh,* 100–119; and Staley, *Margey Kempe's Dissenting Fictions,* 30–38, who advances the idea that the scribe is a necessary fiction of the text that validates Kempe's story and functions as a screen for her social and ecclesiastical criticism.

91. Felicity Riddy, "Text and Self in *The Book of Margery Kempe*," in *Voices in Dialogue*, 438.

92. Lochrie offers the helpful reminder that "writing was viewed as a separate skill in itself (from reading) and one which required a good deal of sheer physical labor" (*Margery Kempe and Translations of the Flesh*, 103).

93. For the view that the second scribe's failure is a result of his lack of grace and not the illegibility of the writing, see Lochrie, *Margery Kempe and Translations of the Flesh*, 99–100.

94. For the argument that Kempe possibly paid the priest for his labor, confirming his primary role as a scribe, see Watson, "The Making of *The Book of Margery Kempe*," 407–10.

95. Staley, *Margery Kempe's Dissenting Fictions*, 36. Staley's comment is apt in the context of Kempe's particularly unusual spirituality, but it would not necessarily seem applicable to other women writers such as Julian of Norwich, who wrote without the intervention of a male scribe.

96. Lochrie, *Margery Kempe and Translations of the Flesh*, 100.

97. For a discussion of how the scribe's doubt about Kempe ultimately works to confirm her saintliness, see Janet Wilson, "The Communities of Margery Kempe's *Book*," in *Medieval Women in Their Communities*, ed. Diane Watt, 155–85 (Toronto: University of Toronto Press, 1997), 161–62.

Chapter Five

1. For a study approaching the York cycle not as a false image of civic unity but as a performance thoroughly implicated in the city's cultural conflicts and material realities, see Sarah Beckwith, *Signifying God: Social Relation and Symbolic Act in the York Corpus Christi Plays* (Chicago: University of Chicago Press, 2001).

2. On the dramatic representation of poverty in the *First Shepherd's Play*, see Ruth Nissé, *Defining Acts: Drama and the Politics of Interpretation in Late Medieval England* (Notre Dame, IN: University of Notre Dame Press, 2005), chap. 4. Nissé argues that the Wakefield master prioritizes poverty and prophecy in polemical opposition to the urban context of the York cycle, which gives preference to visual representation and material labor. While exploring the urban milieu of the York cycle, my reading of the York plays differs from Nissé's: I find the drama's interest in visuality essential to its ultimate critique of the socioeconomic practices in which the plays participate.

3. On the similarities between urban culture and the feudal system, see Christopher Dyer, *Standards of Living in the Middle Ages: Social Change in England, c. 1200–1520* (Cambridge: Cambridge University Press, 1989), 24; John Merrington, "Town and Country in the Transition to Capitalism," in *The Transition from Feudalism to Capitalism*, ed. Rodney Hilton, 170–95 (London: Verso, 1978); and Beckwith, *Signifying God*, 52.

4. On York's governmental structure, see Maud Sellers, ed., *York Memorandum Book Lettered A/Y in the Guildhall Munimaent Room,* 2 vols., Surtees Society Publications (Durham: Andrews, 1912–1915), 2:iv–xii; D. M. Palliser, *Tudor York* (Oxford: Oxford University Press, 1979), 68; Heather Swanson, *Medieval Artisans* (Oxford: Basil Blackwell, 1989), 121–23; Alexandra Johnston and Margaret Rogerson, eds., *Records of Early English Drama: York,* 2 vols. (Toronto: University of Toronto Press, 1979; hereafter *REED: York*), 1:x; and Beckwith, *Signifying God,* 49. In his discussion of the council of forty-eight, even Jeremy Goldberg, who emphasizes the agency and autonomy of the artisan guilds, acknowledges that "it would be unsafe to suggest that crafts . . . carried much authority"; see P. J. P. Goldberg, "Craft Guilds, the Corpus Christi Play, and Civic Government," in *The Government of Medieval York: Essays in Commemoration of the 1396 Royal Charter,* ed. Sarah Rees Jones, 141–63 (York: Borthwick Institute of Historical Research, 1997), 154–55.

5. For discussions of the freedom and the mercers' manipulation of it, see Heather Swanson, *Medieval British Towns* (London: Palgrave Macmillan, 1999), 68–71, and R. B. Dobson, "Admissions to the Freedom of the City of York in the Later Middle Ages," *Economic History Review* 26 (1973): 1–22. On the city's labor structure, see Swanson, *Medieval Artisans,* 110, 113, 125–34; Heather Swanson, "The Illusion of Economic Structure: Craft Guilds in Late Medieval English Towns," *Past and Present* 121 (1988): 29–48; and Beckwith, *Signifying God,* 48–53. For arguments against Swanson and the dominance of the mercantile elite within the craft system, see Goldberg, "Craft Guilds, The Corpus Christi Play, and Civic Government"; P. J. P. Goldberg, "Performing the Word of God: Corpus Christi Drama in the Northern Province," in *Life and Thought in the Northern Church,* ed. Diana Wood, 145–70 (Woodbridge: Boydell, 1999); and Kate Giles, "Framing Labour: The Archaeology of York's Medieval Guildhalls," in *The Problem of Labour in Fourteenth-Century England,* ed. James Bothwell, P. J. P. Goldberg, and W. M. Ormrod, 65–84 (Woodbridge: York Medieval Press, 2000), 68–69. For the argument that guild systems beyond York were not imposed on artisans from above, see Gervase Rosser, "Crafts, Guilds, and the Negotiation of Work in the Medieval Town," *Past and Present* 154 (1997): 3–31.

6. Swanson, "Illusion of Economic Structure," 33.

7. See Swanson, *Medieval British Towns,* 48–49, and Swanson, *Medieval Artisans,* 8, 25.

8. For discussions of the guild system and the conflicts endemic to it, see Swanson, "The Illusion of Economic Structure," passim and especially 33–39; Swanson, *Medieval Artisans,* 30–32, 48–49, 59, 99; Beckwith, *Signifying God,* 49–51.

9. Beckwith, *Signifying God,* 51.

10. See, for example, Martin Stevens, *Four English Mystery Cycles: Textual, Contextual and Critical Interpretations* (Princeton: Princeton University Press, 1987), 51, and Nissé, *Defining Acts,* 33–39.

11. In this sense, the *Entry* offers a contrast to Wycliffite and antifraternal writings, which insist on the predetermined perfection of the evangelical church. This reading complicates Nissé's illuminating view of the pageant, which emphasizes how it features a hermeneutic ideal sympathetic to Wycliffism's promotion of biblical translation and lay exegesis. See Nissé, *Defining Acts,* 23–39.

12. Richard Beadle, ed., *The York Plays* (London: Edward Arnold, 1982), lines 16–17. Hereafter cited parenthetically by line number.

13. Phillip also declares that they are carrying out Christ's command because of the prophecy (46–49).

14. Nissé, *Defining Acts,* 35.

15. *Middle English Dictionary,* 2(b); 4(a).

16. On the different conceptions of foreignness or strangeness, see Derek Pearsall, "Strangers in Medieval London," in *The Stranger in Medieval Society,* ed. F. R. P. Akehurst and Stephanie Cain Van D'Elden, 46–62 (Minneapolis: University of Minnesota Press, 1997). Palliser, *Tudor York,* 147, also discusses the term noting that it could mean a non-freeman.

17. On the increasing anxiety about Scots in the wake of Henry V's Normandy campaign, see Goldberg, "Craft Guilds, the Corpus Christi Play, and Civic Government," 156.

18. Sellers, *York Memorandum Book,* 2:86; this is my translation.

19. Ibid., 2:207.

20. Ibid., 2:209.

21. Nissé, *Defining Acts,* 38.

22. See chap. 3.

23. See Mark 10:46 and Luke 18:35.

24. This kind of suspicious representation of poverty can be found in the Chester cycle, which devotes a single play to the healing of the blind man, who is heard begging for alms. On this pageant and its concern with deserving need, see Goldberg, "Performing the Word of God," 165.

25. See chap. 3.

26. See chap. 3.

27. *REED: York,* 1:20.

28. Nissé, *Defining Acts,* 34.

29. Stevens, *Four Middle English Mystery Cycles,* 59.

30. Nissé, *Defining Acts,* 34.

31. Swanson, *Medieval British Towns,* 116. She notes that "Any estimate of the proportion of the population who made up this sector of the very poor is basically guesswork."

32. Though a rather late record, the Housebooks of 1561 offer an example revealing how the guilds' trading practices could have adverse effects on the poor. Presenting a picture of conflict between poor people fishing for their own consumption or limited trade and the official members of the fishmongers' guild, the

record declares: "from hensforth none of the fysshmongars or others shall exact or tak of any poor folk bryngyng lamprayes smeletes or suche lyk freyssh watir fyssh in tyme of yer to sell within this Cite any pageant" (*REED: York,* 1:333).

33. Swanson, "Illusion of Economic Structure," 40. On the financial demands of guild membership, see also Swanson, *Medieval Artisans,* 111.

34. Swanson, *Medieval British Towns,* 132.

35. Rosser, "Craft, Guilds, and the Negotiation of Work," 30. Rosser makes these comments even as he argues that the guilds allowed for social diversity, "cut[ting] across ostensible horizontal distinctions of status" (19). See also Giles, "Framing Labour," 79–82.

36. This extreme sense of division can be seen within the composition of urban society itself. As Swanson explains, "The sheer scale of the wealth of the richest townsmen meant that within the larger urban parishes there was a greater gulf between rich and poor than there was likely to be in rural parishes" (*Medieval British Towns,* 127).

37. Stevens, *Four Middle English Mystery Cycles,* 75.

38. Nissé, *Defining Acts,* 39.

39. Stevens, *Four English Mystery Cycles,* 30.

40. Kathleen Ashley, "Sponsorship, Reflexivity and Resistance: Cultural Readings of the York Cycle Plays," in *The Performance of Middle English Culture,* ed. James J. Paxon, Lawrence M. Clopper, and Sylvia Tomasch, 9–24 (Cambridge: D. S. Brewer, 1998), 21.

41. J.W. Robinson, "Ad Majorem Dei Gloriam," in *Medieval Drama: A Collection of Festival Papers,* ed. William A. Selz, 31–37 (Vermillion: University of South Dakota Press, 1969), 35.

42. Stevens, *Four Middle English Mystery Cycles,* 30.

43. On the audience's primary role as both witnesses to the crucifixion and participants in it, see Beckwith, *Signifying God,* 69–70.

44. Ashley, "Sponsorship, Reflexivity and Resistance," 20. For a helpful discussion of the play's complex engagement with penance, see Beckwith, *Signifying God,* 90.

45. Ashley, "Sponsorship, Reflexivity and Resistance," 20.

46. Compare these lines with the half-acre episode in *Piers Plowman* when initially "Vch man in his manere made hymsulue to done"; William Langland, *Piers Plowman: The C-Version; Will's Visions of Piers Plowman, Do-Well, Do-Better, Do-Best,* ed. George Russell and George Kane (London: Athlone Press, 1997), VIII.117.

47. Beckwith, *Signifying God,* 53–54.

48. Ibid., 66.

49. Because the actors would perform the pageant (and thus the work of crucifixion) numerous times at different stations, the structure of the cycle confirms the quotidian dimensions of the soldiers' labor.

50. On Christ's body as a prop, see Beckwith, *Signifying God,* 66.

51. Ashley, "Sponsorship, Reflexivity and Resistance," 21, notes that the soldiers possess a "concern with craftsmanship, with using the proper tools and materials, and completing the job to specifications—which the guilds were organized to promote and monitor."

52. Sellers, *York Memorandum Book,* 2:282–83.

53. Ibid.

54. It is interesting that once the cross has been elevated, the audience members, in a sense, assume the role of searchers, examining the final product of the soldiers' labor.

55. Claire Sponsler, *Drama and Resistance: Bodies, Goods, and Theatricality in Late Medieval England* (Minneapolis: University of Minnesota Press, 1997), 148.

56. As in the gospel account, the soldiers draw straws for Christ's clothing, his last remaining possession (290–98).

57. Beckwith, *Signifying God,* 69, notes that the cross is made so heavy by Christ bearing the burden of human sin.

58. Ibid., 66.

59. Sponsler, in *Drama and Resistance,* chap. 6, makes a relevant argument in viewing Christ's broken and bleeding body as a challenge to the labor laws' insistence on work as an all-important activity.

60. Beadle offers another relevant meaning of "travail" as the work of redemption. See his "The York Cycle," in *The Cambridge Companion to Medieval English Theatre,* ed. Richard Beadle, 85–108 (Cambridge: Cambridge University Press, 1994), 103.

61. Thomas of Wimbledon, *Wimbledon's Sermon: Redde Rationem Villicationis Tue,* ed. Ione Kemp Knight, Duquesne Studies 9 (Pittsburgh: Duquesne University Press, 1967), 110, ll. 779–81.

62. 1 Corinthians 12:26.

63. On the York Cycle's engagement with the legal processes employed to condemn heretics, see Beckwith, *Signifying God,* chap. 6.

64. Swanson, *Medieval Artisans,* 113.

65. On the soldiers' ignorance of their role and how the staging compounds their unawareness, see Sarah Beckwith, "*Sacrum Signum*: Sacramentality and Dissent in York's Theatre of Corpus Christi," in *Criticism and Dissent in the Middle Ages,* ed. Rita Copeland, 264–88 (Cambridge: Cambridge University Press, 1996), 273–74.

66. On the mercers' guild and their powerful position in York's political hierarchy, see Sellers, *York Memorandum Book,* 2:iv–xii; Palliser, *Tudor York,* 68; Swanson, *Medieval Artisans,* 121–23; Beckwith, *Signifying God,* 49; and Dobson, "Craft Guilds and City," in *The Stage as Mirror,* ed. Alan Knight, 91–106 (Woodbridge: D. S. Brewer, 1997), 105.

67. On God's *memento mori* speech, see Pamela Sheingorn and David Bevington, "'All This Was Token Domysday to Drede': Visual Signs of Last Judgment in the Corpus Christi Cycles and in Late Gothic Art," in *Homo, Memento Finis: The Iconography of Just Judgment in Medieval Art and Drama,* ed. David Bevington, 15–58 (Kalamazoo: Medieval Institute Publications, Western Michigan University Press, 1985), 42.

68. Beckwith, *Signifying God,* 275, notes that Christ is the only character in the pageant who is capable of rendering infallible acts of judgment.

69. "The Sermon of William Taylor," in Anne Hudson, ed., *Two Wycliffite Texts,* EETS o.s. 317 (Oxford: Oxford University Press, 1925), 17/520–31.

70. See "The Sermon of William Taylor," 15/450–61, and my discussion of Luke 14 in chap. 3.

71. The importance of this charitable vision can be seen in the wider community. For example, it was given material representation in York's Church of All Saints where there was a window depicting the works of mercy described in Matthew 25. See Swanson, *Medieval British Towns,* 127.

72. Wimbledon's sermon, 65–68, usefully illustrates how conceptions of social unity are not necessarily egalitarian. Throughout the sermon Wimbledon advocates the social boundaries of the estates model by urging "eueri man [to] trauayle in his degree" (68).

73. Dobson, "Craft Guilds and City," 105. See also Stevens, *Four Middle English Mystery Cycles,* 34.

74. Simon Shepherd and Peter Womack, ed., *English Drama: A Cultural History* (Oxford: Blackwell, 1996), 15.

75. Beadle, "The York Cycle," 94. For a complete list of the guild's props list see, *REED: York,* 1:55–56.

76. Meg Twycross comments briefly on the "spectacle" and "sense of wonder" created by the pageant. See "The Theatricality of Medieval English Plays," in *The Cambridge Companion to Medieval English Theatre,* 48. Goldberg, "Craft Guilds, the Corpus Christi Play, and Civic Government," 145, also notes the "considerable expense" of the play "reflected in continual expenditure on maintenance and repairs noted in the mercers' company accounts."

77. Shepherd and Womack, *English Drama,* 15.

78. Stevens, *Four Middle English Mystery Cycles,* 34.

79. Alan Justice, "Trade Symbolism in the York Cycle," *Theatre Journal* (March 1979): 47–58, at 56.

80. According to the document, the scrutatores "dicunt quod Willelmus [de Hugate, mercer] pondera sua eis liberari renuit and recusavit. Et cum dicti scrutatores pondera ibidem ceperint, ipse Willelmus ea ab eis violenter eripuit, et fecit eis rescussum in contemptum etc." [The searchers "said that William [de Hugate, mercer] objected and refused to release the weights. And when the said searchers seized the same weights, William violently took the weights from

them and dismissed them in contempt, etc.] (Sellers, *York Memorandum Book,* 2:9), my translation.

81. Swanson, *Medieval Artisans,* 125.

82. Richard Homan, "Ritual Aspects of the York Cycle." *Theatre Journal* 22 (1981): 303–15, at 311. This acknowledgement comes despite Homan's larger argument that "the play cycles provided a mechanism . . . by which the tension implicit in the diachronic rise and fall of occupational communities could be confronted and worked out" (315). For a critique of Homan's and other idealized accounts of the ritualizing power of theater, see Beckwith, *Signifying God,* 23–41, 49.

83. Swanson, *Medieval Artisans,* 130, explains that "mercantile capital was directed toward monopolizing wholesale supplies and the distribution system. The artisan all too often was dependent on a supplier who thereafter was exonerated from responsibility for the quality of the finished product."

84. See Palliser, *Tudor York,* 106, 160.

85. Dobson, "Craft Guilds and City," 105.

86. The mercers' charter is the document most relevant to the guild's foundations and objectives. Because they oversaw the policies and practices of the city's entire labor system, the mercers did not need to develop their own set of ordinances. Their charter was held directly from the king. On the status and significance of this document, see Sellers, *York Memorandum Book,* 2:xxx–xxxi.

87. Ibid., 2:xxx–xxxi.

88. Ibid., 2:xxxiii. Sellers adds that "Members of the mercers' mystery were ipso facto members of the mercers' guild, and their religious, social and charitable undertakings were not merged in a separate organization; the master of the mystery controlled both the mercantile and the religious policy."

89. Ibid., 2:135–36; translation mine.

90. Ibid., 2:xxx–xxxi.

91. Ibid., 2:xxxi.

92. Sellers notes that "the mercers followed prescribed medieval etiquette in this verbose attempt to hide self-seeking under the cloak of charity" (ibid., 2:xxx–xxxi). She adds that "The successful business man of the twentieth century creates an atmosphere of capital around him; the medieval trader's chief object was to create an atmosphere of poverty" (2:xxxi). The strategic declaration of impoverishment is also a common trope in a city's request for aid from the crown (2:xxiv).

93. My argument here is not intended to dismiss or reject the acts of charity performed by members of the mercers' guild in their daily lives. What primarily interests me is the tension between the organization's official vision of poverty and the charitable lessons of the pageant that this organization sponsored. I discuss this perspective further at the conclusion of this chapter.

94. Swanson, *Medieval Artisans,* 118. Goldberg, in "Craft Guilds, the Corpus Christi Play, and Civic Government," 154, argues against Swanson in

suggesting that the guilds were not, in fact, financially burdened by the plays that they voluntarily agreed to produce. He reads any expressions of hardship as strategic declarations aimed at securing funds to be used for other purposes. If one is persuaded by Goldberg's hypothesis, then it is notable that the guilds' claims of poverty are particularly flexible in that they bear little relation to actual forms of need said to be caused or exacerbated by the plays. See also Goldberg, "Performing the Word of God," 152.

95. On the economic decline of York, see Palliser, *Tudor York,* chap. 8. He notes that "the city's fortunes seem to have been at their lowest from about 1510 to 1560 (211).

96. These industries became centralized in the areas of the West Riding and London respectively, which offered better resources and waters that were more easily navigable. See Palliser, *Tudor York,* 162, 208–11, who also notes that during this period other crafts such as leather-making actually expanded.

97. While the date of this ordinance and some of the others I cite is unknown, the precise moment of the guild record within the identifiable date range of the cycle's performance is less important than the overall emergence of a distinctive discourse of poverty and charity relevant to a variety of craft guilds that sponsored individual pageants.

98. The date of this ordinance is unknown.

99. Palliser, *Tudor York,* 164–65, discusses the wealth of the goldsmiths and notes that they were the "most powerful" of the "household crafts."

100. Sellers, *York Memorandum Book,* 2:123–24; trans. *REED: York,* 2:732.

101. See for instance, the armorers' ordinances (1444), *REED: York,* 1:62; the spicers' ordinances (1433), *REED: York,* 1:54; and the cordwainers' ordinances (date unkown), *REED: York,* 2:624.

102. For a helpful example illustrating the artificiality of the labor divisions and the conflicts these produced, see the discussion of the sausage-makers' guild in Swanson, "Illusion of Economic Structure," and Beckwith, *Signifying God,* 50.

103. See, for example, records pertaining to the cutlers (1445), *REED: York,* 2:742; the glovers (1475), *REED: York,* 1:105; the girdlers (1484), *REED: York,* 1:136–37; and the skinners (1517), *REED: York,* 1:214.

104. These alternate terms for charity are taken from the armorers plea to the city government (1444), *REED: York,* 1:62. Citing some sixteenth-century guild records, Alexandra Johnston, in "The City as Patron: York," in *Shakespeare and Theatrical Patronage in Early Modern England,* ed. Paul Whitfield White and Suzanne R. Westfall, 150–75 (Cambridge: Cambridge University Press, 2002), 157–60, demonstrates that the city directed certain guilds/pageants to distribute money to other guilds in need of financial support. While Johnston's discussion focuses in part on the redirection of funds originally allocated to pageants discontinued after the Reformation, her reading of other records tends to view these mandated inter-guild transactions as a benevolent means of maintaining the viability of pageants assigned to needy guilds. She does not consider the oligarchy's

potential complicity in creating or exacerbating such need, viewing it instead strictly as the unavoidable consequence of York's overall economic decline.

105. Palliser, *Tudor York,* 106, notes that in the sixteenth century, more craftsmen had a share in the city government: "seventy-four (70%) of the aldermen were merchants and wholesale traders, while six more were lawyers and gentlemen, but the other twenty-six were craftsmen and retailers." Overall, he remarks that "the Tudor age was clearly an ebb period for the influence of York's merchants, falling between two more prosperous periods." This period of decline for the merchants, did not, however, radically change the socioeconomic structure of the city. As Palliser explains, "in their own city the York merchants were dominant. Numbering a tenth of all freemen, they provided half the Tudor mayors and aldermen; and for eleven years in the sixteenth century the mayor of the city and the master of the mercers' guild were one and the same" (160). Additionally, in terms of the distribution of wealth in the city, Palliser points out that in 1524 "seven per cent of York's taxable population owned exactly half of the taxable goods" (138).

106. On the increasing numbers of poor people who came to York during its decline, see Palliser, *Tudor York,* 213–14. Palliser also notes that at the height of the economic crisis, the dissolution of religious houses in the Reformation also included the closure of many of the city's hospitals, which offered relief to the poor (222).

107. Swanson, *Medieval Artisans,* 111, notes that the carpenters' ordinances make a distinction between the terms "occupacion" and "brotherhood." This differentiation, she suggests, implies an awareness of the divisions between fraternal aspects of guild and the mystery itself.

108. Describing how guilds directed charity to their own members, Antony Black, in *Guild and State: European Political Thought from the Twelfth Century to the Present* (New Brunswick: Transaction, 2003), 27, remarks that "their success as *milieux morales* depended entirely on the degree to which producer and consumer interests were compatible." Rosser, "Crafts, Guilds, and the Negotiation of Work," 27–28, sees in a guild's provision for its own members a form of social inclusivity as it extends the same privileges to masters and dependent laborers alike.

109. Sellers, *York Memorandum Book,* 2:279. Swanson, *Medieval British Towns,* 129, doubts that this charitable provision could have been sustained for any significant period of time.

110. *York Memorandum Book,* 2:280.

111. This stipulation is reminiscent of demands frequently made in reference to modern forms of social aid that the poor should not waste welfare money or other financial donations on things like alcohol, drugs, or cigarettes.

112. *York Memorandum Book,* 2:xxxvi.

113. Ibid., 2:280.

114. Ibid.

115. Goldberg, "Craft Guilds, the Corpus Christi Play, and Civic Government," 160, certainly sees no discrepancy between the play's calls to charity and the mercers' activities. After quoting Christ's recitation of the charitable works performed by the good souls, he concludes that "These words were taken very seriously and indeed literally. [T]he mercers' own guildhall was built above the Trinity hospital of their foundation." While I do not dispute the guild's extensive charitable activities, Goldberg neglects to discuss the specificities of the pageant's account of charity. This account entails a radicalism not likely to be found in an institution's practice of social aid, given the widespread tendency to insist on discrimination in giving.

116. For examples of such charitable giving recorded in the wills of merchants from York, see Ann Warren, *Anchorites and Their Patrons in Medieval England* (Berkeley: University of California Press, 1985), 242. For charitable giving as recorded in the wills of the laity more generally, see P. H. Cullum and P. J. P. Goldberg, "Charitable Provision in Late Medieval York: 'To the Praise of God and the Use of the Poor,'" *Northern History* 29 (1993): 24–39.

117. On the craft groups in York and their association with religious guilds, see Goldberg, "Craft Guilds, the Corpus Christi Play, and Civic Government," 144. On the devotional concerns of guilds more broadly, see Goldberg, "Performing the Word of God," 151–52.

118. See, for example, Rosser, "Going to the Fraternity Feast: Commensality and Social Relations in Late Medieval England," *Journal of British Studies* 33, no. 4 (1994): 430–46. In discussing how fraternities invited the needy to celebratory feasts, Rosser makes two important caveats. First, he notes that "in a rare instance every poor person was said to be welcome." And second, he also acknowledges that the "practical scale of immediate relief . . . was evidently less important than the ritually enhanced force of the example" (436). See also Frank Rexroth, *Deviance and Power in Late Medieval London*, trans. Pamela Selwyn (Cambridge: Cambridge University Press, 2007), chap. 6, for an account describing how guild-sponsored almshouses made sure to cater to the deserving and respectable poor.

119. On the nostalgic reenactment of York's Corpus Christi plays in the modern era, see Beckwith, *Signifying God*, chap. 1.

120. Ashley, "Sponsorship, Reflexivity and Resistance," 20.

Epilogue

1. *Nickel and Dimed* received the *Los Angeles Times* book prize, and it was named as a *New York Times* notable book. As of October 2006, *Nickel and Dimed* had spent 109 (nonconsecutive) weeks on the *New York Times* best-seller list; see http://ehrenreich.blogs.com/barbaras_blog/2006/10/nickel_and_dime.html.

2. The schools that have assigned *Nickel and Dimed* as summer reading include the University of North Carolina at Chapel Hill, Lehigh University, Miami University (Ohio), Southern Oregon University, Ohio State University, Appalachian State University, Ball State University, Fairfield University, Indiana State University, Siena College, Davidson College, Virginia Commonwealth University, and Rollins College.

3. In discussing the methodology of *Nickel and Dimed*, critics align the book with much later texts written in the journalistic tradition of "muckraking." See, for example, Alex Feerst, "Bowery Beautiful: Progressive Slumming and Ghetto Aesthetics, 1880–1930" (Ph.D. diss., Duke University, 2005), 14–19. For comparisons of *Nickel and Dimed* to Jack London's *The People of the Abyss*, George Orwell's *Down and Out in Paris and London*, Jacob Riis's *How the Other Half Lives*, and John Howard Griffin's *Black Like Me*, see Scott Sherman, "Class Warrior: Barbara Ehrenreich's Singular Crusade," *Columbia Journalism Review* 42, no. 4 (2003): 34–41; Lowell Ponte, "Cash and Carry: Propaganda for Fume and Profit," *FrontPageMag.com*, 24 August 2001, available at http://97.74.65.51/readArticle.aspx?ARTID=21687; Roxanne A. Donovan and Mary Crawford, review of *Nickel and Dimed*, *Sex Roles: A Journal of Research* 46, nos. 3–4 (2002): 129–30; and James Fallows, "Working Classes," *Atlantic Online*, 2 May 2001, available at http://www.theatlantic.com/unbound/fallows/jf2001-05-02/.

4. The 1996 Welfare Reform Act essentially mandated that all able-bodied adults must work after receiving welfare benefits for two years. Among its other notable provisions, the law restricted lifetime welfare benefits to a total of five years, though it gave states the option to decrease this time limit. The law also offered states cash rewards for reducing the number of people on their welfare rolls. For the text of the law itself, see http://thomas.loc.gov/cgi-bin/query/z?c104:H. R.3734. ENR:.

5. For an altogether different ethical framework highlighting the dependence and vulnerabilty that necessarily defines all human experience, see Alasdair MacIntyre, *Dependent Rational Animals: Why Human Beings Need the Virtues* (Chicago: Carus, 1999).

6. Committee on Ways and Means, U.S. House of Representatives, "Summary of Welfare Reforms Made by Public Law 104-193" (Washington, D.C.: U.S. Government Printing Office, 1996), available at www.access.gpo.gov/congress/wm015.txt.

7. Barbara Ehrenreich, *Nickel and Dimed: On (Not) Getting by in America* (New York: Henry Holt, 2001), 1996. Hereafter cited parenthetically by page number.

8. For an insightful account of *Nickel and Dimed* and the problems that Ehrenreich's method of research generates for reviewers, see Feerst, "Bowery Beautiful," 1–20. While Feerst's project does not pursue *Nickel and Dimed*'s connections to medieval poverty debates, it similarly focuses on the ethical and

epistemological difficulties embedded in Ehrenreich's experiment. For this reason, I have found Feerst's perspective on *Nickel and Dimed* to be extremely valuable and influential on my own reading of the text.

9. On Ehrenreich's crafted social mobility, see also Feerst, "Bowery Beautiful," 7–10, discussing Ehrenreich's self-conscious claims of "distance and intimacy" primarily in relation to Jim Fallows's interview with Ehrenreich in "Working Classes."

10. Cara Spindler, review of *Nickel and Dimed, Z Magazine,* May 2001.

11. Linda Brebner, "Taking the Down Escalator," *Newsletter of the Evangelical and Ecumenical Women's Caucus* 26 no. 2 (2002), available at http://www.eewc.com/Reviews/Summer2002Escalator.htm.

12. Spindler, review of *Nickel and Dimed.* For a discussion of Spindler's review focusing specifically on the critic's additional charges that Ehrenreich goes "slumming" by engaging in an experiment not designed "to change anything," see Feerst, "Bowery Beautiful," 3–4.

13. John Cooke, *Brill's Content,* quoted in *Slate,* 19 May 2001, available at http://www.slate.com/id/106108/.

14. Lillian Daniel affirms this perspective when she praises Ehrenreich's "refusal to be pious about her own efforts" as "the book's greatest strength"; review of *Nickel and Dimed, Christian Century* 118, no. 22 (2001): 30.

15. Donovan and Crawford, review of *Nickel and Dimed.*

16. Ehrenreich, *Nickel and Dimed,* 22, 123–25, 127–28, 135, 145–46, 149–50, 209–12. See also Ehrenreich's more recent book, *Bait and Switch: The Futile Pursuit of the American Dream* (New York: Henry Holt, 2005), which argues that white-collar workers have also become subject to the same workplace practices that have been used to discipline low-wage laborers.

17. Steven Malanga, "The Myth of the Working Poor," *City Journal* 14, no. 4 (2004), available at http://www.city-journal.org/html/14_4_working_poor.html.

18. Ponte, "Cash and Carry."

19. Mark D. Fefer, "Slumming for Dollars," *Seattle Weekly,* 11–17 July 2001, available at http://www.seattleweekly.com/2001-07-11/arts/slumming-for-dollars.php.

20. Review of *Nickel and Dimed,* brothersjudd.com, available at http://brothersjudd.com/index.cfm/fuseaction/reviews.detail/book_id/5/Nickel%20and%20D.htm.

21. Michael Tremoglie, "Barbara Ehrenreich: Nickel and Diming Truth," *FrontPageMag.com,* 22 July 2003, available at http://www.frontpagemag.com/Articles/Read.aspx?GUID=7C7D42E2-7138-4F13-B35C-2718557CDD55.

22. Quoted in Elizabeth Crawford, "Book Choice for Summer Reading Program Again Stirs Controversy in North Carolina," *The Chronicle of Higher Education,* 11 July 2003.

23. *News & Observer* (Raleigh), 9 July 2003.

24. Quoted in Crawford, "Book Choice for Summer Reading Program."

25. "The Sermon of William Taylor," in Anne Hudson, ed., *Two Wycliffite Texts,* EETS o.s. 301 (Oxford: Oxford University Press, 1993), 18/570–76.

26. Joni Scott, review of *Nickel and Dimed, Humanist* 61, no. 5 (2001): 40–41.

27. Frederic and Mary Ann Brussat, review of *Nickel and Dimed, Spirituality and Practice,* May 2002, available at http://www.spiritualityandpractice.com/books/books.php?id=2805.

28. Jimmy Dorrell, "*Nickel and Dimed*: The Working Poor Don't Need Handouts Just Livable Wage," *The Waco Tribune-Herald,* 22 December 2002. For another review seeing *Nickel and Dimed* as a call to Christian ethics, see Peter Petshauer, Review of *Nickel and Dimed, National Women's Studies Association Journal* 14, no. 2 (2002), 225–27.

29. William Langland, *Piers Plowman: The C-Version; Will's Vision of Piers Plowman, Do-Well, Do-Better, Do-Best,* ed. George Russell and George Kane (London: Athlone Press, 1997), XIII.241–42.

WORKS CITED

Primary Texts

Aquinas, Thomas. *Catena Aurea*. 4 vols. London: J. H. Parker, 1841–45.

Armstrong, Regis J., and Ignatius C. Brady, eds. *Francis and Clare: The Complete Works*. Mahwah, NJ: Paulist Press, 1982.

Arnold, Thomas, ed. *Select English Works of John Wyclif*. 3 vols. Oxford: Clarendon Press, 1869–71.

Augustine. "Homilies on the Gospel of St. John." In *Nicene and Post Nicene Fathers*, edited by Philip Schaf. 10 vols. Grand Rapids, MI: William B. Eerdmans, 1956.

———. *On Christian Doctrine*. Translated by D.W. Robertson. Upper Saddle River, NJ: Prentice-Hall, 1958.

Barr, Helen, ed. *The Piers Plowman Tradition*. London: J. M. Dent, 1993.

Beadle, Richard, ed. *The York Plays*. London: Edward Arnold, 1982.

Bevington, David, ed. *Medieval Drama*. Boston: Houghton Mifflin, 1975.

Bible. The Douai-Rheims Version.

Biblia Latina cum glossa ordinaria. 4 vols. Brepols: Turnhout, 1992.

Bonaventure. "The Defense of the Mendicants." In *The Works of Bonaventure*. Translated by José de Vinck. 5 vols. Patterson, NJ: St. Anthony Guild Press, 1966.

Bridget of Sweden. *The Liber Celestis of St. Bridget of Sweden*. Edited by Roger Ellis. EETS o.s. 291. Oxford: Oxford University Press, 1987.

Bullarium Franciscanum. Edited by Conrad Eubel. Rome: Typis Vaticanis, 1898, vol. 5.

Dean, James, ed. *Six Ecclesiastical Satires*. Kalamazoo: Medieval Institute Publications, 1991.

Denis the Carthusian. *Opera Omnia*. 42 vols. Monstrolii: Typis Cartusiae S. M. De Pratis, 1896.

English Economic History: Select Documents. Edited by A. E. Bland, P. A. Brown, and R. H. Tawney. London: G. Bell and Sons, 1915.

FitzRalph, Richard. *Defensio Curatorum*. In *Trevisa's Dialogus*, edited by John Perry. EETS o.s. 167. Cambridge: Cambridge University Press, 1925.

———. *De pauperie salvatoris.* In John Wyclif, *De domino divino,* edited by R. L. Poole. London: Wyclif Society, 1890.

———. "An Edition of Richard FitzRalph's *De pauperie salvatoris*: Books V, VI, and VII." Russell Oliver Brock, Ph.D. diss., University of Colorado, 1953.

Francis of Assisi: Early Documents. Edited and translated by Regis J. Armstrong, J. Wayne Hellman, and William J. Short. 3 vols. Hyde Park, NY: New City Press, 1999–2001.

Friedberg, Emil, ed. *Corpus Iuris Canonici.* 2 vols. Leipzig: Tauchnitz, 1879.

Hereford, Nicholas. "Nicholas Hereford's Ascension Day Sermon, 1382." Edited by Simon Forde. *Medieval Studies* 51 (1989): 205–41.

Hervaus Natalis. *The Poverty of Christ and the Apostles.* Translated by John D. Jones. Toronto: Pontifical Institute of Medieval Studies, 1999.

Heyworth, P. L., ed. *Jack Upland, Friar Daw's Reply, and Upland's Rejoinder.* London: Oxford University Press, 1968.

Hudson, Anne, ed. *Selections from English Wycliffite Writings.* Toronto: University of Toronto Press, 1997.

———, ed. *Two Wycliffite Texts.* EETS o.s. 301. Oxford: Oxford University Press, 1993.

———, ed. *The Works of a Lollard Preacher.* EETS 317. Oxford: Oxford University Press, 2001.

Hudson, Anne and Pamela Gradon, eds. *English Wycliffite Sermons.* 5 vols. New York: Oxford University Press, 1983–96.

Huyskens, Albert, ed. "The Letter of Conrad of Marburg." *Quellenstudien zur Geschichte der hl. Elizabeth Langaräfin von Thüringen.* Marburg: N. G. Elwert, 1908.

Jacobus de Voragine. *The Golden Legend.* Translated by William Granger Ryan. 2 vols. Princeton: Princeton University Press, 1993.

Jacques de Vitry. "The Life of Marie d'Oignies." In *Two Lives of Marie d'Oignies,* translated by Margot H. King. Toronto: Peregrina, 1998.

Johnston, Alexandra, and Margaret Rogerson, eds. and trans. *Records of Early English Drama: York.* 2 vols. Toronto: University of Toronto Press, 1979.

Kempe, Margery. *The Book of Margery Kempe.* Edited by Lynn Staley. Kalamazoo: Western Michigan University, Medieval Institute Publications, 1996.

Langland, William. *Piers Plowman.* Edited by Elizabeth Salter and Derek Pearsall. Evanston: Northwestern University Press, 1967.

———. *Piers Plowman: An Edition of the C-text.* Edited by Derek Pearsall. York Medieval Texts, 2d ser. London: Arnold, 1978. Corrected ed., Exeter: University of Exeter Press, 1994.

———. *Piers Plowman: The B Version.* Rev. ed. Edited by George Kane and E. Talbot Donaldson. London: Athlone Press, 1988.

———. *Piers Plowman: The C Version; Will's Visions of Piers Plowman, Do-Well, Do-Better, and Do-Best.* Edited by George Russell and George Kane. London: Athlone Press, 1997.

Matthew, F. D., ed. *The English Works of Wyclif.* EETS o.s. 74. London: Trübner, 1880.

The Parliament Rolls of Medieval England. Edited by C. Given-Wilson et al. Woodbridge: Boydell, 2005. Also available on CD-ROM; Leicester: Scholarly Digital Editions, 2005.

Pearsall, Derek, and Kathleen Scott, eds. *Piers Plowman: A Facsimile of Bodleian Library, Oxford, MS Douce 104.* Cambridge: D. S. Brewer, 1992.

Prudentius. "*Psychomachia.*" In *Prudentius,* edited and translated by H. J. Thomson. Cambridge, MA: Harvard University Press, 1949; repr. 1969.

Richard of Maidstone. *Protectorium Pauperis. Carmelus* 5 (1958): 132–80.

Sellers, Maud, ed. *York Memorandum Book Lettered A/Y in the Guildhall Munimaent Room.* 2 vols. Surtees Society Publications. Durham: Andrews, 1912–15.

Statutes of the Realm. Edited by A. Luders et al. 11 vols. London: 1810–28.

"Summary of Welfare Reforms Made by Public Law 104–93." Committee on Ways and Means, U.S. House of Representatives. Washington, D.C.: Government Printing Office, 1996.

Taylor, William. "The Sermon of William Taylor." In *Two Wycliffite Texts,* edited by Anne Hudson. EETS o.s. 301. Oxford: Oxford University Press, 1993.

Thomas de Cantimpré. *The Life of Margaret of Ypres.* Translated by Margot H. King. Toronto: Peregrina, 1990.

Thomas of Wimbledon. *Wimbledon's Sermon: Redde Rationem Villicationis Tue.* Edited by Ione Kemp Knight. Duquesne Studies 9. Pittsburgh: Duquesne University Press, 1967.

Thorpe, William. *The Testimony of William Thorpe.* In *Two Wycliffite Texts,* edited by Anne Hudson. EETS o.s. 301. Oxford: Oxford University Press, 1993.

Wenzel, Siegfried, ed. *Fasciculus Morum.* University Park: Pennsylvania State University Press, 1989.

———, ed. *Summa virtutum de remediis anime.* Athens: University of Georgia Press, 1984.

William of Ockham. *Work of Ninety Days.* Translated by John Killcullen and John Scott. 2 vols. Lewiston: Edwin Mellen Press, 2001.

Wyclif, John. *De blasphemia.* Edited by Michael Dziewicki. London: Wyclif Society, 1893.

———. *De civili dominio.* Edited by Reginald Poole. London: Wyclif Society, 1890.

———. *De domino divino.* Edited by R. L. Poole. London: Wyclif Society, 1890.

Secondary Texts

Adams, Robert. "The Nature of Need in *Piers Plowman XX.*" *Traditio* 34 (1978): 273–302.

———. "Piers's Pardon and Langland's Semi-Pelagianism." *Traditio* 39 (1983): 367–418.
Aers, David. "Chaucer's Tale of Melibee: Whose Virtues?" In *Medieval Literature and Historical Inquiry: Essays in Honor of Derek Pearsall*, edited by David Aers, 69–82. Cambridge: D. S. Brewer, 2000.
———. *Community, Gender, and Individual Identity: English Writing, 1360–1430.* London: Routledge, 1988.
———. *Faith, Ethics, and Church: Writing in England, 1360–1409.* Cambridge: D. S. Brewer, 2000.
———. "John Wyclif: Poverty and the Poor. *Yearbook of Langland Studies* 17 (2003): 55–72.
———. *Piers Plowman and Christian Allegory.* New York: St. Martin's Press, 1975.
———. "*Piers Plowman* and Problems in the Perception of Poverty: A Culture in Transition." *Leeds Studies in English* 14 (1983): 5–25.
———. Review of *The Laborer's Two Bodies,* by Kellie Robertson. *Yearbook of Langland Studies* 19 (2005): 226–36.
———. *Sanctifying Signs: Making Christian Tradition in Late Medieval England.* Notre Dame, IN: Notre Dame University Press, 2004.
———. "Walter Brut's Theology of the Sacrament of the Altar." In *Lollards and Their Influence in Late Medieval England,* edited by Fiona Somerset, Jill C. Havens, and Derrick G. Pitard, 115–26. Woodbridge: Boydell, 2003.
Amos, Mark Addison. "The Naked and the Dead: The Carpenters' Company and Lay Spirituality in Late Medieval England. In *The Middle Ages at Work: Practicing Labor in Late Medieval England,* edited by Kellie Robertson and Michael Uebel, 91–110. New York: Palgrave Macmillan, 2004.
Ashley, Kathleen. "Historicizing Margery: *The Book of Margery Kempe* as Social Text." *Journal of Medieval and Early Modern Studies* 28, no. 2 (Spring 1998): 371–88.
———. "Sponsorship, Reflexivity and Resistance: Cultural Readings of the York Cycle Plays." In *The Performance of Middle English Culture,* edited by James J. Paxon, Lawrence M. Clopper, and Sylvia Tomasch, 9–24. Cambridge: D. S. Brewer, 1998.
Aston, Margaret. "'Caim's Castles': Poverty, Politics, and Disendowment." In *The Church, Politics, and Patronage in the Fifteenth Century,* edited by Barrie Dobson, 45–81. New York: St. Martin's Press, 1984.
Atkinson, Clarissa. *Mystic and Pilgrim: The Book and World of Margery Kempe.* Ithaca: Cornell University Press, 1983.
Austin, J. L. *How to Do Things with Words.* Edited by J. O. Urmson and Marina Sbisa. Cambridge, MA: Harvard University Press, 1962.
Barr, Helen. *Signes and Sothe.* Cambridge: D. S. Brewer, 1994.
———. "Wycliffite Representations of the Third Estate." In *Lollards and Their Influence,* ed. Fiona Somerset, Jill C. Havens, and Derrick G. Pitard, 197–216. Woodbridge: Boydell, 2003.

Beadle, Richard. "The York Cycle." In *The Cambridge Companion to Medieval English Theatre,* edited by Richard Beadle, 85–108. Cambridge: Cambridge University Press, 1994.

Beckwith, Sarah. *Christ's Body: Identity, Culture, and Society in Late Medieval Writings.* London: Routledge, 1993.

———. "*Sacrum Signum*: Sacramentality and Dissent in York's Theatre of Corpus Christi." In *Criticism and Dissent in the Middle Ages,* edited by Rita Copeland, 264–88. Cambridge: Cambridge University Press, 1996.

———. *Signifying God: Social Relation and Symbolic Act in the York Corpus Christi Plays.* Chicago: University of Chicago Press, 2001.

Bennett, Judith, "Conviviality and Charity in Medieval and Early Modern England." *Past and Present* 134 (1992): 19–41.

Black, Antony. *Guild and State: European Political Thought from the Twelfth Century to the Present.* New Brunswick: Transaction, 2003.

Bloomfield, Morton W. *Piers Plowman as a Fourteenth-Century Apocalypse.* New Brunswick: Rutgers University Press, 1961.

Boanas, Guy, and Lyndal Roper. "Feminine Piety in Fifteenth-Century Rome: Santa Romana." In *Disciplines of Faith: Studies in Religion, Politics, and Patriarchy,* edited by Jim Obelkevich, Lyndal Roper, and Raphael Smith, 177–93. London: Routlege and Kegan Paul, 1987.

Bolton, J. L. *The Medieval English Economy, 1150–1500.* London: J. M. Dent, 1980.

Bossy, John. "The Mass as a Social Institution 1200–1700." *Past and Present* 100 (1983): 29–61.

Bourquin, Guy. *Piers Plowman.* 2 vols. Paris: Champion, 1978.

Bowers, John M. *Chaucer and Langland: The Antagonistic Tradition.* Notre Dame, IN: University of Notre Dame Press, 2007.

———. *The Crisis of Will in Piers Plowman.* Washington DC: Catholic University of America Press, 1986.

———. "*Piers Plowman* and the Police: Notes Toward a History of the Wycliffite Langland." *Yearbook of Langland Studies* 6 (1992): 1–50.

Brebner, Linda. "Taking the Down Escalator." *Newsletter of the Evangelical and Ecumenical Women's Caucus* 26, no. 2 (2002).

Brothersjudd.com. Review of *Nickel and Dimed.*

Brussat, Frederic and Mary Ann. Review of *Nickel and Dimed. Spirituality and Practice,* May 2002.

Clopper, Lawrence. "Franciscans, Lollards, and Reform." In *Lollards and Their Influence in Late Medieval England,* edited by Fiona Somerset, Jill C. Havens, and Derrick G. Pitard, 177–96. Woodbridge: Boydell, 2003.

———. "The Life of the Dreamer, the Dreams of the Wanderer in *Piers Plowman.*" *Studies in Philology* 86 (1989): 276–79.

———. "Need Men and Women Labor?: Langland's Wanderer and the Labor Ordinances." In *Chaucer's England: Literature in Historical Context,* edited by Barbara Hanawalt, 110–29. Minneapolis: University of Minnesota Press, 1992.

———. *Songes of Rechelesnesse: Langland and the Franciscans.* Ann Arbor: University of Michigan Press, 1997.

Coghill, Neville. "The Character of Piers Plowman Considered from the B-text." *Medium Ævum* 2 (1933): 108–35.

Cole, Andrew. "Langland and the Invention of Lollardy." In *Lollards and Their Influence in Late Medieval England,* edited by Fiona Somerset, Jill C. Havens, and Derrick G. Pitard, 37–58. Woodbridge: Boydell, 2003.

———. "Scribal Hermeneutics and the Genres of Social Organization in *Piers Plowman.*" In *The Middle Ages at Work: Practicing Labor in Late Medieval England,* edited by Kellie Robertson and Michael Uebel, 179–206. New York: Palgrave Macmillan, 2003.

———. "William Langland's Lollardy." *Yearbook of Langland Studies* 17 (2003): 24–54.

Coleman, Janet. *Piers Plowman and the Moderni.* Rome: Edizioni di storia e letteratura, 1981.

———. "Property and Poverty." In *The Cambridge History of Medieval Political Thought,* edited by J. H. Burns, 607–48. Cambridge: Cambridge University Press, 1988.

Crawford, Elizabeth. "Book Choice for Summer Reading Program Again Stirs Controversy in North Carolina." *The Chronicle of Higher Education,* 11 July 2003.

Cullum, P. H. "'Yf lak of charyte be not ower hynderawnce': Margery Kempe, Lynn, and the Practice of the Spiritual and Bodily Works of Mercy." In *A Companion to The Book of Margery Kempe,* edited by John H. Arnold and Katherine J. Lewis, 177–93. Cambridge: D. S. Brewer, 2004.

Cullum, P. H., and P. J. P. Goldberg. "Charitable Provision in Late Medieval York: 'To the Praise of God and the Use of the Poor.'" *Northern History* 29 (1993): 24–39.

Daniel, Lillian. Review of *Nickel and Dimed. Christian Century* 118, no. 22 (2001): 30.

Dawson, James Doyne. "Richard FitzRalph and Fourteenth-Century Poverty Controversies." *Journal of Ecclesiastical History* 34 (1983): 315–44.

———. "William of Saint-Amour and the Apostolic Tradition." *Medieval Studies* 70 (1978): 223–38.

Delany, Sheila. "Sexual Economics, Chaucer's Wife of Bath, and *The Book of Margery Kempe.*" In *Writing Woman: Women Writers and Women in Literature Medieval to Modern,* edited by Sheila Delany, 76–92. New York: Schoken Books, 1983.

Despres, Denise. "Margery Kempe and Visual Meditation." *Fourteenth-Century English Mystics Newsletter* 11, no. 1 (1985): 12–18.

Dickens, A. G. *The English Reformation.* University Park: Pennsylvania State University Press, 1989.

Dickman, Susan. "Margery Kempe and the Continental Tradition of the Pious Woman." In *The Medieval Mystical Tradition in England,* edited by Marion Glasscoe, 150–68. Cambridge: D. S. Brewer, 1984.

Dobson, R. B., ed. "Admissions to the Freedom of the City of York in the Later Middle Ages." *Economic History Review* 26 (1973): 1–22.

———. "Craft Guilds and City." In *The Stage as Mirror,* edited by Alan Knight, 91–106. Woodbridge: D. S. Brewer, 1997.

———, ed. *The Peasants' Revolt of 1381.* London: Macmillan, 1983.

Dolan, T. P. "Langland and FitzRalph: Two Solutions to the Mendicant Problem." *The Yearbook of Langland Studies* 2 (1988): 35–45.

Donaldson, E. Talbot. *Piers Plowman: The C-text and Its Poet.* New Haven: Yale University Press, 1949.

Donovan, Roxanne A., and Mary Crawford. Review of *Nickel and Dimed. Sex Roles: A Journal of Research* 46, nos. 3–4 (2002): 129–30.

Dorrell, Jimmy. "*Nickel and Dimed*: The Working Poor Don't Need Handouts Just Livable Wage." *Waco Tribune-Herald,* 22 December 2002.

Doyle, A. I. "An Unrecognized Piece of *Pierce the Ploughman's Crede* and Other Work by Its Scribe." *Speculum* 34 (1959): 428–36.

Duffy, Eamon. *The Stripping of the Altars: Traditional Religion in England, 1400–1580.* New Haven: Yale University Press, 1992.

Dyer, Christopher. *Making a Living in the Middle Ages: The People of Britain, 850–1520.* New Haven: Yale University Press, 2002.

———. *Standards of Living in the Later Middle Ages: Social Change in England, c. 1200–1520.* Cambridge: Cambridge University Press, 1989.

Eagleton, Terry. *After Theory.* New York: Basic Books, 2003.

Ehrenreich, Barbara. *Bait and Switch: The Futile Pursuit of the American Dream.* New York: Henry Holt, 2005.

———. *Nickel and Dimed: On (Not) Getting by in America.* New York: Henry Holt, 2001.

Ellis, Deborah. "Margery Kempe and King's Lynn." In *Margery Kempe: A Book of Essays,* edited by Sandra J. McEntire, 139–63. New York: Garland, 1992.

———. "The Merchant's Wife's Tale: Language, Sex, and Commerce in Margery Kempe and in Chaucer." *Exemplaria* 2 (1990): 595–626.

Fallows, James. "Working Classes." *Atlantic Online,* 2 May 2001.

Farmer, Sharon. *Surviving Poverty in Medieval Paris: Gender, Ideology, and the Daily Lives of the Poor.* Ithaca: Cornell University Press, 2002.

Feerst, Alex. "Bowery Beautiful: Progressive Slumming and Ghetto Aesthetics, 1880–1930." Ph.D. diss., Duke University, 2005.

Fefer, Mark D. "Slumming for Dollars." *Seattle Weekly,* 11–17 July 2001.

Fowler, David C. *The Life and Times of John Trevisa, Medieval Scholar.* Seattle: University of Washington Press, 1995.

Fradenburg, Louise. "Needful Things." In *Medieval Crime and Social Control,* edited by Barbara A. Hanawalt and David Wallace, 49–67. Minneapolis: University of Minnesota Press, 1999.

Frank, Robert W. "The Conclusion of *Piers Plowman.*" *Journal of English and Germanic Philology* 49 (1950): 309–16.

———. "The 'Hungry Gap,' Crop Failure, and Famine: The Fourteenth-Century Agricultural Crisis and *Piers Plowman.*" *Yearbook of Langland Studies* 4 (1990): 97–104.

———. *Piers Plowman and the Scheme of Salvation.* New Haven: Yale University Press, 1957.

Fryde, E. B. *Peasants and Landlords in Later Medieval England.* New York: St. Martin's Press, 1996.

Galloway, Andrew. "The Economy of Need in Late Medieval English Literature." Medieval Poverty Conference, Cornell University, March 2008.

Gastle, Brian W. "Breaking the Stained-Glass Ceiling: Mercantile Authority, Margaret Paston, and Margery Kempe." *Studies in the Literary Imagination* 36, no. 1 (2003): 123–47.

Gayk, Shannon. "'As Plouȝmen Han Preued': The Alliterative Work of a Set of Lollard Sermons." *Yearbook of Langland Studies* 20 (2006): 42–65.

Ghosh, Kantik. *The Wycliffite Heresy: Authority and the Interpretation of Texts.* Cambridge: Cambridge University Press, 2002.

Giles, Kate. "Framing Labour: The Archaeology of York's Medieval Guildhalls." In *The Problem of Labour in Fourteenth-Century England,* edited by James Bothwell, P. J. P. Goldberg, and W. M. Ormrod, 65–84. Woodbridge: York Medieval Press, 2000.

Goldberg, P. J. P. "Craft Guilds, the Corpus Christi Play, and Civic Government." In *The Government of Medieval York: Essays in Commemoration of the 1396 Royal Charter,* edited by Sarah Rees Jones, 141–63. York: Borthwick Institute of Historical Research, 1997.

———."Performing the Word of God: Corpus Christi Drama in the Northern Province." In *Life and Thought in the Northern Church,* edited by Diana Wood, 145–70. Woodbridge: Boydell, 1999.

Goodman, Anthony. *Margery Kempe and Her World.* London: Longman, 2002.

Gradon, Pamela. "Langland and the Ideology of Dissent." *Proceedings of the British Academy* 66 (1980): 179–205.

———. "Trajanus Redivivus: Another Look at Trajan in *Piers Plowman.*" In *Middle English Studies Presented to Norman Davis in Honor of his Seventieth Birthday,* edited by Douglas Gray and E. G. Stanley, 93–114. Oxford: Clarendon Press, 1983.

Grady, Frank. "The Generation of 1399." In *The Letter of the Law: Legal Practice and Literary Production in Medieval England,* edited by Emily

Steiner and Candace Barrington, 202–29. Ithaca: Cornell University Press, 2002.

———. *Representing Righteous Heathens in Late Medieval England*. New York: Palgrave Macmillan, 2005.

Gwynn, Aubrey. *The English Austin Friars in the Time of Wyclif*. London: Oxford University Press, 1940.

———. "The Sermon Diary of Richard FitzRalph." *Proceedings of the Royal Irish Academy* 44 (1937): 1–57.

Hanawalt, Barbara. "Reading the Lives of the Illiterate: London's Poor." *Speculum* 80 (2005): 1067–86.

Hanna, Ralph. "Will's Work." In *Written Work: Langland, Labor, and Authorship*, edited by Steven Justice and Kathryn Kerby-Fulton, 23–66. Philadelphia: University of Pennsylvania Press, 1997.

Hardt, Michael, and Antonio Negri. *Empire*. Cambridge, MA: Harvard University Press, 2000.

Harwood, Britton J. *Piers Plowman and the Problem of Belief*. Toronto: University of Toronto Press, 1992.

Hatcher, John, and Edward Miller. *Medieval England: Rural Society and Economic Change, 1086–1348*. London: Longman, 1978.

Herzog, Brad. "The Augustinian Subject, Franciscan Piety, and *The Book of Margery Kempe*: An Affective Appropriation and Subversion of Authority." *Philological Review* 30, no. 2 (2004): 67–88.

Hewett-Smith, Kathleen. "Allegory on the Half-Acre: The Demands of History." *Yearbook of Langland Studies* 10 (1996): 1–22.

———. " 'Lo, here lyflode ynow, yf oure beleue be trewe': Poverty and the Transfiguration of History in the Central Visions of *Piers Plowman*." *Chaucer Yearbook* 5 (1998): 139–61.

———. " 'Nede Hath No Lawe': Poverty and the De-stabilization of Allegory in the Final Visions of *Piers Plowman*." In *William Langland's Piers Plowman: A Book of Essays*, edited by Kathleen Hewett-Smith, 233–53. New York: Routledge, 2001.

Holsinger, Bruce. "Lollard Eckphrasis: Situated Aesthetics and Literary History." *Journal of Medieval and Early Modern Studies* 35, no. 1 (2005): 67–89.

Holsinger, Bruce, and Ethan Knapp. "The Marxist Premodern." *Journal of Medieval and Early Modern Studies* 34, no. 3 (2004): 463–71.

Homan, Richard. "Ritual Aspects of the York Cycle." *Theatre Journal* 22 (1981): 303–15.

Hudson, Anne. "Epilogue: The Legacy of *Piers Plowman*." In *A Companion to Piers Plowman*, edited by John Alford, 251–66. Berkeley: University of California Press, 1988.

———. "Hermofodrita or Ambidexter: Wycliffite Views on Clerks in Secular Office." In *Lollardy and the Gentry in the Later Middle Ages*, edited by Margaret Aston and Colin Richmond, 29–40. New York: St. Martin's Press, 1997.

———. "Langland and Lollardy?" *Yearbook of Langland Studies* 17 (2003): 94–105.

———. "A Lollard Sect Vocabulary?" In *Lollards and Their Books,* edited by Anne Hudson, 165–80. London: The Hambledon Press, 1985.

———. "A Neglected Wycliffite Text." *Journal of Ecclesiastical History* 29 (1978): 257–79.

———. "Poor Preachers, Poor Men: Views of Poverty in Wyclif and his Followers." In *Haresie und vorzeitige Reformation im Spatmittelalter,* edited by Frantisek Smahel, 41–54. Munchen: R. Oldenbourg Verlag, 1998.

———. *The Premature Reformation: Wycliffite Texts and Lollard History.* Oxford: Clarendon Press, 1988.

Johnston, Alexandra. "The City as Patron: York." In *Shakespeare and Theatrical Patronage in Early Modern England,* edited by Paul Whitfield White and Suzanne R. Westfall, 150–75. Cambridge: Cambridge University Press, 2002.

Jones, Edward. "Langland and Hermits." *Yearbook of Langland Studies* 11 (1997): 67–86.

Jurkowski, Maureen. "Lollardy and Social Status in East Anglia." *Speculum* 82 (2007): 120–52.

Justice, Alan. "Trade Symbolism in the York Cycle." *Theatre Journal* (March 1979): 47–58.

Justice, Steven. "Lollardy." In the *Cambridge History of Medieval English Literature,* edited by David Wallace, 662–89. Cambridge: Cambridge University Press, 2002.

———. *Writing and Rebellion: England in 1381.* Berkeley: University of California Press, 1996.

Kaminsky, Howard. "Wycliffism as Ideology of Revolution." *Church History* 33 (1963): 57–74.

Kane, George. "Some Fourteenth-Century 'Political' Poems." In *Medieval English and Ethical Literature: Essays in Honor of G. H. Russell,* edited by G. Kratzmann and J. Simpson, 82–91. Cambridge: Cambridge University Press, 1986.

Kaske, R. E. "The Character Hunger in *Piers Plowman.*" In *Medieval English Studies Presented to George Kane,* edited by E. D. Kennedy, R. Waldron, and J. S. Wittig, 187–97. Woodbridge: Boydell and Brewer, 1988.

Kerby-Fulton, Kathryn. *Books Under Suspicion: Censorship and Tolerance of Revelatory Writing in Late Medieval England.* Notre Dame, IN: University of Notre Dame, 2006.

———. "Langland and the Bibliographic Ego." In *Written Work: Langland, Labor, and Authorship,* edited by Kathryn Kerby-Fulton and Steven Justice, 67–143. Philadelphia: University of Pennsylvania Press, 1997.

———. "*Piers Plowman.*" In the *Cambridge History of Medieval English Literature,* edited by David Wallace, 513–38. Cambridge: Cambridge University Press, 1999.

———. *Reformist Apocalypticism and Piers Plowman.* Cambridge: Cambridge University Press, 1990.

Kerby-Fulton, Kathryn, and Denise Despres. *Iconography and the Professional Reader.* Minneapolis: University of Minnesota Press, 1999.

Kim, Margaret. "Hunger, Need, and the Politics of Poverty in *Piers Plowman.*" *Yearbook of Langland Studies* 16 (2003): 131–68.

Kirk, Elizabeth. "Langland's Plowman and the Recreation of Fourteenth Century Religious Metaphor." *Yearbook of Langland Studies* 2 (1988): 1–21.

Ladd, Roger A. "Margery Kempe and her Mercantile Mysticism." *Fifteenth-Century Studies* 26 (2001): 121–41.

Lahey, Stephen. *Philosophy and Politics in the Thought of John Wyclif.* Cambridge: Cambridge University Press, 2003.

Lambert, Malcolm. "The Franciscan Crisis under John XXII." *Franciscan Studies* 32 (1972): 123–43.

———. *Franciscan Poverty: The Doctrine of the Absolute Poverty of Christ and the Apostles in the Franciscan Order, 1210–1323.* St. Bonaventure, NY: Franciscan Institute, 1998.

Lampe, David. "The Satiric Strategy of *Peres the Ploughman's Crede.*" In *The Alliterative Tradition in the Fourteenth Century,* edited by Paul E. Szarmach and Bernard S. Levey, 69–80. Kent: Kent State University Press, 1981.

Lawler, Traugott. "Harlot's Holiness: The System of Absolution for Miswinning in the C Version of *Piers Plowman.*" *Yearbook of Langland Studies* 20 (2006): 141–89.

Lawton, David. "English Poetry and English Society." In *The Radical Reader,* edited by Stephen Knight and Michael Wilding, 145–68. Sydney: Wild and Woolley, 1977.

———. "Lollardy and the Piers Plowman Tradition." *Modern Language Review* 76 (1981): 780–93.

Leff, Gordon. *Heresy in the Later Middle Ages.* 2 vols. Manchester: Manchester University Press, 1967.

Levinson, Marjorie. "What is New Formalism?" *PMLA* 122, no. 2 (2007): 558–61.

Lis, Catharina, and Hugo Soly. *Poverty and Capitalism in Pre-Industrial Europe.* Translated by James Coonan. Atlantic Highlands, NJ: Humanities Press, 1979.

Little, Katherine. *Confession and Resistance: Defining the Self in Late Medieval England.* Notre Dame, IN: University of Notre Dame Press, 2006.

Little, Lester. *Religious Poverty and the Profit Economy in Medieval Europe.* Ithaca: Cornell University Press, 1978.

Lochrie, Karma. *Margery Kempe and Translations of the Flesh.* Philadelphia: University of Pennsylvania Press, 1991.

Lutton, Robert. *Lollardy and Orthodox Religion in Pre-Reformation England.* Woodbridge: Boydell and Brewer, 2006.

MacIntyre, Alasdair. *Dependent Rational Animals: Why Human Beings Need the Virtues.* Chicago: Carus, 1999.

Malanga, Steven. "The Myth of the Working Poor." *City Journal* 14, no. 4 (2004).

Mann, Jill. *Chaucer and Medieval Estates Satire.* Cambridge: Cambridge University Press, 1973.

———. "The Nature of Need Revisited." *Yearbook of Langland Studies* 18 (2004): 3–29.

Masciandaro, Nicola. *The Voice of the Hammer: The Meaning of Work in Middle English Literature.* Notre Dame, IN: University of Notre Dame Press, 2007.

McIntosh, Marjorie. *Controlling Misbehavior in England, 1370–1600.* Cambridge: Cambridge University Press, 1998.

McRee, Ben. "Charity and Gild Solidarity in Late Medieval England." *Journal of British Studies* 32, no. 3 (1993): 195–225.

Merrington, John. "Town and Country in the Transition to Capitalism." In *The Transition from Feudalism to Capitalism,* edited by Rodney Hilton, 170–95. London: Verso, 1978.

Middleton, Anne. "Acts of Vagrancy: The C-Version Autobiography and the Statute of 1388." In *Written Work: Langland, Labor, and Authorship,* edited by Stephen Justice and Kathryn Kerby-Fulton, 208–317. Philadelphia: University of Pennsylvania Press, 1997.

Moisa, Maria. "Fourteenth-Century Preachers' Views of the Poor: Class or Status Group?" In *Culture, Ideology and Politics,* edited by Ralph Samuel and Gareth Stedman Jones, 160–75. London: Routledge and Kegan Paul, 1982.

Mollat, Michel. *The Poor in the Middle Ages.* Translated by Arthur Goldhammer. New Haven: Yale University Press, 1986.

Moorman, John. *A History of the Franciscan Order from Its Origins to the Year 1517.* Oxford: Oxford University Press, 1968.

Newhauser, Richard. "On Ambiguity in Moral Theology: When the Vices Masquerade as Virtues." Translated by Andrea Nemeth-Newhauser. In *Sin: Essays on the Moral Tradition in the Western Middle Ages.* Variorum Collected Studies Series, essay I. Aldershot: Ashgate, 2007.

Nissé, Ruth. *Defining Acts: Drama and the Politics of Interpretation in Late Medieval England.* Notre Dame, IN: University of Notre Dame Press, 2005.

Norwood, Sam. "Wandering 'Wastours': Medieval and Early Modern Portrayals of Itinerant Laborers, Minstrels, Merchants, and Thieves." M.A. thesis, Lehigh University, 2006.

Ovitt, George. *The Restoration of Perfection: Labor and Technology in Medieval Culture.* New Brunswick: Rutgers University Press, 1986.

Palliser, D. M. *Tudor York.* Oxford: Oxford University Press, 1979.

Parker, Kate. "Lynn and the Making of a Mystic." In *A Companion to The Book of Margery Kempe,* edited by John H. Arnold and Katherine J. Lewis, 55–73. Cambridge: D. S. Brewer, 2004.

Parsons, Kelly. "The Red Ink Annotator of *The Book of Margery Kempe* and his Lay Audience." In *The Medieval Professional Reader at Work: Evidence from Manuscripts of Chaucer, Langland, Kempe, and Gower*, edited by Kathryn Kerby-Fulton and Maidie Hilmo, 143–216. University of Victoria, 2001.

Pearsall, Derek. "Langland and Lollardy: From B to C." *Yearbook of Langland Studies* 17 (2003): 7–24.

———. "Lunatyk Lollares in *Piers Plowman*." In *Religion in the Poetry and Drama of the Late Middle Ages*, edited by Piero Boitani and Anna Torti, 163–78. Cambridge: Cambridge University Press, 1989.

———. "The Piers Plowman Group." In *Old English and Middle English Poetry*. London: Routledge and Kegan Paul, 1977.

———. "Poverty and Poor People in *Piers Plowman*." In *Medieval English Studies Presented to George Kane*, edited by E. D. Kennedy, R. Waldron, and J. S. Wittig, 167–85. Cambridge: D. S. Brewer, 1990.

———. "Strangers in Medieval London." In *The Stranger in Medieval Society*, edited by F. R. P. Akehurst and Stephanie Cain Van D'Elden, 46–62. Minneapolis: University of Minnesota Press, 1997.

Petshauer, Peter. Review of *Nickel and Dimed*. *National Women's Studies Association Journal* 14, no. 2 (2002): 225–27.

Plumb, Derek. "The Social and Economic Spread of Rural Lollardy: A Reappraisal." *Studies in Church History* 23 (1986): 111–29.

———. "The Social and Economic Status of the Later Lollards." In *The World of Rural Dissenters*, edited by Margaret Spufford, 103–31. Cambridge: Cambridge University Press, 1995.

Ponte, Lowell. "Cash and Carry: Propaganda for Fume and Proft." *FrontPage Mag.com*, 24 August 2001.

Postan, M. M. *The Medieval Economy and Society: An Economic History of Britain in the Middle Ages*. London: Weidenfeld and Nicolson, 1972.

Putnam, Bertha. *The Enforcement of the Statute of Laborers during the First Decade after the Black Death*. New York: Columbia University Press, 1908.

Quilligan, Maureen. *The Language of Allegory*. Ithaca: Cornell University Press, 1979.

Rexroth, Frank. *Deviance and Power in Late Medieval London*. Translated by Pamela E. Selwyn. Cambridge: Cambridge University Press, 2007.

Riddy, Felicity. "Text and Self in *The Book of Margery Kempe*." In *Voices in Dialogue: Reading Women in the Middle Ages*, edited by Kathryn Kerby-Fulton and Linda Olson, 435–53. Notre Dame, IN: University of Notre Dame Press, 2005.

Robertson, D.W., and Bernard F. Huppé. *Piers Plowman and Scriptural Tradition*. Princeton: Princeton University Press, 1951.

Robertson, Kellie. *The Laborer's Two Bodies: Labor and the "Work" of the Text in Medieval Britain, 1350–1500*. New York: Palgrave Macmillan, 2006.

Robinson, J.W. "Ad Majorem Dei Gloriam." In *Medieval Drama: A Collection of Festival Papers,* edited by William A. Selz, 31–37. Vermillion: University of South Dakota Press, 1969.

Rogers, William. *Interpretation in Piers Plowman.* Washington DC: Catholic University of America Press, 2002.

Rosser, Gervase. "Crafts, Guilds, and the Negotiation of Work in the Medieval Town." *Past and Present* 154 (1997): 3–31.

———."Going to the Fraternity Feast: Commensality and Social Relations in Late Medieval England." *Journal of British Studies* 33, no. 4 (1994): 430–46.

Rubin, Miri. *Charity and Community in Medieval Cambridge.* Cambridge: Cambridge University Press, 1987.

Salih, Sarah. "Margery's Bodies: Piety, Work and Penance." In *A Companion to The Book of Margery Kempe,* edited by John Arnold and Katherine Lewis, 161–76. Cambridge: D. S. Brewer, 2004.

Salter, Elizabeth. *Piers Plowman: An Introduction.* Cambridge, MA: Harvard University Press, 1962.

Scase, Wendy. *Literature and Complaint in England, 1272–1553.* Oxford: Oxford University Press, 2007.

———. *Piers Plowman and the New Anticlericalism.* Cambridge: Cambridge University Press, 1989.

———. "Two *Piers Plowman* C-text Interpolations: Evidence for a Second Textual Tradition." *Notes and Queries* 232 (1987): 456–63.

Scattergood, John. "*Pierce the Ploughman's Crede*: Lollardy and Texts." In *Lollardy and the Gentry in the Later Middle Ages,* edited by Margaret Aston and Colin Richmond, 77–94. New York: St. Martin's Press, 1997.

Schacher, Yael. Review of *Nickel and Dimed. Slate,* 19 May 2001.

Scott, Anne M. *Piers Plowman and the Poor.* Dublin: Four Courts Press, 2004.

Scott, Joni. Review of *Nickel and Dimed. Humanist* 61, no. 5 (2001): 40–41.

Sheingorn, Pamela, and David Bevington. "'All This Was Token Domysday to Drede': Visual Signs of Last Judgment in the Corpus Christi Cycles and in Late Gothic Art." In *Homo, Memento Finis: The Iconography of Just Judgment in Medieval Art and Drama,* edited by David Bevington, 15–58. Kalamazoo: Medieval Institute Publications, Western Michigan University Press, 1985.

Sheneman, Paul. "Grace Abounding: Justification in Passus 16 of *Piers Plowman.*" *Papers on Language and Literature* 34 (1998): 162–78.

Shepherd, Geoffrey. "Poverty in *Piers Plowman.*" In *Social Relations and Ideas,* edited by T. H. Aston, P. R. Cross, and C. Dyer, 169–89. Cambridge: Cambridge University Press, 1983.

Shepherd, Simon, and Peter Womack, eds. *English Drama: A Cultural History.* Oxford: Blackwell, 1996.

Sherman, Scott. "Class Warrior: Barbara Ehrenreich's Singular Crusade." *Columbia Journalism Review* 42.4 (2003), 34–41.

Shogimen, Takashi. *Ockham and Political Discourse in the Late Middle Ages.* Cambridge: Cambridge University Press, 2007.

Simpson, James. *Burning to Read: English Fundamentalism and Its Reformation Opponents.* Cambridge, MA: Harvard University Press, 2007.

———. *Piers Plowman: An Introduction to the B-text.* New York: Longman, 1990.

———. *Reform and Cultural Revolution.* Oxford: Oxford University Press, 2002.

Smith, D. Vance. *Arts of Possession.* Minneapolis: University of Minnesota Press, 2003.

———. *The Book of the Incipit.* Minneapolis: University of Minnesota Press, 2001.

Smith, Wilfred Cantwell. *Faith and Belief: The Difference Between Them.* Oxford: Oneworld Publications, 1998.

Somerset, Fiona. *Clerical Discourse and Lay Audience in Late Medieval England.* Cambridge: Cambridge University Press, 1998.

———. "Excitative Speech: Theories of Emotive Response from Richard FitzRalph to Margery Kempe." In *The Vernacular Spirit: Essays on Medieval Religious Culture,* edited by Renate Bumenfeld-Kosinski, Duncan Robertson, and Nancy Bradley Warren, 59–82. New York: Palgrave, 2002.

———. "Expanding the Langlandian Canon: Radical Latin and the Stylistics of Reform." *Yearbook of Langland Studies* 19 (2003): 73–92.

———. "'Mark Him Wel for He is On of þo': Training the 'Lewed' Gaze to Discern Hypocrisy." *English Language History* 68 (2001): 315–34.

Spearing, A. C. *Medieval Dream-Poetry.* Cambridge: Cambridge University Press, 1976.

Spindler, Cara. Review of *Nickel and Dimed. Z Magazine,* May 2001.

Sponsler, Claire. *Drama and Resistance: Bodies, Goods, and Theatricality in Late Medieval England.* Minneapolis: University of Minnesota Press, 1997.

Staley, Lynn. *Margery Kempe's Dissenting Fictions.* University Park: Pennsylvania State University Press, 1994.

Stevens, Martin. *Four English Mystery Cycles: Textual, Contextual and Critical Interpretations.* Princeton: Princeton University Press, 1987.

Swanson, Heather. "The Illusion of Economic Structure: Craft Guilds in Late Medieval English Towns." *Past and Present* 121 (1988): 29–48.

———. *Medieval Artisans.* Oxford: Basil Blackwell, 1989.

———. *Medieval British Towns.* London: Palgrave Macmillan, 1999.

Szittya, Penn R. *The Antifraternal Tradition in Medieval Literature.* Princeton: Princeton University Press, 1986.

Tierney, Brian. "The Decretists and the 'Deserving Poor.'" *Comparative Studies in Society and History* 1, no. 4 (1959): 360–73.

———. *The Idea of Natural Rights: Studies on Natural Rights, Natural Law and Church Law, 1150–1625.* Atlanta: Scholars Press, 1997.

———. *Medieval Poor Law: A Sketch of Canonical Theory and Its Application in England.* Berkeley: University of California Press, 1959.

Tolmie, Sarah. "Langland, Wittgenstein, and the End of Language." *Yearbook of Langland Studies* 20 (2006): 115–39.

Tremoglie, Michael. "Barbara Ehrenreich: Nickel and Diming Truth." *FrontPageMagazine.com*, 22 July 2003.

Tywcross, Meg. "The Theatricality of Medieval English Plays." In *The Cambridge Companion to Medieval English Theatre*, edited by Richard Beadle, 37–84. Cambridge: Cambridge University Press, 1994.

Von Nolcken, Christina. "*Piers Plowman*, the Wycliffites and *Pierce the Ploughman's Crede*." *Yearbook of Langland Studies* 2 (1988): 71–102.

Wallace, David. "Mystics and Followers in Siena and East Anglia: A Study in Taxonomy, Class, and Cultural Mediation." In *The Medieval Mystical Tradition in England*, edited by Marion Glasscoe, 161–91. Exeter: University of Exeter Press, 1982.

Walsh, Katherine. *A Fourteenth-century Scholar and Primate: Richard FitzRalph in Oxford, Avignon, and Armagh*. Oxford: Clarendon Press, 1981.

Warren, Ann. *Anchorites and Their Patrons in Medieval England*. Berkeley: University of California Press, 1985.

Watson, Nicholas. "The Making of the *Book of Margery Kempe*." In *Voices in Dialogue: Reading Women in the Middle Ages*, edited by Linda Olson and Kathryn Kerby-Fulton, 395–434. Notre Dame, IN: University of Notre Dame Press, 2005.

Whatley, Gordon. "*Piers Plowman* B 12.277–94: Notes on Language, Text, Theology." *Modern Philology* 82 (1984): 1–12.

White, Hugh. *Nature and Salvation in Piers Plowman*. Cambridge: Cambridge University Press, 1988.

Wilks, Michael. "Predestination, Property, and Power: Wyclif's Theory of Dominion and Grace." *Studies in Church History* 2 (1965): 220–36. Reprinted in *Wyclif: Political Ideas and Practice* (Oxford: Oxbow Books, 2000), 16–32.

Wilson, Janet. "The Communities of Margery Kempe's *Book*." In *Medieval Women in Their Communities*, edited by Diane Watt, 155–85. Toronto: University of Toronto Press, 1997.

Wolf, Kenneth Baxter. *The Poverty of Riches*. Oxford: Oxford University Press, 2003.

Zeeman, Nicolette. *Piers Plowman and the Medieval Discourse of Desire*. Cambridge: Cambridge University Press, 2006.

INDEX

KATE CRASSONS

is assistant professor of English at Lehigh University.